Freaks of Fortune

Freaks of Fortune

THE EMERGING WORLD OF
CAPITALISM AND RISK IN AMERICA

Jonathan Levy

Harvard University Press
Cambridge, Massachusetts,
and London, England

First Harvard University Press paperback edition, 2014

Library of Congress Cataloging-in-Publication Data

Levy, Jonathan, 1978-
Freaks of fortune : the emerging world of capitalism and risk in America / Jonathan Levy.
    p.   cm.
Includes bibliographical references and index.
ISBN 978-0-674-04748-8 (cloth : alk. paper)
ISBN 978-0-674-73635-1 (pbk.)
1. Capitalism—United States—History—19th century.   2. Risk-Sociological aspects—
    History—19th century.   3. Risk-taking (Psychology)—United States—History—
        19th century.   4. United States—Economic conditions—19th century.
        5. United States—Social conditions—19th century.   I. Title.
                        HC105.L48 2012
            330.12'2097309034—dc23   2012014805

For my parents,
Joanne and Martin Levy

Contents

. . . this savage's sword, thought I, which thus finally shapes and fashions both warp and woof; this easy, indifferent sword must be chance—aye, chance, free will, and necessity—no wise incompatible—all interweavingly working together. The straight warp of necessity, not to be swerved from its ultimate course—its every alternating vibration, indeed, only tending to that; free will still free to ply her shuttle between given threads; and chance, though restrained in its play within the right lines of necessity, and sideways in its motions directed by free will, though thus pre-scribed to by both, chance by turns rules either, and has the last featuring blow at events.

—Herman Melville, *Moby-Dick*

Prologue

Voyage

Sail forth! Steer for the deep waters only!
Reckless, O soul, exploring, I with thee, and thou with me;
For we are bound where mariner has not yet dared to go,
And we will risk the ship, ourselves and all.
          —Walt Whitman, "Passage to India" (1871)

I N THE NINETEENTH-CENTURY UNITED STATES, voyage was an image that Americans invoked time and again to capture what it was like to live on the stormy seas of capitalism. In 1871 Walt Whitman offered a maritime allegory of the experience of individual freedom. To do so he evoked risk. Long a technical concept in the financial arena of marine insurance, at the end of the eighteenth century "risk" still simply referred to the commodity bought and sold in an insurance contract. Outside the world of long-distance maritime trade risk had very little meaning or use.

Sometime during the nineteenth century it became all but impossible to imagine the modern condition without the word "risk." By 1871 Whitman was able to invest risk with great lyrical power. Capitalism—an economic system that thrives off radical uncertainty—was asserting control.[1] Meanwhile, men had begun to insure their own lives, brokers had begun to sell mortgage-backed securities, and farmers were beginning to buy commodities futures contracts. Uncertainties and anxieties—some old, some new—had to be managed and coped with, perhaps even capitalized upon. Risk management was born.

The spread of capitalism had brought the insecurity of the sea to the land. Human beings had long associated the power of chance with the capricious tides of the high seas. Now the image of the ship on stormy waters became a powerful metaphor for the perils and possibilities of life under capitalism. Nineteenth-century Americans spoke of howling winds, thunder claps, unknown breakers, and tempests and storms and cyclones that swept over the deep—for which they were not responsible. But they had to learn to cope with them, and even to profit from them. As daunting as the task of managing risk could be, there was also the existential thrill of taking a risk. That tension was at the very operational and moral heart of both capitalism and a rising liberal order.

In the nineteenth-century Americans had their own term for this tension, for all of the sudden economic twists and turns, booms and busts, and ups and downs that were newly and inexplicably in their midst. They called them "freaks of fortune."

Within the context created by the freaks—by the economic chance-world of capitalism—the history of risk comes into view. The notion that risk has a history might come as a surprise. Or, it may seem that an obsession with risk is recent, dating to some time after the 1970s and the onset of crisis for industrial capitalism in the West. An era of pervasive insecurity ensued, one in which risk had to be "embraced."[2] Newly emboldened entrepreneurs began to take "risks." Sociologists began to speak of "risk society." Engineers began to practice "risk assessment." Financiers began to promise "risk management." As the contemporary sociologist François Ewald explains, risk was now "in human beings, in their conduct, in their liberty, in the relations between them, in the fact of their association, in society."[3] Since risk is now so ubiquitous, it might seem impossible to write its history.

Yet, risk does have a history. As a human invention, as a historical protagonist, risk has a biography. In the United States, the most decisive chapters in risk's history were written in the nineteenth century. For by the end of that century, much like throughout the world today, risk was in fact everywhere. Before that century of capitalist transformation, however, it was not. But risk did not appear out of nowhere. It was born on the deep, in the act of maritime voyaging.

Risk was first synonymous with marine insurance—a financial instrument for coping with the uncertainty of transporting commercial goods across maritime space. Buying and selling "risks," long-distance trading merchants purchased from each other financial compensation in the contingent event that a "peril of the seas" or an "act of God" struck their long-distance voyages and destroyed their property. Risk did not then mean extreme peril, hazard, or danger.[4] It did not refer to the immaterial fear of an undesirable event. Rather, it originally referred to something material: a financial instrument for coping with the mere *possibility* of peril, hazard, or danger.

The etymology of the word reflects this historical origin. It can be traced back to the sixteenth-century French *risqué,* and even further to the thirteenth-century Italian *rischio.* Beyond that, all possible roots, including the likely Arabic candidate, appear in maritime "commercial contexts." It is possible that mariners invented the term to refer to uncharted waters upon which they would not voyage. The *Oxford English Dictionary* emphasizes that risk connoted the possibility of "damage to merchandise when transported by sea."[5] Risk made its appearance in the English language in the sixteenth century, but in the United States even as late as the 1820s it had yet to be fully anglicized from "risque"— the commodity exchanged in a marine insurance contract. Then, rather suddenly, risk exploded in everyday language. So would financial risk management.

Risk management was one way to cope with an uncertain future. But at the opening of the nineteenth century there were other ways to do the same. Commerce was ever-present, but America was still very much a rural and hierarchical society. The large majority of persons were legal dependents: wives, children, servants, and slaves. Households and communities achieved social security by coping with the burden of peril together. For men who were masters of households, the ownership of physical forms of capital and wealth—slaves and above all land—anchored economic security. Risk management was for offshore hazards, inapplicable to dangers onshore, where men might tremble before "acts of God" instead of commodifying them. Many onshore dangers—fire, disease, a bad harvest, a premature death—were after all still biblical in nature. Religious authorities counseled that in the end divine providence ruled over the future. And if the future was certain because God determined it, then risk management might be unnecessary, if not all together wrong. After migrating inland risk management competed with other ways to cope— socially, economically, culturally—with the perils of an uncertain future. It would always remain in competition.

Nevertheless, across the nineteenth century Americans began to react to the insecurities of capitalism and its "perennial gale of creative destruction" in a new way.[6] As slavery was abolished and the United States became more urban and industrial, increasingly men began to hedge the perils of life under capitalism by using financial instruments born of capitalism itself. Finance transformed perils, hazards, and dangers— some perennial, some new because of capitalism—into risks. An insurance policy offset the risk of losing the ability to earn income in a market economy; a derivatives contract hedged against the risk of future market price volatility. Nonfinancial collective strategies did not completely die off. Families still shouldered burdens together. Many individuals still believed in an otherworldly fate. But this transformation was ultimately momentous, marking the emergence of risk as we know it today.

The world of capitalism and risk thus formed as nineteenth-century Americans became ever-more dependent upon new financial institutions, markets, and forms of wealth for their security. These included insurance policies, savings accounts, government debt markets, mortgage-backed securities markets, bond markets, futures markets, and stock markets. With this, the corporation became risk management's institutional home ground. Corporate risk communities offered a new form of social security. To provide economic security, corporate actors accumulated financial forms of capital and wealth. Doing so corporations also brought about a cultural transformation. They became the reserves of new probabilistic, statistical explanations of future change that secularized old providential beliefs. In sum, by the opening of the twentieth century the modern American corporate financial system had come to life.

Risk thus recasts the history of American capitalism from the standpoint of powerful new financial corporations. Finance is an expansive terrain. But analyzing the nitty-gritty details of new financial practices demonstrates how risk burrowed into popular consciousness. Moreover, following risk across many registers of thought, action, and experience captures much of the human drama of capitalist transformation. The spread of commerce; the rise and fall of American slavery; the Industrial Revolution; the economic development of the West; the ascendance of the corporation—all were at stake in the rise of corporate risk management. But so was how Americans thought about the future, felt about the future, acted upon it, managed it, and sometimes simply resigned themselves to it.

The thread that runs most consistently through risk's history is a moral one. For risk triumphed in the nineteenth-century United States in the context of the nation's moral struggle over freedom and slavery. A generation—financiers, abolitionists, actuaries, jurists, preachers, legislators, corporate executives, philosophers, social scientists—developed a vision of freedom that linked the liberal ideal of self-ownership to the personal assumption of "risk." In a democratic society, according to the new gospel, free and equal men must take, run, own, assume, bear, carry, and manage personal risks. That involved actively attempting to become the master of one's own personal destiny, adopting a moral duty to attend to the future. Which meant taking risks. But it also meant offloading one's risk onto new financial corporations—like when a wage worker insured his productive labor against workplace accident, an ex-slave opened a savings account, or a Wall Street financier hatched a corporate profit-sharing and employee benefit plan. A new vision of what it meant to be a free and secure actor thus took shape in the new material and psychological reality created by the modern American corporate financial system.

Liberal notions of selfhood had long emphasized the need for self-mastery, even in the face of uncertainty. But only in the nineteenth century did self-ownership come to mean mastery over a personal financial "risk." The moral conundrum that posed, and still poses, is that individual freedom required a new form of dependence. A dependence, that is, upon a new corporate financial system, the central nervous system of a rising capitalism that fed off radical uncertainty and ceaseless change.

Therefore corporate risk management time and again manufactured new forms of uncertainty and insecurity.[7] That was the essential truth taught by the freaks—economic events that eluded the grasp of corporate risk management. As free men began to assume their own personal risks, old forms of security and dependence perished. Not assuming risk, that is, no longer became an option. Whitman was right. Once at risk the only thing certain on life's voyage would be uncertainty itself. Within the economic chance-world of capitalism, desire for risk management and longing for the freaks of fortune constitute one and the same history.

CHAPTER 1

The Assumption of Risk

Safety from an evil which may lurk in the future is as real as any
other commodity.

  —Elizur Wright, "Life Insurance for the Poor" (1876)

IN 1836, NICHOLAS FARWELL WAS AN ENGINE-MAN on the one-year-old Boston and Worcester Railroad when a train ran off the tracks because a fellow employee mislaid a switch. Farwell and his car were thrown from the rail, and the railcar crushed and permanently destroyed his right hand. His career as an engine-man over, Farwell asked the Railroad for compensation but it refused. Farwell hired a lawyer and took his case eventually all the way to the Massachusetts Supreme Court. He valued his right hand at $10,000.

Chief Justice Lemuel Shaw's 1842 decision in *Farwell v. Boston and Worcester R.R. Corp.* ruled that Farwell himself was responsible for the "peril" that had destroyed his right hand.[1] Farwell therefore also personally assumed a "risk." By invoking risk Shaw's decision rested upon precedents in the international law of marine insurance.[2] In 1842 railroad wage work was new. Maritime commerce was old. Shaw granted "that the maritime law has its own rules and analogies" not always applicable to other "branches of law." Applying the moral logic of risk to a dispute concerning an industrial workplace accident followed no direct legal precedent. But Shaw still held it a "good authority" for the case at hand. To grapple with a novel aspect of American economic life, Shaw invited risk inland.

In ruling Farwell personally responsible for the "risk," Shaw also led the wage worker, almost by the nose, to a fledgling corporate financial system. There the wage worker might offload, commercially, that same personal "risk"—just like merchants offloaded the risks of long-distance trade. *Farwell* was thus an early and emblematic agent of the larger dynamic that launched risk's national history in the United States, which eventually drew almost all Americans within its orbit. Shaw attached "risk" to the very meaning and substance of Farwell's personal freedom, empowering both his individual autonomy and what would become, by the end of the nineteenth century, modern American corporate risk management. Therefore *Farwell* provides the opportunity to concretely establish the historical problem of risk.

The Massachusetts Court ruled against the crippled workingman. According to Shaw, Farwell, in contracting out his productive labor, had taken "upon himself the risks and perils incident to his situation" as an engine-man. The two words "risk" and "peril" did not then have the same meaning, and Shaw was not being loose with language. The peril of the accident, Shaw reasoned, was already priced into Farwell's wage, which was higher than the wages paid to workers who were engaged in less hazardous tasks. Within his two-dollar-per-day wage was a "premium for the risk which he thus assumes." Therefore, the railroad corporation was responsible to Farwell for no further compensation.[3]

Farwell stated that as a free man the plaintiff was a proprietor of a personal "risk." The risk he assumed was an element of his self-ownership—the same as the productive labor embodied in his now mangled and disabled right hand. No different than his own body, Farwell's "risk" was part of his selfhood. Like his productive labor, it was his private property, a thing over which he held absolute dominion. The peril was not conceived along propertied terms.

Shaw arrived to this ruling in a series of related moves. For one, Farwell became the owner of what might be termed a downside risk. He became responsible for the possibility of an abnormal future peril, hazard, or danger. The cost of this industrial accident was his own, and the Boston and Worcester Railroad owed him no compensation for his injury. It was a "pure accident," Shaw declared, as the freak event was neither the fault of Farwell nor of the railroad corporation.[4] But Farwell was ruled responsible for its consequences.

Yet, as a free man, Farwell also owned an upside risk—an equally abnormal and corresponding future pecuniary reward. In this case, it was represented monetarily in his higher wage. Both Farwell and the Boston and Worcester Railroad were ruled free and equal contracting parties in like pursuit of commercial gain. In contracting out his productive labor for the new, hazardous employment of railroad work, Farwell—Shaw held—had bargained for extra money compensation for "the risk which he thus assumes." This was a moral idea, the notion that more "risk" assumed justified more reward. As a free man, Farwell was entitled to an upside. But, for the same reason, he assumed a downside. Linking together freedom, self-ownership, and the personal assumption of risk, it was as if Shaw had enclosed a new "risk" within the sphere of Farwell's individual autonomy.

"Enclosure" is a term than can only be historically associated with one specific kind of commodity: land. In England, from the fifteenth to the nineteenth centuries, parliamentary magistrates, lawyers, landowners, mortgage lenders, and enterprising farmers conducted the slow process of "enclosing" a common-fields system that dated back to early medieval times. Land previously held in commons became the exclusive property of private individuals. The word "enclosure" referred to the techniques of demarcating newly private property—the building of hedges, fences, and drainage canals, or the filings and petitions of lawyers and magistrates— along the way to the creation of early modern English agrarian capitalism. By the nineteenth century, the crazy quilt of mutualist obligations that was early modern landed property was all but gone. An old set of hedges that had allocated some land to individual households and some to broader collectivities was replaced by a new set demarcating absolute, and therefore alienable, individual property rights.[5]

In the seventeenth century, when English colonists arrived on American shores, one of the first things they did was to begin to enclose the land, and to claim it as their own. Some New England villages had a full-blown common-field system, and all colonies to some degree maintained collective use-rights in land. They did so through a blend of customary practices that treated the land as a social good as much as an individual commodity. But in America as well, by the nineteenth century a not too dissimilar set of actors had enclosed the land.[6]

Farwell provided a legal technique for an analogous, later enclosure. "Risk," the commodity long exchanged in a marine insurance contract, was something that a person could in fact "assume" and own, alienate, or contract out to another to "carry." And yet, in the early modern period, outside the world of long-distance trade the notion that the cost of a contingent event could be priced and enclosed into a commodity that could then be offloaded through a financial instrument called "insurance" would have baffled most people. At least a fence, a hedge, or a drainage canal could demarcate an enclosed piece of land for the naked eye to see. But a future peril was much more abstract and ephemeral.

A legal precedent, however, could do something like the boundary work of a physical hedge. Enclosed "marine risks" had existed for centuries. In 1842, Shaw enclosed the new personal "accident risk" of the modern industrial workplace. Just as Farwell could sell his productive labor to a boss, so could he sell his accident risk to an insurance corporation. Farwell's employment implicated two commodities which existed in tandem—his productive labor and now the "risk" attendant to its hire. *Farwell* perfectly captured the capitalist approach to peril: commodify it.

To do so Shaw first had to dispense with a legal principle in which the burden of hazard was held in common, much like the land had once been. If the early modern enclosure of land had commodified the commons, then Shaw's enclosure of an "accident risk" commodified a contingency. The common-fields system was after all a form of safety-first agriculture, a communal hedge against the danger of a bad harvest or a bad market.[7] Farwell had sued under the English common law rule *respondeat superior,* which rendered "masters" responsible for accidents caused by their "servants." The paternalist legal rule was premised upon a status-based hierarchy, and was typical of the many highly personal, if asymmetrical, social bonds that persisted into nineteenth-century America. Such bonds achieved social security but were not predicated upon the demand for individual autonomy—and certainly not the individualist moral logic of risk. To understand just how remarkable a decision *Farwell* was, consider that according to the international law of marine insurance—at the time Shaw handed *Farwell* down—a seaman's wages were not legally insurable. As Shaw's contemporary Theophilus Parsons wrote in 1859, masters were legally responsible to directly care for and compensate a seaman who became "sick, or wounded, or maimed in the discharge of his duty" provided it was "not by his own fault."[8]

Shaw departed with *respondeat superior*. Speaking of the "pure accident" that had befallen Farwell, he snapped one chord in the dependent bond between "masters" and "servants," enshrining the Nicholas Farwells of the world as masters and proprietors of their own personal risks. Having personally assumed a risk, Farwell appeared to have no social recourse whatsoever.

For this reason, through the years *Farwell* has struck many as a callous decision—an early blow to the incipient American working class, an implicit subsidy for nascent railroad corporations. That it was, although for what it is worth in the end the Boston and Worcester Railroad, seemingly from charitable impulses, provided Farwell some compensation, even if it was far less than the $10,000 he thought he was owed. And, over time, American courts would begin to recognize employer negligence and liability for some categories of workplace accident. Further down the road, railroad brotherhoods, a new collective strategy, would cope with the individual cost of workplace accident. In time, in the early twentieth century, states would pass workmen's compensation laws.[9]

All of these paths run through *Farwell* and have been illuminated by historians with great care. The reason to linger over *Farwell*—besides, at the outset, to emphasize the crucial role of the law in setting the working rules of risk—is to pin down the maritime source of its individualist logic. But it is also to underscore the practical endpoint it implied: the potential offloading of Farwell's freshly minted personal risk onto a financial corporation.

An "assumption of risk" occurred because Farwell was a free man. But that very same freedom suggested a financial solution for the peril at hand. Departing with the domestic law of master–servant relations, Shaw sure enough turned to the international law of marine insurance. Marine insurance had for centuries offered long-distance trading merchants financial compensation in the contingent event their cargoes were lost to the "perils of the seas." One merchant assumed another merchant's risk. Shaw cited an 1841 decision of his own, *Copeland v. New England Marine Ins. Co*, in which he held that a marine insurance corporation was responsible for a cargo lost due to the "insanity" of the ship's captain. The owner of the ship was bound *"in the first instance,* to provide the ship with a competent crew; but he does not undertake for the conduct of the crew in the subsequent part of the voyage."[10] Likewise, the fellow servant responsible for mislaying the switch that destroyed Farwell's hand was by all accounts "a careful and trustworthy servant."[11] The loss thus fell with Farwell; unless he had insured it. Notably, Shaw equated Farwell not with a waged seaman, but with a ship's owner—the railroading wage not with the seafaring wage (which was not then legally insurable) but with the ship's cargo (which was). Farwell's productive labor was lost, Shaw analogized, to the "perils incident" to his industrial employment.

Shaw had further ruled that Farwell's wage had a "premium" in it—monetarily representing a slight but ideologically significant upside—representing the risk he had assumed. If Farwell had absolute dominion over the assumed risk, why could he not alienate a portion of his upside—just like merchants insured their cargoes? Shaw did not say so, but presumably Farwell could have taken the "premium" paid to him in the labor market and through an insurance contract financially offset the potential loss of his productive labor. There was only one problem: there were no accident insurance corporations in the United States when Shaw issued his opinion in 1842.

By 1846 there would be such corporations, present on both ends of Farwell's old line in Boston and Worcester. The legal precedent of *Farwell* helped drag railroad workers to the front doors of the new accident insurance corporations that first sprung up in the United States during the 1840s. In 1850 the *American Railway Times* reported that one "Mr. W. Richardson, a conductor on the Worcester and Norwich Railroad, received Two Hundred Dollars from the Franklin Health Assurance Company for injury received at Fisherville, by the cars falling through the bridge." He had been "insured at that office against railroad accidents, and paid but fifteen cents for his policy."[12]

Wage workers could now insure their newly coined personal risks against workplace accident. *Farwell* thus hedged a risk, as in to enclose and bound a future contingency within the inviolate sphere of self-ownership. But it also suggested the second historical meaning of the word "hedge." For the outcome of the decision was that the same personal "risk" could be offloaded onto an insurance corporation and thus hedged financially. An accident insurance policy could not bring back Farwell's right hand. The peril inextricably rested with him. But the risk did not have to.[13]

Shaw found a solution to a pressing new legal problem—fashioning a new legal doctrine, the personal "assumption of risk." He articulated a new model of liberal economic personhood in which the moral logic of risk was central. That logic cannot be uncritically assumed to have applied to the particular case at hand. Shaw had to work to insinuate risk into the wage relation. *Farwell* thus looked backward to risk's maritime origins, but also forward to the end of the nineteenth century. By that time modern American corporate risk management would be in place—there to serve the imperatives of a triumphant liberal creed. As *Farwell* well illustrates, from the start the identification of running one's own risk with personhood and freedom went hand in glove with new efforts to financially manage that very same risk.[14]

The task now is to explore in greater depth and detail, across many levels of thought, action, and experience, this double arc: the emergence, in tandem, of a new individualism and a new corporate financial system in nineteenth-century America. To do so will require enlisting a wider cast of characters in addition to the jurist and the wage worker—the rebellious slave, the abolitionist actuary, the proslavery ideologue, the financial speculator, the farm housewife, the fraternal brother, the corporate executive, and even, as risk became increasingly politicized, the occasional president.

That double arc spawned a double freedom. A liberal freedom, that is, *from* traditional, often authoritarian, patterns of social life that achieved security as security moved into the new corporate financial system of risk management. The freedom *from,* as it were, that was declared in *Far-well* when Shaw rejected the legal principle of *respondeat superior.* But the other side of the same coin was the freedom *to* call one's upside risks—however freakish—one's own. Therefore what must now be considered is the ideological significance and economic function of the upside.[15]

The economic phenomenon we call "risk-taking" is as old as commerce itself. For-profit commercial transactions very often involve contingent outcomes.[16] Commercial profit-making feeds off and breeds uncertainty—like the uncertain fate of a long-distance sea voyage.[17] In this sense to some degree every commercial exchange is a speculation.

Seemingly every theorist of capitalism—from Marx to Hayek, Weber to Sombart, Schumpeter to Keynes, Knight to Braudel—has taken the next step and argued that capitalism thrives off unceasing and unpredictable historical change. Noting this fundamental indeterminacy, Keynes most memorably referred to a "radical uncertainty." By this he meant future uncertainties that are qualitative in kind—future possibilities that cannot be assigned a "calculable probability" by any forward-looking agent. A future, that is, whose content "We simply do not know." It is this quality of the future that capitalism is constantly seeking to generate, manage, and exploit.[18]

Nineteenth-century Americans created for themselves a radically uncertain future, although not from whole cloth. From the earliest of colonial times America was a commercial society. Many of its members—willingly or not—had left an old world behind for a new. Yet, when *Farwell* came down in 1842 commerce newly flourished in Jacksonian America. A remarkable surge of commercialization was responsible, but so was the speculative itch of a democratizing culture. The continued rise of American democracy made the social order more liquid, tempting individuals to chase the possibility of a better future state of affairs through commercial gain.[19]

In antebellum America, more and more men were reaching for the main chance via commerce. Southern slave masters feverishly raised cotton for sale on world markets. Free farm households produced great marketable surpluses of grain. Americans flocked to cities and their commercial emporiums, which spread the dominion of the emerging national market economy westward. Linking that economy together was an ongoing transportation revolution—new roads, turnpikes, canals, and even railroads, like Farwell's employer, the Boston and Worcester. In the Northeast, there were the beginnings of industrialization.[20]

In this era, one of staggering wealth creation, most Americans believed that wealth and value were the products of human labor.[21] Part of the upside vision however was that commercial risk-taking—speculation—could be "productive labor."[22] When Anglo-Americans and European immigrants conquered, settled, and economically developed an entire continent, at the cutting edge was land speculation. When southerners built one of the richest plantation societies the world had ever known, at the cutting edge was a speculative market in human chattels. When railroad directors constructed a transcontinental railroad network, at the cutting edge was financial speculation. For every confidence game that was never more than a figment of the imagination, a future projection became real—a Pacific venture, a railroad, a city of Chicago. Later, looking back at a century of capitalist transformation, Charles Hamill, president of the Chicago Board of Trade, explained before Congress in 1892:

> It is too late, in view of what has been accomplished, to deprecate speculation in its proper sense as an element in mercantile life. It has uncovered resources . . . it has created values; it has quickened industry . . . awakened ambition, augmented the comfort of life; it has introduced delicacies and luxuries, it has brought refinement and development to human character, built churches, constructed railroads, discovered continents, and brought together in bonds of fellowship the nations of the world; it is aggressive, courageous, intelligent, and belongs to the strongest and ablest of the race; it grapples undismayed with possibilities; it founded Chicago; it rebuilt a great city upon smoldering ruins, and impels it in the march of progress. Whenever this kind of speculation is denounced it is misunderstood, and it is often decried by those who unconsciously share its benefactions.[23]

Perhaps there were better ways to have economically developed the American continent.[24] But the nineteenth-century American economy was a textbook case of private, speculative-driven "creative destruction," to invoke Schumpeter, producing hitherto unimaginable levels of economic growth and material wealth. Higher money incomes made it possible for many individuals to newly purchase economic security from financial corporations.[25]

Nevertheless, moral, productive risk-taking could pass an elusive threshold and become immoral, unproductive gambling. Indeed, the gambler and the confidence man were the nagging evil alter egos of the productive risk-taker.[26] In particular, many Americans, especially those who worked with their hands, were always suspicious that financiers—who often did nothing but take risks—were unproductive "parasites" on the "real" economy. And yet, pure muscle-and-brawn producerism—the kind that demonized all commercial risk-taking—while present, was never dominant. It was more critical of the "money power" than opposed to the economic activity of risk-taking per se. The reams upon reams of religious and political jeremiads against gambling and "overspeculation" in the nineteenth century were evidence of acute anxiety about the proper scope of commercial risk-taking, but hardly a demand for its wholesale eradication. If anything, such anxiety and unease was evidence of its proliferation.

By the mid-nineteenth century, with commerce expanding and intensifying in a democratic society, in the United States an old commercial truism was becoming an essential ingredient of a new liberal creed. Productive risk-taking was the rightful activity of a free man. "A man has a right," wrote Edwin Freedley, as if stating the obvious in his popular 1856 *A Practical Treatise on Business,* to "risk his own capital." Commercial "gain" was the product of "risk." An individual who took a risk was responsible for a moral/pecuniary reward. He had earned it, no differently than if by the sweat of his own brow. The risk taken was an element of self-ownership. To run commercial risks was part of what it meant to be, as nineteenth-century Americans put it, "independent."[27]

Given a radically uncertain future, from where exactly this moral/pecuniary reward for risk-taking came was, and still is, a contentious subject.[28] For individual risk-taking to be productive, some of the reward—some of the profit—had to be attributable to human faculties: prudence, effort, intelligence, foresight. The market economy was, after all, a field of competition between men, a test of skill. Blind, reckless overspeculation or gambling could only lead to something for nothing, or nothing itself.

Providentialist explanations of future change persisted within nineteenth-century American economic culture. The upside might be evidence of God's inscrutable grace. "God," once said John D. Rockefeller, "gave me my money." Meanwhile, some began to naturalize, in a newly scientific tone, the competitive market economy. Religious and scientific appeals could mix together but free men took risks within an increasingly naturalized abstraction—what would later be known as "the market" or "the economy."[29]

Perhaps it was, in the end, all a game of chance. Fortuna, a "fickle goddess," as a New Orleans newspaper explained in an 1861 article entitled "A Lucky Freak of Fortune," possessed a capricious mood. For no reason, "she snatches some unfortunate mortal, and drags him down to obscurity, and then she raises some humble child of poverty and insignificance to affluence and social distinction." The amorality is striking. Providence too posited a mysteriously working cosmic order, but it was ultimately a just one. If the future was ruled by pure chance, reward for risk-taking was simply a serving of moral luck. Or perhaps the psychological labor of assuming a risk in a market economy governed by brute luck alone warranted an economic desert? The novelist William Dean Howells, in his *A Hazard of New Fortunes* (1890)—in which the waning of providence and the impotency of human will were both great themes— spoke of the power of an "economic chance-world." Perhaps going toe to toe with it alone merited a moral/pecuniary reward.[30]

Still, to many nineteenth-century Americans, the original antebellum mix between chance, a competitive marketplace, and democracy was a potent ideological brew. Chance struck a blow at the kind of aristocratic, hierarchical social order detested by so many antebellum Americans busily on the make. In the nineteenth century freaks of fortune were in fact a common literary plot device—the democratic *deus ex machina*.[31] Freaks were a more preferable source of power and authority compared not only to a king, but also a father, a husband, a town elder, or a slave master. Better to let the freaks, who could in fact energize the democratic will, have at one's fate. Tocqueville already wrote in 1835 that Americans enthused at "all undertakings in which chance plays a part." Americans were "all led to engage in commerce, not only for the sake of the profit it holds out to them, but for the love of the constant excitement occasioned by that pursuit." Life became a "vast lottery," a "game of chance."[32]

Many nineteenth-century Americans continued to invoke a "providential hand" guiding the centrifugal forces of their republic. But they also invoked the wheel of fortune—a long-enduring, originally maritime image—to describe the secular voyage of a commercial, democratic social order, buzzing with so many uprooted and masterless people.

Nevertheless, in 1839 when the newspaperman John O'Sullivan announced the "Manifest Destiny" of the American republic to conquer the West, guided by God's beneficent hand, the title of the article was "The Great Nation of Futurity." The United States was said to have plenty of room for upside risk—in every possible sense of the term—for many, if by no means all, of its members. To assume a risk, to take it, make it your own, to master it, or even just to enjoy the existential thrill of it, was a birthright of the democratic soul, a soul born in commerce.[33]

What follows however is the history of the nineteenth-century American countermovement against the generative insecurity and radical uncertainty of capitalism, as corporate risk management—through a proliferating series of profit-seeking and offsetting financial transactions, calculations and counter-calculations—increasingly insinuated itself into the equation.

The term "countermovement" invokes Karl Polanyi's celebrated notion of a "double movement." Polanyi argued that what propelled nineteenth-century liberal capitalism forward was the simultaneous expansion of markets on the one hand and a countermovement that checked that expansion on the other. Through this dynamic, "Society protected itself against the perils inherent in a self-regulating market system." Polanyi focused on the commodification of land, labor, and money. But nineteenth-century liberal capitalism proved equally insistent upon commodifying Polanyi's "perils" into financial "risks." That effort—to depart from Polanyi's dichotomist and moralistic framework, with the "great and permanent evils" of "the market" in pitched battle with the "self-protection of society"—must be taken up on its own terms. For in the end capitalism itself assumes risk. It assumes, in other words, that financial instruments of its own making can adequately stabilize its own unpredictable rhythms. Projecting its own vision of security, stability, and control, corporate risk management was a candidate in the broader countermovement against the perils of capitalism.[34]

Ultimately, in tandem with a new liberal creed corporate risk management came to life. But that outcome was not foreordained, and to address it on its own terms is not to assume its success. Polanyi's skepticism of what he called the utopian elements of the "self-regulating market" is worth keeping in mind. For the upside had widespread allure to many nineteenth-century Americans. That was especially true if the downside could be offloaded to others, ideally the state, without cost.[35] But risk-taking came with dangers, perils, and hazards, which—everyone agreed—had to be coped with. And, as much as the freaks of fortune were welcomed, trailing after them was a long admonitory tradition abounding with storm-tossed marine imagery, with one clear message: do not look to markets, which are perilous, for protection from the perils of markets. It was one thing to be involved in the commercial game but it was quite another to take the game too far, and become fully dependent upon its vicissitudes. That was a life of economic and also existential risk.[36]

Risk's history was thus marked by tension and oftentimes conflict. In this history financial panics and their aftermath—1837, 1873, 1893, and 1907 being the great ones—loom large. Corporate risk management actually spread its wings in the aftermath of the panic of 1837. But so too did other collective strategies. The countermovement of landed independence, premised upon land ownership, not self-ownership, asserted itself. So did the countermovement of slave mastery, premised upon slave ownership, until it met its fate in the Civil War. Later, following the panic of 1873 there was an outgrowth of new fraternal societies. After the panic of 1893, with the Populist Revolt, landed independence made its last political stand. But then the trust question—whether or not an industrial economy of corporate ownership could adequately stabilize capitalism—took center stage. By the opening of the twentieth century, and following the panic of 1907, with the increasing politicization of risk the state began to make its presence felt in the business of risk management.

Nevertheless, by the end of the nineteenth century the American corporate financial system was in place. But in the end risk management—as much as it could offer its own brand of security—worked to obscure the clean moral accounting of risks and rewards, costs and benefits, that the attachment of "risk" to individual freedom had promised. For in the very act of *under*writing liberal self-ownership the financial system also had the capacity to *over*write it.

The evolving corporate financial system opened up new pathways for the accumulation of financial capital. That meant opportunities for speculative profit-making by powerful finance capitalists.[37] Freedley's *A Practical Treatise on Business* stated that a man had a moral "right to risk his own capital."[38] But he had "no right to risk the property of others." There would have to be new legal and political regulations of this kind of financial behavior—while not denying the financial system its lifeblood of circulating capital. If not, Americans would learn the hard way that financial dispossession and plunder would accompany the assumption of risk. Risk management, that is, put financiers in possession of other people's money.

At the same time, the new financial system of corporate risk management constructed abstract, highly mediated, and seemingly unreachable financial circuits. Another crazy quilt, this one of financial obligations, was stitched together. In a turbulent and panic-ridden century, new financial instruments—government debt, railroad bonds, commodities futures, mortgage-backed securities, corporate stocks—multiplied and circulated at an astonishing frequency and speed. The intricate web ultimately made risk systemic, enveloping everyone—including that system's very architects. Risk management constantly manufactured new forms of uncertainty and insecurity—freaks of fortune.

But this flashes ahead to the end of risk's nineteenth-century drama. To enter that history, what is first needed is an excursion back to the maritime world that Shaw drew upon in *Farwell* to enunciate a new vision of personal freedom. That excursion, curiously enough, leads directly to the history of New World slavery.

CHAPTER 2

The Perils of the Seas

It may, in general, be said that everything happening to a ship, in
the course of her voyage, by the intermediate act of God, without
the intervention of human agency, is a peril of the sea.

—*American Ship-Masters Assistant* (1807)

R ISK'S HISTORY BEGAN with the extension of commerce over space,
with the daring and audacity of long-distance seaborne trade. Risk
was the fruit of merchant capital—of the early modern networks of mercantile commerce and credit that mobilized and knitted together different geographical arenas of economic production.[1] The specific branch of
merchant capital that invented risk management was marine insurance.

In North America, the great colonial merchants were the first men to
commodify perils into financial "risks"—or "risques," as they were known
in the seventeenth and eighteenth centuries. Through marine insurance
they purchased from one another financial compensation in the event
that their property was lost to a "peril of the seas," or an "act of God." A
storm destroyed a vessel, a ship was seized by pirates—the merchant-
insurer provided the merchant-owner compensation for the lost value of
his cargo. To cope with the perils of seaborne trade, the insurance principle was born.

From the ports of Boston, New York, Philadelphia, Baltimore, and
Charleston colonial merchants exported the great American staples—
fish, timber, rum, tobacco, indigo, rice, and later cotton. They brought
to the New World the European indentured servants and the African
slaves whose labor was required to produce them. Insuring the passage

of their cargoes, merchants sold their "risks" to each other: risks on timber bound from New England to the West Indies; on rice bound from the Carolinas to London; on slaves bound from West Africa to the Chesapeake. Much like there was a commercial trade in rice, so was there a commercial trade in risk.

Merchants thus turned the for-profit engine of a financial market into a collective strategy for economic security. Running the risks of long-distance trade, they strained to foresee, control, and manipulate the contingent link between present and future. They also sought to profit from it.

Merchants formed what might be termed "risk communities"—collectivities that socialized personal financial "risks." When used in conjunction with security the term "community" often connotes traditional, noncommercial values rooted in specific places. But community in that sense of the word was after all an invented tradition of the nineteenth century. The term "risk community" is therefore meant to invoke risk management's countermovement against capitalism's generative insecurities and radical uncertainties—in particular the abstract social interdependencies created by the commodification of peril and the financial circulation of risk.[2]

By the time of the American Revolution, the North American British colonies had become strikingly commercial in their character.[3] Yet, the insurance principle was still a rather unique response to hazard. It was "Merchants only that make Insurances," as one English merchant explained in 1720. The same could be said, more or less, in the America of 1800.[4] In subsequent chapters there will be the occasion to examine in depth the late antebellum collision of a number of collective strategies with the evolving corporate financial system of risk management, so dependent upon the insurance principle. But first the origins of the insurance principle must be explored in long-distance seaborne trade.

Within this maritime history are also the roots of the nineteenth-century marriage of risk with liberal notions of self-ownership and freedom.[5] Those roots intertwined, it turns out, with merchant capital's inhuman embrace of New World slavery. For before men became the proprietors of "risks" on their own free selves, they first owned the "risks" on the bodies of their slaves. Before risk was an element of self-ownership, that is, it was an element of slave ownership.[6]

One episode draws together all of these currents, charting risk's winding maritime origins up to the final antebellum decades—when the idea of the personal assumption of risk began to express a new vision of freedom. In October of 1841 the brig *Creole* set sail from Norfolk, Virginia, bound for New Orleans with a cargo of 135 slaves. The lives of the slaves, for the duration of their transit, had been insured by their masters. None of this was unusual and the voyage of the *Creole* is a fitting entry point into both the transnational maritime origins of risk and its subsequent nineteenth-century career in the United States.

Out on the Atlantic, nineteen male members of the cargo of 135 mounted a successful insurrection. Taking control of the brig, the rebels sailed to freedom in the Bahamas, a British possession where slavery had been abolished by act of Parliament in 1833. Back in New Orleans, the owners of the *Creole* slaves sued their marine underwriters for financial compensation for the lost value of their slave property. The case ended in the Louisiana Supreme Court in 1845. With lawyers quoting English, French, Dutch, Spanish, Portuguese, and Italian treatises, cases, and ordinances stretching back centuries, the transcript of *Thomas McCargo v. The New Orleans Insurance Company* alone is an adequate history of risk's centuries-long maritime origins. Yet the decision itself took shape in a roundabout way, when the Louisiana Supreme Court faced the vexing question of whether or not a slave revolt was one of the "perils of the seas." Was a slave revolt an act of God?

The brig *Creole* sat moored near Norfolk, Virginia, on October 31, 1841, with a cargo of tobacco in addition to 135 slaves. Its captain was Robert Ensor. Zephaniah C. Gifford was first mate. Onboard were five white mariners, a free black cook, and a slave overseer named William Henry Merritt. There were also a number of free white passengers, including Captain Ensor's family and Theophilus McCargo, the son of Thomas McCargo, who owned twenty-six of the slaves. In the United States' thriving domestic slave trade—a forced migration of somewhere between 750,000 and 1.2 million—the large majority of slaves traveled overland. Yet, there was a riverine trade on the Mississippi linking the Upper and Lower South, and a larger coastwise trade connecting the Eastern seaboard with the Gulf of Mexico. Norfolk to New Orleans was a common route among others. No less than 38,000 slaves passed through U.S. waterways from 1817 to 1852.[7]

Having set sail for New Orleans on November 6, 1841, the *Creole* experienced nothing out of the ordinary until the night of November 7.[8] The crew secured the slave women in the afterhold and the men in the forehold. Only the men were occasionally permitted on deck, although the house slaves of the McCargo family slept in the main cabin. The night of November 7 was First Mate Gifford's watch. At nine o'clock, the slave Elijah Morris informed him that a male slave was in the afterhold with the women, which was strictly forbidden. Gifford roused the slave overseer William Merritt from his sleep. Merritt descended into the hold, lit a match, and found Madison Washington.

Washington was a Virginia slave who had once escaped to Canada. He returned to Virginia in search of his wife but had been recaptured and sold to Thomas McCargo. "Madison," Merritt shouted, "is it possible that you are down here! You are the last man on board of the brig I expected to find here." Washington responded, "I am going up, I cannot stay here," and leapt on deck. Gifford chased him, but then a pistol fired, the ball grazing the back of Gifford's head. Most likely, Morris fired the shot. Stunned, Gifford retreated back to the main cabin and sounded the alarm. Washington proceeded to the forehold shouting, "We have commenced, and must go through. Rush, boys, rush aft. We have got them now!"[9]

Nineteen slaves, all male, gathered on the deck. The women remained in their hold—the whites would later recall hearing them crying and praying during the fateful moments of the mutiny. The slave overseer Merritt somehow had escaped from the women's hold and slipped into the main cabin. Gifford, after sounding the alarm, climbed up the rigging to the main-topsail, where he hid. Now, with Merritt in the main cabin were the young Theophilis McCargo and his house slaves, a free black cook, and the white passengers. The group of nineteen closed on them. A white passenger, John R. Hewell, an owner of slaves onboard, grabbed a musket, opened the cabin door and fired. He drew a knife and plunged forward and the nineteen men seized upon him with their bare hands. Hewell staggered back into the cabin and later bled to death. Everyone in the main cabin now surrendered, except for Merritt who hid under a blanket. Washington ordered them all into the forehold.

Captain Ensor, asleep in his private quarters with his family, had heard the alarm. Now he appeared on deck calling his crew to fight. Only two sailors showed (one stayed at the wheel, all the others hid in the riggings). These two were knocked down to the deck but not further harmed. Ensor was stabbed numerous times before he too escaped to hide in the main-topsail. Washington, Morris, and two other slaves, Ben Blacksmith and Doctor Cuffin, searched for Merritt and finally found him in the main cabin hiding underneath the blanket.

When Merritt was discovered, he assumed he would be killed. But instead Washington directed him into the main cabin with the slaves Blacksmith, Cuffin, and a few others—to "have a conversation." Washington demanded that Merritt navigate the *Creole* to Liberia. Merritt said there was not enough water or provisions. Blacksmith and Cuffin and the others then demanded to go to a British possession. They insisted, according to Merritt, that, "they did not want to go anywhere else but where Mr. Lumpkin's negroes went last year," referring to the 1840 shipwreck of the *Hermosa,* also bound from Virginia to New Orleans with a slave cargo.[10] British wreckers carried the *Hermosa* slaves to the port of Nassau in New Providence, where British authorities pronounced them free. Ninety of the 135 slaves onboard the *Creole* came from Robert Lumpkin's infamous Richmond, Virginia, slave pen. Obviously, they knew of the *Hermosa*. Merritt grabbed a chart and illustrated the route to Nassau.

The group of nineteen put their former overseer in charge of the *Creole*'s navigation. Shouting upward into the sails, they persuaded the remaining white crewmembers to descend from the riggings and to assist Merritt. The sailors later said they feared for their lives. But Morris, when asked once by a sailor if the whites would be killed, reportedly responded, "No, I expect we shall rise again among ourselves, but the white people will not be hurt." The whites, including the captain, were allowed to dress their wounds and they dined and drank in the main cabin with the group of nineteen, who told them "all they had done was for their freedom." The slaves who did not participate in the mutiny were not allowed out of the hold and supposedly "behaved precisely as they had done before the mutiny."[11]

At ten o'clock at night on November 8, the *Creole* arrived at the port of Nassau in New Providence and a ship with a free black pilot and crew greeted the brig. A quarantine boat, with a white officer, also came alongside. In a daring move, First Mate Gifford jumped from the *Creole* and into the boat. He was ferreted off to the American consul and the two proceeded to the governor of the Bahamas, demanding a guard placed over the vessel and its "cargo." The governor sent a guard of twenty-four black, uniformed soldiers with a white commanding officer who all openly fraternized with the insurrectionists. In the next few days, British magistrates boarded the *Creole* and deposed the white crew and passengers.[12]

While the *Creole* then sat, the American consul hatched a secret plan. The captain and crew of the American bark *Louisa* would surprise and forcibly retake the *Creole*, which would then sail to Indian Key where a U.S. vessel of war awaited. On November 12, the *Louisa* crew rowed out to the *Creole*. But they were too late. That morning a crowd, mostly black, gathered on shore in sight of the brig. A number of boats, all manned by blacks armed with clubs, had encircled the *Creole*, and were shouting instructions to those onboard. The Americans were turned back without a fight.

The British had not been caught by surprise by the arrival of the *Creole*. Only two years before, in 1839, the Colonial Office dispatched from London instructions on how to proceed in such an event. Before British emancipation, two slave-laden American vessels—the *Comet* and the *Encomium*—had wrecked in the British Bahamas and a number of American slaves had gone free (146 from the *Comet*, thirteen from the *Encomium*). After British emancipation, a third vessel, the *Enterprise*, was driven by "stress of weather" to the Bahamas and all of its slaves were pronounced free. The U.S. government had requested compensation from the British for the American owners of slaves on all three lost vessels. Parliament agreed to compensate the owners of the *Comet* and the *Encomium* slaves at their insured value but not those of the *Enterprise*, which landed in the Bahamas after British emancipation. The Colonial Office then issued instructions that when American slave vessels entered British ports, for whatever reason, at "that moment" the slaves "were Free, as Slavery had been abolished throughout the British Empire, and they had acquired Rights which the Courts there were bound to recognize and protect." That was why the *Hermosa* slaves subsequently found freedom on British soil. The Colonial Office added only one caveat. With respect to fugitive slaves, officials might not "shield" a "Criminal from Justice" and must return slaves guilty of "Murder," "Rape," or "Arson." Thus British officials held the *Creole* four days, deposing white crew-members. They were investigating the possible murder of the white passenger John R. Hewell.[13]

Likely perturbed at American duplicity, at two o'clock on November 12 British magistrates arrived onboard the *Creole*. The attorney general, G. C. Anderson, ordered the blacks on the surrounding boats to throw their weapons into the sea. He put the nineteen into custody. First Mate Gifford later swore that Anderson told the remaining *Creole* slaves they were "free to go as they please." Anderson later swore he said, "that, as far as the authorities of the island were concerned, all restrictions on their movements were removed." Three cheers went up from the boats and a British official waved them up alongside the *Creole*. They carried the former cargo of the brig to land and freedom. Ever persistent, Gifford would later attempt to smuggle them back onto the brig but the "threats of the people on shore" prevented him. Most would soon sail to Jamaica, their subsequent fates unknown. Of the group of nineteen, two died in a New Providence prison. The others, on orders from London, were eventually released. But the destinies of those seventeen are unknown as well.[14]

Back on the *Creole*, two female slaves had never left their hold, saying they did not "wish such freedom as there was there." Three of McCargo's six female house slaves, two a mother and child, remained in the main cabin and were "crying, and did not know what to do." They also would never set foot on British soil. In fact, according to British records, five of the 164 *Comet* slaves had chosen to "return to Servitude in the United States," and twelve of the forty-five *Encomium* slaves had willfully "returned with their Owners to the United States." The *Creole* sailed from New Providence bound for New Orleans with a cargo of tobacco and five slaves on November 17, 1841.[15]

The "*Creole* affair" caused a minor diplomatic storm. With Secretary of State Daniel Webster handling the negotiations, the South was in an uproar over the putative British seizure of American private property. John Calhoun led the howls in the Senate. Meanwhile, the embattled American antislavery movement rejoiced. Eventually, the parties submitted to arbitration and in 1853 the United States won financial compensation for the *Creole* slaves' former owners.[16]

The *Creole* insurrection has become a telling episode in the history of slave resistance. And yet, with respect to risk's history the subsequent insurance dispute that wound its way through the Louisiana courts was just as much a telling episode in the history of freedom.[17]

When the Louisiana Supreme Court heard the case of *Thomas Mc-Cargo v. The New Orleans Insurance Company,* the fundamental question was how insuring human chattel was different from insuring other forms of property in motion across the high seas—say, bales of cotton. Obviously, cotton did not mutiny. But for centuries, human chattels had always been objects of risk insured by their owners when in transit, most often across the Atlantic Ocean. Legal disputes over insurance liability for slave revolts in the Atlantic World were not uncommon and the case of the *Creole* was one of the last in a grotesque series.[18]

But the case of the *Creole* was also unique, one-of-a-kind. Not only does it locate the origins of capitalism and risk in New World slavery, it also provided the basis for a legal dispute in an antebellum New Orleans court that signaled the incipient link among freedom, self-ownership, and risk. The court recognized that a slave-owner *ipso facto* owned the "risk" on his slave's life—a logical consequence of slave ownership. A slave, likewise by definition, could not own his or her "risk." His or her fate belonged to his or her master and the "risk" commodified that destiny as the master's private property. But when the *Creole* slaves dared to revolt—chasing the greatest upside of all, their freedom—and succeeded, they had thereby repossessed, reenclosed as it were, their own personal "risks." The court adopted a tellingly circular argument. In their act of revolt, seizing their risks back from their masters, the *Creole* (ex-)slaves now owned themselves. Consequently, their former masters could no longer insure them. The successful revolt voided the insurance contract.

The notion that freedom meant the personal assumption of risk was not merely an abstruse legal question. Inside and outside the courtroom it was one with increasing salience in the final antebellum decades. Nevertheless, while the New Orleans court grappled with the peculiarities of "slave risks," the general features of antebellum American marine insurance were in the background, taken for granted. Therefore, to understand the case of the *Creole*, to appreciate a new vision of personal freedom, what first must be considered is the world of merchant capital in the age of sail.

In 1841, when the *Creole* set sail—even as the age of sail was about to give way to the age of iron, telegraph, and steam, and a new probabilistic, statistical mind-set was about to revolutionize the business—American marine insurance was strikingly consistent with centuries of mercantile practice.

Marine insurance in Europe dates at least as far back as the thirteenth century, and the technique was known to other trading civilizations. Before the commercial revolution of this time, merchants more often traveled with their goods. Increasingly, the great merchants became sedentary, conducting their trades via partners, factors, and agents, while placing their cargoes on ships mastered by captains. Now, from a distance, merchants contemplated the future "perils of the seas" that endangered their commodities in motion. From such anxiety, they commodified their doubts into a new form of private property called "risk." Merchants, in other words, isolated "risk" from physical goods in ways that allowed them to buy and sell that same "risk" independent of those same goods. Insuring their cargoes, they exchanged risks, offloading financial responsibility for their losses. In northern Italy, its apparent birthplace, marine insurance was firmly established by the fifteenth century.[19]

From there marine insurance spread, always to the long-distance, speculative trades—those with the greatest upsides: the Venetian trade with the Levant; the Dutch trade with the East Indies; the Spanish and Portuguese, then the English and French, trade with the Americas. In 1601, at the dawn of the English colonization of the New World, none other than lord chancellor and philosopher Francis Bacon set down the first English Act to recognize "Merchant Assurances." Merchants bought policies of "Assurance" when they made "great adventures," especially to "remote parts." In 1668, the first colonial American maritime code recognized in

Massachusetts Bay Colony the practice of merchant "ensurance." By the 1680s, Edward Lloyd's London coffee house had become the central clearinghouse for the private underwriting of English maritime risks, including American ones. The first colonial American marine insurance merchant-underwriters began to purchase risks in Philadelphia in 1720.[20]

Marine insurance was not much different by the time the *Creole* set sail in 1841. True, there had been some changes. In 1720, American long-distance trade was conducted under the umbrella of post-Restoration, mercantilist British Navigation Laws intended to circumscribe colonial trade within the British Empire. American planters and merchants largely sold colonial staples on their own accounts, increasingly transporting them in American ships but consigning them to commission agents in London. In return, London merchants provided the colonials with a variety of financial services, including capital and credit, and the underwriting of their risks. The London market for American risks dwarfed the colonial market. The system routinized and there ensued the mid-eighteenth-century golden age of American colonial commerce.[21]

The Revolution's disruption brought a flourishing American market for maritime risks. Liberated from the British Empire, American commerce expanded to encompass new ventures to China, India, and the Dutch East Indies, and during the French Revolutionary Wars neutral American merchants seized upon the European carrying trades. Long-distance trade flourished—by 1810 American commercial tonnage was 1.25 million, comparable in size to Great Britain's merchant fleet. American underwriting would become more domestic, and take new institutional forms.[22]

American independence ended imperial restrictions on the chartering of joint-stock corporations. In the midst of a flurry of postrevolutionary incorporations there arose new marine insurance companies. The first was the Insurance Company of North America, chartered by the Pennsylvania legislature in 1792. The New Orleans Insurance Company, which would insure many of the *Creole* risks, dates to 1805. By 1810, the private, individual underwriting of marine risks in America had almost ceased, with a total of twenty-six corporations now buying up maritime risks in the leading ports of Boston, Philadelphia, Baltimore, and New York. By 1837, there were thirty-seven corporations in Boston alone. That year, one London underwriter estimated that American corporations underwrote 95 percent of American maritime risks.[23]

Corporations like the New Orleans Insurance Company gave the financial circulation of risk a new institutional flavor, presaging the corporate nature of American financial risk management. Yet, the early national American insurance companies were simply consortiums of the great proprietary merchants who had already been engaged in private underwriting. In 1841, for instance, the longtime president of the New Orleans Insurance Company was Thomas Urquhart. He and his brother David—the partners T. & D. Urquhart—were two of twenty-one New Orleans merchants, representing ten partnerships who in 1815 owned 50 percent of all New Orleans insurance stock. Ownership was more widespread in the North, but not by much. Marine insurance was still conducted within the tight mercantile networks of long-distance trade.[24]

To begin to pry open that world, consider the Bostonian merchant Joseph Balch. Balch was born in the town of Newburyport, Massachusetts, long a center of the fish and rum trades. He descended from a line of Puritan merchants who first arrived in Massachusetts Bay Colony in 1630. His father was a private marine underwriter. Balch first arrived in Boston in 1810, working under another private underwriter. In 1818, he became the first president of the newly chartered Merchants' Insurance Company of Boston, remaining one of the leading insurance men in antebellum America until his death in 1849. His brokerage journal from 1813–1823 survives. Within it, the logic of maritime risk comes to life.[25]

Balch's journal tells the story of a momentous era of American long-distance trade. In the opening pages, Balch underwrote risks himself or brokered them between merchants and other private underwriters. By the end, he bought risks for a corporation, the Merchants' Insurance Company. After 1815, European peace ushered in a new era of competition in the Atlantic carrying trades and many American merchants turned to the Pacific or new trades in the expanding American hinterland. Balch thus insured the China, India, and Dutch West Indies trades. In 1761, the great New York merchant Gerard Beekman lamented that no one in London would "Insure at Any rate to the Mississippi." Balch brokered and purchased Mississippi River risks all the time. The westward commercial expansion of the United States—of which the *Creole* voyage was part—is in plain sight in his brokerage journal.[26]

Balch did not trade "slave risks." He once signed a petition protesting the treatment of free black sailors in the South, but he was not an abolitionist. One of his lines of trade was however "cotton risks," as slave-produced cotton was fast becoming America's leading export. By 1823, as cotton cultivation spread west, information concerning short-staple cotton flooded his pages and the Port of New Orleans fell under his gaze. Balch obsessively tracked levels of cotton imports at Liverpool and their point of origin, whether from America, the Levant, or Bengal. Apart from shipments to industrializing England, Balch also monitored the coastwise shipment of cotton to the nascent textile mills of New England. Pushed out of the Atlantic trades, a good portion of American merchant capital was now being invested in the Northeast. Foresight was Balch's greatest asset. He envisioned the entire global cotton trade in order to enclose pieces of the contingent future into risks.[27]

In Balch's day, as it had been for centuries, a series of basic rules governed the commodification of the perils of the seas and the financial exchange of maritime risks. These rules emerged from mercantile practice but were also governed by the international law of marine insurance. Ultimately, the law set the working rules of risk. In the early modern era, the most fundamental legal rule was that a "risk" only existed if it maintained a relationship to a primary, underlying piece of corporeal property. A risk was the product of a double commodification—thus Balch's nomenclature "cotton risks."

Balch commodified the perils threatening a primary, underlying asset in motion on the high seas. The primary commodity was the cotton. The secondary, financial commodity was the "risk." The risk detached from the cotton, or the physical commodity referred to as the merchant's "interest." The financial exchange of "the risk" then proceeded along its own distinct temporal and spatial path. The cotton might be bound from Savannah to Liverpool but the risk found its way to Boston (and ultimately to wherever the shareholders of the Merchants' Insurance Company resided). An 1809 Philadelphia translation of a famous 1655 commercial treatise published in Naples explained that with marine insurance, the "goods themselves are not bought and sold." Rather, "merely the obligation is transferred, to meet the risque." And so, in merchant vernacular, a risk could be "run" or "carried" by the owner of the primary, underlying asset. Or, the risk could be "thrown" to another merchant and insured. Risks were conceptual, but originally they were not mere figments of imagination. They required material, corporeal foundations.[28]

Early modern merchant vernacular reveals how the two commodities operated in tandem. The key term was the expression "Risque and Account." Take for instance the business correspondence of the eighteenth-century Charleston, South Carolina, merchant and insurance broker, and later jurist, Robert Pringle. Pringle's letters always first denoted the primary commodity at hand—more often rice, but sometimes slaves—and then upon whose "Risque and Account" the "adventure" was being carried out. Pringle traded as a commission agent but also as an independent proprietor on his own account. The status of the "risque," as he put it—whether it was Pringle's or one of his principals, "thrown" already to another merchant or not—was a consistent theme of his correspondence. In one 1739 letter Pringle informed his brother Andrew, who was in London, that a cargo was bound eastward on the Atlantic "on your proper Risque." Andrew should therefore choose whether to "make insurance" in London. The owner of a commodity in motion on the Atlantic was *ipso facto* the proprietor of a financial "Risque." In search of profit he ran an upside risk. To acquire security, downside protection, a "hedge," he could "throw" a portion of his risk to someone else.[29]

Before the telegraph, there was another trick to the trade. Unless a merchant insured with an underwriter in his homeport, the "advice to Insure" traveled over the same waters as the underlying good itself. In London, Andrew Pringle would receive "advice to Insure" from Robert—the name of the ship, the captain, the route, and often the invoice of the goods—weeks after the ship in question sailed. Robert was always anxious to "receive advice to Insure" with "due Notice" when trading on his own "Risque & Account." Some gamed the system, instructing their brokers at the point of destination to hold off on insuring for a week or two. If no news of arrival came by then, the broker was to then have the cargo insured in London.[30]

Still, with double commodification the financial exchange of "risque" always maintained a foundation, however tenuous, in the fate of the underlying, material, primary commodity. For this reason, Balch necessarily tracked the global cotton trade, as Robert Pringle had tracked the Atlantic rice trade before him. Information was critical. There was never an American equivalent of London's Lloyd's Coffee House. Yet, by Pringle's day, colonial merchants frequented the new coffeehouses of Philadelphia, New York, and Boston. In 1808 on Boston's State Street opened the new "Exchange Coffeehouse," a seven-story building modeled after Lloyd's. The first floor was the merchant's exchange, thronged with merchants, mariners, and underwriters seeking news of ship arrivals and departures, sifting through manifests, bills of lading, and insurance policies. Elsewhere, in Louisiana, the New Orleans Insurance Company was located in the heart of New Orleans' "Exchange Alley," two blocks away from the city's slave pens.[31]

Mercantile customs were ultimately enforced by the international law of marine insurance. Foremost was the legal doctrine of "insurable interest." A merchant could only insure property in which he had a pecuniary "interest." He could not insure another man's ship or cargo, enclosing another man's primary, underlying commodity into a risk of his own. If so, he had not exchanged a risk but rather had simply wagered in favor of a ship's destruction. In colonial America, statutory authority for "insurable interest" resided in the British Marine Insurance Act of 1745. Early U.S. courts would enforce "insurable interest" under the authority of the common law.

The doctrine of insurable interest had emerged over the early modern period. According to the same 1655 Neapolitan treatise, "A wager of insurance among merchants of any sum is valid." In the period before the 1745 British Marine Insurance Act, Lloyd's was famous for such policies. At the end of the eighteenth century, the great European marine insurance treatise writers condemned insuring without interest and the American courts followed. The thingyness of risk was the crucial divide. As one French writer explained, insurance was not a wager but an "aleatory contract," since "the consideration which one part receives is not the price of a thing which he gives but of a risk which he agrees to take upon himself." By the nineteenth century, "insurable interest" was the rule throughout the Atlantic.[32]

Another legal principle guiding double commodification concerned "deviation." A risk only existed when the insured ship or cargo was in motion, along a path agreed to by the underwriter. In 1841, according to his policy with the New Orleans Insurance Company, Thomas McCargo's slave risks began at Norfolk and continued until "said goods and merchandize shall be safely landed at New Orleans." The *Creole* was allowed, only if "obliged by stress of weather or other unavoidable accident," to deviate from this course "without prejudice to this insurance." If there was an unwarranted deviation, the risk was thrown back to McCargo.[33]

A further legal rule prohibited what was called "overvaluation." A merchant could not fraudulently overvalue the "interest" insured. A long tradition of legal prohibition and mercantile custom stood behind this. In the early modern world, customarily merchants ran at least a tiny portion of their own risks. That was no longer true by Balch's day. In twin 1761 and 1766 decisions the British jurist Lord Mansfield had issued a new standard. Merchants acting in "utmost good faith" could value insured property as they saw fit. The question was whether such "valued policies" insured the primary commodity or the contingent expectation of "profit," which did not have enough thingyness to be considered a material and thus insurable thing. As one French treatise writer explained in 1783, the expectation of profit was "a mental figment not existing on board the ship, and consequently cannot be insured." Mansfield adopted the same position, ruling that merchants could not insure against market volatility, or the "loss of a Market" as it was then known. But they could write "valued policies." So could, and did, both Balch and the New Orleans Insurance Company.[34]

The final step in the double commodification was that the risk required a price. That was the "premium" rate, indicating the probability that the ship would perish from one of the "perils of the seas." In 1841, there were still no statistics computing the relative frequency of these events. There was no actuarial knowledge.[35] In an 1839 article in the *Merchant's Magazine and Commercial Review* entitled "Rates of Premium for Marine Insurance," an aging Balch explained that, "Hitherto, the computation of premiums of insurance on marine risks has been on no systematic or regular principles, but on the loose, general, and indefinite impressions of those who make the contracts."[36] The pages of Balch's brokerage journal provide the right image: a messy compilation of numbers, scribbles, and pasted newspaper clippings running over each other, upside down and sideways. Unlike later actuarial tables, no one besides Balch could use this journal to price a risk. Only prudence and foresight distinguished the successful underwriter.

For underwriters had no techniques to price risks unavailable to their original owners. In 1819 the Rhode Island merchant Thomas Thompson wrote to Nathaniel Phillips, then Balch's peer at Providence's Warren Insurance Company. On his Amsterdam-bound cargo, Thompson demanded a "premium of 2 per cent," which was "the premium at which I have insurance affected in this town." Commonly, a clerk transferred a prospective voyage's details to a card which was then presented to Phillips and a number of the insurance corporation's mercantile directors. Each wrote upon the same card the premium he had in mind, before they settled upon a rate or rejected the risk. The double commodification was now complete and a "risk" had come into being.[37]

Of course, given the cost of the premium, merchants would rather not insure and run their risks themselves. Already, there were countless strategies for reducing the size of a singular risk. In Balch's day merchants still commonly divided their "interests" among numerous vessels, lightening their risks. By the nineteenth century, the "sixty-fourth" had become the standard unit of ownership in ship-bottoms and the cargo-holds of vessels were similarly divided into allotments. Or, as Adam Smith wrote in 1776 in *The Wealth of Nations,* "When a great company, or even a great merchant, has twenty or thirty ships at sea, they may, as it were, insure one another." The great early modern joint-stock corporations, like the East India Company, pooled investor capital, lightening potential risk. Furthermore, there were other financial instruments besides insurance with which merchant might hedge, most prominently the custom and law of "general average." If a portion of a cargo was lost in an emergency effort to save the ship, the owners of the surviving cargo (including their insurers) compensated for the loss, proportionate to their share. Merchants insured lines of trade in which their upsides were large—in other words trades that were exposed to great peril.[38]

These were the most precious trades, with the highest value per unit and the most uncertain of fates, usually because they were carried out over the longest of distances.[39] Therefore the Atlantic trades were the most insured lines in colonial America. In the early national period, it was the new Pacific trades and then the burgeoning trade with South America and California. The most speculative trades produced the largest risks.

In this context, the *Creole* risks were no aberration. In the eighteenth century, the Atlantic slave trade was at the very cutting edge of British marine insurance. After the demise of the seventeenth-century Royal

African Company, proprietary merchants dominated the trade. They less often spread their "interests" among numerous ventures and more commonly owned the ship and the entirety of the cargo outright, which produced large risks. Colonial American slavers insured at London. When in 1758 the Rhode Island slaver William Vernon wrote to his London insurance broker reconfirming his "advice to insure," he reminded him, "I never had risqued my interest abroad without insurance." The Atlantic slave trade—which brought 12.5 million Africans to the New World, 450,000 alighting on future or current U.S. ports—was impractical without marine insurance.[40]

So too was the post-1815 renaissance of southern slavery in the United States. The Bostonian Willard Phillips, who in 1823 published the first American marine insurance treatise, maintained a file of a dozen representative American marine insurance policies. It included two domestic slave trade policies. After the *Creole* revolt, the New Orleans slave broker Newton Boley wrote to his client and principal, the Virginia dealer William Crow, relating his shock at the mutiny. But Boley also confirmed to Crow that insurance had been made in New Orleans on fifteen of his slaves—likewise bound from Virginia to New Orleans. Slaves sold to New Orleans down the Mississippi River were also commonly insured. Merchant underwriters had once insured, literally, the possibility of New World slavery. Now, corporations like the New Orleans Insurance Company insured its future in the United States.[41]

Men thus offloaded their risks onto one another through commercial contracts. Financial risks circulated across the Atlantic as mercantile risk communities formed. These collectivities were voluntary, nonhierarchical, and decentralized. Within them, single risks fractured into abstract bits as merchants sliced, repackaged, and resold risks in a dizzying sequence—until risks had been socialized almost beyond recognition. With respect to the onshore society, for centuries—and right up until the time the *Creole* sailed—the social logic of mercantile risk communities was quite unique.

Individual mercantile proprietorship thus led to complex forms of collective action to cope with, and profit from, uncertainty. In the *Creole*'s day, a heroic American discourse began to celebrate the "great merchant," the courageous, lone risk-taker. The truth was that there was no such thing as a Robinson Crusoe in the world of long-distance trade.[42]

Further, it was not the case that one individual sold his risk to another and then the music stopped—not with multiple underwriting and "reinsurance." Underwriters usually did not purchase the full value of a risk. They hedged their own bets, insuring only portions of individual risks. In the 1760s, for instance, the Philadelphia broker Benjamin Fuller once acquired thirty-four separate underwriters for one single risk.[43] Whether bought whole or in parts, risks could then be passed through to other buyers in what was called reinsurance. One of those thirty-four underwriters could sell an already chopped up risk to yet another merchant (or chop it up yet again and resell it to multiple parties). The game stopped only when news concerning the ship's fate landed at the door of the man holding the final bit of the original risk.

The British 1745 Marine Insurance Act barred reinsurance. But after the Revolution, American merchants brought it back. Soon, the United States was known for its thriving reinsurance market. One single risk could circulate and fracture up and down the Atlantic seaboard, even across the ocean itself. When a ship was lost, it might take years to fully unwind the series of transactions. This was why merchants were so fastidious in their correspondence to establish the status of the "Risque." The original proprietor often had no clue as to who, in the end, owned his personal risk.[44]

Postrevolutionary corporate underwriting reformulated the old system and injected it with new potential. Corporations still underwrote portions of singular risks, although more often they insured the whole. Since the ownership of insurance company stock was at first highly restricted within the hands of the mercantile directors, incorporation itself was a new form of multiple underwriting. Reinsurance would only burgeon and expand with the rise of corporate underwriting. But joint-stock insurance corporations harbored a new element. As *DeBow's Commercial Review* put it in 1846, "The great New York merchant, Astor, cannot pass a ship load of cotton safely over the ocean, without adding a few mites, at the same time, to the treasury of the poor old widow, that has invested her every farthing in the company which guarantees his adventure." By 1840, for instance, the combined capitalization of Boston insurance corporations was $61.5 million (compared to $200.5 million in Boston's commercial banks). Insurance corporations began to accumulate financial capital, as risk was spread outside the mercantile community.[45]

Despite the abstractions and complexity, the obligations that bound these risk communities were concrete. They had the force of merchant custom, but ultimately also the law behind them. Early modern merchants not only suffered from anxiety concerning the fate of their ships, but also the trustworthiness of their counterparties. For this reason, commerce often filtered through kinship, ethnic, and friendship networks. In his correspondence, Robert Pringle instructively marked various merchants throughout the British littoral as either "strangers" or "friends." Legal contracts provided another source of confidence. When disputes occurred, merchants commonly resorted first to private arbitration. That failing, they resorted to courts, and the early federal U.S. courts were clogged with marine insurance cases. There, merchant-owners and merchant-underwriters met as formal equals. The coercive authority of the law secured the sanctity of their risk communities.[46]

The marine insurance contract thus provided a form of economic and also social security. The practice became a structural necessity of long-distance trade—as well as a standard against which to measure a merchant's prudential duty to attend to the future. In his 1601 "Act touching the policies of Assurances used among Merchants," Bacon had explained that with a "policy of Assurance:"

> it cometh to pass upon the loss or perishing of any ship there followeth not the undoing of any man, but the loss lighteth rather easily upon many than heavily upon few, and rather them that adventure not than those that do adventure, whereby all merchants, especially of the younger sort, are allured to venture more willingly and more freely.[47]

Without marine insurance, long-distance trade would not flourish. Merchants would simply refuse to run the risks themselves.

At the same time, marine insurance was a for-profit commercial transaction. It itself was therefore fundamentally uncertain. From the underwriter's point of view, "Insurance," as Lord Mansfield famously put it in 1766, was "Speculation." To follow the early modern mercantile linguistic conventions, marine insurance was the original form of "risque" taking. Mansfield was aware of the gambling manias that had gripped Lloyd's of London in the era of the South Sea Bubble. Later, by the time of the *Creole* a small American public had begun to speculate on the fluctuations of marine insurance stocks. These were all predictable consequences of the effort to acquire economic security in a financial market. That effort, time and again, led to new forms of speculative risk-taking which required new efforts at risk management—which led to more new forms of speculative risk-taking. Risk management manufactured insecurity. The dynamic, on ever grander scales, extends across the centuries.[48]

But in the early U.S. republic, a risk community was still rather distinctive. Only compare marine insurance to more traditional collective strategies that coped with the burden of peril without commodifying it into a financial risk. They too were present on the ships that crossed the high seas, although they squared better with onshore social logics. These collective strategies consisted of social relations—masters and slaves, masters and servants, husbands and wives, parents and children—that were more local and personal. Premised on hierarchy, many operated through the paternal and noncommercial exercise of mutual duties and obligations. Rather than contract and consent, they were often enforced by coercion, even interpersonal violence. But they too were ultimately enforced by the law.

Take, for example, the ship's captain and crew—masters and seamen. Captains, and less often crewmembers, could be "co-adventurers." They had the privilege to carry goods on their own "risk and account." But the crew was more often compensated with wages. Wages were *not* insurable. There was concern that if seamen insured their wages they would take less care with the ship. But the real reason, as one late eighteenth-century French treatise writer explained, citing codes in France, Antwerp, and Amsterdam, was that wages (like profits) did not "form a physical object which exists on board a ship." There was no double commodification at stake. The Bostonian Theophilus Parsons' 1859 *Treatise on Maritime Law* declared that, "the insurance of the wages of mariners or masters" are "held to be illegal and void." Wages were not "things," the way bales of cotton or human chattels were. Wage earners—even at sea—were not yet proprietors of financial risks.[49]

Instead, if wages were lost through no fault of the mariner—if, say, a mariner was injured and could not work—it was the obligation of his employer to compensate him or, in the event of his death, his household members. The rule flowed from the legal relation of "master" and "servant," a subset of the law of "domestic relations." The relations between master and mariner, a commanding 1802 treatise on the subject explained, were like those of "a parent over his child." As Parsons wrote in 1859, masters were customarily and ultimately legally responsible to directly care for a seaman who became "sick, or wounded, or maimed in the discharge of his duty"—again provided it was "not by his own fault." The hierarchical and personal relationship between master and crew was unlike the abstract financial exchange of maritime risk.[50]

Wage compensation for sick, injured, or even deceased seamen became a contentious issue for the early American courts. In a widely cited 1800 Pennsylvania case, *Walton v. Neptune*, the seaman John Walton had perished from "accidental illness" while in port in Havana. The owners of the ship *Neptune* refused to pay his surviving dependents "for the whole voyage." Judge Richard Peters ordered a full payment, as if Walton had met "the fate of the ship." Peters admitted there was no law on the books codifying the "benevolent principle" he was enforcing. But it was enough to cite the "provisions of the general maritime laws," as his decision reached back all the way to the *Digest of Justinian*. He reenforced the paternal bond of master and servant, cutting into the profits of the owners of the ship *Neptune*. Decades later, in *Farwell,* the Massachusetts jurist Lemuel Shaw would take the opposite tack, applying the contractual logic of marine insurance to new onshore, industrial wage relations.[51]

The case of *Walton v. Neptune* implicated another form of human community. It was Walton's household dependents who had pursued their deceased paterfamilias' wages. Merchants, masters, and seamen were all very likely masters of households. Throughout the age of sail, merchants were known to remove wealth from the speculative arena of long-distance trade and to invest in land (in America also slaves), a far more secure form of wealth for their families to inherit. As for mariners, stricken households like Walton's pursued lost wages. Young widows might remarry. Some might extend the business activity—boarding, garden keeping—begun while their husbands were at sea. In worst cases, they depended upon the charitable support of local communities. In 1845 the *New York Evangelist* carried the article "The Perils of the Seas," an excerpt from the address of the Reverend John C. Abbott to the "New York Mariners' Family Industrial Society." Abbott lamented the plight of the perished mariner's widow and orphan. Charitable mariners' societies were in every seaport town, offering subsistence for the destitute. They, and the poor laws, were the last resort in the seafaring community.[52]

There is one final collectivity to consider—the slaves onboard the brig *Creole.* Their insurability as chattels classified them together as one. But that commercial classification elided much. Nineteen males of the 135 *Creole* slaves shared the ultimate risk of revolt. Their premeditation indicates that somehow—whispers in Robert Lumpkin's Virginia slave pen?—they had come together to strike for "their freedom." Somehow they knew about the wreck of the *Hermosa,* and that American slaves had found freedom on British soil. Running alongside the mercantile financial networks that insured slave cargoes were different flows of information, the undercurrents of a rebellious Atlantic world.[53]

Yet, there were also fissures onboard the *Creole.* One hundred and sixteen slaves reportedly did not join the revolt, remaining in their holds. Forty-five were women and children, perhaps sharing blood or intimacy with the nineteen. Regardless, the entire group still found freedom on British soil. According to one source, many laughed out loud and rejoiced from their holds as the nineteen steered the *Creole* into the British port. In every possible sense, they were free riders. But what about the five slaves who would make their way back to Louisiana, as they did not desire "freedom?" Their risks remained under the dominion of their masters.

Before returning to the case of the *Creole,* one final aspect of early modern risk demands attention. It concerns issues of worldview—or beliefs about the nature of contingency. The worldview at hand isolated the events that merchants could insure against: the "perils of the seas."

Those perils lead back to the case of the *Creole,* where the question was whether or not a slave insurrection was one of them.

What were the "perils of the seas?" The clause found in Thomas Mc-Cargo's policy with the New Orleans Insurance Company read:

> Touching the adventures and perils which the New Orleans Insur-ance Company of New Orleans is contended to bear and take upon itself in the voyage, they are of the sea, men of war, fires, enemies, pirates, rovers, thieves, jettison, letters of mart and countermart, surprizals, takings at sea, arrests, restraints, and detainments of all kings, princes, or people, of what nation, condition, or quality so-ever, barratry of the master and mariners, and all other perils, losses, and misfortunes that have or shall come to the hurt, detriment, or damage of the said goods and merchandize, or any part thereof.

This was a list of all the perils that merchants, stretching back to the fourteenth century, had agreed to transform into insurable risks. Over time, the clause was standardized, culminating in the above wording first set down in the 1779 common policy of Lloyd's of London. McCar-go's clause was a verbatim copy. Yet, despite appearances, the "perils of the seas" clause was not a list. The "perils of the seas" was a concept with an exegesis.[54]

By the time the *Creole* voyaged, the clause meant that underwriters were liable for any "accident" or "fortuitous event" outside the scope of the foresight, volition, and responsibility of the ship's captain and crew-members who were, in this context, extensions of the insured merchant owner's moral agency and legal responsibility. Foresight, volition, and responsibility constituted a legal checklist for insurance liability.

The "perils of the seas" thus set the limit on the moral autonomy of an archetypically free agent. According to an 1850 Boston translation, as a much-cited French treatise put it in 1783: "Accidents *(cas fortuits)* are those events which no human prudence could foresee. Superior force, *vis major,* cannot be foreseen or resisted. The two commingle. By accident *(cas fortuits)* is meant a superior force which cannot be resisted." But this was not every loss. "There is a great difference between a fortuitous case, and a *case unforeseen.*" For the loss "that happens through the

imprudence or unskilfulness of the captain is unforeseen, but is not fortuitous. In a word, we place in the category of fortuitous cases only those
which happen in spite of all human prudence." If the peril was one the
captain and crew should have foreseen, and thus averted, then legal liability fell back upon the insured merchant. The rule placed limits on the
commodification of peril.[55]

The French treatise told Americans what a peril of the sea was not.
Another often-cited definition, this one British, said what a peril of the
sea was. As the English jurist Lord Kenyon explained in the 1792 case
Green v. Elmslie:

> It may, in general, be said that everything happening to a ship, in the
> course of her voyage, by the intermediate act of God, without the
> intervention of human agency, is a peril of the sea. Thus, every ac-
> cident happening . . . which human prudence could not foresee,
> nor human strength resist, may be considered [a peril of the sea] . . .
> within the meaning of such a policy; and the assured must answer
> for all damages sustained, in consequence of such accidents.

This passage was reprinted in antebellum American marine manuals
and was often presented as the working definition of the "perils of the
seas" in federal and state courts. As a lawyer explained before the New
York Supreme Court in 1816, citing *Green v. Elmslie,* there were the insurable "acts of God," and then there were the noninsurable "acts of
man." Lord Kenyon too marshaled a prudential model of human agency
that consisted of foresight, volition, and ultimately moral/legal responsibility. Maritime risks existed because human agency was sometimes foiled
by unforeseeable, irresistible "acts of God." The first risks were thus
enclosed within a providential horizon—enclosed pieces of God's will,
exercised from a realm beyond and outside of secular time, inscrutable
to human agents until the very moment it struck.[56]

For this reason, at its emergence in the fourteenth century marine
insurance had encountered theological hostility within the Catholic
Church. Many religious thinkers condemned the trade as usury. God's
will determined future events and only God could foresee His foreordained future. To traffic upon God's will was immoral. By the seventeenth

century, another set of thinkers had effectively countered that critique by redefining the very meaning of insurance. Insurance was only another aleatory contract of purchase and sale, with its own discrete object, a "risk"—the theological contribution to the enclosure of maritime risk. No different than a bushel of corn, a risk was just another commodity.[57]

Lord Kenyon and his Americans followers were constructing a working judicial rule, not a metaphysics. To them, to say "act of God" was to create a residual category of contingent events not possibly attributable to the human agency of the insured, like unforeseeable and irresistible tempests, pirate marauds, or the seizures of foreign governments—the classic "perils of the seas." Nevertheless, the phrase "acts of God," connoting a providential horizon, persisted.

Early modern maritime risks had circulated on the margins of onshore societies in which the term "act of God" was not yet the half-dead metaphor uttered by Lord Kenyon. Consider the late-seventeenth-century Puritan merchant John Hull. Hull, a Bostonian, traded furs to England and provisions to the West Indies, often insuring his cargoes. Pious, he believed that the entire cosmos was nothing but a continual "act of God." The Puritans in fact led the Protestant reaffirmation of the authority of divine providence over the future. As Uriah Oakes, president of Harvard College, put it in his 1677 *The Sovereign Efficacy of Divine Providence,* the world was determined by the "providence of God ordering and governing time and chance according to His own good pleasure." Furthermore, providence justified a hierarchical social ladder. As another Puritan thinker put it in 1676, it was not "the result of time or chance that some are mounted on horseback while others are left to travel on foot." Divine providence determined the paternalist ethos that some were masters, in charge of caring for servants, wives, children, and slaves—the religious origins of the benevolent principle,[58] not the insurance principle.

Puritan merchants like Hull might suffer from a double doubt and anxiety. There was the perilous passage of their ships and cargoes, which they insured. But what did the fate of those voyages signal about the fate of their predestined souls? Puritans often interpreted shipwrecks as evidence of God's displeasure with the excessive pursuit of profit. Hull, in one occasion when two of his cargoes were seized by Dutch privateers, reminded himself that "the Lord made up my lost goods in the two vessels last year by his own secret blessing, though I know not which why"—a case of insurance by divine intervention. Hull ran his commercial risks in a providential horizon. Religious and commercial doubts swirled together and bred an anxious commercial striving.[59]

Such strivings contributed to the commercial character of the eighteenth-century Atlantic, as the "shedding of the religious conception of the universe"—at least the religious conception held by Hull— proceeded. One historian marks the 1740s as the moment when commerce "displaced providence" in New England popular consciousness. From the pulpits, jeremiads on God's will still ripped through congregations and local communities. But what judges, drawing from the Atlantic-directed, international law of marine insurance, considered to be "acts of God" began to carry competing social and cultural authority.[60]

Eighteenth-century American mercantile correspondence, a different genre than either religious sermons or legal decisions, contains strikingly few references to God. They do contain many references to "luck" and "chance." In 1834, Benjamin Balch (no relation to Joseph Balch), the president of New York's Commercial Insurance Company, wrote to the Boston underwriter Moses Hale (Joseph Balch's former clerk) lamenting "that it is next to impossible to make any money" in the business of marine insurance "except by sheer good luck." By the time the *Creole* voyaged in 1841, the notion of an "act of God" still limped alongside an increasing appreciation for the power of chance. Soon a new probabilistic, statistical understanding of contingency would transform this cluster of ideas and beliefs.[61]

Nevertheless, across time, a notable feature of the insurance principle was its drive to render the future subject to human manipulation and control. In this period, that drive was understood as masculine.[62] Through the financial exchange of risk, even as the limits of individual human agency were identified the capacity of collective action to reach beyond those limits seemingly expanded. Yet, since the desire for control was inseparable from the drive to profit, uncertainty—whether it was the acts of His will or the whims of Fortuna—could not be altogether suppressed. Marine insurance rendered long-distance seaborne trade manageable enough to be profitable.

These aspects of the "perils of the seas" clause were all fully on display in the journals, ledgers, and correspondences of antebellum
American underwriters. The tempest was the classic peril of the sea and
attempting to foresee the weather was an obsession. Balch kept a running log of "meteorological observations" in his journal. Underwriters
also monitored political conditions meticulously. Balch kept a list of
U.S. custom-house regulations, in addition to "French ordinances re-
specting" whaling, or the details of Russian tariffs. Conversely, underwriters wanted to know the assumed scope of moral responsibility.
Therefore, they followed the outcomes of legal decisions closely.[63]

In the end the law ultimately determined the distinction between an
insurable "act of God" and an uninsurable "act of man." Underwriters
often refused claims (a continuity in the entire history of insurance). The
captain should have known better; he should have done more. What
damaged the thing insured was no "act of God." Over the centuries,
courts, from the Rota of Genoa to the Supreme Court of Massachusetts,
grappled with unending variations on the same theme. What was the
scope of human agency and thus liability? A tempest destroyed a ship.
Was it a "peril of the sea" or should the navigator have redirected the
route? Saltwater destroyed a hogshead of sugar. Again, was it a "peril of
the sea" or had the captain improperly stored the cargo? From thousands upon thousands of these cases, courts, moving through the checklist of foresight, volition, and responsibility, created an archetype: the
risk-running, free agent, buffeted by a larger, external authority. Only
when a contingent event struck from outside that agent's sphere of autonomy was another man—the insurance underwriter—morally responsible, legally liable, for its outcome.[64]

Not surprisingly, there was no greater advocate of the scope of human
agency than a sued insurance company. Just as, for the same reason,
there was no greater advocate for the "acts of God" than the insured
owner of a destroyed cargo. There was one legal dispute that posed the
question in the familiar way, but which also leads finally back to the case
of the *Creole*.

The case was a British one, regarding the infamous 1781 voyage of the
slave-ship *Zong*. The Liverpool owners of the *Zong* and its cargo of 442
slaves were insured in London. Adrift off the coast of Jamaica, against

winds and currents, running low on water and provisions, Captain Luke Collingwood and the *Zong* crew "jettisoned" 132 slaves, dragging them up from out of their holds, removing their chains, and pitching them into the sea. When the *Zong* finally arrived in Jamaica, the Liverpool syndicate of William Gregson filed an insurance claim seeking compensation for all 132. The underwriters refused.[65]

The legal question was simply whether a "peril of the seas"—a sudden, unforeseeable, irresistible shift in winds and currents—had diverted the *Zong* from Jamaica, warranting the jettison. Scouring the record, historians have found no other instance of a slave jettison in the Middle Passage. But "jettison" clearly was a sacrifice for which insurers were then liable. "Jettison" was even listed as one of the "perils of the seas" in Thomas McCargo's policy with the New Orleans Insurance Company. The lower British court held against the underwriter but the case was appealed to the Court of the King's Bench.[66]

There, Lord Mansfield presided over a routine discussion of the "perils of the seas" clause. Even the underwriters admitted jettison was authorized as a "last necessity." But Mansfield had his doubts. Had the ship sailed from Africa with enough water onboard? Was a preventable navigational error, rather than winds and currents, liable for the *Zong* being stranded off Jamaica in the first place? Suspicious, Mansfield ordered a new trial to determine if a "peril of the seas" had truly led to the *Zong* jettison. No retrial however would ever take place as it seems Gregson withdrew the claim.

The case of *Gregson v. Gilbert* simply took the form of a normal marine insurance dispute.[67] There was nothing to indicate that the insurance of slave property was any different from the insurance of other forms of private property—that a "slave risk" was unlike a "cotton risk." Outside the London courtroom, however, matters were different. Abolitionists brought the *Zong* to public light and, far from an "act of God," they maintained it was an act of man—an act of murder. The *Zong* became one spark in the public mobilization of British antislavery which made it so that in 1841 the nineteen sailed the brig *Creole* to free British soil, instead of New Orleans.[68]

Only the Union Army would destroy slavery in Louisiana. But in saying something fundamental about the kind of freedom that would emerge after the destruction of slavery, the case of the *Creole* did do something that the *Zong* did not. For the case of the *Creole,* unlike the *Zong,* was preoccupied with "the peculiar nature of the property insured."

That preoccupation distinguished the case of *Thomas McCargo v. New Orleans Insurance Company* from other Atlantic slave-insurance disputes. The result was an articulation of freedom in a commercial vernacular, which implied that to be *unfree* was for another man to own your risk, while to be *free* was to own that risk yourself. Risks had first been originally enclosed in a providential horizon, repossessed from the will of God. Now, the Louisiana Supreme Court had to consider whether the revolt of the group of nineteen was an "act of God" or an act of free men. Had the nineteen in the act of revolt repossessed their risks from their earthly masters? Or did their masters still own these risks, leaving the underwriter responsible for the loss of their property on free British soil?

The legal argument took this turn because of a remarkably heretical brief submitted on behalf of the underwriters by the New Orleans lawyer Judah P. Benjamin. A Sephardic Jew, Benjamin was born in 1811 in the British West Indies. He spent his childhood in the Carolinas, studied law at Yale, and settled in New Orleans in 1832. He purchased a sugar plantation and began to buy slaves. After the *Creole* ruling, Benjamin entered politics, taking a seat in the lower Louisiana chamber as a Whig. Never quite comfortable as a slave master, in 1850 he sold his plantation and 150 slaves. Two years later he became a U.S. senator. Twice he turned down presidential offers to sit on the U.S. Supreme Court. With the outbreak of the Civil War, Benjamin became the first attorney general of the Confederacy. A confidant of Jefferson Davis, he would hold the Confederate posts of both secretary of war and secretary of state. After the collapse of the Confederacy, Benjamin fled to England where he once again set up a thriving commercial law practice. Nothing in this biography, besides an evidently ingenious legal mind, prepares one for the argument Benjamin submitted to the Louisiana Supreme Court in 1845.[69]

As his opposing counsel—lawyers for Thomas McCargo and his fellow *Creole* slave owners—complained, Benjamin rested his argument "wholly on the peculiar nature of the property insured." The policies at hand contained the clause: "But warranted by the assured free from elopement, insurrection, and natural death." The clause, a common one, acknowledged the humanity of the slaves while stripping them of the very qualities that made them human. If slaves did not run away, rebel, or die, how were they not like the cotton they labored to produce? The *Creole* slaves, at least nineteen of them, had mounted an insurrection. The case seemed clear and the policy was void. But the lawyers for McCargo argued otherwise. In their view, it was not the insurrection but rather a "peril of the seas" that had led to the destruction of their property. That peril was the "British seizure" of their property at New Providence, an irresistible act that Captain Ensor and his crew could not be held responsible for. Which was it, a British seizure or insurrection? Was it an act of God or an act of man?

In arguing for insurrection, Benjamin underscored the *Creole* slaves' personhood, not their status as property.[70] As Benjamin explained to the Louisiana Supreme Court:

> Will any one deny that the bloody and disastrous insurrection of the Creole was the result of the inherent qualities of the slaves themselves, roused not only by their condition of servitude, but stimulated by the removal from their friends and homes, for the purpose of sale by their owners in an unknown land . . . ?

Benjamin flagged the "inherent qualities of the slaves themselves" and the term "inherent" was no accident. In the law of marine insurance "the inherent vices of the subject insured" was its own special study. Commodities with "inherent vices" were ones somehow perishable in nature—a piece of rotten fruit, a diseased horse or pig, or a dead slave. As Benjamin had explained to the lower New Orleans Commercial Court, insurance underwriters were only responsible for "external accidents," the "perils of the seas." By law, they were not liable for "inherent vices." By this logic, a deceased slave—the peril of "natural death" as the McCargo policy put it—was no different from a rotten piece of fruit.[71]

Fruit went bad, but it did not insurrect. It was on this "inherent vice" that Benjamin had much to say. In the lower Commercial Court, the slave owner and future leading Confederate Benjamin submitted to the court on the subject of the *"vice proper de la chose"* of the slave:

What is a slave? He is a human being. He has feelings and passions and intellect. His heart, like the white man's, swells with love, burns with jealousy, aches with sorrow, pines under restraint and discomfort, boils with revenge, and ever cherishes desire for liberty.

In his subsequent brief to the Supreme Court, Benjamin expounded on the slave's desire for liberty. Within "the nature of the slave" was an "ever wakeful and ever active longing after liberty." In the very nature of things the slave was always "ready to conquer his liberty where a probable chance presents itself."[72]

Benjamin had simply applied the insurance liability checklist of foresight, volition, and responsibility—distinguishing an insurable "act of God" from a noninsurable "act of man"—to the thing insured itself. First, the group of nineteen's prudent exercise of foresight, their contemplation of a "probable chance," was crucial. Their mental "preparation" for the *Creole*'s voyage was in fact superior to that of Captain Ensor. With a "probable chance" assessed, slaves possessed "passions," likewise generated "by nature," which sprung their wills into action to "conquer" their "own liberty." At that moment, the night of November 7, 1841, "the blacks asserted their freedom"—a moral capacity for freedom that was only dormant until then. They performed like men, not property, and their risks were no longer insurable by their masters, no matter what the policy said. They had been repossessed by their slaves, the rule of double commodification was broken, and there no longer being slaves there could no longer be "slave risks." By foreseeing a probable chance, acting upon it, and becoming responsible for the event afterward, the *Creole* slaves simply did what free men do.[73]

Benjamin was quick to sink one possible counterargument. Slaves or not, "blacks" were capable of running risks and becoming free. Black slavery was countenanced by civil law, but not the "law of nature." There were "vast numbers of free blacks in the United States." In truth, "if the black population of the world be taken in view, the vast majority are freemen." Thus, "the fact that the insurgents on the Creole were blacks can make no difference in principle." According to a friendly biographer, Benjamin uttered these words with sympathy, as a member of the long-oppressed Jewish people. Benjamin's discourse on "What is a slave?"

was an unmistakable allusion to Shylock's "Hath not a Jew eyes?" monologue in *The Merchant of Venice*. But Benjamin was also a smart lawyer
cynically defending his client. Years later, Senator Benjamin would rise
before the Senate and mock the abolitionist falsehood that slavery was
not "protected by international law." For slaves were "just as much private property as any other merchandise or any other chattel."[74]

Regardless, the most pressing argument for Benjamin to rebut was British seizure. Had the *Creole* slaves become free before the events at New
Providence? Both parties agreed to the same common law principle—*In
jure non remota causa, sed proxima spectator*—codified in 1597 by the
same Francis Bacon who in 1601 legally codified the practice of "Merchant Assurances." To put forth his application of the doctrine of "proximate causation," Benjamin presented to the Louisiana Supreme Court
the 1785 British case, *Jones v. Schmoll*.[75]

Jones v. Schmoll was another British slave-insurance case that had come
before Lord Mansfield, two years after the *Zong*. Another slave ship was
bound from West Africa to the West Indies, insured in London. The disputed policy said the underwriters were "not to pay" for "suicide,"
"natural death," or "for mortality by mutiny, unless the same amount to 10
per cent." That 10 percent clause was a standard British provision. When
rebellion occurred, "the crew were forced to fire upon the slaves and attack them with weapons." According to the court reporter:

> Several slaves took to the ship's sides, and hung down in the water
> by the chains and ropes, some for about a quarter of an hour: three
> were killed by firing and three were drowned; the rest were taken in,
> but they were too far gone to be recovered: many of them were des-
> perately bruised; many died in consequence of the wounds they had
> received from the firing during the mutiny; some from swallowing
> salt water; some from chagrin at their disappointment, and from
> abstinence; several of fluxes and fevers; in all to the amount of 55,
> who died during the course of the voyage.

The 10 percent threshold appeared to be met.[76] The legal question was
one of "remote" versus "proximate" causation in the deaths of the slaves.

Mansfield's courtroom discourse on the metaphysics of causation led the jury to decide that a slave's decision to swallow salt water was a "proximate" cause.[77]

Benjamin cited *Jones v. Schmoll* to argue that the *Creole* mutiny was indeed the "proximate" cause. But what made Benjamin's argument so striking was that he considered the foresight of the "thing insured." Morally, that the group of nineteen had foreseen a "probable chance" of revolt, thus leading them to act, had located the "proximate" cause of their lost value within their very "assertion of freedom." Once the insurrection occurred, there was nothing else left for the British authorities to do. The *Creole* slaves had already become free.

From the other side, Benjamin's opposing counsel argued that the British seizure of American property was a "peril of the seas" and therefore the "proximate" cause of their clients' loss. It was no different than if for some unforeseeable, irresistible reason a ship laden with a cargo of horses was forced to touch at the port of Nassau and the British had allowed the horses to run free across the island. For, on principle, "blacks" could not "assert their freedom." Slaves were private property that belonged to their masters, and no rebellion could change that.

Counsel for the *Creole* owners had their own interpretation of what happened out on open waters the night of November 7, 1841. Black slaves possessed "capacity to commit offenses," and as "chattels" they "possessed a value that belongs to someone else." By rebelling, the *Creole* slaves had stolen the property of their owners. "Robbery" on the high seas was "piracy," a classic "peril of the seas." And so the group of nineteen were pirates.[78]

The *Creole* lawyers presented the 1776 French case of the slave ship *Comte d'Estaing*. On the Atlantic, the slaves took advantage of a sickened crew and successfully revolted. But they were ignorant of the "art of navigation" and crashed upon the rocks of Turk's Islands in the French West Indies. French inhabitants captured eight of the slaves. One, to "escape slavery," threw "himself into the sea and drowned." The others "perished from want." In court, the underwriters claimed they did not know it was slaves they were insuring. "Negroes were men," and were "incapable of forming the subject of insurance." The French Admiralty court shot back that slaves were *"chattels, moveables,* and *merchandize"* and could be insured. The "revolt of negroes" was an insurable *"fortune de mar."* The *Creole* slave owners' lawyers put a name to this peril: piracy.[79]

Still, the central claim of the slave-owners was that "British seizure" was the "proximate" cause of their destroyed property. In their view, the law of marine insurance demonstrated that whenever a "concurrence of perils was present," it was always "the last one which operates" that was "considered the cause of the loss, and is termed its proximate cause."[80]

The only question was this: At what point was the insurable property destroyed? The notion that a mutinous slave—even if he exhibited prudent foresight, a bold will, and the capacity for moral responsibility—was *ipso facto* "free" contradicted the very legal foundation of chattel slavery. Insurrection alone could not sever "the tie of slavery which bound the slaves to their owners." When the nineteen pirates acquired a "temporary control of the brig," there had been no "extinction of this species of property"—the double commodification was still in place. None of the slaves died on account of the insurrection or were "disabled" by it in any way. (Plaintiff's counsel on this point too cited *Jones v. Schmoll.*) The "insurrection of the 19" did not deprive "the slaves insured of all value." The slaves were not yet "worthless" at Nassau harbor. The loss occurred only when British authorities pronounced them free on the morning of November 12, the "proximate" cause of the loss.[81]

The events of that morning were decisive evidence. The American consul had conspired to retake the *Creole* in Nassau harbor by force. Only the presence of a fleet of black-manned boats surrounding the *Creole* that morning foiled the attempt. That was the first act of "British interference." Moments later, the British attorney general came onboard and told the *Creole* slaves they were "free." Now, the tie between master and slave was severed and the "destruction" of the insured property accomplished. The moral agency of the slaves—their performance on the Atlantic—was immaterial. Cotton could not assert freedom and neither could the *Creole* slaves. They needed the British to assert their freedom for them.[82]

Thus "the great question," Justice Henry Adams Bullard surmised, was "whether the loss of the slaves was caused by the insurrection, or by illegal and unauthorized interference on the part of the authorities of

New Providence?" Bullard was born in Massachusetts in 1788. After graduating from Harvard he studied law in Boston and then opened a commercial law practice in Philadelphia. In 1813, he joined a failed military expedition to Texas but landed on his feet in New Orleans. On the bench, Bullard's commercial law library was renowned throughout the South. He had all of the great eighteenth-century European marine insurance treatises. After the *Creole* case Bullard would join Benjamin in Louisiana's congressional delegation to Washington, DC.[83]

Bullard first took up Benjamin's argument that "the slaves on board the Creole became free, *de facto*" by "their successful mutiny." He was unequivocal. Even after the mutiny brought the brig to New Providence, "We regard them still as slaves." Was it not but a short step from Benjamin's claim to the conclusion that all rebellious slaves were "free, *de facto?*" Incredibly, Benjamin had cited in his favor the 1836 Massachusetts case *Commonwealth v. Aves*. In that suit, Bullard's Massachusetts counterpart—Chief Justice Lemuel Shaw—held that a New Orleans slave girl brought to Massachusetts by her master could sue for freedom under Massachusetts law. Shaw acknowledged that his ruling did not apply to "fugitive slaves." Grounds for their return were in the U.S. Constitution's Fugitive Slave Clause. Still, by Benjamin's lights the *Creole* slaves in port at Nassau were no different than the New Orleans slave girl in a Boston parlor. Later, both Congressman Bullard and Senator Benjamin joined together to pass the draconian Fugitive Slave Act of 1850. But in 1842 Bullard maintained, against Benjamin, that mutinous slaves had not "ceased to be the property of their masters."[84]

So was British seizure a "peril of the seas"? No—the weight of testimony, Bullard ruled, indicated that the British attorney general did not pronounce the *Creole* slaves "free." Rather, he pronounced all British "restraint" upon their movements lifted. With "restraint" removed, the *Creole* slaves continued along the course they had set for themselves during the insurrection—to British soil and freedom. Rebellion, an act of man, was the "proximate" cause. To establish insurrection as the proximate cause, Bullard too had turned to the moral agency of the group of nineteen. In the end, he too linked self-ownership, freedom, and risk.[85]

Property had turned itself into "free persons." Bullard used the same checklist: foresight, volition, responsibility. To him, as it was to Benjamin, the foresight exhibited by the nineteen was a crucial piece of evidence. The insurrection was "brought about so suddenly, and yet with such evident readiness of preparation at the first signal, as to leave no doubt that the arms used were already loaded, and the plot formed." The slaves had acted with foresight and prudence. Ascertaining their chances, with daring and audacity the nineteen had set their plot in motion. Their moral agency was responsible for the destruction of insured property. "Slave risks" had dissolved into thin air. The *Creole* slaves' destinies were now in their own hands to plot and direct. With one stroke Bullard had acknowledged the legal foundations of chattel slavery as he upheld the northern obligation to return fugitive slaves. With another he had agreed with Benjamin: black slaves were capable of running their own risks. The very nature of the *Creole* mutiny evidenced, and achieved, their freedom.[86]

Bullard's ruling, however, elided much. What about those who did not join the group of nineteen in the revolt and remained in the hold until arrival at New Providence—the free riders? What of the weeping slaves who returned with the *Creole* to New Orleans and slavery? The abstract financial risk at stake was not the same thing as the felt experience of the slaves—who faced the peril of revolt long before Bullard ruled that they had repossessed the risk. Did any of the *Creole* slaves feel as though they were free at any time before they finally touched British soil? Bullard could not, or did not, take up these questions.

What he and Benjamin did do was to articulate freedom in the financial vernacular of long-distance trade. That was a world centuries in the making, and very much responsible for the very existence of New World slavery. Merchant capital provided the cognitive materials for the future Confederate Secretary of War Benjamin to mount his case and Bullard had bought it—with an important caveat. Both men had deep roots in the world of Atlantic commerce, deeper than in the world of the plantation, the heart of southern slave society. Indeed, proslavery ideologues howled in the southern press that Benjamin and Bullard had sided with the "misguided fanatics" of the North who would abolish the "rational freedom" of slavery. Northern abolitionists wanted to abolish the benevolent "domestic" affection of the master–slave relation that was providentially determined and "demanded by the security of society."[87]

Nevertheless, Benjamin and Bullard had argued that to be a slave was to have someone else own the risk on your life. To be free was to own that personal risk yourself. The mutinous slave wrested a risk out of the hands of his master and thus remade his destiny into his own.

The ship voyaging on the high seas would remain an abiding image of the link among freedom, self-ownership, and risk. The voyage of the *Creole* alone was a powerful image. In 1852, for instance, the escaped slave and famous abolitionist Frederick Douglass wrote the novella *The Heroic Slave,* a fictionalization of the *Creole* drama. The insurance controversy could not have been farther from Douglass's mind, and men like Benjamin and Bullard were his sworn mortal enemies. Yet, like the case of the *Creole,* Douglass too was preoccupied with the moral foundations of personal freedom.[88]

The narrative of the *Heroic Slave* centers on the bravery of Madison Washington. But before leading the insurrection, Washington first resolves himself, in a private moment of reflection, to one day rebel and become a free man. It was then that Washington "vanquished a malignant foe; for at that moment he was free, at least in spirit. The future gleamed brightly before him, and his fetters lay broken at his feet." With this psychic breakthrough, the slave was able to foresee himself as a free man and thereby to chart his own destiny. And with that thought, Douglass wrote, "at that moment he was free." The idea was not unlike Benjamin's notion that the group of nineteen's contemplation of a "probable chance" at successful revolt was a crucial element in their "assertion of freedom."[89]

Douglass had already developed this theme in his own autobiographical works, written after his escape from slavery in Maryland in 1838. He recalled of his slave days, "I longed to have a *future*—a future with hope in it." To Douglass, the possession of a future, even the subjective ability to foresee it, was as much a component of self-ownership and freedom as was his bodily integrity. Certainly, Douglass never failed to acknowledge the power of the master's lash over his body. But he also remembered that his master advised him "to complete thoughtlessness of the future, and taught me to depend solely upon him for happiness." If "I would be happy," Douglas recalled, "I must lay out no plans for the future." This kind of mental submission could "make a contended slave." In Douglass's account of his own path to freedom, a crucial step was when he achieved the ability to foresee, and long for, his own future as a free man—a future not fated by his master.[90]

In perhaps the most riveting scene in his autobiography Douglass wrote of standing "all alone upon the loft banks" of "the Chesapeake Bay, whose broad bosom was ever white with sails from every quarter of the habitable globe." Like the fictionalized Madison Washington standing alone in a Virginia forest, Douglass faced the Chesapeake where the "beautiful vessels, robed in purest white, so delightful to the eye of freemen, were to me so many shrouded ghosts." With "saddened heart and tearful eye," he wrote, the "sight of these always affected me powerfully. My thoughts would compel utterance; and there, with no audience but the Almighty, I would pour out my soul's complaint, in my rude way, with an apostrophe to the moving multitude of ships." He would shout:

> You are loosed from your moorings, and are free; I am fast in my chains, and am a slave! You move merrily before the gentle gale, and I sadly before the bloody whip! You are freedom's swift-winged angels, that fly round the world; I am confined in bands of iron! O that I were free! O, that I were on one of your gallant decks, and under your protecting wing!

The ocean-going ships which carried so many millions of Africans to New World slavery had become, at least to this one slave, "shrouded ghosts," but also the foremost symbol of freedom. In *The Heroic Slave,* after the insurrection Washington taunts First Mate Zephaniah C. Gifford, "Mr. mate, you cannot write the bloody laws of slavery on those restless billows. The ocean, if not the land, is free."[91]

Standing at the Chesapeake, Douglass decided: "Get caught, or get clear, I'll try it." And yet he also appealed to God to ensure his deliverance. "O God, save me! God, deliver me! Let me be free!" As a slave boy, Douglass had learned that a "God, up in the sky" had predestined him to be a slave. He had to unlearn this, to discover that "not *God,* but *man*" was behind "the existence of slavery." Douglass would say time and again that his escape from slavery was fated by divine providence. That belief had only strengthened his own will to escape. Guiding Douglass's path toward freedom was something "more intelligent than *chance,* and something more certain than *luck.*" He quoted Hamlet, for whom there was a "Divinity that shapes our ends / Rough hew them as we will." Douglass credited the "special interposition of Divine Providence" for his freedom. Douglass had acted; divine providence had ensured.[92]

Eliminate the interposition of the slave master, Douglass was saying, and providence and free will would harmonize into a free society. But the freaks of fortune, as he himself was to learn, would have their say as well.

CHAPTER 3

The Actuarial Science of Freedom

God has not launched our globe on the ocean of space and left its
multitudinous crew to direct its course without his interference.
He is at the helm. His breath fills the sail. His wisdom and power
are pledged for the prosperity of the voyage.

—*Cotton is King, and Proslavery Arguments* (1860)

THE BRIG *CREOLE* HAD SET sail for New Orleans in 1841. In 1844
another ship sailed on Atlantic waters, this one carrying the noted
American abolitionist Elizur Wright to the city of London. Wright traveled there to solicit the support of his British antislavery brethren. But to
earn extra money, he had agreed to take notes on English actuarial science on behalf of a fledgling Boston life insurance corporation and bring
them back to America.[1]

In a London alley near the Royal Exchange, Wright came upon a scene
that to his eyes appeared all too much like slavery. It was an outdoor auction block. One man after another stepped upon the block as buyers
placed their bids. Free Englishmen were reselling their own life insurance policies because they could no longer afford to pay their premiums.
They sold their policies to men Wright called "speculators." The new
holder of the policy would pay the premiums until the insured died. And
the sooner that death came the better. The shorter the life of the insured,
the higher the profit for the speculator on death. Wright, who had insured his own life before the voyage, recoiled. Later he would recall: "I
had seen slave auctions at home. I could hardly see more justice in this
British practice." There were of course no real slave auctions in London.
But there were in America—like the New Orleans slave market for which

the *Creole* slaves had been bound. Wright "resolved" that when he "returned to America" life insurance "should be otherwise here, if my voice could avail."[2]

When he did return, Wright's career shifted from antislavery to the new American business of life insurance, to the enclosure of a new financial commodity: the free "life risk." Not only did Wright bring back English actuarial tables under his arm, he subsequently Americanized the science. For math was the weapon he chose to rid the financial exchange of "life risks" of the stench of slavery. Wright became America's leading, and arguably first, professional actuary.

In 1844, however, compared to England where there was already over £150 million of life insurance in force and somewhere in the neighborhood of 150,000 policies, there was very little life insurance in America. In 1825 there had been fewer than 100 policies in the United States with about $168,000 of life insurance in force (in 1860 dollars). In 1840, there was $4.5 million. By 1870, however, there would be $2.3 billion and 800,000 policies in existence, or roughly 1 in 3 for every adult male in the Northeast. Soon America would have, by any measure, the largest amount of life insurance in force of any nation in the world.[3]

Premised upon the principle of self-ownership, life insurance was a liberal form of economic security. The underlying primary asset of this new double commodification was the human capital of a free man. Upon insuring it, his dependents—at first his creditors but over time overwhelmingly his wife and children—acquired financial compensation in the contingent event of his death, and therefore the lost value of his future productive labor. Life insurance thus commodified self-ownership into a financial abstraction. Its sale provided economic security for middling households in the commercializing cities of the antebellum Northeast, while the increasing association of life insurance with domesticity gave the "life risk" a moral valence that "marine risks" had lacked. Meanwhile, new risk communities emerged onshore that shared the contractual, nonhierarchical, and abstract qualities of the mercantile risk communities of the high seas.

The northern life insurance industry took off in the aftermath of the financial panic of 1837. Without the panic, it is impossible to understand a sudden inflection in the rise of corporate risk management—with the new practice of financial self-insurance at its center. At the time, a mix of political and religious idioms dominated public debates concerning who or what was responsible for the bust. The lesson learned, however, was that many Americans, especially those who lived in cities, increasingly led lives that were dependent upon markets. New safeguards—novel forms of wealth, community, and belief—were needed to help cope with a rising economic chance-world.[4]

As new uncertainties washed over the land, financial entrepreneurs brought the insurance principle inland. But they also fundamentally transformed it. As commodities, life risks were priced differently than maritime risks. Corporations newly priced them according to probabilistic, statistical measurements, creating for the first time actuarially defined risk communities. After the financial panic of 1837, the evolving corporate financial system mobilized the new intellectual standard of probabilistic certainty as a new bulwark of security, stability, and order.

Yet, in the wake of the panic of 1837 the new life insurance embodied only one countermovement against the generative insecurities and radical uncertainties of capitalism. When Wright voyaged crossed the Atlantic, most working Americans were not the urban merchants, doctors, lawyers, artisans, and clerks that first purchased life insurance policies. The 1840s and 1850s featured the most rapid phase of American urbanization before or since, the context for the urban flourishing of life insurance. But with 60 percent of the workforce employed in agriculture in 1860, America was still a predominately rural society.[5]

In the northern countryside, land ownership was still the dominant foundation of security, grounding an ethos of landed independence. Hardly immune from peril, many commercial farmers had a distinct sense of what it meant to be a free and secure actor. They looked to their lands and the collective strategies of the farm household to mount their countermovement.

Further, in the largely agricultural South, the master class developed a countermovement of its own. Enjoying the continued commercial renaissance of chattel slavery, invoking the providential paternalism of the master-slave relation, many white southerners hedged against the perils of capitalism by owning slaves. In the final antebellum decades, both freeholders and slave owners sharply distinguished their economic forms of life from northeastern urban dwellers. Antebellum corporate risk management was in competition and conflict.

With respect to risk's history, the juxtaposition between self-ownership and slave ownership is most telling. For centuries, New World slavery had fueled the early modern Atlantic commercial revolution. Slave ownership had been at the cutting edge of the insurance principle. In late antebellum America, the insurance principle suddenly transformed free society's most cherished ideal: self-ownership. Something new was afoot in the North as life insurance corporations began, slowly at first, to accumulate fresh stores of finance capital. Meanwhile, the Old South accumulated capital in the physical form of black slaves. The addiction of the white master class to a particular form of social power rooted in the dominions and dependencies of slave ownership intensified. The antagonism between free North and slave South sharpened. Slave society was to be destroyed amidst the carnage of the Civil War. Financial self-ownership would only continue to burgeon across centuries, as the dynamic of a new individualism and a new corporate financial system operating in tandem was set in motion. The ethos of landed independence would persist into the postbellum era but it too would succumb to the same dynamic.

The abolitionist actuary Wright was always quick to underscore the growing antagonism between free society and slave society. He was in fact an agent of it. For self-ownership was not only the material foundation of the new life insurance. It was a bedrock principle of the new radical antislavery.[6] This was what so shocked Wright about the London life insurance auction block. The self-insurance of men—against premature death but also industrial accidents, sickness, even old age—was to be the new liberal/financial response to the perils of life under capitalism. To find it embodying the scourge of slavery was abhorrent. In America, Wright would never find physical life insurance auction blocks. But the practice of selling one's policy in the open market, known as "assignment," became popular before his eyes.[7] Corporate risk management manufactured a disquieting form of speculative risk-taking.

And so Wright joined to his crusade against chattel slavery an actuarial crusade to abolish the secondary marketplace in free "life" risks. To him, the line separating freedom and slavery was sharp. But that normative distinction was about more than chattel slavery and the growing sectional divide between North and South. In 1837, Wright wrote in the *Anti-Slavery Record:*

> The line which runs between the pro-slavery, and the anti-slavery camps, is not a geographical, but a moral line. The two principles are at irreconcilable war—the two parties cannot peacefully coexist; either the one must be driven from the geography of the globe, or the other must be wholly and permanently brutified, or the conflict must be eternal.[8]

Here was the moral foundation of Wright's future actuarial science of freedom.

If self-ownership meant that men had absolute, exclusive property rights over their own persons, and if a "risk" was an element of that self-ownership, then Wright sought to actuarially demonstrate that a policyholder had a property right to an equitable cash "surrender value" from an insurance company if he no longer desired, or was able, to pay the premiums on his "life risk." Wright's actuarial calculations would abolish the secondary market for free "life risks." He used science and later as the insurance commissioner of Massachusetts the coercive arm of the state to insert entitlements in the contractual relation between policyholder and insurance corporation. He sought to place limits on the financial commodification of human life in a free society—salvaging along the way the incipient corporate financial system's countermovement to the perils of life under capitalism.

Ultimately, Wright's prosaic actuarial science of freedom shared something with the dramatic *Creole* revolt. To future Confederate Attorney General Judah P. Benjamin, the *Creole* slaves had removed "slave risks" from the marketplace, making their risks their own and asserting and achieving their freedom. The future wartime Insurance Commissioner of Massachusetts Wright removed free "life risks" from a marketplace that to him was tantamount to the logic of slavery. In the emerging world of capitalism and risk, at stake in each instance was the new nineteenth-century link among freedom, self-ownership, and the personal assumption of risk.

Elizur Wright, Jr. was born February 12, 1804, in a farmhouse in northwest Connecticut. Descending from a long line of Puritan stock, his father was a town elder of nearby South Canaan and a deacon in the Congregationalist church. Like so many of his generation Wright made his way to the city. But in the countryside, American farmers still pursued a distinct form of economic life which might be called landed independence. It is worth pausing for a moment to explicate its logic. For the persistence, in fact *resurgence*, of landed independence in an era of rapid commercial change frames the rise of a new form of economic life in northeastern antebellum cities and the significance of the sudden explosion there of a new type of financial, rather than landed, economic security.

Landed independence had roots in the earliest of colonial times.[9] American freeholders held absolute, alienable property rights in their lands and colonial America was already distinctive for its extreme commodification of landed property.[10] Land ownership always provided the potential basis for commercial risk-taking and land speculation itself was always ubiquitous. In antebellum America, the typical male freeholder still had command over his own labor and—in theory—paternal command over the labor of his household dependents. Therefore, he controlled the resources of his farm and most often engaged in "mixed" or "safety-first" agriculture—usually with sixty to 120 acres at his disposal, he mixed subsistence or "household" goods along with market goods in the diversified production of grains, meat and dairy products, and other food and household items. The "marketable surplus" generated money income for the household. Antebellum farming was fundamentally a commercial enterprise.

Yet, to many the land was a special form of property uniquely capable of providing a baseline sense of economic and existential security. The stolidity of the land itself, the household unit of production, the endurance of subsistence cultivation at the margin, and the farmer's dependence upon the cyclical rhythms of the natural world all contributed to a distinct sense of what it meant to be a free and secure actor. It was this countermovement that Wright left behind in the countryside.

Indeed, when Wright voyaged to England in 1844 the American economy had only recently emerged from the bust that followed the financial panic of 1837. In this context, farmers reasserted the ethos of landed independence. Many late antebellum farmers cast a jaundiced eye at the cities. The urban market system held out the possibility of more riches but it was fundamentally more precarious and insecure. The farmer's way of life stood on more solid ground—a literal terra firma apart from the perilous seas of an extending and intensifying national market economy.

Farmers reached for the metaphor of voyage as they tapped a new word in antebellum vernacular: "risk." A farmer of the Genesee Valley in upstate New York, a region of striking agrarian commercialization, explained in 1838 why "mixed farming" made all the difference. The peril of farming with "exclusive reference to a single object," he wrote, was that the farmer committed "all to a single risk—in a nautical phrase, embark all in one bottom." He continued:

> If the venture be in sheep, a revolution in the pecuniary world may (as at present), destroy the market for wool; if it be in the cultivation of wheat . . . the worm, may doom the granary to emptiness. . . . Where a course of mixed husbandry has been pursued, the risk is less. When one vessel has parted, another may hold [another product]. Each adds to our chances of safety.

This farmer championed two types of diversification: cultivating more market crops than one and producing nonmarket goods for direct consumption. Landed independence promised scope for commercial risktaking but also a more stable and predictable fate than the one enjoyed by more specialized, urban commercial proprietors—whose very subsistence and success depended upon the purchase of commodities.[11]

These agrarian voices rang loudest after 1837, as they had after the panic of 1819. Another Genesee farmer in 1838 found the agrarian ethos "verified by the events of the past year, and the present situation of our country." Who had suffered the "shipwreck of their fortunes?" Not the farmer but the "merchant, the speculator, the manufacturer." As still another farmer put it in 1840, the panic had led "a great many to resort to farming as the surest means of procuring a subsistence, if not to increase their wealth." Merchants lived a life of "restlessness and anxiety," argued a New York farmer in 1838, creating men of "feverish ambitions," all of whom *must* engage in "hazardous experiments." The only foundation for a stable economic selfhood was land ownership. The rhythms of planting and harvest taught farmers the "cardinal element of a well adjusted character" which was "patience." Patience was a difficult virtue to cultivate in the booming and busting economic chance-world of the cities.[12]

To maintain their economic security, many farmers attempted to avoid complete dependence upon the financial circuits of the urban market system. True, some had begun to invest in financial assets or even to hedge certain risks financially. Fire insurance slowly spread from town to country, introducing the insurance principle. The old Boston marine insurance hand Joseph Balch in fact incorporated one of the largest fire insurance companies in Massachusetts.[13]

Yet, in general, extra money income in the countryside did not purchase financial assets. Very few antebellum farmers purchased the new life insurance policies. There were no rural depository savings banks. Antebellum agrarians largely stored their wealth and accumulated their capital in land—a fixed, physical, rather than financial, asset—either by acquiring more acreage or improving their farms. In this, the Massachusetts farmer John Sleeper explained in 1841, a man had "made a safe investment." In an era of all too many bank failures, the farmer watched not with complete but relative "indifference." Unlike a bank deposit, "the soil itself" could never vanish. "Greater riches" were possible in other branches of trade "where there is more risk to encounter." But the farmer invested his money "in that best of all banks, a bank of earth." Economic security was literally right under the farmer's feet. In 1850, almost 50 percent of total national wealth was held in farm property. Land values dwarfed the amount of wealth held in financial assets, including the meager $100 million of life insurance then in force.[14]

In 1850, the politician and local dairy farmer George S. Boutwell addressed the Agricultural Society of Concord, Massachusetts, and summed the situation up. Boutwell shared an ideological pedigree with Wright. A Van Burenite Democrat with Free Soil sympathies, in 1851 he became governor of Massachusetts. In 1854 he would help to found the Republican Party which Wright would quickly join. Boutwell proclaimed to the

Concord gathering that the farmer was far more "independent" than the urban mercantile proprietor. He had less "anxiety than men in other pursuits" as farming offered the "certainty of a competence." Farmers were not like "merchants," a class of men perpetually "tempest-tossed" by forces outside their "control." There were, Boutwell argued, "great and necessary risks of business from which the farmer is exempt." "Agriculture" and "commerce" were not the same thing: the latter form of life was "dependent" while the former was "independent." An urban proprietorship was inherently more perilous than a landed one. In the countryside, this sentiment echoed with astounding uniformity and frequency.[15]

Landed independence should not be romanticized. The land itself was a site of tremendous conflict—between squatters and speculators, not to mention the Indians who were so often violently removed by white settlers. No doubt, many antebellum farmers all too quickly mythologized their countermovement and its supposed traditional basis, rooting their communal longings for security in specific places, their lands. But farmers were of course hardly immune from peril, even commercial peril. They too went bankrupt and were subject to financial ruin, if the natural world itself was not hazardous enough. Further, while many agrarians looked to the cities and saw insecurity and panic many city folk (a good number former farmers) looked to the countryside and saw closed horizons, mind-numbing boredom, and back-breaking labor, not to mention the oppressive authority of a father or a town elder—not enough, in every possible sense of the term, upside risk.

Farming still relied upon the gender-based unit of the household— fathers, mothers, daughters, and sons. Personal relations of dependency bred collective strategies that coped with the burden of peril without having to commodify it. For instance, the accumulation of landed wealth and related patterns of partible inheritance provided many farmers with a hedge against the perils of old age. Nevertheless, that hedge was already tenuous, if only because the economic chance-world of the cities lured so many sons and daughters away precisely because the economic life of the cities was so uncertain—if one could not determine one's own destiny on the farm, then let the freaks of fortune have at it in the towns. Farming was no secure, primordial paradise.[16]

Furthermore, antebellum commercial farming was not static. Farmers were not detached from the expanding urban market system, nor did the great majority want to be. They needed finance and credit to get their crops to expanding markets and in many instances to purchase and improve their land. Antebellum landed independence thus rested on increasingly shaky foundations. Farmers demanded the "internal improvements" necessary to get their surpluses to buyers in urban markets. The result of the transportation revolution that followed was by the 1850s a band of specialized wheat and corn farms that stretched from the mid-Atlantic seaboard to the western prairies. Voiding "safety-first" and exploiting virgin soils, many migrating Yankee farmers put as many acres as possible into commercial staples. They drove northeastern farmers into more specialized forms of fruit, dairy, and vegetable farming. In 1850, Boutwell warned the farmers of Concord that fast encroaching upon them was the mercantile logic of "competition" and specialization. Tellingly, the kind of "Agricultural Society" that Boutwell addressed, which was only decades old, existed not only to extoll landed independence but also to promote a more mechanized, efficient, and commercial agriculture.[17]

Nonetheless, late antebellum farming was still a distinct form of economic life. Land ownership provided many households a potential flight to safety outside markets. In the northern countryside peril and possibility, opportunity and danger, still combined into a definite pattern. The available evidence confirms that antebellum farmers did forego more profitable opportunities in the urban commercial and industrial trades in pursuit of the "certainty of a competence." Farmers were likely to earn less money income but they did on average own more wealth than nonfarmers, distributed more equitably. Antebellum farming straddled the fence between a way of life and a sheer business enterprise.[18]

Boutwell was not the only politician to link landed independence with political ideology, a marriage at least as old as Jeffersonian republicanism. After 1837, the politics of landed independence got a new lease on life. Notably, a number of states passed homestead laws that newly protected farmers' lands from creditors and overturned laws, some of colonial origin, that protected creditors. Landed independence actually surged in response to increased economic volatility.[19]

But as important as political ideology was a religious worldview. The popular 1819 *Farmer's Manual,* adopting an old Calvinist phrase, called the harvest the bounty of God's "common providence." Biblical perils— floods, draughts, insects—were actually virtues, illustrating mankind's fundamental "dependence upon God." Farming therefore cultivated stoicism, not anxiety. Many agrarian ideologues cited the biblical promise to Noah after the flood in the book of Genesis. Even Boutwell reminded, "The cultivation and the cultivators of the land have been eminently blessed by Divine Providence. God had spoken to the husbandman, and said, *Seed-time and harvest shall never fail.*" In 1853, three years after Boutwell's address, Edwin Freedley's popular *A Practical Treatise on Business,* a how-to success manual on urban commercial life, posed the question: "How can independence be attained with the greatest certainty?" Land ownership was the answer. This was because the farmer "receives a real increase of the seed thrown into the ground in a kind of continued miracle wrought by the hand of God." In 1844, when Wright voyaged back from London over the Atlantic deep he had already left this world behind.[20]

Wright had roots in the countryside. But the financial entrepreneurs responsible for organizing the new life insurance corporations of the 1840s largely did not. Their ties were firmly in the commercializing, bustling American cities, if not literally in seaborne Atlantic trade. In 1840, the American urban population stood at 11 percent. By 1860 it had almost doubled to 20 percent—from 2 to 6 million Americans. New York City mushroomed from a city of 350,000 to nearly 1 million inhabitants. Within such cities, a self-conscious "middle class," who would purchase the new life insurance policies, emerged. With the spread of American commerce towards its hinterland, they lived in the urban nodes that integrated a new national market system. The era of the great proprietary merchant gave way to a world of more specialized wholesalers, bankers, manufacturers, clerks, jobbers, dealers, plungers, retailers, grocers, peddlers, drummers, brokers, agents, auctioneers, and bookkeepers. In 1839, a new periodical, *Hunt's Merchants Magazine,* declared the arrival of a new "commercial class."[21]

After 1840, a handful of companies chartered as corporations in Boston, New York, Hartford, and Newark arose and transformed the business. Precedents were in abundance. The marine insurance of human chattels had long existed and still did. Over the centuries, the marine insurance of free lives—across space, not time—was not unknown. In his 1810s journal, Balch noted that, "A life may be insured for a single voyage," either against death or pirate capture. Up through the eighteenth century, however, in continental Europe life insurance on free men was illegal. In 1783, the great French insurance treatise writer Emerigon wrote, "The life of man is not an object of commerce, and it is odious that his death should form matter of mercantile speculation." That double commodification was immoral.[22]

England was the great exception. There, in the era of the South Sea Bubble, life insurance thrived. Often it was unabashed third-party speculation on death. The industry shrank after the bubble burst in 1720 but in 1762 the first actuarial life insurance company was founded in London and soon other firms also flourished. By the time Wright voyaged to London in 1844 there were nearly 100,000 English life insurance policies.[23]

Life insurance thus came to America from long-enduring practices of Atlantic commerce, but also from an already commercialized England where the urban population reached 40 percent in 1700—a threshold the United States would not cross until 1870. The same outfit that had hired Wright to bring back the English actuarial tables, the New England Mutual Life Insurance Company, was a prototypical American corporation. Its founder was Willard Phillips, the author of the first American legal treatise on the international law of marine insurance and a private arbiter of marine insurance disputes. Clearly, he saw new potential for the old insurance principle.[24]

Entrepreneurs like Phillips chose the corporate legal form for their businesses.[25] The lax charters of all of the 1840s life insurance corporations, the New England Mutual included, with their calls for small capital reserves or their loose provisions for boards of directors read much like the charters of the marine insurance companies of the 1810s and 1820s. The first New England Mutual policies, sold in 1844, were similar to the marine policies Phillips collected while researching his marine insurance treatise. The policy listed the beneficiary of the insurance and the underlying commodity insured. Firms adopted the rule of "insurable interest" although it then had no legal basis in the United States. The policy listed the sum insured and the term covered, which at first was between one and seven years. It listed the contingencies that dissolved "the risk," harking back to the maritime rules of both "deviation" (the insured could not travel outside certain geographical limits) and the "vice of the thing insured" (he could not die by his own hand or in the act of committing a crime).[26]

In the coming decades, as the industry matured it became less local and personal and more impersonal and routine. At first, prospective customers contacted firms directly. The insured filled out a questionnaire concerning their health, habits, and character, and submitted testimonials from reputable friends and a personal doctor. By 1870, firms had developed an agency system that spread across the continent, aggressively marketing policies. Companies hired their own doctors to perform medical examinations or dispensed with them all together. No longer were personal testimonials required. Travel restrictions were lifted. In 1866, 93 percent of policies, according to Wright, were now "whole life." Life insurance corporations became formidable organizations stocked with executives, clerks, accountants, actuaries, and lobbyists. In 1860, there were forty-three American life companies. By 1870, there would be 163.[27]

But the growth of American life insurance, while sudden, was not all smooth. In 1845, just after returning from London, Wright received a letter from his fellow antislavery agitator Julius L. Mayne. Wright was now an agent of the same New England Mutual and he had sent Mayne a copy of the firm's 1844 circular. Mayne responded, "I do not approve of any such schemes" against "the ways and dealings of providence." "'Tis God alone," Mayne charged, "who holds the key of Life or death." His was not a lone voice. The criticism echoed that life insurance was an impious commercialization of the ways of providence.[28]

Clearly, many were unaware of long-practiced mercantile techniques and did not understand the insurance principle. They thought marine insurance promised to secure the safe passage of a voyage and that life insurance promised to extend life. Mayne decried insurance against all "acts of God"—including marine insurance. Only God "may shorten or lengthen" life. Humankind could not "by an act miscalled insurance . . . prolong vitality a single day." An 1848 letter writer to Chicago's *Christian Advocate* argued that "our lives are in the hands of God, and may be required in ten minutes, though they be insured for ten years." Meddling with the divine author's plan was not only foolish but also perverse. It only tempted providence to malevolently strike.[29]

Others understood clearly yet still dissented. The worldly repercussions of death, if not shipwreck, should remain in God's hands. "Ten years ago," the *Merchant's Magazine* explained in 1849, life insurance was "scarcely known in this country." "The masses" regarded it "with pious horror, as implying a distrust of God's providence in the affairs of men." In this context, often cited was the biblical injunction against "thought for the morrow." Life insurance, according to one voice, was a "sinful distrust of Providence." In an 1846 fictional dialogue in the middle-class periodical *Columbian Lady's and Gentleman's Magazine*, one critic said that to "assure one's *life* seems to me to be wicked." There was a distinction between the insurance of inanimate property and the insurance of "life." The contingent workings of the world could be commercialized, manipulated—up to a point. Commercial risk-taking was the rightful activity of free men. But death, the very passage of one's soul, was different.[30]

The disquietude contained traces of an old providential worldview. Recall the pious Boston merchant John Hull, who in the late seventeenth century insured his overseas cargoes while fervently believing that the entire world was a perpetual act of God, and that the passage of his goods somehow inscrutably reflected the fate of his predestined soul. Unlike Wright's friend Mayne, Hull was not hostile to marine insurance. His piety, far from breeding fatalism, had emboldened an anxious, commercial striving. But death, in the Puritan providential horizon, was different.[31]

Advocates of life insurance fought the moral battle on numerous fronts. They would champion life insurance policies as lone bulwarks of family security in the rising economic chance-world of the cities. They would argue that its actuarial basis—premised upon a probabilistic, not providential form of epistemological certainty—was increasingly necessary given the full flight of the economic chance-world. But first life insurance advocates marshaled a new vision of the ways of providence at work in liberal Protestantism which emboldened rather than constrained free will. In this, they drew upon powerful religious currents running through the national religious revival known as the Second Great Awakening.[32]

Consider one 1848 religious defense of life insurance published in the newspaper the *New York Evangelist.* An editorial spoke of "the analogy between the plan of salvation and this scheme of life insurance." For "the infinite sacrifice, the atoning blood of Christ, represents the infinite, paid-up capital in that office in which the Redeemer is president and sole director." That capital was "ample enough for the whole world of sinners. They became ours by subscribing with our own hands to the Lord's. The promises of Jehovah are the policy of insurance." Sinners achieved salvation by "subscribing" with their own hands. Human agency was the proximate cause, the independent variable. Salvation was something the sinner himself had to foresee, to act upon, and to become responsible for. It was as if the sinner had to bear the downside risk of his soul's damnation. Salvation—the ultimate upside—was something only God could insure through His grace. The analogy was clear. The imposition of the will upon the sacred future legitimated life insurance's attempt to manipulate and control the secular future.[33]

The *New York Evangelist* was founded in 1831 by Joshua Levitt. Like Mayne, Levitt was another of Wright's antislavery brethren. He had started the newspaper to publish the words of the great revivalist preacher Charles Grandison Finney. Finney, a lawyer with no formal theological training, famously preached the gospel of personal responsibility. Individuals, relying upon their own moral agency, were personally responsible for achieving their future salvation. In 1835, the *New York Evangelist* was the first to publish Finney's classic *Lectures on Revivals of Religion.* Finney asserted that the sinner's salvation "never rests on . . . the influence of the Spirit, but on the powers of moral agency." He drew human agency into the foreground; the Holy Spirit was not absent, and still necessary, but in the background, an assuring, emboldening presence. Preaching sudden, immediate conversion, Finney and others led a national surge of religious revivals.[34]

To many orthodox thinkers this was heresy, although the relationship between free will and divine providence was a perennial Calvinist dilemma.[35] What Finney did was not simply to tip the scales in the precarious balance providence and free will, dependence and independence. He—and the *New York Evangelist* author writing on the score of life insurance—reformulated the very workings of the will of God. The ways of providence not only reigned down from a transcendent, omniscient, inscrutable wellspring, cowering mankind. Providence had now slipped behind the human agent, emboldening the will, emboldening salvation, and legitimating the enclosure of a new financial commodity.

The power of the new religiosity was evident in the early life of Wright. He had first left the farm in 1822 to attend Yale College. His father had encouraged him to join the ongoing revivals at Yale but Wright could only feign religious awakening. His favorite subject was math, not theology, which he taught at Ohio's Western Reserve College after graduation. His true conversion experience occurred there, in 1832, when he read the Bostonian William Lloyd Garrison's *Thoughts on African Colonization*. Garrison's scathing polemic called for the immediate, unconditional abolition of the national sin of slavery. Wright, like many others, heard in Garrison's call something like the revivalists' cry for the immediate, willed redemption of the individual soul. Without having to pretend, Wright instantly converted to immediatist antislavery. In 1833 he wrote his own tract, *The Sin of Slavery,* which garnered him a name in the movement. That same year, Wright and Garrison were in Philadelphia together for the founding of the American Anti-Slavery Society.[36]

Wright took a leadership position, becoming the organization's secretary. He edited and wrote for the society's many publications. In one of his most urgent pieces, the 1836 "Slavery and its Ecclesiastical Defenders," Wright asked whether the Bible condoned slavery. He argued that what proslavery thinkers referred to as "slavery" in the Bible was in fact "servitude." Servants worked at will in return for wages and were thus "free labor," whereas slaves did not. Wright surmised that even the prophets converted by the proximate cause of a "willing and cheerful obedience to God," a form of "voluntary labor." Free labor paid in wages; God paid in salvation. The master–slave relationship, however, was one of complete dominion and dependence. In the proslavery view, the prophets were not the "'servants of Jesus Christ', but the 'slaves of Jesus Christ'." Men were not so dependent upon God that they were His unwilling slaves. The proximate, independent variable in the world was individual human agency which was what God—His assuring, if not ensuring, presence in the background—wanted.[37]

The new, emboldening notion of the ways of providence was put to work not only in antislavery but also in the 1840s moral legitimation of life insurance. As one critic complained in 1848, employing the old Puritan terminology of divine "first causes" versus human "second causes": "The erection of, and dependence on, life insurance companies takes away dependence upon the first Cause, and bestows it upon secondary causes." That it did. The loudest ministerial voice championing life insurance was the celebrity preacher Henry Ward Beecher—son of Wright's former college mentor, Lyman Beecher. Beecher was paid to do so by a corporation, New York's Equitable Life Assurance Society. In 1867, the same year life insurance in force reached $1 billion, Beecher asked: "But has a man a right to take the future out of God's hands? Ought we not to trust in Providence?" His answer: "A man . . . does all he knows how to do." Nobody "has a right to trust in Providence." Providence, Beecher concluded, "did not pay a premium on indolence." A new cluster of ideas—gathering around a new emphasis on free will—hung together, warranting free men to enclose financial "risks" on their own lives.[38]

At the foundation of the new financial commodification of a personal "life risk" was the Yankee principle of self-ownership. If the new emboldening notion of providence was one thrust of the late antebellum promotion of life insurance, another countered the second note in Mayne's critique. Life insurance was not the commercialization of death. Rather, it was the old mercantile rule of double commodification applied to the free male body, the contingent human capital of a productive life. As Wright described it:

> Life insurance comes in as a financial invention, by which capital in the shape of a productive life—a life controlling and directing some branch of the wealth-begetting or wealth-distributing machinery of the age—can perpetuate itself, or convert a part of its productive energy into a contingent fund, that will be immediately available in case of death.

Mayne had the same wrong idea as the fourteenth-century theologians who had criticized marine insurance. An insurance contract was not a wager—whether on the passage of a voyage or the passage of a soul. It was a contract of purchase and sale, with a distinct form of alienable private property—a "risk"—as the object of exchange.[39]

On this point, advocates of life insurance were emphatic. The inaugural 1846 prospectus of the Connecticut Mutual explained that the firm insured not death but "the value of the *future* exertions of an individual." Drawing from the medical theory of vitalism, Edward Jarvis, a noted Massachusetts doctor and advocate of life insurance, explained that physiologically "the constitution of man" was an average quantum of "vital force." "Vital force," the "capital of life," as it were, was simply now insurable. Tellingly, many of the early personal insurance corporations— some of which insured productive labor against accident, in addition to death—called themselves "health" insurance companies. As *Hunt's Merchants Magazine* put it in 1843, life insurance "renders contingent property nearly equal, in point of security, with absolute property." Like with the "absolute property" under the farmer's feet, now the holder of a life policy found security through a financial abstraction of his own contingent human capital.[40]

The underlying asset of that abstraction circles back yet again to Wright's antislavery. In the 1837 *Anti-Slavery Record,* Wright had asked: "Are men naturally, necessarily, and in all circumstances, the rightful owners of themselves?" The answer "lies so deep among self-evident, and therefore undemonstrable truths, that we shall have to assume it." Self-ownership, that "every man belongs to himself," was a liberal "axiom." Later, speaking about life insurance, Wright insisted that "productive energy or capital" resided within the free, self-owning male person. Other antislavery thinkers besides Wright saw that self-ownership inherently entailed ownership of a financialized "life risk." In 1850, Garrison's *Liberator* editorialized:

> Every man has a certain capacity for production, upon which, usually, others besides himself are more or less dependent, which ceases with his life, and in many cases thereby leaves those dependent ones helpless . . . But this terrible necessity can be avoided, and a man's

productive power prolonged, so to speak, after his death, by the system of Life Insurance.

Life insurance did not commodify death; it commodified life. As one life insurance advocate put it, "Life is not only property, but always the best property a man has."[41]

Once insured, that property became a new form of capital. In the antebellum cities, for instance, men now spoke of the "perils of the credit system." That credit system holding together a proliferating series of market transactions existed because antebellum America was relatively poor in finance capital. Much of the nation's wealth was in the physical capital of land and slaves. At first, the beneficiaries of life policies were not family members but rather one's creditors—who had an "insurable interest" in the continued lives of their debtors. The 1840 edition of Phillips's *Treatise on the Law of Insurance* called this the primary reason to take out a life policy, to transform contingent human capital into working credit. In the way farmers mortgaged their land or slaveholders their slaves, the male commercial proprietors of the urban middle classes began to insure their lives. The financial commodification of contingent human capital was thus an instrument of a primitive, highly leveraged form of antebellum capital formation.[42]

How much the contingent human capital of a free man was worth was another question. Unlike with land or slaves, there was no actual marketplace that valued the underlying asset of contingent human capital. Slavery, Wright wrote in 1836, was the *"absolute ownership of the person,"* the complete violation of the "axiom" of self-ownership. Therefore, he argued that life insurance should only commodify contingent "productive energy" and nothing more.[43]

Once again, the law provided a working rule. The leading precedent became the 1856 Massachusetts case *Loomis v. Eagle Life and Health Insurance Company.* Chief Justice Lemuel Shaw issued the decision. The case concerned a complicated policy on the life of the twenty-year-old Freedom Keith. In 1849, Keith left his home in the textile mill town of Manchester, Connecticut, to join the California Gold Rush. Because he was not yet twenty-one, his father insured his life for $500. When

Keith died upon reaching San Francisco, the Massachusetts' Eagle Life and Health Insurance Company refused the claim, maintaining that Keith's life had been overvalued. The argument harkened back to the world of maritime risk where the "overvaluation" of the underlying asset was strictly prohibited.[44]

Was Keith's life worth $500 in five months? At that date, he turned twenty-one and became an "emancipated" adult, after which time his father no longer maintained an "insurable interest" in his life. Shaw said it was and presented a general rule: "every man has an interest in his own life to any amount in which he chooses to value it, and may insure it accordingly." Shaw reasoned that "by working a few weeks or days in a gold mine, or by a lucky hit in a single day," Keith might have struck "gold enough to make his share exceed the whole sum insured." Freak events were at least "possible." Therefore it was up to the contracting parties to determine a life's contingent value. Shaw's ruling stands to this day.[45]

Of course the premiums one could afford to pay still set a limit. The typical antebellum policy was in the range of $2,000 to $3,000. For most this would not replace a lifetime of expected income. *Hunt's Merchant's Magazine* declared that a family of four, for "plain living," required an annual income of $1,500. The "middle class" then lived within the range of $500 to $4,000 of income. If the new life policies did not fully replace a life of foreshortened earnings, they did transform contingent human capital into a meaningful stake of wealth. In 1860, 42 percent of the white population had wealth of less than $100. Tellingly, antebellum life insurance policies—even expensive ones—have been linked to men with no accumulated wealth whatsoever. To them, "life" had become not just the "best" but also the only form of property they owned.[46]

To import the maritime rule of double commodification, the price of a "life risk" still required a premium rate priced according to the expectation of a contingent event. Death, in the end, was that event—another reason why Mayne's religious critique might have echoed. Unlike the old marine insurance, the new life insurance priced risk actuarially according to the European science of probability. Actuarial science provided a new technique for the financial enclosure of a "risk." It was an epistemological countermovement, so to speak, against the radical uncertainties of capitalism.

The application of probability theory represented a great departure in risk's history. In American culture, life insurance corporations first introduced probability theory—a new worldview concerning the contingent link between present and future. Slowly, from this one small corner of commercial practice probability theory would help disenchant the old providential horizon, as it promised to help tame the rising economic chance-world and newly order a liquid, liberal social order. On behalf of the fledgling New England Mutual, Wright voyaged back to America in 1844 with actuarial life insurance premium tables under his arm.

In its opening 1844 advertising circular, the New England Mutual explained that with the "assistance of scientific gentlemen" the company had formed a "scale of probability of life." Premiums rates corresponded to the insured's age. A table was presented illustrating the "comparative chance of life at different ages." The chance, that is, that a man aged n years would live $n + 1$ years. From it, the "yearly chance of life" and the "average chance of life" were knowable. For example, a man aged thirty, to secure a $100 policy, paid a premium of $2.06. A person who was forty paid $2.85. The variable was pure, abstract, and homogenous time—a simple but radical departure.[47]

At a given age, every "life risk" was the same—an astonishing intellectual act of abstraction. Earlier, in the centuries-long world of maritime risk, merchants like Joseph Balch had prudentially calculated premium rates according to each particular voyage across space. No two "risks" could be the same. The hasty sideways scribbles of Balch's insurance journal contrast to the clean parallel and perpendicular lines of the premium table of the New England Mutual, a table its directors might consult but did not have the mathematical ability to create. A new form of systemic, actuarial foresight was now on the scene.

Actuarial science had two historical foundations. The first was the existence of mortality statistics. The second was a probability theory that could transform them into average life expectancies. Originally tools of statecraft, mortality tables appeared in the mid-seventeenth century, and classical probability theory dates to the same era. In 1756, the Englishman James Dobson, a student of mathematical probability theory, published his *First Lectures on Life Insurance.* In 1762 he founded London's first actuarial insurance company. After a century of delay, formal probability theory had entered the world of commercial practice.[48]

The history of probability theory and statistics is an enormous and complex subject.[49] But only one historical probability idea requires exegesis: the idea of "unity." It was the basis for the calculation of life probabilities, but also for the subsequent expansion of the actuarial framework for it also contained a worldview, an epistemology concerning the contingent link between present and future. Wright, in the popular republication of his *Annual Reports* as insurance commissioner of Massachusetts during the 1860s, explained it succinctly: "the value of a chance or probability may be expressed by a ratio or fraction, certainty being expressed by unity." The "numerical value" of unity was 1, a standard of complete epistemological certainty against which probabilities could be confidently quantified as ratios. What Wright was saying was no different from saying the probability of a coin flip coming up heads can neither be less than 0 percent nor greater than 100 percent. Furthermore, in this example, if the probability of heads is 50 percent, then the probability of tails must be 50 percent. The events were also "disjoint": the coin could not come up both heads and tails. And the probabilities accounted for all possible outcomes. A coin could only come up heads or tails. So, the probabilities of heads or tails must add up to 1, or "unity"—complete certainty. The seeming simplicity of this cluster of ideas, given these assumptions, only underscores its subsequent historical triumph.[50]

Actuaries like Wright approached a mortality table as if life and death were a series of yearly coin tosses. The mortality table was perfectly suited to probabilistic transformation. Assuming that a variable of pure time was no different than the act of flipping a coin, each year a life either perished or it did not. There was no other possible outcome. And the events were "disjoint," as it was not possible to be both dead and alive. Finally, the probability of death some day represented "unity," or 1. Thus, Wright explained how to determine a life probability:

If it has been observed that of a certain number, *a*, of persons aged *n* years, *b* persons, and no more, have lived to complete the age of *n* + *q* years, and we assume this particular fact to represent a natural law or general fact, then the numerical value of the chance of a person aged *n* years living through *q* more years is the ratio or fraction *b* / *a*, and if *b* = *a*, *b* / *a* = 1 is the numerical value of certainty.

Belief that probabilities conformed to "natural law" was the final kicker. Probability theorists originally pursued a singular "law of mortality." Unity—certainty, the number 1—was both an epistemological tool and a metaphysical creed. Jarvis, the Massachusetts doctor and probability enthusiast, added the qualifier that statistical law had nothing to do with any mysterious interposition of "Providence." But apparently the universe still preferred a standard of perfect certainty. In this framing, the mathematical computation of probabilities left no room for qualitative and radical forms of uncertainty.[51]

These ideas were evident in the New England Mutual's 1844 premium rates. From various European sources the Harvard mathematician Benjamin Pierce had constructed the premium table. There was no widely agreed upon American mortality table in circulation until after 1870, despite some individual efforts to collect mortality statistics and translate them into rates. Because Americans were so mobile, finding anything like a "stationary population" in the United States—to measure births against deaths within the same population—was a fool's errand. Regardless, antebellum Americans preoccupied with vital statistics, mostly insurance men and medical doctors, had imbibed an epistemological confidence in the "law of mortality." Soon actuaries would begin to classify distinct populations according to familiar markers of identity. But at the outset, to many if the average life expectancy for a forty-year-old man in the small English hamlet of Carlyle was 23.82 it was not entirely unreasonable to believe it to be the same for any forty-year-old man in America. The law of mortality was a natural law, a universal law.[52]

Actuarial premiums had one final, seemingly innocuous but enormously consequential trait. Premiums were "level." A life probability normally decreased over time and so yearly premiums increased over the same duration. "Level" premiums "leveled" payments into the same annual figure. Wright's favorite example was a five-year term, $1,000 policy on a man thirty years old. The "natural" premiums would be: $8.93, $9.12, $9.31, $9.53, $9.74. Transformed into "level" premiums it became five payments of $9.31. As the industry moved towards "whole life" policies the gap grew starker. Early "level" premiums paid for future years of coverage and actuarially the trick was to factor into the premiums the interest that accumulated on the front-end payments, money held in the company's "reserve." Wright was conservative, always choosing a 4 percent return on company investments. (Given the dearth of money capital in the United States, antebellum interest rates then hovered around 6 percent). There were no probabilistic projections—not yet—for future interest rates.[53]

In other words, to cover future liabilities level-premium life insurance corporations accumulated financial reserves. The science demanded the accumulation of financial capital—to be invested somewhere or another. State legislatures passed laws constraining insurance corporations' options (most legislatures wanted funds invested within their respective states). Regardless, corporations had limited choices. The private corporate securities market was small, undeveloped, and fluctuating. With defaults on municipal and state debt after the panic of 1837, insurance corporations shied away from such assets. The Jackson administration had retired, for a short time, the entire federal debt. State legislatures restricted corporations from owning real estate, which smacked of a new, corporate landed aristocracy. What was left then were farm mortgages. In 1860, about 80 percent of life insurance assets—$35.6 million total—were invested in farm mortgages. Ironically, at first the new financial self-insurance provided working capital for aspiring farmers, many in pursuit of the economic and existential rewards of a landed independence.[54]

Nevertheless, probabilistic certainty would from now on permanently color the intellectual life of risk. Of course, old providential worldviews were not eclipsed overnight, especially since old conceptual structures endured within putatively new scientific beliefs. Probabilistic certainty was first an epistemological tool for commodifying certain perils into risks. To flourish it did not have to destroy providentialist explanations each and every time a contingent event struck. It is doubtful whether families began to find comfort in the existence of mortality statistics when burying their loved ones, even if their lives were insured. Coping with peril was not the same as managing risk.

Nevertheless, probability ideas harbored a new determinism. In 1846 Wright wrote that, "We have great respect for Christianity." But as "much as we respect it, we should dread to see it rush into an encounter with arithmetic." Actuarial science was "perfectly sure." "The only chance Christianity has, is to alter the law of mortality, and that is a slim one." Quickly, some began to mull over the perennial problem of free will not in the context of predestination but rather statistical law. *Merchant's Magazine* speculated in 1847 that with the "law of average" it seemed that "fate" was "unveiled." Soon thereafter, Ralph Waldo Emerson, in an essay on "Fate," cited the growing authority of the "new science of Statistics." By then probability thinkers were in pursuit of a litany of objective, long-run statistical frequencies. In addition to the "law of mortality," Americans read about so-called regularities governing the incidences of murder, suicide, and even the infamous number of dead letters in the Paris post office. In 1839, the old marine insurance hand Joseph Balch called for the collection of shipwreck statistics and the actuarialization of marine insurance premiums. If not by divine providence, free will was now buffeted, if not undermined, by another external power.[55]

Yet, newly discovered statistical laws could also be tools of an emboldened, expanded human mastery. Prudence, the moral duty to attend to the future, demanded that men take heed of probabilistic discoveries. In 1844, tapping the maritime metaphor and speaking of the necessity of actuarial life insurance, the *Christian Register* explained:

> No man of common prudence sends a vessel or a cargo to sea without
> first effecting an insurance upon them. Yet, the dangers of the sea
> have been all explored, its rocks and shoals laid down in charts . . .
> In the voyage of life there are perils against which no foresight can
> guard, unknown breakers, and whirlpools in the ocean before us . . .

The radical uncertainty of life was all the more reason to depend upon the foresight of the actuary. Noting a commercial world of unforeseeable booms and busts, in 1862 the New York Equitable Life Assurance Society agent Samuel Smith proclaimed in a letter to prospective customers: "Of the 1,000,000,000 on earth, it is estimated that 33,333,333 die every year, 91,824 every day, 3730 every hour, 60 every minute, or 1 every second." The farmer looked to land ownership and the timeworn, certain, providentially determined rhythms of the natural seasons. With the double commodification of his life, the policy owner offloaded his risk to a corporation, looking to statistical law for both economic security and an existential sense of certainty.[56]

The farmer championed landed independence after the sudden wreckage of the panics of 1837 and 1857. So after these two events did advocates of life insurance champion the epistemological authority of probabilistic certainty. Life insurance corporations too seized upon the metaphor and imagery of voyage, harkening back to the "perils of the seas." The Equitable wrote in an 1857 circular of the destruction of all property values, "all in an unexpected moment, as the tornado, with irresistible force, passed over us." There had long been the "human lottery of the sea." In 1847 Wright, looking at the perilous commercial world around him, reflected on the need for life insurance and ominously declared: "To a great part of the people who live, life is but a lottery." For one's dependents, a life insurance policy financially offset the cruelest of life's blows.[57]

Finally—just as was the case with land ownership—the security of the life policy granted many Americans the very ability to play the great commercial game. With a life insurance policy one could chase the upside of a liberal, commercial social order, enjoying the booms and riding out the busts with a greater sense of calm. One's dependents—creditors, wives, children—had a potential flight to safety in a financial asset. Some did bemoan, as did the transcendentalist Henry David Thoreau in 1854 (near the same patch of ground where Boutwell had proclaimed the virtues of landed independence) that "so many are ready to live by luck." Thoreau likewise detested commercial insurance, a death knell for "self-reliance." Writing on civil disobedience, he lashed out at the "American" who "ventures to live only by the aid of the mutual insurance company." But in the end, no matter the scruples of Calvinist orthodoxy or New England transcendentalism, the takeoff of life insurance was a testament to the allure of the upside and the status of the independent commercial proprietor in an energizing, democratizing commercial society.[58]

It remained to be seen what kind of hedge financial self-insurance actually would be, as insurance policies proliferated within an emerging corporate financial system. For no matter the new probabilistic certainty, this was still the pursuit of economic security in a financial market. That marked an important threshold—the full absorption of security into the stream of commerce, a flight to safety within the market economy itself. Continuing the pattern, corporate risk management would provide new opportunities for speculative risk-taking, manufacturing insecurity in the process. But that was not clear at the outset.

Here is what Wright had to say about the new corporate risk communities formed by self-insurance in 1865:

> While all other sorts of communism interfere too much with individual liberty to be widely or long tolerated, here is a form of it, which allows unrestrained individualism, without the penalty of beggary entailed upon dependents or descendents.[59]

As a collective strategy, it was not uncommon for early personal insurance to be compared with the utopian socialism of Robert Owen or Charles Fourier, let alone with communism. In 1846, *Hunt's Merchant's Magazine* spoke of the new "arrangement of society" in which all were "left to take care for himself." What was needed was a "social liberty" to compensate for the "terrors of uncertainty." The "Fourierists" and "Socialists" went too far. The answer was to get "society united on the basis of mutual insurance." Indeed, the new life insurance companies of the 1840s were organized on a "mutual" basis, rebating their profits to policyholders not stockholders. In its early days, self-insurance, much like the countermovement of landed independence, attracted communal longings.[60]

If personal insurance was a sort of communism, however, the solidarity operated rather passively. Actuarial science transformed the nature of risk communities. The insurance principle remained voluntary and contractual. But it was also now premised upon the probabilistic law of large numbers—an objective average that operated naturally, whether men liked it or not. The insurance principle did not create communities that could be located in actual, fixed places.[61] It was difficult to even imagine such communities. Risk communities became even more abstracted from place, as actuarial science plucked individual lives out of their local worlds, spawning webs of statistical interdependence between them. Security and certainty now depended upon an average rate of death among men who did not know each other. The mortality table, potentially transcending ascriptions and allegiances, could take various forms of human capital—the mental acuity of the merchant, the muscle of the manual laborer—and render them actuarially commensurable.

Over time, the abstractions—the epistemological authority of statistical law, the professional competence of actuaries like Wright—displaced the communal rhetoric. That displacement was never complete, however, as insurance corporations, pleading with men to offload their personal risks onto them, never gave up on the imagery of mutualism. Life insurance corporations also mobilized domestic, seemingly noncommercial sentiments. Overwhelmingly the new insurable object was the male body. As the beneficiaries of the life policy increasingly became familial dependents the life risk moralized.

Life insurance helped transform the households of the countryside to the more purely affective families of the city. Families were now dependent upon each other, however imperceptibly, through the grand operations of the law of mortality. Looking back to his own roots, Wright explained how the farm household's "estate or source of income"—the land—could not "be buried with him." Now, husbands earned money income in the market while the "staff and shuttle" dropped from the hands of "millions" of wives, sons, and daughters. Wives became the bearers of a new domesticity. Wright in fact instructed corporations to never insure women's lives. He was utterly blind to the value of productive labor performed by women outside the nexus of market exchange. But he was also thinking prescriptively. Ideally, the female body should lack the kind of "productive energy" that earned money income in a market economy. Released from farm labor, boys should attend school, thereby accumulating their own human capital in preparation for adulthood. Daughters should prepare to become wives. This was the new middle-class ideal, exploited by insurance corporations' mawkish advertising campaigns. As the *New England Family Magazine* asked in 1845, "are you to trust the comfort of your family to a chance?" For "in this trying world—it seems so indispensable . . . to have *something* certain." Of course, members of many working-class families still scraped for survival. But that was all the more reason why life insurance policies fast became status symbols of middle-class respectability—not too much unlike the bric-a-brac of the mid-nineteenth-century Victorian parlor.[62]

Paralleling the passage of state homestead laws, after 1840 many states passed laws protecting life insurance policies from the deceased's creditors if the named beneficiaries were widows and/or orphans. Often citing these laws, state judges determined that wives and children by "nature" had an "insurable interest" in the continued life of the male head of household. With a propertied claim on the male productive body, they did not have to "prove" an active "pecuniary" interest in it—as merchants long before had to prove ownership of the cargoes they insured against the perils of the seas. Eventually, the U.S. Supreme Court announced the same standard and very soon the overwhelming majority of life insurance policies were male productive bodies insured on behalf of their putatively unproductive familial dependents.[63]

All told, "life insurance," Wright declared, was "working out the great problem" of how "to secure individual independence by means of general dependence." The answer was simply for free, self-owning men to offload their personal risks onto an evolving corporate financial system of risk management. To many, Wright included, the insurance principle was full of liberal promise.

Therefore it is not difficult to understand why the outrage Wright felt in 1844 before the London auction block continued to stay with him. There, one man truly had gambled on the death of another. Something other than contingent "productive energy" had been commodified, threatening to cross the threshold separating freedom from slavery. The speculation on death had carried no actuarial price. Finally, replacing potential widows and orphans, the speculator himself became the new beneficiary of the policy.

Back in America, there were never any physical life insurance auction blocks. Yet, third-party "assignment," as it became known, was a common practice. In 1855, a New York court adopted an English precedent. So long as "the policies were valid in their inception" they were assignable to third parties with no restrictions. The court added, "It has been said, that without the right to assign, insurance on lives lose half their usefulness." Assignment allowed the insured to cash out the policy if he could no longer afford to pay the premiums—enabling him to salvage a portion of the premiums he had paid into the policy. To the beneficiary of the assignment, however, insurance resorted back to speculation.[64]

More than speculation, to Wright assignment mirrored the fully commodified logic of chattel slavery. Therefore he hoped to abolish the practice. Meanwhile, during the 1850s—when Wright went to work on his solution, an actuarial science of freedom—the white master class of the Old South was developing its own response to the perils of capitalism: not self-insurance, not landed independence, but slave mastery.

The final antebellum decades witnessed the resurgence of chattel slavery in a highly capitalistic form—fueled by the twin cotton booms of the 1830s and 1850s and chastened only by the twin financial panics of 1837 and 1857. The place of the Old South in the nineteenth-century development of capitalism has long posed an interpretive conundrum for historians.[65] From the perspective of risk, late southern slave society harbored a distinct countermovement against the generative insecurities and radical uncertainties of capitalism. Moreover, the character of this countermovement helps isolate the particular developmental dynamic of the Old South, in growing contrast to the emergent free society of the North. Freedom—newly reliant upon corporate risk management—emerges as the truly peculiar institution.

The voyage of the *Creole* well illustrates that there was plenty of room for the insurance principle in the commercial interstices of slave society. The destiny of a slave could be commodified into a "risk," the private property of his or her master, and exchanged in a financial market. The new "life insurance" found some room in the Old South. In 1852, the Mutual Benefit Life of New Orleans, the first corporation of its kind in the city, opened for business. It offered "Insurance on the lives of White persons and Negroes" and its president was John Hagan—the same John

Hagan who was the insured owner of many of the *Creole* slaves. Through-out the South, northern and even British firms successfully solicited both southern "free" and "slave" risks. In the 1840s and 1850s at least sixteen homegrown southern life insurance companies opened for business.[66] But almost all of them quickly failed. Notably, life insurance did not take root in the plantations, the heart of the Old South. Slave ownership had once been at the cutting edge of the insurance principle. No longer was that the case. Self-ownership, through self-insurance, propelled a new regime of flexible, financial capital accumulation, as slave society only ramped up its addiction to a physical form of capital: slaves.

After the panic of 1837 proslavery ideologues reaffirmed what was distinctive about their particular hedge and thus their particular form of economic life. They did so far more vehemently, and far more infamously, than late antebellum northern freeholding farmers, not to mention the southern yeoman class.[67] White slave masters knew well that they were fundamentally commercial risk-takers—chasing upsides in the world cotton market, speculating on slave values. The South had a sophisticated banking sector, with slaves as the dominant form of collateral. White masters often mortgaged their black slaves to raise critical cash and credit.[68] Yet white southerners, with their paternalist insistence on mutual obligations, rights, and responsibilities—in tandem with the violence of the lash—spoke of a noncommercial hedge.[69] In the face of an economic chance-world, only the master–slave relation—providentially determined—could provide an adequate flight to safety. Many members of the white southern ruling class looked to the free society of the North and saw financial innovation compensating, rather weakly, for the "social given" of the master–slave relation.

White southerners underscored the social logic of a providential paternalism. Late proslavery ideology was brashly unapologetic, stridently rejecting silly liberal notions that "all men were created equal," or that polity, society, and economy, let alone the family or even the soul's salvation were products of willful consent. Writing in the famous 1860 proslavery anthology *Cotton is King,* the Old School Presbyterian Charles Hodge, a northerner who was head of the Princeton Theological Seminary, rested his apology for slavery upon the "Great First Cause" of the universe. As for the future, "Nothing is by chance," Hodge proclaimed. "Nor is the world in the hands of its inhabitants." "God's universal providence" determined the seemingly contingent workings of the world. Passages of *Cotton is King* read more like Cotton Mather than Thomas Jefferson, let alone Charles Finney (Hodge assaulted Finney's heretical Arminianism). To Hodge, there was certainly no need for the epistemological authority of the new science of probability, and no possibility at all of seizing the risk of one's own salvation. Such future contingencies were not the private property of individuals. A worldview of providential certainty was revarnished, set in defense of slave society.[70]

Hodge was not alone. His noted Old School Presbyterian peer, South Carolinian James Henley Thornwell, asked in his famous 1850 sermon "The Rights and Duties of Masters": "What is it that makes a man a slave?" "We answer, the obligation to labour for another, determined by the Providence of God, independently of the provision of a contract." It was "Divine will" that the slave submitted to the master's will. Only this hierarchical chain of being achieved the general "security of the social order." As Hodge put it, "The obedience which slaves owe their masters, children their parents, wives their husbands, people their rulers, is always made to rest on the divine will as its ultimate foundation." Thornwell complained that in the North "society" was becoming the mutable "machinery of man" rather than adhering to the "original plan" of providence. Abolitionists preached "social anarchy." To men like Thornwell the racial inferiority of blacks indicated God's design for black slavery. But providential certainty was the metaphysical foundation of a coherent proslavery worldview that saw the free North as letting the genie of chance rush out of the bottle.[71]

In this line of thought, the paternalism of slave mastery ensured for everyone a baseline economic security—that great chestnut of late proslavery ideology. The editor's 1860 introduction to *Cotton is King* spelled out the "true definition" of slavery. The abolitionist notion, that slavery was the complete ownership of a person, was a fiction. Rather, "Slavery is the duty and obligation of the slave to labor for the mutual benefit of both master and slave, under a warrant to the slave of protection, and a comfortable subsistence, under all circumstances." The slave's subsistence was said to never be in doubt. Further, the master did not steal the fruit of the slave's labor—an abolitionist slander. Rather, the slave had to "repay the advances made for his support in childhood, for present subsistence," and to "accumulate a fund for sickness, disability, and old age." The slave labored for a customary "right" to the master's unerring provision.[72]

In this context, two proslavery thinkers explicitly counterpoised the hedge of slave mastery to the ongoing financial innovation of the free North. One was the eccentric Virginian George Fitzhugh, the other the equally eccentric Mississippian Henry Hughes, author of the 1854 *Treatise on Sociology*, published the same year as Fitzhugh's *Sociology for the South*. Free society, Fitzhugh warned, tapping the maritime metaphor, was going to "wreck." "What a glorious thing to man is slavery," he declared, "when want, misfortune, old age, debility and sickness overtake him." In the North, he added, personal insurance corporations increasingly provided the "security" that free society itself had "ceased to render." All the worse, insurance companies, being in the market, "often fail." What he called "Slavery insurance," on the other hand, "never fails, and covers all losses and misfortunes." "Domestic slavery," Fitzhugh concluded, "is nature's mutual insurance society." The southern household—in white and black—coped with the burdens of peril collectively. Financial insurance was a "vain" attempt to "imitate or to supply its place." Fitzhugh classed life insurance companies with "Mobs," "voluntary unions," "social and communistic experiments," and a "thousand other isms that deface and deform free society."[73]

Hughes corporatist vision was equally forward-looking. In the collective strategy that was the master–slave relation, the master always "takes" the "risk." The slave labors to provide a "premium" of "insurance" for the master to provide him future "subsistence" in the event of youth, old age, sickness, or any other "bodily inefficiency" like a disabling workplace accident. By definition, the master "insures" and the slaves "are insured." No financial instrument was required. "The Free-labor form of society," Hughes wrote, "must be abolished." It "must progress to the form of mutual-insurance or warranteeism"—"mutual-insurance" was Hughes's synonym for southern slavery. The only adequate hedge was the direct, authoritarian bond between master and slave.[74]

Meanwhile, southern voices echoed that in free society no one was guaranteed anything. Tellingly, in this critique proslavery ideologues did not target northern freeholders. They targeted self-ownership, often the plight of northern independent commercial proprietors, decrying their existential dependence upon markets. But more often they took aim at the incipient class of northern industrial hirelings—the bastardized artisans of New York and Philadelphia or the mill hands of industrial towns like Manchester, Connecticut, and Lowell, Massachusetts, whose only access to a secure subsistence was to sell their labor-power. Many worked in textile factories that processed southern cotton.

Next to them, slaves came out better in the wash—both economically and existentially. Fitzhugh entitled a chapter of *Sociology for the South* "The Free Laborer's Care and Anxieties." The popular 1856 extended poem by William John Grayson, *The Hireling and the Slave,* chastised the "Abolitionist denouncers of Providence." In the South, "by God's decree" and not by "chance," the slave escaped "the perils of the poor." "The Master's providence" always provided for the slave while free societies consisted of "anxious multitudes." Or, as the New Orleans lawyer George Sawyer explained in the 1858 *Southern Institutes,* free society did not supply the "majority of laborers" with wages above subsistence needs. And, unlike the slave, free laborers must "sustain all losses from sickness, want of employment, &c." Hardly masters of their futures, free laborers were "constantly weighed down with cares and anxieties for the welfare of themselves and families in sickness and other misfortunes." Yet slaves were relieved of "dark forebodings of the future" knowing they had "sure support, in sickness and health, in infancy and old age." Fitzhugh added, alluding to personal insurance, that when the slave "comes to die, he feels that his family will be provided for."[75]

Much of this was nothing more than the self-serving claptrap of a white master class. Fitzhugh and others simply redescribed many of the hard-won customary rights achieved by black slaves, as they focused upon only one side of the paternalist coin—domestic benevolence, not sadistic violence. Like northern freeholders, the slaveholders too mythologized the traditional character, let alone effectiveness, of their countermovement. Slave mastery, put bluntly, was as modern as corporate risk management.[76] Nevertheless, without indicating that slave ownership was less perilous, even on its own terms, than self-ownership, late proslavery touched upon some important truths about the dynamics of peril and possibility, opportunity and danger, in a society where productive property was dominated by a physical form of capital: human chattels. Those truths throw in sharp relief the novelty and character of the emerging corporate financial system of the North.

For one, American slave masters practiced a variety of safety-first agriculture, being much less focused on market production than their Atlantic peers. American plantations were largely self-sufficient units as the majority of output—corn, vegetables, meat, clothes, construction materials, farm implements—was directly consumed. As Hughes explained, the only way to make economic life "certain, unvarying, positive, absolute, and unconditional" was for men to "receive directly, their share of produce." The larger the plantation (or the further west) the more likely it was that more acreage was in the great southern staple of cotton. And when the price of cotton spiked cotton acreage increased. But when it plummeted, rather than doubling down on cotton production, masters shifted acreage back into subsistence production, as they did after the meltdown following the panic of 1837—the famed "retreat to subsistence." To be sure, planters were not unaffected and many, especially those who had mortgaged their slaves, were bankrupted. This was one of the potential perils of a highly capitalistic form of chattel slavery. But on balance the slave owners weathered the aftermath of 1837 relatively well.[77]

These dynamics alone explain slaves' vaunted subsistence guarantee. Slaves were promised cradle-to-grave security because they worked, very nearly, cradle-to-grave. Prime hands cultivated cotton but masters squeezed labor across the life cycle. The young, disabled, and elderly produced for subsistence—hoeing gardens, fishing streams, tending livestock, performing needlework. Masters ceded slaves customary rights to "Negro plots" through which they supplemented their subsistence (and sometimes even engaged in production for markets). By one estimate, only a third of the average slave's labor time was spent cultivating cotton. Individual slaves here or there might be carried on the master's dole. But all in all there was very little need for masters to transfer wealth within, or to, the slave community.[78]

That is why life insurance made so little inroads into southern plantation. Slaves were capital assets and there was no reason not to insure them as such. But American slave mastery bred its own distinct form of economic security. Given the high fertility rate of American slaves, on large plantations—with twenty or more slaves—masters simply hedged their capital assets by distributing them along the life cycle. That cold economic calculus could dovetail perfectly with a master's paternalist self-image. As Fitzhugh put it, "masters, mistresses, and slaves" will never "be all sick, or die at once." The young and the elderly tended to the plantation's subsistence. The prime adult hands cultivated cotton, chasing upside risks in markets for their masters.[79]

Owning wealth in the form of human chattel was the foundation of the Old South's form of economic security/insecurity. The social psychology of the master-slave relation constituted its existential form. After the panic of 1837, land ownership and the farm household, self-ownership and corporate risk management, had equally asserted themselves. The three different countermovements fueled different forms of capital accumulation. Slaves and land were physical assets. In 1860, the total value of slave property was $3 billion. The nation's farm property stood at $6.6 billion. By comparison, the nation's industrial capital stock—factories and railroads—was $2.2 billion. In 1860, the accumulated financial capital of life insurance companies was a paltry $35.6 million. It purchased for the most part northern farm mortgages. But it could in principle be invested anywhere. The South had fostered its own unique capitalist dynamic. But it was addicted to slave property and had a voracious appetite for fresh western lands (slave society needed a western safety valve far more than free society). It was not in the business of accumulating flexible forms of financial capital.[80]

This also meant that southern urbanization and industrialization famously lagged behind the North, despite an effort at invigoration in the final antebellum decades. Industrial slavery was where life insurance made its greatest inroads in the South, especially for masters who owned only a few slaves, and often "hired them out" to third-parties to work in coal pits and iron foundries or on railroads and steamboats, not inconsequential phenomena. Southern courts created a specific law of industrial accident for slave ownership. There was a future in store for life insurance in the field of industrial slavery.[81]

Furthermore, urban and industrial or not, most slave masters did not run large cotton plantations and owned small numbers of slaves. The incentive to insure the lives of their one or two slaves was greater than on large plantations. But with extra cash, southerners usually purchased more slaves, passing them along to their progeny. The Old South was addicted to a category of wealth and capital, but also to a form of social power. Both provided white masters a distinct sense of themselves as free and secure actors.[82]

The Old South, in the end, put all of its chips in chattel slavery. In his famous 1850 sermon, Thornwell invoked providence one final time, summoning the metaphor of voyage: "God will vindicate the appointments of His Providence—and if our institutions are indeed consistent with righteousness and truth, we can watch the storm which is beating furiously against us, without terror or dismay." The great existential peril of the master class was that their chosen species of private property would be destroyed.[83]

There were of course other existential perils in the Old South. Consider once again the former slave Frederick Douglass. Douglass experienced both plantation and urban slavery. While living in the city of Baltimore he was hired out as a ship's carpenter, but meanwhile back in the Maryland countryside of his youth his master died intestate. Douglass returned to the plantation for the valuation and distribution of the old man's property. Douglass himself, it turned out, functioned like his master's life insurance policy.[84]

Douglass recounted the experience in his 1857 *My Bondage and My Freedom,* in a chapter entitled "The Vicissitudes of Slave Life"—a striking foil to the "The Free Laborer's Anxieties and Cares" chapter in Fitzhugh's 1854 *Sociology for the South.* With this experience, Douglass gained new "insight" into "the unnatural power" of the slave master. He parted from his "dear Baltimore mistress" weeping bitterly, not knowing "among which pile of chattels I should be flung." He "got a foretaste" of the "painful uncertainty which slavery brings to the ordinary lot of mortals." "Sickness" and "death" afflicted all, Douglass noted, but only the slave knew the "added danger of changing homes, changing hands, and of having separations unknown to other men"—the peril of a sudden and total alienation from a known social world. In the Old South, most slaves would not live to thirty-five without being sold at least once, in some instances because, especially during the run-up to the panic of 1837, their master had mortgaged them to raise cash and credit, only to bust. This was one of the slave's great existential perils.[85]

An hour passed between the valuation and the division. For Douglass, it was one of "distressing anxiety." "Our destiny was now to be *fixed for life,* and we had no more voice to the decision of the question, than the oxen and the cows that stood chewing at the haymow." "We were all appalled before that power, which, to human seeming, could bless or blast us in a moment." When it was all over a new owner sent Douglass back to his Baltimore overseer. Douglass considered it "thanks to a kind Providence." Still, the "slave's life is full of uncertainty" and yet another master's sudden death ultimately led him back to the countryside. It was the same grand moral theme of Douglass's autobiographical writings. Well fed or not, he was not enough the master of his own personal destiny—upside, downside, and all.[86]

Perhaps, Wright began to think, the slaveholders had got something right. The rising class of northern industrial hirelings was suffering from a kind of unfreedom, even if, morally, comparing them to slaves was a fundamental category mistake.[87] Very few antebellum Americans cherished the status of wage laborer. Wage laborers were a minority of the antebellum working population—and many of them were already dependent women and children—but they were a growing minority, and evidently a class of permanent industrial hirelings who would never join the cherished ranks of independent proprietors was forming. In this context, Wright began to wonder, "whether the system of work to the lowest bidder, which has been adopted throughout the civilized world as an improvement upon slavery and feudalism" was after all "the perfection of freedom?" The final cornerstone of his actuarial science of freedom was now set.[88]

Wright decided that without personal insurance there would be "wage slavery." Only financial innovation could salvage free labor. Double commodification would transform the future "productive energy" of the hireling into a form of "capital." For, as Wright wrote, "it will always require some capital to make a man owner of his own labor. . . . capital he must own, or be himself a tool." Wright looked to life insurance, but also to the further extension of the insurance principle to self-ownership. In the 1840s and 1850s, new "health insurance" companies began to form in the Northeast. Coming in the aftermath of *Farwell,* they paid benefits in the event of workplace accident. But they also paid sickness benefits, or for any "accident" that temporarily destroyed one's productive labor, leading to unemployment. The idea of old-age insurance even began to circulate. Wright championed all forms of male, personal insurance.[89]

Yet, it slowly dawned upon Wright that limiting the extension of the insurance principle was the same root cause that led Englishmen to the life insurance auction block and Americans to "assign" their policies. Hirelings were, by definition, poor. And in that era if a man could not pay his premiums, insurance corporations simply forfeited his policy. The premiums paid in were all lost, an outcome prescribed in the "forfeiture clause." For this reason, the rising northeastern working class was not turning to personal insurance but rather to a new network of northeastern working-class savings banks, founded in the same era. At the savings bank, this month's deposit was not lost if no deposit was made next month. In this way, wageworkers began to accumulate financial savings to hedge against the perils of premature death, sickness, accident, or unemployment. But, much to Wright's lament, they did not insure their own contingent productive labor.[90]

In this context, Wright decided the "forfeiture clause" was thievery. But the theft was only visible actuarially for the key was the nature of "level premium" life insurance. "Leveled" premiums meant that each year the premium was the same amount. But the cost of insurance each year was not the same, as it increased with age. So, in the early years of a policy a man overpaid for coverage. It was that accumulating overpayment that was the true, actuarial "value of the policy"—the money value of the personal "risk" still belonging, by right, to the policyholder. It was really an accumulated "savings" above the cost of present insurance to pay for future insurance. Corporations, Wright held, should repay the sum to those who wanted to surrender their policy before term—a "surrender value." That value was the insured's "risk," an element of his self-ownership—no different than if a boss refused to compensate a hireling with wages for his productive labor. With it there would be no need for the life insurance auction block or the practice of "assigning" policies to speculators on death. A snap actuarial pricing prevented the overcommodification of a free life.

It was a simple idea, containing enormous ideological significance. Likewise, it had important implications for financial corporations' accounting standards and the extent of their accumulations of financial capital. If a forfeiting policyholder received no "surrender value," his premiums simply forfeited to corporation's growing capital reserves. Wright also declared that the "value of the policy" determined the amount of capital corporations should hold in "reserve" to meet their future obligations to their policyholders—for if they could not the economic security of a life insurance policy was worthless. The "value of the policy," in other words, was not only an actuarial emblem of self-ownership but also a measure of corporate financial solvency. Without knowing the actuarial "value of each policy on its books," Wright declared in 1852, "A navigator might as safely be ignorant of his latitude in mid-ocean."[91]

In 1855, Massachusetts created the first state insurance regulatory office. Soon Wright, now an unemployed abolitionist, proposed in the *American Railway Times* that Massachusetts should hire "a single person of proper mathematical attainments" to create a "Life Insurance Registry." The registry would list the "value" of every policy in the state. Wright had just published his *Valuation Tables,* listing the outstanding "value" of thousands of hypothetical policies. He wrote the bill and presented it to the state legislature himself, and it passed. Lacking the "mathematical attainments," other potential candidates declined the post of insurance commissioner. In 1858, therefore, Wright became the new insurance commissioner of Massachusetts.[92]

The 1858 registry law did not demand "surrender values." So immediately Commissioner Wright called for another law to secure them. His 1860 report as commissioner calculated that of 38,231 Massachusetts policies in force in 1858, 850 lapsed to the company, with no compensation offered—a number that did not include an unknown number of policies "assigned" to third parties. Wright demanded that corporations return the actuarial "value" of these policies to their forfeiting policyholders.[93]

The emerging life insurance industry fought Wright tooth and nail. In calculating his "surrender values," they argued, Wright did not account enough for corporate operating expenses. Insurance corporations needed money to advertise and hire agents or else not enough men would purchase policies and the law of mortality would not work. Further, Wright assumed 4 percent returns on the investments of company assets. But as one fellow actuary asked Wright: "you make no reference to the risk of . . . financial disturbance." Wright pulled back, admitting "there is always a class of perils beyond those which can be foreseen." Finally, the "forfeiture clause" was clearly stipulated in the policy contract—the policyholder knowingly assumed the risk of forfeiture.[94]

Nevertheless, Wright's "surrender value" bill became Massachusetts law April 10, 1861. The bill passed only because of Wright's impeccable antislavery credentials, as the insurance commissioner was in favor with the Republican state house. Wright was only half satisfied however as the law only secured four-fifths of the full "value of the policy" and not as a cash payment—the four-fifths was commuted to a policy of term insurance.

On April 12, 1861, two days after the bill passed, shots were fired at Fort Sumter. From his perch as insurance commissioner, Wright thought the Civil War would end quickly. He wrote pamphlets calling for immediate slave emancipation, and advocated for black civil and political rights and the redistribution of southern land to former slaves.[95]

Meanwhile, Wright soon became the leading public authority on life insurance in America. Life insurance sales exploded during the 1860s as insurance in force leapt from just over $100 million to over $1 billion. Demand was so heavy for Wright's annual commissioner reports— which included dense statistical tables but also stirring editorials on the necessity of self-insurance—that in 1865 they were collected into a single volume. The work popularized life insurance and its appendix became the first technical American actuarial treatise. Wright believed he was securing the financial foundations for the kind of free society that would emerge from the Civil War.[96]

After the war, the governor of Massachusetts did not renominate Wright for the post of insurance commissioner. A rising corporate insurance lobby did not like his continued calls for full cash "surrender values" and the momentum he had achieved with the 1858 and 1861 Massachusetts laws had stalled. Wright left however with a parting shot. "If unrestrained life insurance is destined to withdraw from the pockets of the people," then it would be better to have the "Federal government" enter "the field" as the "insurer itself." Wright's career as a state regulator was over.[97]

Afterward, Wright earned his living as an actuarial consultant. He continued to push for the cause of full cash "surrender values," publishing a number of books, pamphlets, and newspaper articles. He warned of the power of the vast accumulations of financial capital in the hands of private corporations, much of it consisting of forfeited policies. He wrote on "Life Insurance for the Poor," urging for the extension of the insurance principle to the perils of wage work, and also of old age. In 1875 he ran for the Massachusetts State Senate on a personal insurance platform and lost. The next year he incorporated his own "self-insurance" company which quickly failed for lack of business.[98]

The scene was thus bleak when, that same year, Wright finally scored a victory in the 1876 U.S. Supreme Court decision *New York Life Insurance Company v. Statham*. *Statham* was a consolidation of numerous cases that concerned the status of southern life insurance policies purchased from northern financial corporations before the outbreak of Civil War.[99]

In 1851, the New York Life Insurance Company had sold a $5,000 whole-life policy to A. D. Statham of the state of Mississippi. Statham's wife was the beneficiary and the policy contained the standard "forfeiture clause." Statham paid his premiums until the outbreak of the Civil War. After 1861, both Union and Confederate nonintercourse laws barred him from making payments. Statham died in 1862 and after the war his widow sued the New York Life, arguing that the war was an "act of God." It had suspended rather than annulled the original contract. The corporation therefore owed the widow $5,000, less the unpaid 1862 premium. The New York Life argued that life insurance was a series of yearly "executory contracts." Each year's premiums paid for that year's insurance. The 1862 premium was not paid, the contract was broken, and so Statham's widow was owed nothing.[100]

Justice Joseph Bradley delivered the opinion of the court. He quickly dispensed with the New York Life's argument. In a "level" premium life insurance company, policyholders purchased with their premiums future years of coverage. Next, Statham's 1862 nonpayment was in fact "caused by an event beyond the control of either party," although Bradley left the question of whether or not the Civil War was "an act of God" unanswered. Statham's widow was not entitled to the full $5,000. Rather, she was "entitled to have the equitable value of his policy." The "value" of the policy was the insured's "property." It was only estimable with an actuarial calculation. Thus Bradley remanded the case, asking the Appeals Court to figure out the precise valuation. If Bradley sounded like Wright, it was no accident. Days after the case, Bradley wrote a letter to the former insurance commissioner:

> Dear Sir, I enclose you a full copy of the opinion recently delivered by me in the Supreme Court on Life policy lapses by the war. I would place much value on your approbation of its principles. If attacked because it gives the assured something I think it will find a defender in you, since, according to my recollection our views on this subject are in accord.

Statham was a victory for the actuarial science of freedom but also for the professional standing of actuarial science.[101]

Statham emboldened Wright. He publicized the ruling hoping to mobilize support in state legislatures for full cash "surrender laws." In 1878, California passed a law to his liking and in 1880 Massachusetts followed. But Wright was routed in the crucial state of New York, whose insurance corporations now dominated the national field. With their vast accumulations, they had bought off the state legislature in Albany. In 1879, New York passed a law with a 33.3 percent surrender charge which granted no cash "surrender value." Even this law did not apply if the "forfeiture clause" was printed in "red ink."[102]

The Supreme Court's decision in *Statham* only applied to former Confederates. And so the irony was that the abolitionist luminary turned leading actuary had secured his cherished "surrender values" almost exclusively for the white citizens of the former Confederacy.

Wright, needless to say, was disappointed. But now at the end of his life, his attention had turned elsewhere. He had become a fervent atheist and in his final years, while personal insurance burgeoned—bearing yet lacking his mark—it was God that most preoccupied his thoughts. He wrote that religion assumed that, "the whole universe was created and is governed by a person of immaterial Will, named God." But the universe was not an unceasing act of God. Thankfully, "science" was now "relegating the human imagination to its proper sphere." The new "doctrine of chances" supplied "to mankind, in regard to a great many subjects, a sort of substitute" for the "fore-knowledge, or prophetic power" of God. No longer believing in the ways of providence, Wright, the former evangelical abolitionist, died an atheist actuary.[103]

CHAPTER 4

The Failure of the Freedman's Bank

The sudden [financial] panic . . . has come into our city like one of those cyclones of which we read in the Eastern seas, which occasionally sweep over the deep with such violence as to leave it strewn with wrecks. Vain is the power of man in struggling with such a tempest.

—"The Panic," *The New York Evangelist,* September 25, 1873

A T THE CLOSE of the American Civil War, 4 million newly emancipated slaves entered the brave new world of capitalism and risk. Yankee emancipators believed that the freedmen should offload their freshly minted personal risks onto the evolving northern corporate financial system, as a consequence of their newfound freedom. A financial experiment was launched as the 1865 Freedman's Savings and Trust Company, otherwise known as the Freedman's Bank, was incorporated. Directed by northern white abolitionists, the freedpeople would save their wages, using a financial corporation to hedge themselves against the perils of freedom and of the rising economic chance-world of capitalism.

As for that economic chance-world and its imprint upon the moral texture of the future, the Civil War was a turning point for providential worldviews in American culture. In 1861, many northerners and southerners marched off to battle believing, or at least having been told, that God was on their side. By the time it was all over some 620,000 were dead and the Union Army had destroyed southern slavery.[1]

To northern abolitionists and African-Americans it was the vindication of God's design. Clara Jones, a North Carolina freedwoman, reflected: "The white folks went off to the war. They said they could whup, but the Lord said, 'No,' and they didn't whup. They went off laughing, and many did not come back." African-American voices declared the coming of a foreordained Jubilee. As James Lynch, an African Methodist Episcopal minister, preached: "the hand of Providence was in the election of Mr. Lincoln to the Presidency." It was "Divine Providence" that brought about "the deliverance of the slave from bondage."[2]

The sentiment was not unique to the African-American people. In 1865, the Princeton theologian Charles Hodge, Old School Presbyterian and former northern contributor to the 1860 proslavery compendium *Cotton is King*, published a tribute to the assassinated president, once again revarnishing old Calvinist doctrines, but now in defense of freedom's triumph. Divine providence, he declared, still assured that "nothing happens" by "chance." God "governs free agents with certainty, but without destroying their liberty." Even the former apologist for slavery admitted that the triumph of freedom was divinely ordained and providentially secured.[3]

These voices rang loudly in the era of Appomattox. But already a new timbre portended the fragility of providential beliefs. As the war toll worsened, a tortured President Lincoln had privately meditated on the inscrutable workings of God's will. At the Second Inaugural, with victory in sight and with none other than Frederick Douglass watching from the audience, Lincoln speculated that the rise and bloody demise of slavery had all come "in the providence of God." And yet, Lincoln's invocation of "Divine attributes" was posed in the form of a question. Privately and publicly, Lincoln edged toward the brink of agnosticism.[4]

Elsewhere, the war bred an even greater skepticism. Many thinkers became fascinated with the blind force of chance. Some, like Elizur Wright, turned to scientific explanations of contingency, spawning new forms of determinism both soft and hard. War-weary Americans did not all become atheists and the postwar generation exhibited pronounced longings for religious regeneration. But one kind of divine master did begin to recede from public view just as the slave master lost his private dominion. In this context, there echoed throughout the land Lincoln's call at Gettysburg for a "new birth of freedom."[5]

Slave society was no more. Its bedrock, the master–slave relation—a social bond southern divines had once declared the handwork of an omniscient God—was torn asunder in a spectacular destruction of private property. As a sympathetic former Confederate warned Union officials on the ground in South Carolina in 1865, "The past cannot be recalled."

The very project of slave emancipation consisted of a radical "uncertainty." It was a "gigantic experiment" charged with bringing "order" out of "chaos." Emancipation, according to a critical 1864 War Department document, "cannot safely be left undirected and uncared for, to work itself out, drifting on at haphazard, according to the chance shiftings of the current of daily events." The federal government—newly expansive over the course of the war—was to navigate the passage from slavery to freedom, as Yankee emancipators took upon themselves the daunting task of constructing a free society from the ground up.[6]

The federal government would have to ensure the former slaves' newfound self-ownership. In this spirit, emancipators enclosed the risks of an entire people. Slaves became formal proprietors over their own persons and therefore now assumed their own personal risks. "In slavery," Yankee General Rufus Saxton lectured the freedmen, "you did not think of the future." "In freedom," he warned, "you must have an eye to the future, and have a plan and object in life." The moral weight of the future pressed down on any free agent.[7]

The dominant Yankee free-labor vision directed the freedpeople to continue to crop the white man's cotton. But they would be paid for their labor in money wages, through contracts—representing a slight but ideologically significant upside. Likewise, they assumed a downside. In sickness, disability, or old age the freedman—not his former master, not the federal government—would support himself and his familial dependents.

Self-ownership proceeded down the path of finance, a path cleared with great care by Yankee emancipators. On March 13, 1865, President Lincoln signed a law chartering the Freedman's Bank, a nonprofit savings bank directed by white northern philanthropists. In the urban North, savings banks had for decades targeted the bourgeoning industrial white working class. In the Freedman's Bank, the freedpeople could save their wages and begin to take charge of their own futures.[8]

The freedpeople themselves did not at first clamor for savings accounts. They had their own vision of economic freedom: landed independence rather than financial independence. They wanted the lands they had labored upon as slaves. "Gib us our own land and we take care ourselves," a South Carolina freedman told one white northern journalist. The freedpeople had their own sense of what it meant to be a free and secure actor. Like virtually all Americans, they desired the means of commercial risk-taking on their own account. But ex-slaves also wanted a bulwark of economic and existential security outside the grasp of markets—not to mention the clutches of their former masters. Famously, in the fateful years of 1865 and 1866 they failed in their quest for land. And so a new class of black sharecroppers would turn to the Freedman's Bank. By 1873, it had received a staggering $50 million from nearly 100,000 depositors.[9]

That $50 million was an emblem of the nineteenth-century liberal experiment that made free men personally responsible for assuming their own risks but then encouraged them, if not forced them, to offload those same risks onto financial corporations. Piddling in their individual amounts, Freedman's Bank deposits, premised upon the Yankee ideals of self-ownership and personal responsibility, created a distinct new form of social dependence residing in the opaque sinews of financial intermediation. The bank's white directors pledged there would be "no speculation" and "no risk." Black depositors should have complete faith and trust in the white-run institution. The ethos was philanthropic, a benevolent "trusteeship." But the finance committee of the Freedman's Bank would have to invest the deposits somewhere. In 1868, Henry Cooke, a partner in his brother's great investment bank Jay Cooke & Co., took charge of investing the freedpeople's savings on their behalf. With the direct power and authority of the slave master lifted, the former slave, in order to realize his newfound freedom, joined the evolving American financial system. A "new birth of freedom" gestated in the emerging world of capitalism and risk.[10]

Slavery had been destroyed. Providence waned. With its own novel, energizing, and frightening temporal rhythms, the economic chance-world waxed—in awesome fashion during the panic of 1873. Amidst it all, the United States became for the first time a self-professedly free society.

The Freedman's Bank was a product of the attempt to impose northern free-labor practices on the war-torn South. The Civil War, explained one of the bank's founding trustees, the Boston textile manufacturer Edward Atkinson, was "a war for the establishment of free labor."[11]

Atkinson embodies the triumphant Yankee of 1865. He was not a freeholding farmer or, like his father, a general-trades merchant. He was a precocious industrialist. In 1851, at age twenty-four, he was already the manager of a textile mill. By 1860 Atkinson oversaw six cotton mills for Boston-area corporations. He had also become a radical abolitionist, even raising funds in 1855 for John Brown's raid on Harper's Ferry. Meanwhile, that decade witnessed a surge in northeastern industrialization—in the new mill towns and one-industry cities of New England, or in the more diversified metropolitan centers of Boston, New York, and Philadelphia. Atkinson spread the new factory system, personally overseeing a labor force that tended to 70,000 spindles and 1,500 looms. Spreading the gospel of free labor, he represented a new form of industrial capital. With the slaveholders defeated, men like Atkinson were suddenly in the saddle.[12]

To Atkinson's crowd, free laborers, by definition, were savers. The proof was the flourishing network of working-class northeastern savings banks which counted $246 million of deposits in 1865—about half of total private money savings in the United States, including the $55 million of life insurance reserves. Not only a trustee of the Freedman's Bank, Atkinson would soon become president of his hometown Brookline Savings Bank, serving Boston-area textile wage earners. Freedom meant financial intermediation.[13]

Unlike slaves free men enjoyed self-ownership.[14] Free laborers, proprietors of their own persons, were proprietors of their own labor power, a commodity sold on the market for a money wage to an employer in a consensual, contractual exchange. That wage contained a "premium"—to recall the word Justice Lemuel Shaw chose in *Farwell*—to compensate the wage earner in the events of disability, sickness, death, or old age. Further, with enough savings the wage earner might leave the ranks of dependent hirelings and become an independent proprietor. Wright hoped to extend the insurance principle to the working masses. Most abolitionists, however, were like Atkinson. They directed industrial wage earners to the savings banks.

For Union officials, the question was simple. Would black slaves work for wages and save for the future? They answered with a resounding yes. "That which savings banks have done for the working men of the north," declared John W. Alvord, the founder of the Freedman's Bank, "they are capable of doing for these laborers." Alvord and others drew that conclusion as confident adherents of free labor and prideful observers of the financial success of northern working-class savings banks. But they also drew from the wartime experiment with black free labor in the Union-held territories of the Confederacy.[15]

That experiment produced the first black savings banks, predating the 1865 Freedman's Bank. Months after Lincoln's Emancipation Proclamation, in March 1863 the War Department created the "American Freedmen's Inquiry Commission." Three men of impeccable antislavery credentials—among them the Bostonian Samuel Gridley Howe, another future founding trustee of the Freedman's—set about grappling with the impending problem of emancipation. Howe and his two peers traveled through the Union-occupied strongholds of Virginia, South Carolina, Louisiana, and Tennessee. They walked in the refugee camps of runaway-slave "contrabands" that had swelled within Union picket lines. They inspected the government-run plantations. Of the some 4 million southern slaves, an estimated 475,000 were not only set free before the war's end but had also performed some form of compensated labor. The emancipators asked: What were black slaves like? Were they capable of foreseeing, willing, and becoming responsible for a future of their own reckoning? Were they, in other words, capable of freedom?

Yankees confronted widespread southern racial stereotypes which must have haunted them. Without their masters' provident guiding hand, Confederates taunted, black slaves would not work to produce anything above their immediate subsistence. They certainly would not save. In 1866 an embittered George Fitzhugh explained that, "Negroes will not provide in summer for the wants of winter, nor in the youth for the exigencies of age, unless compelled to do so." Only the "white race" was naturally "provident and accumulative." Racial inferiority demanded that ex-masters continue to manage their ex-slaves' futures.[16]

Most Yankees had their own notions of black inferiority. But still to many the root cause of the black slave's disregard of the future was not race. It was slavery. In 1865, the superintendent of negro affairs in Virginia explained to the Freedmen's Inquiry Commission that, "Their past education," not their race, had "taught them to have no care for the future."

Earlier, in June 1863 the commission visited the city of Beaufort, South Carolina, where tens of thousands of slaves were under the jurisdiction of General Saxton. They reported that slavery had produced "submission, humility, resignation, reliance on Providence, obedience to masters." In 1865, two of Saxton's lieutenants reported in the eminent *North American Review* that, "Under slavery, so much does man take the place of God, and his law and his care that of God's law and providence, that the will does not find its natural exercise." That was why the slave "lacks forethought and finish."[17]

These were typical antislavery views. Saxton, one of the more idealistic of Union officials, sounded them directly to the freedpeople. Under slavery, Saxton lectured in 1865, "Having nothing to hope for beyond the present, you did not think of the future but like the ox and the horse, thought only of the food and work for the day." Slaves, to become free, would require a strengthened will directed toward a this-worldly future. Saxton thus commanded the freedpeople to develop an "eye to the future."[18]

To the Yankee eye, there were already glimmerings that black slaves were willing and capable risk-takers. The slave refugee camps existed because thousands upon thousands of slaves had run away from their masters. Howe and the Freedmen's Inquiry Commission concluded that, "Southern slaves as a body do desire release from bondage." They had after all run grave risks to gain their freedom. One South Carolina slave had run away from his master, "determined to risk his life in an attempt to escape." The Bostonian lawyer Edward Pierce—at Port Royal in early 1862 on behalf of Treasury Secretary Salmon P. Chase—observed that, "The desire to be free has been strongly expressed." "Every day almost adds a fresh tale of escapes, both solitary and in numbers, conducted with a courage, a forecast, a skill worthy of heroes." These arguments were not unlike those that circulated around the case of the *Creole*. The master misjudged the slave.[19]

What was more, once under Union command the slaves appeared willing to work for wages and even to save them. "Do these people," the Freedmen's Inquiry Commission inquired of Captain E. W. Hooper, an aide to Saxton, "work willingly for wages?" Yes. Wage payments from the northern entrepreneurs who ran the government-controlled plantations were "more than sufficient for their wants, and they save." The Freedmen's Inquiry Commission published a preliminary report in June of 1863. Slaves, it assured, would willingly work for wages. And they would willingly save: "working for wages, they soon get an idea of accumulating. Saving banks will be popular with them when their confidence is won."[20]

Yankee emancipators were glad to reach that conclusion. They knew that freedom demanded a total reconstruction of risk, which would require new financial institutions in the South. Already during the war, Union officials had created three savings banks for ex-slaves in Norfolk, Virginia; New Orleans, Louisiana; and Beaufort, South Carolina.

The most revealing wartime bank was the Free Labor Bank of New Orleans, created by General Nathaniel P. Banks, the former governor of Massachusetts who had had once appointed Wright insurance commissioner. In 1861 President Lincoln appointed Governor Banks a general of the Volunteers Corps and in January of 1863 Banks took command in New Orleans, with 150,000 Louisiana slaves within his lines. In October of 1864, Banks returned to Boston to give a public lecture on his system of "Emancipated Labor."[21]

"The problem," Banks explained, was to "apportion the risk between capital and labor" while establishing the federal government's "authority" as "superior." Slaves now ran the risks of free labor—the risk of being "unable to labor" whether because of sickness, old age, disability, or infirmity. Then there were the "risks incurred in the investment of capital"— the capital of either resident southern planters who had thrown in with the Union or northern leasers of abandoned plantations. For capital there was the general "insecurity" of war. Northern and southern planters all complained of the "the risks of the system"—from the Confederate "guerillas," to the "dishonest lessees," to the "failure of the crop," to black laborers who came and went as they pleased. Banks's task was to create an authoritative government framework for the free management of risk.[22]

The slave "unable to labor" was by far the most pressing problem in Louisiana, and for that matter in all the Union-occupied territories. Northern capitalists were chasing the upside, planting cash staples like sugar, cotton, or rice. Unlike the slave master, they had no reason to practice a "safety-first" agriculture, to distribute their workers across the life cycle, to mix subsistence production (largely performed by the young, the infirm, or the elderly) with staple production (largely performed by the prime hands). For their part, the former slaves still felt entitled to the subsistence goods of the plantation—food, clothing, shelter, and medical care. Even southern planters understood the new logic quickly, often turning out the young, sick, and elderly. As one Louisiana planter claimed, "When I owned niggers I used to pay medical bills and take care of them; I do not think I shall trouble myself much now." In September of 1863, one of Banks's aides wrote to him of the legion of "old, sick, disabled, or children, with a few women, whose husbands are in the army" all banished by their former masters. Banks's aide asked for authorization "to send back these old and disabled people to the plantations where they belong, and let their masters support them." They had spent their productive years working for them and now "masters should be made to support them in their old and disabled condition."[23]

In this context, Banks proceeded to violate a number of free-labor precepts. His field order of February 1864 declared that for the time being capital would provide for the support of "the workman and his family, in sickness or in health." Without this provision, Banks estimated that some 75,000 would be "thrown upon the Government for support." Yet, Banks also attended to the risks of capital. Laborers were coerced to enter yearlong contracts which they could not break. Violating the rising free-labor doctrine of "employment at will," capital gained a more certain productive input. Clearly "Emancipated Labor" and "Free Labor" were not the same thing.[24]

The passageway to freedom was opened with the Free Labor Bank, also created in the same field order of February 1864. In time, Banks lectured to his Boston audience, the freedman was to "labor for his own support," and for the support "of his family or the helpless portions of his race." Banks had this goal in mind when he himself set the wage rates for field hands. He had added to "the price of wages to be paid in addition to the support of each individual labor" a premium for the "maintenance of the infirm, the sick, the aged, and the young." With such a wage, the laborer "could provide for himself, and for them in the future." In that future, blacks would not rely upon their former masters. They would not form a permanent mass of burdensome dependents on the federal dole. The emancipated laborer only required an institution by which he "shall make good the excess of wages." That was the Free Labor Bank, the ideological and practical solution to the shortcomings of "Emancipated Labor."[25]

The path required financial intermediation—ex-slaves' savings, that is, had to land somewhere in the capital market. Six months after Banks created the Free Labor Bank, in October 1864 Saxton founded the South Carolina Freedmen's Savings Bank with similar intentions. By the end of December 1865 Saxton's institution had $170,000 in deposits, an enormous figure. There is no record of where it came from but most was probably black military pay or money hoarded under slavery. Regardless, in May of 1865 the *New York Times* printed: "Jay Cooke reports the subscriptions to the Seven-Thirty Loan yesterday at $15,411,800. Among the subscriptions were $80,000 by the Freedmen's Savings Bank, of South Carolina."[26]

The Philadelphia banker Jay Cooke was a private advisor to Treasury Secretary Salmon P. Chase, and the general subscription agent for an exploding Union war debt. By 1865 he and his 2,500 subagents had sold over $1 billion of U.S. bonds directly to the American people, a watershed moment in American financial history which ballooned the federal debt to hitherto unimaginable proportions. According to one of Cooke's agents, to purchase a war bond was to show confidence in "the justice of our cause, and, we firmly believe, the protection of Divine Providence." War bonds were marketed to citizens as a form of "forever safe" savings. One of Cooke's 1865 New York "Victory Loan" posters advertising the seven-thirty bonds was entitled "The Working Men's Savings Bank!" Meanwhile, according to Saxton, the South Carolina Freedmen's Savings Bank was proof that "some of the freedmen, at least care for the future, and not all of them, as is frequently asserted, think only of to-day."[27]

In sum, as the Civil War gave way to Reconstruction it was clear that savings banks would play a critical ideological and institutional function. Yet a federally chartered Freedman's Bank was more than a continuation of wartime trends. Modeled on a successful northern institution, it was in line with the original spirit of Reconstruction. In May 1864 the

Freedmen's Inquiry Commission concluded that while slave emancipation could not be left to "work itself out" according to "the chance
shiftings of the current of daily events," at the same time an excessive
"guardianship" of the freedman was itself perilous. "The risk is serious
that, under the guise of guardianship, slavery in a modified form, may
be practically restored." The trick was to weigh appropriate federal
power against excessive "guardianship."[28]

Congress had been debating the appropriate balance. The wartime
Republican Congresses had dramatically expanded federal power and
in June 1864 Senator Charles Sumner of Massachusetts brought to the
Senate floor a bill, following the Freedmen's Inquiry Commission's recommendation, to create a temporary Freedmen's Bureau. Even the
staunch antislavery Iowa Senator James W. Grimes protested. The only
"way to treat these men is to treat them as freemen." The freemen "will
be jostled as we are all being jostled through this life" but soon enough
"they will settle down into the position that Providence has designed
that they shall occupy under the new condition of affairs in this country." Recalcitrant Democrats were far less cooperative. Months earlier a
democratic Congressman asserted that blacks, slaves or not, would forever require white rule and reminded that, "The law of providence is
inequality." Vain were those who thought they could "improve upon the
workmanship of the Almighty."[29]

On the Senate floor, Sumner countered. He called the Freedmen's
Bureau a necessary "bridge from slavery to freedom." "The Senate,"
Sumner analogized, "only a short time ago was engaged for a week con-
sidering how to open an iron way from the Atlantic to the Pacific. It is
now to consider how to open a way from Slavery to Freedom." Sumner
was referring to a second wave of federal support for the new transcontinental railroads. Congress had just granted 47 million acres, in the largest giveaway of public lands ever, to one corporation, the Northern Pacific Railway. The bill had passed the Senate without protest, following
the Pacific Railway Act of 1862, which had provided land grants and also
federally secured and subsidized thirty-year, 6 percent bonds to the
Union Pacific and Central Pacific railroads. As for the freedman, Sumner continued, "the National Government must interfere in the case,
precisely as in building the Pacific Railroad." Both slave emancipation

and the transcontinental railroad, he surmised, were far too perilous endeavors to undertake without government backing. President Lincoln signed into law the Freedmen's Bureau on March 3, 1865.[30]

That very same day, Lincoln signed another law, this one chartering another corporation, the Freedman's Bank. It too had emerged from Sumner's Select Committee on Slavery and Freedom. The Freedman's Bank's corporate charter also passed with hardly a murmur. It had been brought to Sumner by the aforementioned Alvord.

Alvord was no financier. Born in Connecticut, he was an ordained Congregationalist minister. He joined the radical antislavery cause in 1833. During the Civil War traveled within General William T. Sherman's lines, distributing religious tracts to the troops and teaching slave refugees how to read. He became friends with one of Sherman's most trusted generals, Oliver O. Howard, who shared Alvord's evangelical fervor. In March 1865, Howard was put in charge of the Freedmen's Bureau and he would soon name Alvord the bureau's first inspector of schools and finances. In 1864, Alvord had observed Saxton's South Carolina Freedmen's Bank and got the idea for a general Freedman's Bank. "Slavery," he declared, had "prevented all forecasting of thought." But "a change has come." In January 1865, Alvord was in New York City, convening a group of twenty-two men to found a mutual savings bank for former slaves. The group proposed a charter and Alvord traveled with it in hand to Sumner.[31]

It was an almost boilerplate copy of New York City savings banks' corporate charters. A "savings bank" was then different from a "commercial bank." Commercial banks existed to turn profits. There were private banks like Jay Cooke & Co. or corporate banks that paid dividends to stockholders. Like savings banks, commercial banks took deposits. But they made most of their profits by performing "general" banking services: trading and discounting bank notes and bills of exchange, making personal and business loans. They were risky, and that was the point. They failed all the time. Savings banks were meant to stand apart from the commercial banking system.[32]

In the late 1810s prominent northeastern philanthropists had begun to incorporate "savings banks." The original idea was English, dating from the same time. The first American savings bank was the 1816

Provident Institution of Savings of Boston. One of Provident's trustees, Amos A. Lawrence, was another Boston textile manufacturer and another founding trustee of the Freedman's Bank. Soon American savings banks outstripped their English peers. Taking deposits, savings bank trustees promised to invest in conservative assets, rebating all returns to their depositors as interest. The original point, explained Emerson Keyes, long a New York state banking official, looking back from 1876, was working-class "security."[33]

The antebellum savings bank was originally a class-based institution. Its founding idea was charity, not profit, and the banks existed for the lower orders of society. The early relation between trustee and depositor, Keyes surmised, was like that between "patron" and "dependent." The first trustees did not draw salaries and many savings banks capped deposits in order to maintain a working-class clientele. A savings account, in hard times, might prevent laborers from resorting to private charity or the public dole—a widespread fear of Northern officials. The inculcated spirit of "independence," aided by further accumulations, might lead to upward mobility and the cherished status of independent proprietor. To Yankee emancipators this was just the right amount of federal intervention. "This is a benevolent institution" declared an early piece of bank literature. But it was not excessive "guardianship."[34]

In truth, the benevolent ethos of the Freedman's Bank was already anachronistic. Between 1850 and 1860 active deposits in New York mutual savings banks surged from 68,000 to 196,000. In that time $13.5 million on deposit became $43.7 million. Savings banks were becoming crucial financial intermediaries in the local capital market, often tied at the hip to profit-hungry commercial banks. The Bowery Savings Bank of New York, for instance, was founded in 1834—according to its president for the workingman to protect himself against all "vicissitudes." By 1861, the Bowery was the largest savings bank in the city with 44,000 accounts open and $10.3 million on deposit. But it was essentially an arm of the commercial Butcher's and Drover's Bank. (The Bowery's president publicly disavowed himself of any "benevolent feelings.") Savings bank officials had begun to draw salaries, as they moved their assets out of government bonds and into more risky securities like commercial bank deposits and call loans. The line between commercial and savings banks blurred. Once again, the countermovement of corporate risk management had created new opportunities for speculative risk-taking.[35]

The Congregationalist minister Alvord, and other founders with little banking experience, were perhaps ignorant of this trend. Others, like Atkinson, trustee of the Brookline Savings Bank, were probably not. He and his industrialist peers probably drafted the corporate charter.[36]

The original federal charter of the Freedman's Bank contained two crucial provisions. Section 5 read that the bank was to receive deposits "by or on behalf of persons heretofore held in slavery in the United States, or their descendents, and in investing the same in the stocks, bonds, treasury notes, or the securities of the United States." Jay Cooke's war bonds were then still widely available. But section 6 of the charter already contained an out. Copying a common New York and Massachusetts provision, it allowed for a third of the bank's deposits, called an "available fund," to be invested anywhere. Massachusetts savings banks were already investing in the most speculative assets of all—railroad bonds. The same clause was bringing together New York commercial and savings banks in a warm embrace. The new Freedman's Bank was to be headquartered on Wall Street.[37]

The Freedman's Bank was however a strikingly unique financial institution. For one, it carried a federal charter—the only federally chartered bank allowed to open local branches and the first since the Second Bank of the United States. Further, there were no true "savings banks" in the South. Southerners had stored their wealth largely in their slaves or in their lands, rooting security in fixed and physical forms of capital, not finance capital. For that matter, savings banks were almost unheard of in the countryside, North or South. The West had its "wildcat" commercial banks but freeholders largely stored their wealth in land and land improvements—the logic of landed independence. Like antebellum life insurance, antebellum savings banks were an urban phenomenon. The effort to create a rural savings bank in the largely agricultural South expressed the profound confidence of Yankee emancipators in their worldview (and the tilt toward the free-labor rather than Free Soil wing).

Put everything in place—self-ownership, free labor, savings banks—and freedom would flourish. So would the capital market—although this was not said out loud or even fully realized by men like Alvord.[38]

For the first two years after its creation the Freedman's Bank largely stood idle. The chaotic nature of early Reconstruction was in part responsible but the freedpeople simply did not clamor for savings accounts. They wanted land. They did not have the money to purchase their own farms, and there were few willing white sellers. If there were to be black freeholds, the federal government would have to intervene.

The possibility was not entirely outrageous. During the war many slaves had already seized "abandoned" plantations. Some were granted autonomy, some even credit and capital, to operate government farms. Some simply squatted. Then, the March 1865 law creating the Freedmen's Bureau promised forty-acre plots carved out of the 858,000 acres of abandoned lands under the bureau's jurisdiction. The freedpeople not only desired land but expected it as just compensation for unrequited toil and military loyalty. "[T]he negro," reported bureau official and future Freedman's Bank trustee Colonel Alexander P. Ketchum in 1865, "regards the ownership of land as a privilege that ought to be co-existent with his freedom." Throughout 1865, rumors raced throughout the South of an impending and seismic Christmas-day land redistribution. The fate of the Freedman's Bank would not be determined until the resolution of the "land question."[39]

The most dramatic battlefront concerned the infamous and often-told story of "Sherman's reserve." After a devastating march to the sea, General William T. Sherman's army had arrived in Savannah in December 1864. Scores of fleeing slaves had sought refuge and freedom within his lines. On January 12, 1865, Sherman met with twenty local black religious leaders who told him, "We want to be placed on land until we are able to buy it and make it our own." Relieving his army of a dependent population, Sherman issued Field Order 15 which covered 400,000 acres of rich coastal land running from Charleston, South Carolina, to the St. John's River in northern Florida. Under federal protection, black families could acquire "possessory" titles to forty-acre plots—"possessory" meaning that outright ownership required a final congressional and presidential seal of approval.[40]

Sherman's reserve—almost half the 858,000 acres under bureau control—would prove to be a great breeding ground for future Freedman's Bank depositors dispossessed of forty-acre farms. But it was also a breeding ground for future Freedman's Bank officials. Alvord was travelling in Sherman's lines when Field Order 15 was issued. Saxton, a future bank trustee, administered Sherman's reserve. His closest aid was Ketchum, a young New York lawyer from a prominent antislavery family. Ketchum's older brother Edgar, another lawyer, would become a particularly active trustee. Also there in coastal South Carolina was the younger brother of Freedmen's Bureau commissioner Oliver Howard, Charles, another of Saxton's aides. Charles would soon direct the branch operations of the Freedman's Bank, one of a handful of its most important executives. These men—Saxton, the Ketchums, the Howards— were some of the staunchest northern advocates of land redistribution. Foiled in their initial quest for land, freedmen and Freedmen's Bureau officials alike would turn to the Freedman's Bank.

Field Order 15 renewed an ongoing contest in coastal South Carolina, which had revealed the freedmen's desire for land but also anxieties within the Yankee camp about whether they should get it. The Treasury Department had taken control of 40,000 acres of forfeited Confederate property in the South Carolina Sea Islands with the intention to auction them off for outright, "fee simple" ownership. In March 1862 Saxton had argued in a Boston periodical for the redistribution of "the fertile lands on these islands among the different families in lots large enough for their subsistence." "The great gain to humanity," Saxton had judged, "would far outweigh the loss in cotton."[41]

Saxton's was hardly the prevailing Yankee view, however. Atkinson for instance had different designs, first announced in the 1861 pamphlet "Cheap Cotton by Free Labor." Atkinson, along with another Boston industrialist and founding trustee of the Freedman's Bank, would lead a consortium of Boston textile firms who purchased eleven Sea Islands plantations. Edward Philbrick, the young assistant superintendent of the Boston & Worcester Railroad—Nicholas Farwell's old line—took charge of what he and Atkinson hoped would become model free-labor plantations. Much to his chagrin, the ex-slaves resisted Philbrick's authority. Meanwhile, Saxton complained to his superiors that the "great bulk of lands" had come "into the hands of speculators" whose only interest was "the profit to be derived from labor at the lowest price." Indeed, in the first year Philbrick himself turned a handsome profit of $80,000. Ketchum wondered if the former slave was to remain nothing more than "a mere laborer for the white man and subject to his will." Less than 4 percent of lands auctioned under the Direct Tax Act of 1862 were sold to former slaves.[42]

But Field Order 15 reshuffled the deck. Saxton, with Ketchum his point man, meant to carry it out and had Commissioner Howard's full support. Significant administrative hurdles stood in the way and southern white resistance often took violent turns, but in June 1865 Saxton reported to Howard that 40,000 former slaves had been settled throughout the reserve. In July 1865 Howard issued Circular 13, again ordering all abandoned and confiscated lands under the bureau's jurisdiction allotted to ex-slaves or white refugees. In August 1865 Saxton moved Ketchum to the district of Savannah where he quickly shepherded 397 titles granting 7,841 acres to 1,592 former Georgia slaves. At this moment—within limits, as the bureau controlled less than 1 percent of all Confederate lands—some form of land redistribution was no pipe dream.[43]

The freedpeople wanted land not only because they felt they deserved it. They said time and again that they desired a life of "independence." First and foremost, independence meant freedom—for themselves, their families, and their communities—from the power and authority of their former masters. But the black vision of freedom had positive as well as negative content. Much like white freeholders North and South, land-hungry ex-slaves shunned the dependent status of wage worker. In truth, Atkinson and company had sought to transform black slaves into the first permanent American agricultural proletariat. Atkinson pictured the wage workers of his own textile manufactures. He was not thinking of freeholding, family-farm proprietors. Emancipators like Oliver and Charles Howard, sons of a Maine farmer, were more likely to have the ethos of landed independence in mind. Indeed, the freedpeople's hunger for land was yet another variant of the broader nineteenth-century American quest for a landed independence.

Therefore the "land question" not only concerned white property rights and the control of black labor. It also concerned what crops would go into the ground—the timeworn agricultural shuttle between commercial opportunity and baseline security. For their part, Atkinson and Lawrence wanted the black free laborer to produce as much cotton as possible for industrializing New England textile mills. They fantasized about ex-slaves purchasing northern consumer baubles or at least subsistence goods, including western wheat, from national markets. They desired complete absorption of economic life in market exchange—that crucial threshold in the history of capitalism. Alarming men like Atkinson, when freedpeople did get a hold of their own plots they tended to their own subsistence needs first. They raised corn, potatoes, peas, and other vegetables, and hunted, foraged, and fished in the open range. Cash crops—cotton, rice, tobacco, sugar—came next. The freedpeople desired a landed independence and a safety-first agriculture.[44]

Of course, before the war, slave plantations practiced a commercial form of safety-first, and had been relatively self-sufficient units. (This was one reason Atkinson envisioned that free labor would produce more cotton.) Atkinson's free-labor farms would turn out the young, sick, infirm, and elderly, and they would specialize in cotton. They would pay a money wage and the freedman would save it to care for black dependents, as Banks had earlier put it, "unable to labor."

The freedpeople rejected this brave new world. Their rejection had roots under slavery, when plantations had in part acquired self-sufficiency through the "informal" or "slave's" economy—a relatively autonomous sphere of slave production for direct consumption and even market exchange. Many slaves had access to a few acres of their own. They fished, hunted, and foraged. They marketed their goods—wild game, baskets, melons, squash, peas, corn, even some cotton—within the plantation but also in some cases at local markets. A number of slaves maintained extralegal title to property in livestock and farm implements, and stashed away cash and coins inside of trunks and slave cabin walls. Some of this money found its way into the coffers of the Freedman's Bank. Slaves closely guarded the relative independence granted to them by the informal economy and masters had reasons to acknowledge it so long as it aided their own designs.[45]

For a short time, within the small and precarious spaces of the war-torn southern economy—spaces opened by the tenacity of ex-slaves and federal officials like Saxton and Ketchum—there appeared fleeting glimpses of the freedpeople's style of landed independence. It was more communal, more subsistence-orientated, and less commercial than other American variants.

The Atkinson wing of emancipators wanted the freedpeople to produce more cotton than under slavery. The freedpeople wanted to raise less. In 1860, the farm output of "Southeast" plantations with over fifty slaves consisted of nearly 65 percent cotton. In August 1865, in the heart of Sherman's reserve, a Freedmen's Bureau official surveyed sixty-six subdivided plantations on Edisto, Jehossee, Fenwicks, and Little Edisto islands. He counted 3,230 acres, supporting 1,065 black families, a total of 5,440 persons. In a different measure than farm output his survey nonetheless calculated that only 33 percent of "acres under cultivation" were in cotton. Fifty-four percent was in corn, with the rest in various garden vegetables. One subdivided plantation, for instance, supporting eighty-nine ex-slaves with twenty-three unable to work, had sixty-three acres in corn and two and a half in cotton. Strikingly, this pattern of crop diversification resembles that on record for white, free southern family farms in the same period.[46]

Further, in Sherman's reserve and elsewhere land use was more open and more communal. To many ex-slaves, the land was a focal point of kinship and community, a sense of rootedness in place. Some blacks expressed bafflement when offered lands for purchase or settlement other than the land they had labored upon as slaves. The land was not just any commodity and in this context many black land-use practices harkened back to before the enclosure of land, let alone the assumption of risk. Horrified, whites witnessed a return to family and community-based cultivation of unenclosed strips of land scattered about subdivided plantations. Many blacks "clubbed together" resources to purchase and cultivate land communally. The farms identified in the 1865 Sea Islands survey supported anywhere from one to 163 families, usually somewhere between fifteen and thirty. More communal to be sure, but on the whole this was the safety-first logic of landed independence. It kept the freedpeople's downside risks outside the full grasp of markets—which because of their very nature or because of who controlled them were no adequate basis for security. It would certainly prevent men like Atkinson from employing the freedpeople's labor to run upside risks of their own.[47]

The logic was also less commercial compared to the ambitions of the former slave master, the northern industrialist Atkinson, or even the improvement-obsessed Yankee farmer who had far more acres at his disposal. Philbrick compared the prospect of land redistribution to the inefficient "minute subdivision of lands among the French peasantry." To others, like Fitzhugh, it was a return to a barbaric form of subsistence agriculture. Noting the tendency to scatter unenclosed strips for household cultivation, one bureau agent in South Carolina called the freedpeople's land use "contrary to the laws of Nature and Civilization as I understand them." The shock of these men is understandable. They watched ex-slaves plant corn, peas, and melons on what were after all some of the richest and most productive cotton fields in the world.[48]

But even this variant of landed independence still had room for commercial risk-taking, an impulse that white observers were often blind to. The ex-slaves were not hostile to producing cash crops on their own accounts. In Louisiana and Virginia some freedpeople shifted into a form of truck farming, marketing fruits and vegetables to nearby cities. On the Sea Islands, 33 percent of acres in cotton cultivation was still 33 percent. In August 1865, on St. Helena's Island in South Carolina, the ex-slave Jim Cashman took his former master on a tour of his own farm, pointing to what was now his own cotton crop. "The Lord has blessed us since you have been gone. It used to be Mr. Fuller No. 1, now it is Jim Cashman No. 1." In 1865, the freedpeople who controlled land did not grow as much cotton as their former masters had once demanded, or as Atkinson would have liked. But they did grow cotton. Now free, they wanted to earn upside commercial risks of their own.[49]

The new President, Andrew Johnson, called the experiment off. To enable political Reconstruction, Johnson's Amnesty Proclamation of May 29, 1865 promised to the large majority of ex-Confederates the "restoration of all rights of property, except as to slaves." Commissioner Howard ruled that restoration would not apply to land administered by the Freedmen's Bureau, but Johnson disagreed. In September 1865, Howard announced the new policy of the restoration of lands under bureau control. In October, Johnson sent Howard in person to Sherman's reserve to break the news. On October 17, in a bitter, tearful meeting, Howard, in full military uniform, informed a group of Edisto Islanders that their land was to be restored to their former owners. Standing with Howard were three men who would prove to be critical Freedman's Bank officials—his brother Charles, Saxton, and Ketchum.[50]

When Howard broke the news, he was interrupted by a "general murmur of dissatisfaction." There were shouts of "No, never" and "Can't do it." Days later, a committee of Edisto Islanders presented two petitions of protest, one written to Johnson, the other to Howard. The petition directed to Howard struck a more personal tone. "General we want Homestead's," they pleaded, continuing:

> we are at the mercy of those who are combined to prevent us from getting land enough to lay our Fathers bones upon. We have property in Horses, cattle, carriages, & articles of furniture, but we are landless and Homeless, from the Homes we Have lived In In the past we can only do one of three things Step into the public road or the sea or remain on them working as In former time and subject to their will as then. We can not resist It In any way without being driven out Homeless upon the road.

The petitioners pleaded: "You will see this Is not the condition of really freemen." The petition was signed by Henry Bram, Ishmael Moultrie, and Yates Sampson. Moultrie, who was twenty-three years old, was raised on the nearby Clarke plantation where he was secretly taught to read and write by his white mistress. On that plantation, in August 1865, thirteen black families, a total of eighty people, had settled. The Clarke plantation then had 36 1/4 acres in cotton, 25 3/4 in corn, 4 acres in sweet potatoes, 3/4 acre in rice, and 1/4 acre in peas. But it was now destined for restoration to Archibald Clarke. In the petition to Johnson, the committee begged, "We wish to have A home if It be A few acres. without some provision is Made our future is sad to look upon." Even just a few acres, enough to "lay our Fathers bones upon" was more than nothing. For the freedpeople, the land rooted communal longings. It could be a bulwark of both an economic and existential sense of independence.[51]

Oliver and Charles Howard, Ketchum, and Saxton attempted to foil restoration, dragging their feet and protesting to the War Department and Congress. Howard responded to the Edisto petitioners that the "whipping post of which you complain is abolished forever" and that "I will ask for your rights and try to obtain them." Two months later, in December 1865, a bureau official reported that Moultrie was imploring freedpeople not to enter labor contracts with restored owners and assuring them that eventually "the government would give them the lands." Johnson removed the recalcitrant Ketchum from his post in January 1866. The land, with very few exceptions, was restored.[52]

Alvord had been watching these developments. Throughout 1865 he was in correspondence with one of Saxton's aides, Samuel P. Low, who informed him blow by blow of the contested restoration. In December 1865, Alvord traveled from the Freedman's Bank's headquarters in New York to Savannah. There, he met up with Charles Howard and the two addressed a group of Georgia freedmen. Howard spoke on land restoration. The younger Howard would recall in a report to his older brother that Alvord presented the new Freedman's Bank, soon opening a branch in Savannah. From Alvord, "the importance of such an institution to the freedmen" was "strongly urged." He would soon file his own report to the older Howard. "The freedmen," Alvord surmised "have a passion for land." Luckily, there was the Freedman's Bank. Alvord continued:

> I found that the large crowds of negroes who I often addressed spring forward to ideas of industry and economy, that they might save for old age, for sickness, for purchasing homesteads, or other prosperity in the future. Their notion of having land given to them by government is passing away, and we hear them saying, "We will work and save and buy for ourselves." When they know this is what their prosperous friends (the Yankees) have always done, they seem eager to follow the example. . . .

Alvord informed Howard that once small accumulations were made the freedmen would be "ready purchasers" of land. "There are a number of men on Edisto and other sea islands who are only waiting for the action of government in permitting them to have lands." Indeed they were. But if they wanted land, the Edisto freedpeople would have to save their wages. Three years later, in 1868, the petitioner Ishmael Moultrie opened a savings account at the nearby branch of the Freedman's Bank.[53]

Alvord's December 1865 arrival in Savannah ended an on-and-off six-month tour of the South that had opened ten branches of the Freedman's Bank. He began in Washington, DC, in June, forming a committee of black "business men." William "Daddy" Wilson, a free black before the war and later a trustee of Howard University, became the bank's cashier, although black cashiers were rarities in the first wave of branch openings. Most were white Freedmen's Bureau agents or agents of northern charitable societies. Alvord did create powerless local black "advisory boards." Many branches were in cities like Richmond, Charleston, Washington, New Orleans, Baltimore, and Savannah. Others were in more rural areas like the branches opened in New Bern, North Carolina; Vicksburg, Mississippi; or Jacksonville, Florida. By the close of 1865, the bank's deposits stood a shade under $200,000. Saxton's South Carolina Freedmen's Savings Bank, now the Beaufort branch, had provided an infusion of $170,000. The branches of the Freedman's Bank stood awaiting deposits.[54]

In late 1865, with Alvord busily opening branches, Commissioner Howard went about instituting a landless slave emancipation. The message Alvord delivered at Savannah echoed across the South from Howard's agents in the field. The freedman was told he "should work diligently, and carefully save his wages, till he may be able to buy land and possess his own home." Saving wages was the only route to land ownership.[55]

The Freedmen's Bureau had other designs for the freedman's savings. The law creating the bureau charged it with the task of aiding the "destitute," but officials feared the creation of a permanent mass of black dependents. By entering labor contracts and working for wages ex-slaves were to care for their own dependents. The situation on the ground in the early years of Reconstruction was chaotic, with some destitute slaves still under the care of their old masters, some crowded into the bureau's own hospitals and pauper colonies, and others relying upon local networks of kinship and communal support. But the logic of the new order was clear. As a North Carolina bureau official instructed the freedman in 1865: "Your freedom imposes upon you new duties. Some of you have families; it is your duty to support them. Some of you have aged parents and relatives, to whom liberty has come too late; it is your duty to minister to their comfort." A Virginia bureau official added: "You now have no masters to provide for you in sickness and old age; hence you must see the necessity of saving your wages . . . for this purpose." Such were "the responsibilities of [their] new condition."[56]

In the tumultuous years of 1865–1867, the bureau's free-labor vision utterly failed. True, freedpeople entered contracts (whether they liked it or not) for money wages. But southern planters did everything they could to restore the old plantation system of highly regimented and supervised gang labor. Corporal punishment was not uncommon and Black Codes kept ex-slaves on the plantation. Licensing laws and fees often made black commercial proprietorship impossible. Many ex-slaves often resided in the same cabins as under slavery, now deemed part of their compensation as free laborers. Planters provided weekly subsistence rations and in theory fixed monthly or postharvest wages. But that was if blacks were paid at all. Many planters simply refused, as if on principle. The South however was also incredibly cash-poor and credit-strapped. Without slaves and with declining land values, the asset-basis of the southern credit system collapsed. Cotton prices unexpectedly plummeted and the cotton harvests of 1866 and 1867 were abysmal. Planters were in a credit trap. They needed high cotton prices and yields to restore their credit positions but they also needed credit to raise cotton. Even if the harvest was good, black laborers now stood at the end of a long line of factors and creditors. If the harvest was bad, laborers might receive no money compensation at all. The black wage worker assumed much of the downside risk, with no corresponding upside. A panicky Alvord lamented in 1866 that many "laborers were turned off without pay." There was no money for black free laborers to deposit and save.[57]

The freedpeople however resisted the reconstitution of the plantation regime, with some success. A different kind of exploitation emerged in sharecropping—a far cry from what ex-slaves had once hoped for but better than what they had been offered. Freedpeople simply would not work under the supervised gang system, withdrawing their labor from the fields (true for all hands, but especially for women and children). At this stage the household became the crucial battle site. Planters wanted the labor of prime male hands and only when it suited their purposes the labor of anyone else. They also wanted to keep their large plantations intact. Freedpeople asserted that the household be the dominant productive unit, which would effectively break up the large plantations. Black women often demanded that the maintenance of themselves and their family members be a condition of black male employment. By the 1867 harvest, a new order was emerging. There occurred a steady devolution from supervised "gangs" to smaller "squads" and finally to households, working their own enclosed, small parcels of land for a share of the crop. The great plantations were no more.[58]

Hardly victorious, the freedpeople had still achieved a real measure of autonomy and control over their labor. But the division of risk between "capital and labor"—as Banks had put it at the dawn of slave emancipation— was also part of the equation. The laborer who worked for a postharvest wage bore all the uncertainties of the harvest. The sharecropper was not an independent proprietor working on his own account. But a share of the crop brought a larger chunk of the upside. The dynamics of sharecropping would soon give the Freedman's Bank many of its defining characteristics.[59]

Amidst all of this tumult there continued to be little patronage of the Freedman's Bank. Ever optimistic, however, Alvord remained undaunted. In 1866, the bank received a meager $100,000 in deposits, mostly from black military pay, and operated at a loss of $10,000. It paid no interest to depositors. But it opened seven more branches. By 1867 the bank would have twenty-two of them. Its vice president, William Hewitt, a New York clothes merchant, wrote to Alvord: "I feel anxious and sometimes blue, when contemplating the future." Alvord cited a lack of black "confidence" in the bank. True or not, the freedpeople simply had no money to deposit. In 1866, for instance, Alvord opened a branch in Houston, Texas. But a bureau agent had recently toured southeastern Texas and found that two-thirds of the freedmen had not received one cent in wages. Elsewhere, branch cashiers with no funds to deposit blamed black land hunger. Alvord's 1866 report on "Schools and Finances" was mum on the subject of the freedmen's "finances" as there was nothing to say. In January of 1867 the Freedmen Bank's board of trustees narrowly defeated a proposal to close the bank's doors for good.[60]

Facing oblivion, in May of 1867 the Freedman's Bank was essentially refounded. Alvord moved the headquarters from New York to Washington, DC, and the bank's personnel turned over. Absentee New York board members gladly shuffled out. Alvord became the president of the bank and Ketchum, now living in Washington, DC, and acting as an aide to Oliver Howard, became a new board member, as did his brother Edgar. Soon Saxton joined them. So did the first black trustees, two Washington, DC, ministers and two Howard University professors. Below the board, the bank had two working committees: the agency committee that oversaw branch operations and the finance committee that conducted the bank's investments. The new chairman of the agency committee was Charles Howard. The new finance chairman was Henry Cooke.[61]

Henry ran the Washington branch of his brother's investment bank Jay Cooke & Co. (Jay operated out of Philadelphia, the third branch was in New York.) Alvord practically begged Henry to take the reins of the bank's finances. Given both the success of Jay Cooke & Co. marketing war bonds and its close ties to the federal government his desire is understandable. Alvord called Henry "an excellent Christian man, warmly the friend of the Freedmen, and much interested in the success of our institution." Alvord thought he was the type of man who could be trusted. Perhaps Alvord was naive. Perhaps he was oblivious to the shadowy world of Gilded Age finance. Or perhaps he knew that Henry casted a long shadow.[62]

Henry had very little financial talent per se. He was Jay Cooke & Co.'s Washington lobbyist and a good one. His brother called him a spendthrift and speculator. Jay's biographer concluded: "Never can there have been a bank executive who was much less of a banker than Henry Cooke!" That all depended upon one's image of the ideal banker. Henry might have lacked a financial acumen and he might have had a penchant for making bad loans to important politicians. But those loans, and

Henry's "good fellow" social skills, including a reputation for evangelical piety, were often necessary for Gilded Age financial success.[63]

The larger political-economic significance of Henry's career could hardly be exaggerated. His itinerary began with a failed stint as an antebellum San Francisco tradesman before landing back in the brothers' native Ohio. Jay paid off his debts, an abiding family tradition. Henry began to edit a leading Republican newspaper and became a close friend of Salmon P. Chase. When Chase became secretary of the Treasury during the Civil War, it was Henry, now residing in Washington, who played matchmaker between Chase and Jay. Jay marketed Chase's war bonds to the American masses, exploding the federal debt. The political insider Henry maintained the firm's Washington contacts. Spurred on by government debt, a national capital market formed.[64]

During the war, the Cookes chartered the First National Bank in Washington, a commercial bank, in order to hold Treasury deposits. It occupied the second floor of a two-story building whose first story housed the Washington branch of Jay Cooke & Co. Henry was the president of the First National and William Huntington was its cashier. In late 1867, both joined the Freedman's Bank board and finance committee. In January 1868, the board of trustees granted them discretion to buy and sell the "bonds, stocks, or other property owned by this company." By then Henry was a close personal friend of President Grant and Jay Cooke & Co. was still financing the federal debt, the very assets that the Freedman's Bank invested in by charter. The finance committee—usually with only Henry, Huntington, and a third ally, D. L. Eaton, present—began to hold its monthly meetings at the office of the First National Bank.[65]

In hindsight, having Henry at the helm of the finance committee was a bad idea. But at the time, what man in the world had better inside knowledge of the federal bond market? The worst kept secret on Wall Street was that Jay Cooke & Co. was still the Treasury's behind-the-scenes transactional agent, purchasing Treasury securities on its behalf and parking the proceeds in the First National Bank. Henry was personally advising the Treasury secretary George S. Boutwell—the same Boutwell who once celebrated the ethos of landed independence at Concord, Massachusetts. Boutwell was a greenhorn at government finance and in desperate need of advice. Later, a trustee of the Freedman's Bank would admit that he thought Henry, with inside information at his disposal, was turning neat profits for the bank's depositors by purchasing and selling government bonds at timely moments. Or at least that was what he suspected. The real truth he did not care to know.[66]

In any event, the success of the Freedman's Bank after 1867 was astonishing. Not capturing the figures in Table 1 (see Appendix) were deposits made and withdrawn before the year's end, a common occurrence. The bank paid interest ideally every four months—exactly the average length of deposit according to Eaton. All in all, ex-slaves probably deposited some $50 million in the Freedman's Bank, about 1 billion 2012 dollars. In 1874, the bank counted 61,000 active deposits but likely around 100,000 individual depositors patronized it. Already in 1868 the bank declared that the leap in deposits was "irrefutable evidence of the colored man's ability and intention not only to take care of himself, but also to provide for the necessities of the future."[67]

That success, given the relative poverty of the target population, was truly staggering. Yet, the savings rate of all Americans at this time, including the white working class of the industrial North, was equally impressive. Lacking their slaves, the financial savings of the southern ruling class also soared. Indeed, the trajectory of the Freedman's Bank mirrored those of a multitude of new American financial institutions that accumulated private money savings and financial capital. In one estimate, the American savings rate shot upward between 1840 and 1880 from 11 to 23 percent. With that, a new national capital market—in part forged by Civil War finance—absorbed the savings. Men like Henry became the crucial mediators, pulling savings from one region and redirecting it as investments to another.[68]

But if Henry was to invest the freedpeople's savings, first he needed the deposits. That job now fell to Charles Howard and the agency committee. The board granted a $1,500 annual budget to place advertisements in the press and to print circulars, pamphlets, and cards praising the virtues of thrift. In 1868 the bank began to publish its own monthly, the *National Savings Bank,* whose circulation in two years would approach 15,000. If the slave's "past education," as one Yankee emancipator had once put it, taught him not to think of the future, the bank's literature educated the freedman on his newfound obligation to do so.[69]

The bank however continued to dangle out the prospect of black land ownership. The inaugural 1867 circular put forward that the man who saved "would buy his piece of land and become a thriving farmer!" He would no longer work for wages or shares, instead taking his own products to market, expanding his own fields, and ultimately passing along his farm to his offspring. He would run his own upside risks. The *National Savings Bank* boasted that freedmen were now "looking out for the main chance; observing how an honest penny may be turned by taking note of the market—just as other men are doing from day to day and from year to year." With the bank, declared one official in 1870, ex-slaves were "learning to think for the future; learning to do business as other intelligent citizens do it." If the freedman could not afford a forty-acre farm, so be it. Start with "garden patches." Then "Save, save, save." "Let every man strive to become the owner of land—ever so small a tract even."[70]

Land ownership was indeed the great incentive. But there were also the newfound duties and responsibilities of freedom. What must have now sounded like a broken record to the freedmen, the bank lectured: "being your own masters, it is your duty to provide for your settlement in life, for your families, and for old age." Howard had departed from South Carolina and was now working in Washington, DC. He oversaw a Freedmen's Bureau pauper village across the Potomac in Virginia known as "Freedmen's Village." As Howard's agency committee implored the freedpeople to save, Howard personally strove to remove freedpeople from the federal dole. The Freedman's Bank was one solution to the still pressing problem of black dependency.[71]

The freedpeople's own savings accounts would become the bulwark of their independence—a financial, if not a landed, independence. Rhetorically, the bank presented a deposit as perfectly certain and secure, hoping to inspire black confidence in the largely white-run institution. The bank could not appeal to the certainties of probability theory and statistics. Instead, the Great Emancipator's likeness was all over the bank's advertisements and deposit books. The bank came perilously close to claiming government backing. "The Government of the United States has made this bank perfectly safe," claimed one passbook. The bank, according to an 1867 pamphlet, "being authorized by Congress, and approved by the President of the United States," was "the safest place you

can find your money." The bank was unequivocal: "There is no speculation," and "consequently no risk in this Bank." For his part, Alvord truly
believed it. He told the trustees in 1870: "Our institution has been the
child of a protecting Providence . . . *the system* we have adopted seems
as safe as anything of the kind in human affairs *can be.*"[72]

"No risk" was now impossible. Self-ownership, in practice, demanded dependence upon the rising American corporate financial system, the central nervous system of a radically uncertain capitalist economy. Even war bonds fluctuated on the market, revealing an important
truth. Regardless, the bank's finance committee met January 23, 1868, at
the First National Bank. The typical quorum of three (recently reduced
from five) sat down together: Henry, Huntington, and Eaton. According
to the minutes, they met to consider a question posed by Henry: "Are
Pacific R.R. bonds a security contemplated by the charter?" Alvord and
other bank directors were reaching for higher yields. Only recently the
bank had failed to pay interest on its deposits and expenses were still
outrunning revenues. Meanwhile, the federal government was beginning to retire the war debt. The federal bond market was drying up, and
even Jay Cooke & Co. was contemplating a turn to railroad finance.[73]

The answer to the question Henry posed was no. But the finance
committee decided that one specific kind of Pacific Railroad bond—
thirty-year bonds bearing 6 percent interest with repayment guaranteed
by the federal government—was in fact "within the meaning of the law."
The board of directors agreed and at its next meeting it "authorized and
empowered, at their discretion to GET RID three hundred thousand
dollars worth of the present securities by the company at best market
price and invest the proceeds in the bonds issued by the Government to
the Pacific railroad." Henry waited a few months, as Pacific bonds
dipped in the market. But in June 1868, the minutes read that "the finance committee in consultation at the Banking House of Jay Cooke &
Co. on this day decided to invest in Pacific Railway bonds." By the end
of 1868, of $928,063.49 in total bank assets, $355,000 was held in transcontinental bonds.[74]

Government guarantee notwithstanding, railroad bonds were widely
acknowledged as among the most speculative financial assets in existence.
The transcontinental railroads were among the first private companies

to draw from the new national capital market and Henry directed funds from impoverished black sharecroppers to their construction. The freed-people's savings, in however miniscule fashion, contributed to the west-ward rush of a triumphant, industrializing American capitalism. The financial engine revved up again, whistling the same old song. Corporate risk management bred new opportunities for speculative financial risk-taking, and thus new forms of insecurity and uncertainty.

While this was happening the Freedman's Bank lectured the freed-people on the perils of gambling and overspeculation. To run risks in the market and to watch out for the "main chance" was freedom itself. But a cashier's report in Mobile, Alabama, complained that half of the $4,000 of withdrawals in a single month had gone to "speculation." Nothing bothered Alvord more than when freedpeople gambled with their money instead of saving it. Traveling through the South in 1870, he lamented that "One of the worst habits of Freedmen in Augusta is spending money for lottery tickets." There and everywhere, "on every business street," "tempting the unwary" was "this species of gambling."[75]

And yet at the same time Alvord admitted in private to the "irregu-larities" of Henry's investment strategies. He began to lobby Congress to relax the bank's corporate charter. It would be surprising if Henry too was not working his friends in Congress towards the same end.[76]

There was a discrepancy between Henry Cooke's new investment strat-egy and the pledges made to freedmen concerning the absolute certitude of their deposits (not to mention the letter of the bank's corporate char-ter). There was another discrepancy between the bank directors' vision of black freedom and the way freedpeople—men and women—actually put the bank to work in their own local communities.

In the decades after their emancipation blacks tenaciously strove to be-come land owners. In 1867, the Radical Republican Thaddeus Stevens introduced a failed bill in Congress to redistribute forty-acre farms to freedpeople, a last-ditch effort from above. Now the only support extended to land-hungry blacks was the waiting branches of the Freedman's Bank.[77]

Black men used their savings accounts to climb the proverbial south-ern agricultural ladder, hoping to become independent farm proprietors.

Wage labor was the bottom rung, offering seasonal employment mostly to mobile, young, and single males. Next on the hierarchy was the lowest rung of tenancy. On credit, the sharecropper borrowed subsistence goods and the necessary productive implements for his household to work a field and earn an entitlement to a share of the crop—perhaps an eighth. The more a household saved, the more it could provide for its own needs the next year, and the higher the share would be—perhaps up to a half. Even the purchase of a single mule could make a difference. An English traveler in the South in 1871 observed of black sharecroppers:

> The negro begins to deposit usually with some special object in view. He wishes to buy a mule or a cow, or a house, or a piece of land, or a shop, or simply to provide a fund against death, sickness, or accident, and pursues his object frequently until it has been accomplished.

In 1870, the cashier at the Beaufort branch, which still had the largest deposits of any branch, reported that of nearly $1.5 million of drafts since 1865 a third bought "seed, teams, agricultural implements, shops, tools" along with other "business purposes." That figure approximated the very haphazardly collected data at other branches. Of all the branches reporting in 1870, $942,000 of drafts was for productive property, compared to $699,000 for daily consumption (which was money that could replace items carried on credit at the local factor's store). Black men between the ages of twenty and twenty-nine opened more accounts at the Freedman's Bank than any other demographic. At Beaufort, for instance, Caesar Green opened account number 3830 at the branch. He was in his twenties, a farmer who worked "for himself." He had a wife, brothers, and sisters but no children. He was likely saving up, climbing the agricultural ladder.[78]

The final rung was landownership. In the same 1870 count, $663,000 of drafts were for land purchases. The Beaufort cashier estimated that 6.7 percent of drafts purchased land, a figure that loosely held for the other predominately agricultural branches. Of course, blacks were seldom able to purchase fertile forty-acre farms. At Beaufort there were 2,800 purchases of land for a total of 50,400 acres, an average of eighteen acres. At New Bern the average purchase was fifteen acres and at the Charleston branch it was ten acres. In 1870, Alvord continued to observe the communal effort of "clubbing together" for land purchases. By 1870, 1 in 21 rural black families in South Carolina owned land, no matter how small a parcel, in a region where freedpeople fared best. In Alabama, it was 1 in 51. Blacks were offered the worst lands for purchase, if at all. Racism filtered through local and exploitative credit markets, dragging freedpeople down the agricultural ladder, even from its highest rung. The black landowner always depended upon white credit. Any act, even one such as voting the Republican ticket, could imperil one's credit position.[79]

With such obstacles, why bother saving up for the future and striving for a landed independence? The Alabama sharecropper Ned Cobb, looking back from the twentieth century, recalled his father's many missed opportunities to purchase land after his emancipation from slavery. Cobb explained his mind-set. He was "blindfolded." He "didn't look to the future." But there were good reasons, even Cobb admitted, for doing so:

> . . . whenever the colored man prospered too fast in this country under the old rulins, they worked every figure to cut you down, cut your britches off you. So, it . . . weren't no use in climbing too fast; weren't no use in climbing slow, neither, if they was going to take everything you worked for when you got too high.

There was always the peril of getting "cleared out" of everything one had by the white ruling class. Cobb's father managed that risk by never running it.[80]

Against these odds, freedmen made their deposits and saved and strove for land. After 1868, letters arrived at the bank's Washington headquarters from all over the South requesting the opening of branches in black communities—from places like Sherman, Texas; Albany, Georgia; Salisbury, North Carolina; and Selma, Alabama. According to one estimate, between 1866 and 1876 black acreage in the South increased by 400 percent, often aided by bank deposits. After the failure of land redistribution, Alvord's vision was in part realized. Many freedmen did use the Freedman's Bank to acquire homesteads of their own.[81]

Still, perhaps most striking about the Freedman's Bank was what it shared in common with the working-class savings banks of the industrial North. It turns out that most mid-century wage earners did not save to manage the downside risks of accident, sickness, or old age. Like the freedmen, they did so in hopes of acquiring enough productive property to become independent proprietors—to control their own labor and to chase proprietary upsides. At the Dime Savings Bank of Brooklyn, which was directed by two of the founders of the Freedman's Bank, young apprenticed clerks commonly accumulated savings on the path to becoming independent tradesmen. Or, in another parallel, parents commonly opened accounts for children. At Augusta, 25 percent of depositors were children. Andre and Rebecca Bryan opened accounts numbered 3765 and 3766 at Beaufort for their daughters Sally, age three, and Eliza, age one and a half. Likewise, account number 13828 at the Dime Savings Bank was a "lad 10 years old, a Jew boy" whose father was a "tobacconist."[82]

Furthermore, both northern and southern women frequently opened accounts in their own name, North and South. At Beaufort, account 3831 belonged to Peggy Green, resident of Ladies Island. Her occupation was "farming" and she worked for "herself." On the signature book "wife" was crossed out and next to "husband" was written "George Green." The rate of female depositors, often unmarried female domestics, was especially high in the more urban branches—44 percent at Louisville, 20 percent at Richmond. Female domestics were frequent depositors in the urban North. Account 1189 at the Dime Savings Bank was a "colored washerwoman" who had opened an account with $12 in 1859. Even the high frequency of withdrawals and the tiny sums held on deposit exhibited the likeness between the Freedman's Bank and its northern urban industrial peers.[83]

There was however one distinguishing characteristic of the Freedman's Bank. Many accounts held the deposits of black voluntary associations. Moultrie, an author of the 1865 Edisto Islanders' petitions of protest against land restoration, had opened his own personal account in 1868. But in 1866 he had experienced a religious conversion, soon becoming the minister of the Edisto Island Presbyterian Church. He opened another account in 1871, not for himself, but for his church. But the largest class of black associations was mutual-aid societies. Such collective strategies provided local and communal support for the sick, elderly, or otherwise dependent black population. A disproportionate number had female heads. Belinda Brown, treasurer of the Beaufort Baptist Benevolent Society, opened a savings account for the society at the Freedman's Bank. The Memphis branch counted sixty-six accounts of local fraternal societies. Yankee emancipators had not seen this coming.[84]

Black fraternal societies often had beginnings under slavery, when meetings many times occurred secretly under cover of night. Larger than households and kinship ties, these were still small, local, and personal communities. Yet, once their funds were removed from under their treasurer's mattress (or some similar resting place) and deposited at the Freedman's Bank, tight local circles were broken. The fate of these communities now rested in the hands of Henry Cooke—and the economic chance-world Jay Cooke & Co hoped to master. The Beaufort Baptist Benevolent Society was now at risk.

Henry Cooke had taken the reins of the Freedman's Bank's finances in 1867. But with the exception of the purchase of Pacific Railroad bonds in 1868, the bank's portfolio did not change very much, consisting largely of federal bonds. Until 1869, the government bond market was still Jay Cooke & Co.'s specialty. The firm continued to prop up the price of federal bonds on behalf of the Treasury Department. But the government loan business was dissipating and the federal government had begun the decades-long process of retiring its liabilities. That meant there would be fewer federal bonds to buy. With interest rates falling, the federal government would however refund the outstanding debt at lower rates and the firm hoped to be its exclusive underwriter. This effort, not the Freedman's Bank, was Henry's focus, as he extended easy loans to members of Congress. Jay wrote to Henry: "We must take the risk of all the expense" in order to stiffen the "backbone" of Congress. When the brothers' preferred refunding bill failed to pass Congress suddenly Jay Cooke & Co. was in a bind. For lack of government loan business, Treasury deposits at the First National Bank fell from $885,000 in 1867 to $96,000 in 1869. The national capital market was turning to railroad finance, recycling retired federal debt into new railroad bonds. In 1869 Jay Cooke & Co. took the Freedman's Bank along for the ride.[85]

But that would happen only after Jay resisted pressure from his partners to fire his brother. Henry's operations—including the entertainment
of Washington politicians—were a drag on the firm's bottom line. He
made a lot of questionable loans to political insiders with, at least in the
eyes of the New York partners, no returns to show for it. He racked up
tens of thousands of dollars in personal debts which Jay Cooke & Co.
covered. As a profit-making commercial bank, even Henry admitted
there was no reason for the First National Bank to exist. He offered to
close the shop, resign from Jay Cooke & Co, and to remove himself to Europe in exchange for a yearly allowance. But Jay did not accept the offer as
he had decided that the firm would undertake a fantastic new venture
which would require the assistance of Henry's political friends in Washington. Jay had decided to finance the Northern Pacific Railroad.[86]

In 1869, the prospects of the Northern Pacific were dire. It possessed
an immense chunk of land, 47 million acres stretching from Duluth,
Minnesota to the Pacific Coast, granted to it by the federal government
in 1865. But unlike other transcontinentals, it had not secured federal
guarantees for its bonded debt. And much of that land was still controlled by Sioux Indians whose hostility frequently disrupted land sur-
veys. The Northern Pacific had yet to lay a track. Nonetheless, in 1870
Jay entered an agreement with the railroad's directors. Jay Cooke & Co.
would market $100 million of bonds, paying 7.3 percent interest. It would
guarantee the sale of $5 million worth of bonds and advance $5 million
to the Northern Pacific to begin construction. Jay Cooke & Co. acquired
60 percent control of the company's stock. For every bond it sold at par,
the firm earned twelve cents. Henry went to work in Washington seeking to acquire a federal guarantee for the bonds.[87]

In 1870, Henry had another reason to lobby Congress. He and the
Freedman's Bank directors were attempting to liberalize the bank's corporate charter so that it could loan money on real estate security. With the
federal bond market drying up and interest rates falling, the bank's sole
avenue of investment for two-thirds of its assets was shrinking. Even Oliver Howard wrote an editorial in favor of relaxing the investment provisions of the bank's charter, arguing that black depositors deserved a higher
rate of return. Northern savings banks had entered a period of pronounced
competition, with one bank offering better interest rates to its depositors
than the next, all dipping deeper into the far reaches of the capital market

to achieve them. Howard noted that even federal debt had become "a commodity of merchandize for speculation." Not even government bonds could be purchased "without risk of depreciation." It would be better to allow the bank to diversify its assets and to reach for higher yields.[88]

Senator Sumner once again brought the Freedman's Bank's charter to the floor of the Senate. Only one voice objected, the Pennsylvania senator and Lincoln's former secretary of war Simon Cameron—an especially corrupt politician in an era of stiff competition. But Cameron at least had a significant background in banking. On the Senate floor he defended a still vibrant nineteenth-century moral code. It was immoral to take a risk with another man's money. The emancipated slaves' deposits were now "in the hands of persons entirely irresponsible." "They [the finance committee] will be led probably into speculations." Nevertheless, the revised corporate charter passed with hardly a murmur.[89]

Between 1870 and 1872 Henry Cooke transformed the Freedman's Bank into a freewheeling commercial/investment bank. He did not even recognize the provisions of the new charter, which allowed the bank to loan money only on real estate security that doubled the value of the loan. A loan, for instance, was extended to one E. H. Nichols of $175,000, which still had a balance due in 1876, two years after the bank's failure. All that could be discovered was that Nichols "was treasurer of a certain corporation which had to do with Kickapoo land-titles in Kansas." Henry being the man he was, it would be shocking if loans like this lacked a political calculus. These loans were made while the bank, with very few exceptions, refused loans to its black depositors. Black sharecroppers suffered from highly exploitative and localized credit markets, the reason why so many had accumulated savings deposits to begin with. Some attempts were made in the final years of the bank's existence to expand black control over branch operations and to extend loans to blacks but this was largely a sham. The deposits from local branches funneled into Henry's hands and bad real estate loans were the least of his transgressions. He loaned money on stocks and bonds of dubious value, sometimes to himself. His most infamous loan was one of $50,000 to the Seneca Stone Company, a shell of Henry and Huntington. But there were also scores of arcane repurchase agreements between Henry and a number of counterparties with no apparent credible financial purpose. All of this would only be discovered after it was too late.[90]

Much of this can be chalked up to Henry's personal profligacy. But there was a logic to the plundering. Everything led back to Jay Cooke & Co.'s failed effort to finance the Northern Pacific Railroad. In 1870, after Henry had narrowly survived a purge the partners forced Jay to shut down the costly loan operations of the First National. No direct evidence exists but the timing would indicate that Henry and Huntington simply transferred their operations to the Freedman's Bank. The two certainly did move the worst liabilities of the First National and Jay Cooke & Co. onto the Freedman's Bank's books, exchanging cash for worthless First National paper. To top it off, in 1871 President Grant named Henry (his good friend) the governor of the new territory of the District of Columbia. The collateral for many Freedman's Bank loans was notes issued by fly-by-night municipal works projects that Henry believed, with his influence, would soon receive federal appropriations (the same failed business model as the Northern Pacific). Finally, in the most egregious act, the Freedman's Bank now held usually somewhere between $500,000 and $600,000 of its assets in cash deposits at Jay Cooke & Co., which was after all not a depository institution but an investment bank. Jay Cooke & Co. paid 5 percent on these deposits while the Freedman's Bank promised its own depositors 6 percent. The Freedman's Bank had become a backer of the Northern Pacific Railroad.[91]

Jay Cooke & Co. needed those deposits because the Northern Pacific was draining its resources to the bone. Railroad construction not only dragged to a crawl but costs also exploded. By 1872, the Northern Pacific had overdrafts at the Washington branch of Jay Cooke & Co of $2.6 million. Jay had failed to market bonds to rich European or American investors. Drawing upon his Civil War experience, he decided to market directly to small American investors. The old agency force was reactivated and the advertisements once again rolled out. The back pages of a February 1871 New York weekly, for instance, featured an advertisement of the Freedman's Bank—which had opened a branch in New York City—next to an advertisement for Northern Pacific bonds. Northern Pacific bonds, Jay promised, were a "safe, profitable, and permanent investment." The bonds were secured by the government's land grant—"agricultural,

timbered and mineral lands," a most "fertile belt of land" in the western
territories. There was very little risk in the investment: "The land-grant
is absolutely a surety to the bondholders." If the road failed, the bondholder acquired a homestead, making it an attractive investment for "settlers and emigrants." To sell a financial asset, Jay exploited the rhetoric
of landed independence. He claimed to be actively settling the territory
which was not true. Below this, the advertisement for the Freedman's
Bank promised, "All deposits payable ON DEMAND, with interest due."
But that promise now depended upon Jay's ability to sell Northern Pacific
corporate debt.[92]

By 1870 Jay Cooke had many competitors in the field of retail railroad
finance. Many sold bonds below par on roads that actually existed and
brought in revenues. Some had the government backing that the Northern Pacific always lacked (although he fought to the end, Henry failed).
The bonded debt of American railroads surged from $416 million in 1867
to $2.23 billion in 1874 as national railroad track expanded from 35,085
miles in 1865 to 70,784 miles in 1873. But investors, whether small or
large, would not swallow the bonds of the Northern Pacific.[93]

By 1872 the writing was already on the wall. In the fall of that year,
financial markets began to tremble under the burden of the normal extension of credit for the harvest and crop-moving season and the massive
glut of railroad debt. Henry persuaded the secretary of the Treasury to
go into the market and purchase federal securities and thereby increase
liquidity. Yet, no amount of liquidity can compensate for insolvency and
Jay Cooke & Co. itself was tottering. The firm mobilized all available
financial resources. Jay had even recently chartered a life insurance corporation and the firm squeezed as much money out of its reserves as possible. But the Cookes still needed more cash.[94]

Early in 1871, acting as finance chairman of the Freedman's Bank
Henry had begun to loan Freedman's Bank's funds to Jay Cooke & Co.,
presenting Northern Pacific bonds as collateral. To what extent he did
this it is hard to know. But in March 1871, the board resolved that it
doubted "the expediency of investing $50,000 in bonds of the Northern
Pacific R.R. Co., because that road is but begun and is of vast extent in
line and operation and may not be able for years to pay any interest out
of its earnings." The whistle-blower was Edgar Ketchum, the brother

of Alexander Ketchum, the man who had personally filed the land claims of ex-slaves in the ill-fated Sherman's reserve. Ketchum protested Henry's entire loan portfolio and the latter responded with a speech on the sterling prospects of the Northern Pacific (whose transcript does not survive) which persuaded the board. Two months later both Edgar and Alexander Ketchum would resign, apparently in protest, and Saxton soon joined them. Eventually the board did draw the line at Northern Pacific bonds. It demanded that Henry repay the loan and liquidate all the bank's holdings in the Northern Pacific, of whatever form. For months Henry dragged his feet on repaying the $50,000. Finally, seemingly having reached an endgame, in February 1872 Henry and Huntington resigned from their positions at the bank. When the Freedman's Bank failed, congressional inquirers found $200 of worthless Northern Pacific bonds in its vaults.[95]

It is worth pausing to characterize the novel form of social power that Henry exercised over tens of thousands of former slaves in the years 1867 to 1872. Certainly, it was nothing like the direct and personal authority of the slave master. If Henry would have walked the streets of the black neighborhoods of Washington D.C., it is doubtful whether he would have recognized one single black depositor, or if any one depositor would have recognized him—although it is equally doubtful that Henry would have ever gone for such a stroll. The Freedman's Bank was a very different collective strategy for responding to the generative insecurities and radical uncertainties of capitalism. Henry controlled the small funds freedpeople had accumulated themselves in order to fulfill a newfound duty of freedom—which was to assume, and master, their own personal risks. But that had required offloading those risks onto a financial corporation, and ultimately into the hands of Henry himself.

Henry fraudulently dragged the freedpeople headlong into the Gilded Age. He had channeled the small savings of the South Carolina ex-slave turned sharecropper into the construction of the westward-stretching Northern Pacific railroad—a financial intermediation of agricultural savings into the project of American industrialization and the economic development of the West. All of this happened within the short period of five years. Of course, the Cookes believed that they could successfully market Northern Pacific bonds and they hoped to turn a staggering profit for everyone. But it was a risk, one that the depositors of the Freedman's Bank now assumed. Henry exploited the bank's funds for his own designs. But he also submitted the fate of the Freedman's Bank to the rising economic chance-world.

Henry was not in the saddle. Nor, in fact, was anyone truly. The position of Jay Cooke & Co. in the market was untenable. On September 18, 1873, the firm failed, triggering a widespread banking panic. The Northern Pacific was not the only highly leveraged American railroad and Jay Cooke & Co. was not the only highly leveraged American bank. Retiring its debt, the federal government's general policy was to tighten the money supply. When the reputable Jay Cooke & Co. failed, depositors large and small knew that other banks were likely to fall as well. They did not know which banks so they withdrew their deposits from all. This is how entire banking systems crash, as the American banking system did in the fall of 1873. The economy plunged into a brutal decade of economic depression.[96]

Black depositors behaved no differently than white depositors. From September 18 to 20 there was a run on the Washington branch of the Freedman's Bank. Alvord, recovering from a recent nervous breakdown, rushed to New York and cashed in $200,000 of the bank's $487,000 of government securities (purchased after Henry's resignation). In the coming months there would be runs on the Augusta, Savannah, Montgomery, Atlanta, and Memphis branches totaling almost $1 million. In response, the Bank demanded a sixty-day notice for depositors to withdraw funds. Alvord was still in control of the bank, along with two black trustees: Charles Purvis, a medical professor at Howard University; and John Mercer, a Howard law professor. As white trustees fled the bank, black trustees now formed the majority at most board meetings. Congress appointed an auditor to look into the bank's finances as it limped along into 1874. At the March 1874 meeting, the board of trustees removed a mentally frail Alvord as president. They nominated Frederick Douglass to be the new president of the Freedman's Bank.[97]

Douglass had not sought the nomination. The trustees were doing everything they could to boost the bank's credibility within the black community in order to prevent further bank runs. Douglass was willing to oblige them, having moved to Washington, DC, two years before. He wrote in one of his later autobiographical works:

> So I waked up one morning to find myself seated in a comfortable arm chair, with gold spectacles on my nose, and to hear myself addressed as President of the Freedmen's [sic] Bank. I could not help reflecting in the contrast between Frederick the slave boy, running about at Col. Lloyd's with only a linen shirt to cover him, and Frederick-President of a bank counting its assets by millions. I had heard of golden dreams, but such dreams had no comparison with reality.

Perhaps no one else than Douglass had better captured in words the absence of the slave's control over his own destiny and the master's near absolute power over his future. But now, with slavery abolished, and as the president of the Freedman's Bank, Douglass came face to face with a new, abstract, somewhat perplexing form of social power in American life. Taking the job, Douglass knew the bank was in serious financial trouble. But soon after his appointment he wrote that, "I believe that the Institution has done a good work and has yet a good work to do." Douglass even loaned the bank $10,000 of his own money. But Douglass was no banker. Even if he was, he could not have successfully turned back the tide of a financial tempest.[98]

In fact, the Freedman's Bank was already doomed when Douglass took his chair as president. At the behest of Congress the comptroller of the currency issued a damning report on the bank's finances the same week Douglass assumed office. The bank had an unaccountable deficit of $218,000. It had admirably struggled for two years to unwind many of Henry's positions but given the state of the financial world, the awful loans on its books, and the remaining "claims against Jay Cooke & Co.," it would be impossible to liquidate enough of its holdings to meet its obligations to panicky depositors. The bank had 61,114 accounts open with nearly $3 million of obligations. It had sold nearly all of its federal securities and counted $1.2 million of bad outstanding loans, thanks to Henry. It took Douglass two months to realize that the situation was hopeless. Humiliated, he requested that the Senate Finance Committee draft legislation to orderly close the bank. By June the bank could no longer meet its obligations to withdrawing depositors. On July 2, 1874, the Freedman's Bank closed its doors for good.[99]

A series of congressional investigations followed. Nothing much came of them except recrimination. Alvord blamed "The crash of Jay Cooke and Company." Henry testified but his memory was blank. Outside Congress, the southern Democratic press attributed the failure of the Freedman's Bank to a malfeasant Republican Reconstruction—whose lifespan would outlast the Freedman's Bank only by a few years. For their part, black depositors leveled biting and bewildered protests at both the bank and the federal government. On September 14, 1874, outraged Baltimore depositors staged a protest at the former Baltimore branch. Baltimore fraternal societies had lost $50,000 and their work had been "broken up" for "want of means." To wild applause, speeches demanded the money back. A group of Charleston depositors submitted a petition to Congress, stating that the majority of Charleston depositors were of the "laboring classes" and that they had been "induced to place their money in the bank under the impression that it was guaranteed and protected by the General Government." Led by Douglass, for decades depositors would plead with Congress to cover the bank's losses. But the federal government was not in the business of insuring bank deposits. The government subsidized transcontinental railroad construction but it had no safety net to offer to the freedpeople. It did appoint a committee to handle the bank's receivership which would not quit its work until 1919. By that time, of the almost $3 million owed to depositors when the bank failed, just over $1.7 million had been repaid. The loss was 41 percent of deposits at the time of failure and 2.4 percent of the approximately $50 million that were ever deposited at the bank.[100]

The fate of the Freedman's Bank however was not unique. There were few savings bank failures prior to the 1870s. But the panic of 1873 brought down a host of northern savings banks. Henry was not by his lonesome. The Civil War had provided a mountain of federal debt paying high interest rates for savings banks to snap up. When the war ended, with the federal bond market sagging and with deposits accumulating at a remarkable rate, savings banks began to look to invest in more profitable financial assets. Many began to make loans like profit-hungry commercial banks. In 1878, New York banking examiner Keyes wrote: "For the most part . . . the failure of Savings Banks in this country, has been wrought by injudicious investments or loans, made sometimes under the sanction of the law, sometimes without its sanction, and sometimes even in opposition to its mandates." The 1875 failure of the Third Avenue Savings Bank in New York, with $6 million in deposits, was the most spectacular, triggering a broader New York savings bank panic. After a rash of failures, the state of Connecticut conducted an investigation on how to separate savings banks from other "monied institutions," as did Pennsylvania. The savings banks' original reason for existence, said Keyes, was "SECURITY" for the working class. That purpose had been lost in the early flush of the Gilded Age.[101]

The reach of the panic of 1873 into the savings accounts of ordinary Americans tells the broader significance of this particular moment. Certainly, the antebellum panics had generalized out into hard times. But many more Americans were still hedged nonfinancially, even outside markets—slave owners, freeholders, household dependents, slaves. By the 1870s a financial panic mattered more than ever before. Tellingly, the cause of many of the savings-banks runs of the 1870s was not only panic. Depositors drew on these funds to subsist; they had no other ground to retreat to other than their own financial accumulations. Risk was becoming systemic in character—the panic of 1873 would leave in its wake a decade of economic violence and woe unlike the nation had ever experienced.

There were more than social and economic reverberations. The panic of 1873 was a profound cultural event, the coming-out party for the economic chance-world. Compared to the antebellum panics, fewer Americans interpreted this panic in predominately religious terms. Likewise, and surprisingly, given the political corruption at the heart of boom-and-bust railroad finance, much less did it occur in a political idiom. Fewer saw the moral reformation of individual economic character as a solution to the instability of the market economy. Now, more saw the vicissitudes of capitalism as part of a blind, natural world. The Civil War had subtly undermined many providential visions while shattering others. The slaveholders' providential paternalism, for one, lay in ruins. Now, the freaks of fortune looked to fill the breach.[102]

In this context, the metaphor of voyage became only more poignant. The September 1873 *Independent* noted that "Such a thunder-clap" and "such a storm among our bankers and other moneyed institutions" was never before witnessed. Another New York periodical spoke of "the sudden panic which has come into our city like one of those cyclones of which we read in the Eastern seas, which occasionally sweep over the deep with such violence as to leave it strewn with wrecks." This was old imagery, only missing direct allusions to acts of God. Still, like an early modern "peril of the seas," the panic was unforeseeable, irresistible. Individual agents were helpless. Voyage became an image and metaphor for an entire economy in motion, at risk.[103]

Brought to the fore were the same old vexing moral questions, just in new form. In 1880, Henry explained before the Senate that the bank's depositors:

> were the victims of a widespread, universal financial trouble, by which I myself, my firm, have been heavy losers, as well as others, and I have always regarded this trouble of the company as having been the result of a widespread, universal, sweeping financial disaster.

The moral responsibility of the economic chance-world, the metaphor of disaster, had obvious appeal for someone with as much culpability as Henry. But when the black trustee Purvis addressed a group of black depositors at Washington's Union Bethel Church in September of 1874, all angry to know who or what was responsible for the bank's recent failure, he answered that the failure of the Freedman's Bank was the product of both "great rascals" and "the panic." Great rascals to be sure, but the economic chance-world now occupied a new seat of power, authority, and responsibility.[104]

And so the rising American corporate financial system expanded as more and more Americans became both existentially and economically dependent upon its vicissitudes. With the Freedman's Bank no more, black sharecroppers continued to struggle and strive for a landed independence in the face of disenfranchisement, segregation, and violence. By 1890, in a testament to their strivings, 1 in 5 southern black farm operators would be landowners.[105]

Jay and Henry Cooke were bankrupts. Jay lived long enough to regain his fortune by speculating on western mining projects but Henry died a disgraced man in 1881. The Northern Pacific Railroad, bankrupted in 1875, was finally completed in 1883. It spread west from Duluth at the mouth of Lake Superior and across the fertile Red River Valley before reaching the Puget Sound and the Pacific Ocean, sprouting many tributaries along its path. In the decades after the Civil War, along the western railroad lines, many migrating Americans and Europeans would settle, in search of a landed independence of their own.

CHAPTER 5

Betting the Farm

Muscle without brains on the farm is like a ship at sea without a compass. The voyage, to say the least, is very uncertain and is usually attended with humiliation and disaster.

—"Secrets of Success in Farming,"
Wisconsin Farmers' Institutes (1892)

IN 1873, THE GERMAN IMMIGRANTS thirty-year-old Henry Ise and his new eighteen-year-old bride Rosie migrated west from Iowa, settling on 160 acres of fertile western Kansas soil. A veteran, Ise had earned the claim outright fighting for the Union Army in a series of nasty campaigns in Tennessee which had left him with a creaky shoulder. After the Civil War, the freedpeople had failed to get their southern claims as the finance capitalist Henry Cooke channeled their savings into the construction of the western railroad network. But for those willing to head west, even for the trickle of southern black "Exodusters," the Homestead Act of 1862 had promised to open up millions of acres for settlement in clean rectangular 160-acre quarters.[1]

The Ises would succeed in raising a thriving commercial farm. But in 1887, needing $363 to pay a doctor to care for their youngest son John who was stricken with polio, the couple decided to mortgage their homestead to a financial corporation, the Pennsylvania Mortgage Company. It was a fateful decision. According to John's memoir of his childhood experience, the mortgage became the "relentless master of the family destinies." The Ise mortgage entered into a new stream of financial circulation—the "western mortgage market."[2]

Indeed, after 1870 there emerged an American market in what are now called "mortgage-backed securities." New financial intermediaries purchased mortgages on new western farms, guaranteed them, and then mostly passed them through to private and institutional investors in the East or packaged them together into bonds for public sale. Capital consequently flowed westward while wheat, corn, and other staples flowed eastward. By 1890, homesteaders had mortgaged somewhere between 30 and 40 percent of all farm acreage west of the Mississippi River and east of the Rocky Mountains. During the 1880s the "western farm mortgage" craze had spread like a fever among the eastern investing public. But after a series of droughts and the financial panic of 1893 the market collapsed. Yet, by then the logic of American farming had been utterly transformed. The farmer's distinctive hedge—his land—was lost. The countermovement of landed independence was over.[3]

After the Civil War, as before, many commercial farmers migrated west in pursuit of the economic and existential rewards of a landed independence. The Ises' lone-stated aspiration was to become "independent." Clearly, some had other, more narrow goals in mind. There were farmers, for instance, who put all possible acreage into wheat, the great western staple, in search of a short-term upside rather than a sense of long-term economic security. They hoped that rain would follow the plow, and that providence or chance would dispense a friendly fate, rewarding their labors. The 1880 western guidebook *Where to Go to Become Rich* devoted a chapter to plains farming, next to another on southwestern gold prospecting. Western land speculation flourished, as always, and western railroad finance continued to boom and bust. Farmers raised wheat and cattlemen grazed cattle. Gold, copper, silver, and timber beckoned. *Where to Go to Become Rich* followed a long American tradition of chasing upside risk in the West. The chief reason to migrate after all was the promise of a better life. Still, for a large proportion of western migrants in the 1870s and 1880s landed independence remained at least an ideal against which to measure the worth of their economic lives, as it did for Henry and Rosie Ise.[4]

The Ises successfully paid off their debt to the Pennsylvania Mortgage Company. But years later they found themselves in debt again. By his son's account, Henry worried incessantly and was often found sitting in a chair mumbling aloud to himself, counting figures and wondering if he would have enough cash on hand when the note came due. When Henry died in 1900, his son thought him a broken man. Looking back, Rosie described her husband as a terrific "farmer" but a terrible "business man." The opposition between "farmer" and "business man" (the latter a term that had acquired currency only in the 1820s) was telling, suggesting as it did the difference between the pursuit of landed independence and the pursuit of profit as the core principle in operating a farm.[5]

American farm mortgage debt increased by 42 percent during the 1880s, but it was hardly a new phenomenon. Neither was a farmer lamenting his debts. What was new, however, was the financial architecture of the market for western farm mortgages and the larger corporate financial systemization of risk of which it was a part. Until the middle of the nineteenth century there existed a more direct, personal link between mortgage lenders and borrowers. Many if not most farmers knew who owned their mortgage. With the rise of mortgage-backed securities and new forms of financial intermediation this was no longer the case. The relationship between lender and borrower became attenuated. Landed wealth became a dematerialized abstraction in the circulation of a new financial commodity: the "western mortgage." The Ises first mortgaged their farm to a local lender who then sold their mortgage to the Pennsylvania Mortgage Company, a new type of financial corporation that bought individual western mortgages, stapled them together, and resold them to private and institutional investors in the East. As farmers worked harder and longer to repay their debts they became cogs within an increasingly complex financial system. Unlike with the freedpeople, there was no Henry Cooke pulling these strings, reflecting risk's increasingly systemic character. The emerging American corporate financial system allowed a great many Americans the opportunity to be "independent" farm proprietors but it also squeezed their labor and pushed them into world commodities markets. Their land could no longer shield them from those markets' vicissitudes. Western farmers had difficulty wrapping their minds around how such an abstract and impersonal system worked. But clearly they were not in the saddle. Looking into the future, Rosie Ise observed of plains farming, while upsetting her dinner guest, a prominent evangelical minister: "Nobody's responsible."[6]

Ironically, for the economic security their own soil had ceased to provide farmers began to look to a financial instrument within the same system: life insurance policies. Vigorously marketed to farmers for the first time in the 1870s (particularly to those with mortgages), these policies were the ultimate emblem of the inversion of land and labor on the western plains. Self-ownership, not land ownership, became the bulwark of the farm household's economic security as male farmers began to offload their personal risks—a double commodification of their productive labor—onto the emerging corporate financial system.

But forces and agents at work in that same financial system doubled back and knocked on the farmer's door. For it turned out that the same corporation that bought a farmer's "life risk" might also, through a network of financial intermediation, own the same mortgage that led him to insure his life. Indeed, the largest institutional investors in the western mortgage market were eastern life insurance corporations (followed by eastern savings banks). As the mortgage and insurance markets systematized and intersected, western farmers became both agents and objects of a newly abstract financial power.

Not surprisingly, the ever-anxious Henry Ise purchased a life insurance policy. The Ises' story is worth recounting not only because of the family's failed quest for landed independence in the older sense but also because, by monetary measures, their farm was a success. The Ises were never in danger of foreclosure. In fact, however complex the western mortgage market became, the flow of eastern capital onto the prairies and plains had worked to lower western interest rates. Indeed, the far less ambiguous fate of the southern black sharecropper, starving for credit, trapped in exploitative local credit markets, provides a striking opposition. Unlike the Ises, many western farmers observed their rising incomes, soaring land values, and access to new financial forms of economic security and happily proclaimed themselves "independent." Henry Ise still sat in his chair, anxious, worriedly counting figures. Unlike him, other farmers would voice their anxieties in the Populist Revolt, demanding that the federal government, not financial markets, ensure for them the

economic security that land ownership had once provided—an early pre-
monition of risk's politicized twentieth-century history. But first risk's financial systematization eroded landed independence. It also created the
very conditions for the collapse of the first market in mortgage-backed
securities.[7]

A crucial agent of land enclosure in early modern England, the farm
mortgage traveled with European colonizers to the New World. In the
early 1700s, William Penn mortgaged the entire colony of Pennsylvania.
By the mid-eighteenth century the New England and Middle colonies
had created government loan offices that issued paper money to farmers
against their lands as collateral, the money repayable in installments
below market interest rates. These mortgages increased the circulating
medium and often financed capital improvements. But colonial land
banks did not lead to a decline in commercial safety-first strategies.
As late as 1820, on the western frontier government land offices offered
cheap credit to homesteaders and speculators. But neither did this break
the logic of landed independence.[8]

Nevertheless, in early national and antebellum America, farm mortgages played an increasingly large role in the northern countryside. Consider once again the town of Concord, Massachusetts, the same town
where in 1850 the politician, local dairy farmer, and future secretary of
the Treasury George S. Boutwell declared that the farmer had less "anxiety than men in other pursuits" as farming offered the "certainty of a
competence." Unlike merchants who were "dependent" upon the flux of
commerce, only the farmer was "independent."[9]

As Boutwell addressed the farmers of Concord, the quixotic towns-
man Henry David Thoreau was busily revising *Walden*. Despite Boutwell's boasting, Thoreau observed that no Concord tax assessor could
name him a dozen farmers "who own their farms free and clear." To know
the history of Concord "homesteads" was to inquire "as to the bank
where they are mortgaged." To Thoreau, the consequences of mortgage
debt were clear: the felling of forests; the intensification of labor ("work,
work, work," he taunted his neighbors); the reduction of time into money
values; the existential dependency of farmers upon commerce. Farmers

labored "under a mistake," driven "by a seeming fate, commonly called necessity." It was a "fool's life." Thoreau bragged that at Walden Pond he "was more independent than any farmer in Concord" as he was "not anchored" to a commercializing farm. The only possible source of Thoreau's independence was transcendental—"What a man thinks of himself, that is which determines, or rather indicates, his fate." The only source of Boutwell's independence, by definition, could be his land. But as Thoreau noted, the land was already beginning to abstract into the stream of financial circulation.[10]

Regardless, the vision of landed independence espoused by Boutwell in 1850 crystallized into the Homestead Act of 1862, which provided millions of western acres for men like Henry Ise to farm and ultimately to mortgage. No doubt, the Homestead Act did not achieve the fantastic Jeffersonian designs of its authors. But it did create almost 400,000 farms between 1862 and 1890. In the decades following the American Civil War, as the market in western farm mortgages revved up, the fate of landed independence hung in the balance.[11]

The postbellum decades are usually associated with large-scale industrialization and urbanization, as the American industrial corridor, stretching from the Atlantic Ocean to the Great Lakes, formed. During the 1870s, for the first time the percentage of farm property in the nation's total capital stock dipped below 50 percent. In the 1880s, the percentage of Americans employed in agriculture fell below the same symbolic threshold. Meanwhile, between 1860 and 1900 the share of manufacturing in total national output rose from 32 to 53 percent: New England textile factories, New York City sweatshops, Pittsburgh steelworks, Cleveland oil refineries. By 1900 America's industrial proletariat amounted to 25 percent of its labor force, and if first- or second-generation European immigrants like Henry and Rosie Ise trekked onward to the western plains, many more settled down in the industrializing cities. After a stunning great leap forward, in 1900 America would be the largest industrial power in the world.[12]

And yet this era also witnessed a dramatic expansion of American farm acreage, centered on the western prairies and plains. If agriculture declined relatively, its growth in absolute terms was striking. American farm acreage increased by 44 percent during the 1870s and there were 54 percent more farms. If by 1890 farm property was only 39 percent of the total capital stock, it was still double that of all industrial capital. Basically, in these measures by 1890 the industrial sector had replaced the slave sector in the composition of the American economy. Yet, to oppose agriculture to industry, countryside to city, is to conceal the symbiotic nature of postbellum American capitalist development. The same railroads after all brought the many primary products of the West's predominately extractive economy to new urban markets. Further, much of the nation's new industrial capacity, whether it was Minneapolis flourmills or Chicago stockyards, processed agricultural products and byproducts.[13]

The role of the evolving American corporate financial system in all of this was somewhat counterintuitive. Between 1850 and 1895, the relative size of the American financial sector increased by 51 percent. Since the economy was industrializing and urbanizing, it might be expected that finance capital contributed to the rise of industry—in much the same way Henry Cooke directed the freedpeople's agricultural savings into the construction of the transcontinental railroads. In fact the opposite occurred. Industrial capital accumulation—manufacturing firms' retained earnings— was outstripping built manufacturing capacity. Excess capital required outlets. The South, shackled by the sharecropping regime, imported little capital. With impressive fluidity finance capital flowed west, following not only the railroads, but also ranchers, miners, loggers, and farm households like the Ise family. Finance capital had to materialize somewhere.

When it landed on the western prairies and plains, the result was a wave of western farm staples that washed onto American and world markets. Between 1866 and 1886, for instance, the corn output of Kansas rose from 30 million bushels to 750 million. In 1880 the wheat crop of Dakota was not quite 3 million bushels. In 1887 it passed 60 million. These figures had no historical precedent. It took the states of Illinois and Indiana *together* fifty years to reach the level of wheat production that Dakota achieved in seven. Within ten years, bragged the western farm mortgage broker James Willis Gleed in 1890, "the growth which occupied a hundred years in the older States" had been accomplished in the lands north of Chicago and west of the Mississippi River. In turn, western farms quite literally fed eastern industrialization—which entered its most intensive phase in the 1880s. Triumphantly, Gleed concluded, "The mortgage did this." The mortgage was an external instrument capable of doing the work itself. That instrument—a network of abstract financial interdependence—chipped away at the foundations of landed independence.[14]

Western farmers turned to the mortgage market both by choice and from necessity. If from necessity it was partly because western farmers encountered difficulties with the very nature of their new land and climate. East of the Mississippi, plentiful forests and waterways combined with diverse soils and vegetations to provide the basis for commercially orientated safety-first strategies. Forestal areas were more difficult to clear but they were blessed with a more diverse resource base—timber for fuel and construction, cover for wild game. Waterways provided fishing streams, another energy source, and access to commercial markets. The few lands west of the Mississippi that offered this ecology, so familiar to eastern farmers, were the first to be settled. But after 1870 the forestal frontier closed.

Somewhere near the famed 100th meridian, grasslands gave way to plains. Here, the ecological mix necessary for traditional American agricultural practices was absent. There was a reason why, moving west, the Sioux became horse-mounted nomads, terrorizing impoverished Native American agriculturalist villagers. Even, if apart from buffalo chips and nothing more, the plains did offer one thing: virgin, fertile soil ripe for commercial grains. Without waterways, plains farming proved impractical without markets for agricultural products of great geographical scale, together with the railroads to connect them—and also, of course, working capital. On the plains, free soil by itself could not make a farm.[15]

The amount of cash required was varied, but it was far more than most had. The 1880 guidebook *Where to Go to Become Rich* recommended arriving at the Kansas plains with at least $1,000. A thousand dollars allowed a man to purchase 160 acres on a six-year mortgage, paying $150 down.

The "other necessary expenses will run, house building, $250; team and harness, $180; breaking plow, $22; harrow $10; cow, $30; interest payments on land one year from purchase, $35; total, $677. This will leave . . . $323 for seed and to carry him through till the crop can be raised." The sum of $1,000 is not far from the later estimates of historians.[16]

Nevertheless, the hopeful migrating farmer had several options. Henry Ise saved his wages in Iowa and delayed marriage. Tenancy was another avenue. As in the South, an agricultural ladder was at work, ascending along the life cycle from wage work to tenancy and finally proprietorship. The first rung of entry often proved decisive. En route to western Kansas a woman stole $300 from Henry's misplaced wallet. He grumbled about the theft for the rest of his life, especially in periods of debt. Only when possessed of more capital could western farmers climb the ladder and, under competitive pressures, stay there. This was the principal reason to mortgage. An 1890 census sample determined that 83 percent of mortgage debt was for land "purchase money" or "farm improvements." The category of "business" was assigned another 9 percent and "family expenses" 2 percent. The western farm mortgage market, in other words, was a capital market.[17]

But the desire for cash for any reason might lead to a mortgage. As noted earlier, Henry Ise had first mortgaged his homestead to pay a doctor to tend to his polio-stricken youngest son. The consumer goods of the cities were fast becoming emblems of rural status. The Ise family never mortgaged for that purpose but they were conscious of their own expanding consumer desires, and they noticed when for this reason their neighbors mortgaged their farms.[18]

In sum, between 1860 and 1890 total factor productivity—a broad measure of the productivity of all business inputs—soared in the agricultural sector like never before.[19] It was the traditional farm household that was responsible. Despite the bonanza wheat farms of California or the Red River Valley, this same period, which witnessed such a dramatic extension and intensification of American agriculture, also witnessed a decline in the use of agricultural wage labor. The incidence of wage labor in American farming rose from 27 percent to 35 percent between 1860 and 1870 but it fell back to 27 percent by 1890.[20] It was financialization, not proletarianization, that ushered American agriculture into the Age of Capital.

In the 1870s and 1880s western farmers entered a complex series of market transactions that constituted a new systemic structure. It began with taking out a mortgage. Take, for instance, the mortgage on Willis and Mary Olmsted's farm in eastern Nebraska. In 1876 the couple read an advertisement in their local newspaper placed by A. W. Ocobock, a Chicago banker. Chicago was the great intermediary for eastern capital seeking western outlets. Ocobock was offering mortgage loans in their county through an agent named C. C. Cook. The Olmsteds contacted Cook, who contacted Ocobock. Ocobock sent yet another man from the nearby railroad town of David City to inspect the farm. Satisfied with the inspection's results, Ocobock offered the Olmsteds a $400 loan for a term of five years at 10 percent interest. Ocobock instructed the Olmsteds to make their payments by mail to the Corbin Banking Company, a banking and real estate brokerage partnership of New York City. In addition, the Olmsteds agreed to pay Ocobock an $80 commission. The Corbin Banking Company did not own their mortgage however. The bank was the transactional agent of a financial corporation, the New England Mortgage Security Company of Boston. The corporation then stapled the Olmstead mortgage together with other western farm mortgages, securitizing them into bonds for public sale. The man pulling strings behind all of these transactions was the managing partner of the Corbin Banking Company, Austin Corbin.[21]

Corbin was a native of New Hampshire and an 1849 Harvard graduate. He established a law practice in Davenport, Iowa, in 1851 but quickly began to broker Iowa farm mortgages for eastern investors. In 1865 he moved to New York City. The new Corbin Banking Company operated under the 1864 National Banking Act which was initially thought to prohibit commercial banks from owning mortgages. The Corbin Banking Company, incorporated in 1874, became a conduit for institutions that carried mortgages on their own balance sheets. Corbin was a director and the largest stockowner of not only the New England Mortgage

Security Company—but also of the New England Loan Company of Manchester, New Hampshire. He was one of the largest stockholders of the American Mortgage Company of Scotland, a company chartered in Edinburgh for which the Corbin Banking Company acted as an American agent. He had the same relationship with the American Freehold Land-Mortgage Company of London. British capital too found its way to the western plains. Corbin would become a prominent New York financier and philanthropist, once causing a public splash when he imported western buffalo for a preserve on his New Hampshire estate. He would eventually take his mortgage-derived riches into the railroad industry. But in 1876 Corbin himself signed a circular forwarded to Ocobock that instructed the Olmsteds that "interest payable at this office on a day certain" meant money was due *"on that day."* And when not paid *"promptly* we shall return to the owners, and they will send to an attorney for foreclosure." The Olmsteds thus mortgaged their farm.[22]

Their experience was revealing of the dynamics of the western mortgage market after 1870. Thoreau had observed that the history of Concord homesteads was to be discovered at the local bank. That is to say, it was still possible in the 1850s to connect the dots. But in the decades that followed that would no longer be the case. This is what gave the increasingly systematized western farm mortgage market its novelty, distinguishing it from centuries of farm mortgaging. The Olmsteds had to haul Ocobock to court before they even learned of the existence of the New England Mortgage Security Company. When Henry Ise brought a mortgage broker named Armstrong, papers in hand, to inspect the farm Rosie greeted him "with scarcely concealed hostility." Many state homestead laws demanded that wives sign mortgages. To Rosie, Armstrong "the capitalist" embodied the mortgage. But what she actually greeted at her door was an entire network of eastern finance capital. Armstrong passed the mortgage through to the Pennsylvania Mortgage Company. Capital wanted wheat. Mortgage brokers and their agents such as Armstrong accordingly inspected homesteads for their value as capital assets. The western brokerage giant Edward R. Darrow required his agents to take photographs of inspected farms, opening a new chapter in the aesthetic commodification of nature that Thoreau had so detested. Photographic representations of homesteads that had entered the swirl of financial intermediation were filed away in the offices of innumerable brokers.[23]

Other aspects of the Olmsteds' mortgage were likewise emblematic. On average, farmers mortgaged half the value of their farms. Corbin claimed to have never mortgaged more than a third. Most mortgages were for five years and occasionally as low as three. They never extended beyond seven years. The mortgages were not fully amortized and they featured balloon payments in the final year of repayment. As for the interest rate, there were usury laws on the books of every state, many of them a legacy of rates as high as the 40 percent that had been charged by local agents in the 1840s and 1850s. In 1890, the census-recorded interest rate in Kansas was 8.68 percent, below the usury ceiling of 10 percent.[24]

As interest rates plummeted, some voices in these years called for the abolition of state usury laws. The loudest was that of Richard H. Dana, Jr., author of the famous sailing memoir, *Two Years Before the Mast*, and a noted former abolitionist. In 1867 he called upon the Massachusetts legislature to abolish usury laws. In the new era of "competition," the "the borrower is no longer the trembling suppliant at the threshold of the patrician lender." Interest rates rather should be set by "the market of the world," which moved with the "irresistible power of ocean tides." Indeed, many judges enforced usury statutes while characterizing them in the same breath as barbaric relics. Regardless, the western farm mortgage market brought western interest rates down and contributed to the national convergence of regional eastern and western rates.[25]

So measured, the West had become a more efficient capital market, although exploitation was still evident in the commission charges of brokers. Henry Ise was offered a loan at the usurious rate of 15 percent but that included Armstrong's commission. The Olmsteds brought Corbin to trial in Nebraska on usury charges after they failed to make their payment and Corbin foreclosed on them. The Olmsteds paid 10 percent, the legal limit, but they also gave $80 to Ocobock as a commission. They claimed that since Ocobock was the agent of the New England Mortgage Security Company the extra $80 was usury. Corbin countered by describing Ocobock as the agent of the Olmsteds, which meant that the $80 was a fee for the service he had rendered them. The Nebraska Supreme Court sided with the Olmsteds but no judicial standard emerged in Nebraska or anywhere elsewhere. Struggles over usury were local in character and elude generalization. For this reason, statistical totals regarding late nineteenth-century interest rates cannot be trusted. The Olmsted mortgage was not unique but their effort to trace Ocobock back to Corbin was. When Rosie Ise asked Henry if he could do better than 15 percent—a usurious rate—he replied that no one in town would lend for less. The Ises needed the money and the mortgage was signed, as were hundreds of thousands of others in that same decade.[26]

Mortgages passed from brokers to investors. Many mortgages—more than half nationally although a lesser percentage in the West—moved into the hands of individual private investors. It is difficult to know much about the motivations of these men and women. Some of them were speculators, chasing the upside in another installment of the great American pastime of western land speculation. Some still subscribed to the notion that land was relatively still the most secure form of investment. A daily Boston newspaper in 1877 did note the "anxiety" experienced by many of the city's purchasers of western mortgages. In these decades the American savings rate was soaring, and many private savers owned retiring Civil War bonds. At first, many turned to railroad bonds. But after the 1870s railroad bust, in the 1880s it seems western mortgage bonds became a chosen form of investment.[27]

In 1887, between sojourns to the Old World, a twenty-seven-year-old Jane Addams caught the "western farm mortgage" craze. She later wrote of visiting a "western state" where she had "invested a sum of money in mortgages" after her recently deceased father had left her $50,000. Addams was "horrified by the wretched conditions among the farmers"—a result of drought. The scene provoked a moral anxiety. "It seemed quite impossible to receive interest from mortgages placed upon farms which might at any season be reduced to such conditions." Addams withdrew the investment. She bought a sheep farm near her Illinois home instead, a purchase sound "both economically and morally." But she was no farmer and the enterprise "ended in a spectacle scarcely less harrowing than the memory it was designed to obliterate." Addams departed for Europe "sadder for the experience."[28]

Addams's effort to personalize her investment was no ordinary act. Equally extraordinary farmers would occasionally seek out the owners of their mortgages. The broker Edward Darrow warned potential investors of this possibility. Farmers might discover "the name and address of the investor" and "write directly." Any investor, Darrow instructed, "who attempts to deal with the borrower directly under such circumstances is acting against his own interests." A western mortgage was a commodity like any other "regulated by the price of supply and demand." The market, through brokers, brought borrowers and investors together. Direct interaction of any sort was counterproductive.[29]

No matter how hard they tried, sometimes farmers and investors could not find one another. In the 1880s another financial innovation introduced an extra level of mediation. These were financial corporations such as Corbin's New England Mortgage Security Company. They purchased mortgages, which they guaranteed, repackaged together, and then securitized for public sale. Mortgage terms in the 1870s and 1880s prohibited a farmer from the early repayment of his loan's principal, thus stabilizing mortgage companies' cash flows and allowing the process of securitization to proceed. The Olmsted mortgage, which was securitized by the New England Mortgage Security Company, was destined in bits and pieces for eastern holders of such "debenture bonds." Here, the western broker Gleed bragged, the farmer "cannot treat directly with the eastern owner of the mortgage, for he cannot ascertain who that owner is; the assignment from the company to the investor is not recorded." The Olmsteds read the advertisement of Ocobock in their local Nebraska paper. Their mortgage's future owners—perhaps with bread made of western wheat on their dinner tables—read in their own local newspapers of investment opportunities in western mortgages. The New England Mortgage Security commonly advertised ten-year bonds at 5 percent that were backed by western mortgages. Or investors might see circulars such as Corbin's 1872 "Ten Per Cent First Mortgages on Improved Farms in Iowa and Kansas." Mortgage companies flooded the advertising back pages of the eastern press, especially during the latter half of the 1880s, the height of the western farm mortgage "craze." In a single sheet in 1889, *The Independent* featured forty consecutive such ads interrupted by a sole advertisement for safe deposit vaults: "7 percent Kansas Farm Loans;" "All loans made on

Corn Growing lands of the west;" "A solid 9 per cent." The aggressive marketing worked. By 1893 private eastern investors had purchased at least $93 million of mortgage debenture bonds. Individual homesteads were securitized—bundled together, repackaged, sliced, diced, and resold.[30]

The rationale of the debentures was to spread investors' risk—to reduce their anxiety, protect their downsides. According to Gleed, invoking the now protean metaphor of insurance, "the investor is not compelled to stand or fall with one mortgage or one piece of real estate. Each debenture bond is, in a sense, insured by all the rest of the series." Furthermore, companies could engineer bonds whose value was below that of any single mortgage. A Boston newspaper announced in 1887 that a new company was offering debentures as low as $50, enabling "small investors" to get into the game. A 3 to 4 percent spread between western interest rates and eastern bond rates was not uncommon and maturities varied from one to twenty years. An Iowa outfit was the first to sell debenture bonds in 1881. Ten years later, according to New York bank regulators, there were 167 such companies selling bonds in the state. Anecdotal sources testified to hundreds more operating in both the East and West.[31]

The new system suddenly grew in the 1880s and then collapsed after the panic of 1893. The broker Darrow had always detested the new financial engineering. The aim was to manage uncertainty, to hedge risk. But securitization, he thought, created a false sense of security. The multiple layers of interweaving mediation made it too easy for financiers and investors to disregard the underlying, material assets—the farms themselves—and to engage in finance qua finance. Western farms had become so fractured and abstracted that the actual assets were difficult to see. If she had been a debenture bondholder, Addams would have had to spend years searching the western plains; in this market structure, the very notion of locating individual moral responsibility was an absurdity. The investor in "mortgage securities," Darrow surmised, was like a man who bought a horse "without the least examination as to whether the animal was blind, halt or lame." Making a bad situation worse, mortgage originators were often paid upon closing. That is, they had no stake in the loan's future repayment. A few years of drought and then financial panic caused many western farmers to default on their loans. Farmers feared foreclosure but so, in fact, did their creditors. Mortgage companies attempted to turn foreclosed farmers into their tenants but the U.S. Supreme Court had already blocked them and state legislatures were equally unfriendly to that aim. After 1893, almost all of the mortgage-backed securities corporations went bankrupt. Wall Street observers remarked that most of them had been too highly leveraged and too poorly managed. One Wall Street bond rater claimed that western farm appraisements had been "absurd." Many agents "did not know a sand-hill pasture from a bottom-land garden." But this would not be the last time that the financial securitization of mortgages would—quite literally—lose sight of the underlying assets. After 1893, the next time a mortgage-backed securities market of such depth and breadth would blow up would be 2007.[32]

It turned out that the greatest owners of intermediated farm mortgage debt were life insurance corporations. In 1890, for instance, life insurance corporations owned 41 percent of all western intermediated mortgage debt—compared to 23 percent for mortgage companies, 18 percent for savings banks, and 10 percent for building and loan associations.[33] The course of late nineteenth-century American agriculture was unimaginable without the capital accumulations of American financial corporations. In 1865, the total assets of life insurance firms counted $82 million. By 1890, they stood at $809 million (see Table 2 in Appendix). That figure represented almost 10 percent of accumulated private financial savings held in the burgeoning reserves of American financial institutions, including life insurance corporations, savings banks, commercial banks, and new-fangled trust companies.[34]

To arrive at this point, life insurance corporations followed a similar trajectory as savings banks. The Civil War had created gluts of federal debt. In 1865, 33 percent of life insurance investments were held in government debt (including federal, state and municipal debt) compared to virtually nothing before the war. As the federal bond market shrank, amounting to only 7 percent of investments by 1890, life insurance firms turned elsewhere, snapping up a variety of assets including the new western farm mortgages. State laws did control their investments but after the rash of savings banks failures following the panic of 1873, states tied the hands of savings banks far more than life insurance corporations. So it was the many individual Americans who turned to self-insurance in the 1870s and 1880s who seemingly gave the prospect of landed independence a greater lease on life.[35]

Of course, most of the finance capital provided by these financial corporations consisted of the accumulating "level" premiums of predominately eastern, urban policyholders—and also the forfeited premiums that Elizur Wright hoped to transform into "surrender values." But, tellingly, during the 1870s firms began to aggressively market policies to farmers—especially mortgaged farmers in the West.

Life insurance companies had by now perfected their sales pitch. One new corporation that especially sought out farmers was the Travelers Insurance Company of Hartford, Connecticut. With the insurance principle, the Travelers explained, the "income-producing capital" of a free male life could be transformed into a financial asset. It was not a form of gambling on death but a prudent hedge against the uncertainty of the future: "It is not so much the event of death against which life insurance provides, as the uncertainty of life." As for the future, trust in "providence" was a "ruinous fatalism." Premised on the ideal of "personal independence," personal insurance was actually "the realization of the socialistic ideal of a competence for all." The so-called "law of mortality" made the policy perfectly secure. The Travelers concluded that the existential "feeling of security" brought by an insurance policy was worth "more than the money."[36]

Personal insurance was also a necessary hedge against the perils of farm mortgaging. "Good luck cannot always be depended upon," as the Travelers explained, and many young farmers were "so deeply in debt" that if their lives were suddenly taken away they would leave their households with "nothing." To attend to the future now demanded— instead of accumulating wealth by acquiring more land or improving the farm—that the farmer should invest in a financial asset. As one leading New York firm put it in 1874, "a mortgage on real estate ought always to be offset by a policy of insurance on the life of the mortgagor." Farmers began to take note. An 1895 survey of Wisconsin farmers found that 30 percent carried life insurance policies—coincidentally about the same percentage that carried a mortgage.[37]

The circularity and symbiosis is striking. If a man was mortgaged, so it went, the insurance policy became the household's bulwark of economic security. Self-ownership—the ownership of the "life risk"—replaced land ownership. Yet, agrarian policyholders were both saving for the future (there was still a dearth of depository savings banks in the countryside) while they were also, however indirectly, investing in the western farm mortgage market themselves—the market that was the very reason they now insured their lives. One firm, the Northwestern Mutual Life of Milwaukee, set up branch offices throughout the West from where agents solicited both mortgages and life policies.[38] The same man who inspected your farm as a viable capital asset might then turn around and inspect your life as a viable capital asset. Or other life insurance corporations purchased mortgages from their originators or from the new mortgage securitization companies. The security of self-insurance now depended upon the farmer's future mortgage payments.

The Travelers, for instance, told farmers to trust the "integrity" of the corporation's investments. The firm, it turned out, was a heavy investor in western farm mortgages. In 1887 the company reported assets of almost $11 million to the Kansas Superintendent of Insurance. Nearly $4 million of that was held in "loans on bond and mortgage on real estate," although in unspecified locations. But the Travelers' public financial disclosures once listed 496 shares in the Kansas Farm Mortgage Company of Abilene. In 1898, with its assets listed at $17 million, the Kansas Superintendent of Insurance grew suspicious of the Travelers' valuations of its mortgage holdings in Kansas and asked to see the corporations' books. The firm sued for a blocking injunction and ceased to do business in the state for a short period.[39]

The point is that the western farm mortgage market was a vast and intricate financial structure of debt and investment. The farmer's personal risk systematized across each and every inch of it. A mortgage-insurance complex, so to speak, connected farmers with the likes of Ocobock, Corbin, Addams, the New England Mortgage Company, and the holders of mortgage company debenture bonds—along with the stockowners of the Travelers Insurance Company and finally the firm's policyholders who were now often western farmers themselves.

Within this complex, the farmer's life insurance policy was the ultimate emblem of the fate of landed independence. The mortgaged farmer did not own his land outright, to do with what he will. What he did own outright was the financial "risk" on his life. A "man's right to himself and to his own services is unquestionable," the Travelers insisted. He could therefore alienate and insure his personal risk—which only provided more capital for more mortgages. When the Civil War destroyed chattel slavery it had destroyed, in a sudden and violent political conflict, slave society's distinctive countermovement against the generative insecurities and radical uncertainties of capitalism. The fate of landed independence was too marked by political conflict, culminating in the Populist agitation of the 1890s. But it began to pass away first in a far more subtle fashion. Slowly, the mortgaged farmer learned that his own contingent human capital, not his land, was his most important and valuable capital asset. In 1890, a Kansas agrarian periodical carried the shocking title of a Yale professor's recent lecture on agriculture—"Man is worth more than land." Slave ownership first, now land ownership, gave way to the liberal ideal of self-ownership—and a new sense of what it meant to be a free and secure actor. That ideal continued to flourish in tandem with the growth of powerful financial corporations.[40]

The life insurance policy truly was a great boon to the mortgaged farmer. Even agrarian periodicals, famously hostile to eastern financiers, repeatedly extolled the necessity of personal insurance. If the mortgaged farmer experienced a single bad harvest, or a plummet in the wheat market, he might lose his land. A policy now remained a family's sole source of secure wealth. Or, as the Travelers emphasized in 1885—much to the chagrin of a dying Elizur Wright—it could be "assigned" in the open marketplace. Further, the life insurance policy could replace the generational succession of the family farm. In this respect, not only Henry Ise's life insurance policy but also his son John's career as an Iowa state agricultural economist is telling. The Ises had twelve children, nine of whom went to college. Instead of land, Henry gave each of his children $100 when they turned eighteen. One of the Ise boys became a farmer, although by then Henry's original 160 acres was nowhere near a viable holding. The other

Ise children found their way to the cities, and Rosie Ise spent her final years living in her daughter's home in Lawrence, Kansas. This was not just true of the Ise family. Old patterns of generational succession were generally disrupted in the countryside. Fewer farms stayed within families. More often, they were put up for sale to the highest bidder.[41]

In all of these ways, the farm household was breaking apart. Collective strategies that coped with the perils of an uncertain future transformed, and in some instances crumbled. Farmers had long accumulated wealth in farm property—fixed, physical forms of wealth. Now they were accumulating financial assets, transformed by corporations into flexible forms of finance capital. Farmers had followed careful, even delicate, strategies in ensuring the transmission of their farms to their children and, not unrelated, their children's care for them in old age. Now, if the family farm was destined for auction, the life policy became the new dangling carrot. In 1880, the Travelers spoke of a policyholder "absolutely dependent upon his children for support." "Filial affection" aside, his children knew they would be "rewarded pecuniarily for all their trouble by the payment at his death . . . of his life policy." The life insurance policy wedged itself into the farm household.[42]

On behalf of his family, the farmer thus offloaded his personal risk onto the evolving corporate financial system. Security now depended upon the abstract social logic of the insurance principle. The farmer could no longer look directly to his own soil. Contractual, nonhierarchical, actuarial insurance created risk communities by plucking them out of their known social worlds and setting them in relationships of statistical interdependence premised upon the law of large numbers. According to the Travelers, that law was not providentially ordained. But it was "firmly settled as the attraction of gravity." As the corporation concluded in 1878: "Which is better able to take this risk, your family, or the insurance company?" The farm household joined the countermovement of corporate risk management.[43]

The mortgage-insurance complex chipped away at the foundations of landed independence, including the farmer's legendary command over both his own labor and the labor of his household dependents. In the

postbellum decades many farmers, working harder and longer to meet
their mortgage payments, voiced a new sense of time-work discipline.
The mortgage-insurance complex, however impersonal and abstract,
could still squeeze farm labor, exerting a peculiar kind of supervisory
control.

Tellingly, the Travelers' campaign to extend the insurance principle to
the agrarian classes was part of the same effort to bring industrial wage
workers into that same fold. In antebellum America many independent
farm proprietors had celebrated their distinctive economic form of life by
comparing it favorably to the urban mercantile classes, who might have
enjoyed greater potential upsides but did not enjoy the security offered by
the land. Now, only a few decades later, many independent farm proprietors had begun to compare their fates not to the mercantile classes but
rather to the lots of dependent industrial hirelings. The farm household,
in principle, was still intact. It was the new financial structure of debt and
investment that brought about this change in consciousness.

Antebellum farming had straddled the fence between business enterprise and way of life. After the Civil War, the balance finally tipped. In
1887 and 1895 respectively, the labor bureaus of Nebraska and Wisconsin surveyed hundreds of farmers to investigate the sources of agricultural
success and failure. Many farmers voiced typical agrarian discontents:
the nefarious railroads, the eastern moneylenders, the deflationary gold
standard. Others celebrated the virtues of farming, calling the comparison to wage labor preposterous. But everyone, often in the same breath,
announced that farming had newly become a "business." "Farming is
very much like any other business," one Wisconsin farmer bluntly stated.
Farmers must "adopt a system that will in the end secure the greatest
amount of products at the lowest minimum cost of production." They
must employ a "thorough business instinct."[44]

But was the farmer/business man in the saddle? Henry Ise had escaped
the wage labor of his youthful twenties, which was no small feat and one
he cherished. No human boss directed his work but he sensed that he had
acquired a boss of another kind. A popular poem of the day, an exemplar
of a thriving western genre, captured the sentiment. Its author was the
equally popular Midwestern writer Will Carleton, a Michigan native who
grew up watching his father struggle with mortgage debt. In the "Tramp's
Story," published in a book of verse entitled *Farm Festivals,* a father gives

his son a bequest on his wedding day of an eighty-acre farm, one fit for an "independent start." "Land-hungry," the son mortgages the homestead to purchase an adjacent eighty acres. Although skeptical, his wife agrees to work "hard from day to day." For "we knew that life was business, now that we had that debt to pay." There follows a section of the poem that was widely excerpted in agrarian periodicals:

> We worked through spring and winter—through summer and
>   through fall—
> But that mortgage worked the hardest and the steadiest of us all;
> It worked on nights and Sundays—it worked each holiday—
> It settled down among us, and it never went away.
> Whatever we kept from it seemed a'most as bad as theft;
> It watched us every minute, and it ruled us right and left.
> The rust and blight were with us sometimes, and sometimes not;
> The dark-browed, scowling mortgage was forever on the spot.
> The weevil and the cut-worm, they went as well as came;
> The mortgage staid forever, eating hearty all the same.
> It nailed up every window—stood guard at every door—
> And happiness and sunshine made their home with us no more.

"Failing crops" and "sickness" and "foreclosure" brings about the wife's death: "She died of *mortgage*." The widower subsequently falls into alcoholism and becomes a wandering tramp dependent for subsistence upon alms.[45]

Carleton anthropomorphized the western farm mortgage market. Indeed, it exerted supervisory control over the household—"it settled down among us" and "watched us every minute." It "ruled us." Notably, the verses echoed others then capturing the experience of industrial proletarianization in the east. The Ise mortgage "hung like a pall over the spirits of all, even the children." At the supper table, "the family conversation, no matter where it started, usually led finally back to that engrossing and disturbing theme." The mortgage had settled down among them—the "relentless master of the family destinies." Who was that master, the "it"? "It" was very different from the more easily personified boss of the industrial factory. It was not the local, violent, racist, exploitative white southern credit factor. The owners of the Ise mortgage

resided at the end of a winding path of financial intermediation. He or
she did not know that they owned a fractured, chopped-up bit of the Ise
mortgage; Ise did not know the many investors who owned his mortgage's many bits. Yet unlike the factory boss, unlike the local credit factor, the mortgage followed the western farmer out of the workplace, out
of the fields, into his home. It bore into his very psyche.[46]

The mortgage-insurance complex was capital and capital wanted
wheat. In this era, both mechanization (the steel plow, the McCormick
reaper) and biological innovation in crop seeds increased farm productivity. But until the twentieth century brought the tractor and the combine, along with new fertilizers and pesticides, farm households often
raised yields by squeezing their labor. The farmer's captive labor force
of women and children, in fact, was one of the great business virtues of the
farm household. And now, even nonmortgaged farmers had to compete
with those who were working to meet their mortgage payments. In Kansas, the Ise farm suffered because Henry spent too much time reading instead of attending to the business of the farm. To farmers who were critical
of agrarian radicalism, "loafing," "laziness," and "shiftlessness" were to
blame for farm failures. "But to successfully compete with the world nowa-
days," one Wisconsin farmer stated, "one must be awake early and late."[47]

In the cities, antebellum life insurance was complicit in the general
removal of middle-class household dependents from the labor force. For
a mortgaged farm household to do so was economic suicide. In the 1882
Michigan Farmer, an author wrote about the "young girl who married a
poor farmer." She settled down to the "task of paying off a mortgage on
their home." The young wife "likes music, books, pictures and all sorts
of nice things" but instead "plods along year after year, doing lots of
hard, drudging work." It was as if the mortgage had also been placed
"upon her own health and strength." Once again, labor rather than land
was the foundation of the farmer's independence. With the mortgage ultimately paid off, "her face is thin and faded, her form bent, and her
hands brown and calloused." Her "fingers have lost their affinity for the
keys," and she was too coarse to "go out into society." Children were
also busily at work in the fields. The Ises had neighbors who were Swiss
immigrants with "a large family of children" that "worked like beavers"
to pay off a mortgage.[48]

The Ise memoir is likewise no tale of bourgeois domesticity. John Ise, crippled with polio from youth, reflects upon the untiring labor of his father, mother, and siblings with a twinge of guilt. But no less significant than the amount of time spent working was the work's productivity, measured in units of time. The Ises' experience is again instructive. Since the Civil War, Henry had suffered chronic shoulder and stomach problems. With a mortgage, the question of replacing his flagging labor power with that of a youthful hired hand became a constant issue. Prudent calculation was called for. Further, Rosie often complained that Henry got "less work out of hired hands than anyone else in the neighborhood." He was too kind. So she often insisted on doing the work herself. Her work, and the work of her children, was invisible to insurance corporations. But it was necessitated by the demands of capital. The Ises measured the relative value of their productive labor against the general wage force. Rosie was better at this than Henry, as was revealed in their decision to borrow $100 against their land to purchase a windmill. At first, the Ises drew their own water from a well whenever they "wouldn't be doing anything else that counts." But Rosie realized that it would be cheaper to hire extra hands to do that, allowing them to divert the household's labor elsewhere. Finally, she wondered whether a windmill would not be the best solution since it would reduce the cost of boarding hands. She made the appropriate calculations on the back of an envelope. The Ise household's labor was a fungible economic input weighed and considered against others.[49]

On this theme, the new Travelers Insurance Company had much to say. In fact, the corporation burst onto the scene in the 1870s selling a new form of insurance—"accident insurance." True to its namesake the firm was chartered in Hartford, Connecticut, in 1864 to insure railroad travelers against injury, another American imitator of an originally English business model. By the end of the nineteenth century British insurance executives would be travelling to America to study the phenomenal success of the Travelers.[50]

By the mid-1870s the Travelers had begun to specialize in insuring men's contingent human capital against "accident." For decades it dominated the new field of accident insurance, with little commercial competition. By 1885, the Travelers announced it had sold over a million accident policies. Exaggerated or not, no company in the world compared. The Travelers insured $232 million of contingent productive labor against the perils, as it were, of everyday life. It sold, or so it claimed, tens of thousands of policies to farmers.[51]

The object of this new double commodification was contingent male productive labor measured in units of "time," a new approach to temporality for the insurance principle. Accident insurance was "a contract to indemnify for a loss of time in consequence of disabling physical injury." An "accident" was any event that acted immediately to "*totally disable* the person insured from labor or business." The Travelers sold policies valued at $3 to $50 per week for up to twenty-six weeks. An 1885 agent's manual instructed that a policy should never "exceed two-thirds of the actual money value of the insured's time." The female body was considered *ipso facto* uninsurable. And men were only insurable between the ages of eighteen and seventy. People without "visible means of support" or "without occupation" were also uninsurable. For their time was "worthless."[52]

The farmer's future labor time could thus be enclosed into an "accident risk." Accidents might happen, the Travelers reminded:

> to persons traveling on business or pleasure; to the mechanic or artisan working at his trade; to the farmer cultivating his farm; to the operative in mills and factories; to the professional or business man in the active pursuits of life: accidents *may* happen to any man, by his own misfortune or the carelessness of others.

There might be:

> Dislocations, Fractures, Broken Bones, Ruptured Tendons, Bruises, Cuts, Stabs, Gunshot Wounds, Crushing or Mangling, Burns and Scalds, Bites of Mad Dogs or Serpents, Unprovoked Assaults by Robbers or Murderers, Strokes of Lighting, or Drowning.

Accident insurance provided financial compensation in the event of all of these contingencies and more. It did so for anyone who "must obtain the subsistence of their families by some kind of continuous labor." To these men, "Immunity from the risk is out of the question." Free men, possessing productive labor, simply carried the personal risk of "accident" whether they liked it or not. Time out of mind, human beings had been breaking their bones. The genius of the Travelers was to commodify the cost of that future peril into a financial "risk." The peril was a different matter. The Travelers could not, of course, unbreak bones.[53]

The Travelers pitch to farmers went like this. There were "so many ways for a tiller of the soil to get hurt." Indeed, "Farmers who insure against accidents find frequent occasion to call on the Travelers with their little bills for indemnity." An accident policy was a "great help" when a farmer was "disabled." While he recovered, the value of the accident policy could replace his labor with a wage hand's. In 1882, when the Travelers published a pamphlet of 500 representative accident claims, sixty-two were farmers' claims, stretching from New York, to Iowa, Kansas, and California. These included claims for:

> Kicked on leg by horse; struck by lightning; fell from scaffold in barn; fell, and kicked by a horse; burned in prairie fire; injured by railroad accident; stepped in hole in barn floor; barrel of pears rolled on leg.

Any accident that caused the farmer to suffer lost labor time could be subjected to the insurance principle.[54]

Much like early modern marine insurance had once required a definition of the "perils of the seas," accident insurance required a definition of "accident" in everyday life. The law continued to set the working legal rules of risk. The Travelers' policy language shifted in accordance with pivotal legal decisions. An 1872 law review article on the subject concluded that an accident was "any event which takes place without the foresight or expectation of the person acted upon or affected by the event." It was "some violence, casualty, or *vis major*." The standard of "proximate causation" applied. This was much like an old "peril of the sea" absent any reference to "acts of God." One jurist simply spoke of an "unknown cause" in the world. The first treatise on accident insurance, published in 1894, called an accident "something which happens by chance." In 1889, the U.S. Supreme Court provided a catch-all standard. An insurable accident was an "event" that was "unforeseen" and was "an unusual and unexpected result attending the performance of a usual act." A legal construction of individual moral autonomy—the old mercantile checklist of foresight, volition, and responsibility—determined insurance liability in a new setting.[55]

There were still the same caveats. Marine insurance did not insure against the "vice of the thing insured"—rotting fruit, revolting slaves. Accident insurance did not cover "riot, sunstroke, fighting, wrestling, suicide, riding or driving races," or "drunkenness." There was also "unnecessary exposure to danger or peril," a standard of "due diligence" on account of the insured, which the U.S. Supreme Court codified in 1873 with the standard of "limitation of risk." The precedent-setting case however was an 1871 New Jersey one. An insured farmer had built a barn and to view the results of his labor had climbed up onto the top joint. The joint broke and he fell to his death. In attempting to void the policy, his insurer explained to the court that, "[a]t the time of the accident he had on two overcoats, and was said to be an awkward man." The court did not accept the argument but it did hold that there must be some prudential standard, which the Supreme Court soon called "limitation of risk," the everyday complement to the workplace notion of "assumption of risk" announced decades ago in *Farwell*. For the mortgaged farmer, to engage in "unnecessary exposure to danger or peril" at any moment might be to risk the entire farm.[56]

The Travelers maintained that all of the world's true "accidents"—not just workplace accidents—could be reduced to probabilistic, statistical frequencies. While few "have any correct idea as to the probabilities in their case," accidents were nevertheless events that could be "calculated." Yet, in 1894 one observer still lamented that "as yet no accident tables have been published." The Travelers' early rates were probably the informed guesswork of their consultant, who was none other than Elizur Wright. In 1873, it did inaugurate an actuarial department and soon its rates were more discerning and precise. By 1885 it claimed "statistics" were the basis of its premiums tables. When the prospective policyholder sold his "accident risk" to the corporation, he had also seemingly bought into the Travelers' statistical worldview. The farmer who did buy into that worldview, agreeing to forego "unnecessary exposure to danger or peril," did something more. For his premium payments contributed to a systemic process of financial capital accumulation. Self-ownership, probabilistic certainty, and corporate risk management continued to hang together.[57]

Furthermore, the farmer entered into the Travelers' risk communities. By 1885, the company had devised ten classes of "accident risks" ranging from "preferred" to "extra special hazardous," all based upon occupation. The "farmer or farm laborer" fell into the "special" class, the fourth-most hazardous. This meant the farmer's "accident risk" was the same as the "Captain of a vessel or Steamer on Great American lakes" or the "Rail-end Stocker" in a Bessemer Steel Works. An actuarial commensurability brought the western farmer into the same risk community as the Colorado miner or the Northern Pacific Railroad engine-man. Any distinction between independent farmer and dependent industrial wage laborer collapsed. Indeed, the Travelers spoke of the "perils of western mining" in the same breath as the perils of western farm mortgaging. An actuarial equality, as it were, replaced the Jeffersonian vision of a widespread, egalitarian distribution of landed property.[58]

The final foundation of landed independence was the farm household's control over what crops went into the ground. Here a further market-driven dynamic worked itself out. Capital hungered for wheat and despite incipient soil exhaustion and an onslaught of insects and crop diseases western farmers were tempted by wheat monoculture in the 1880s. Less frequently, farmers found security in traditional commercial safety-first practices, including subsistence production at the margin. Perplexed by, if not fearful of, the whims of the world market and a volatile, perilous natural world west of the 100th meridian, many farmers turned to new modes of statistical prediction—spawning further frontiers for the insurance principle.

According to contemporary accounts, mortgaged farmers in the 1880s were more likely to practice monoculture, the "single-crop" or "all-wheat" system. On the nineteenth-century frontier the normal sequence had been for households to move from initial monoculture to a more diversified basket of goods intended for both market exchange and home consumption. After the Civil War, the practice continued along the western edge of the wheat belt. In the 1880s, however, this logic was losing its grip, at least according to the labor commissioners of Minnesota, South Dakota, and Nebraska, and many observers in Iowa and Kansas. The balloon payments due on the final years of mortgages applied great pressure. The harvest in the year before the note came due was a make or break moment. Oftentimes, all possible acreage was devoted to wheat. Crop rotations were also sacrificed. In Wisconsin, a farmer wearily observed that there was "plowing and seeding every year." What was the point of minding future soil fertility if the foreclosed farmer no longer owned the farm?[59]

The result was heightened regional specialization: the "corn belt" of Iowa and Illinois; continuing wheat production on the Great Plains; and dairy farming in Minnesota and Wisconsin. Historians dispute the postbellum western farmer's degree of specialization. It does seem that the nature of diversification, where it continued to be practiced, changed. Instead of mixing a variety of subsistence items with a singular market good, farmers were now more likely to diversify within a wider batch of market goods. Farming itself became a series of offsetting market actions.[60]

In the 1880s western farmers fueled a regional, national, and even global feedback loop of competitive pressure. In the state of Massachusetts price convergence in farm products dated to the early years of the republic. By 1890 the price of wheat in Chicago, New York, and Liverpool had nearly converged. Western grains pushed all of American agriculture towards specialization. Noting a continuation of antebellum trends, the Connecticut Labor Bureau's 1889 report on mortgaged farming—a striking complement to the Connecticut Insurance Department's 1889 report on its financial corporations' investments in western farm mortgages—noted the inability of the "rocky hillsides of Connecticut" to compete with the "fertile prairies of the West" in grains. The "contagious spirit of manufacturing" consequently dominated Connecticut's economy. Landowners now functioned as "real estate dealers" rather than "farmers." Those farms that continued to produce specialized in fruits, vegetables, and dairy goods. The report added that abandoned farms were being sold in small lots to industrial wage laborers who "desire a little land for cultivation." It was now industrial wage workers in other words, not farmers, who engaged in marginal subsistence production as a hedge against their economic lives. Boutwell, retired from his stint as Treasury secretary, described the dynamic in an 1878 essay for the *Massachusetts Ploughman*. He announced that the farmer's chief problem was now "to produce a given quantity at the least cost." In light of western competition dairy farming was the only "certain . . . source of revenue" for the Massachusetts farmer. So much for the "certainty of a competence," which Boutwell had juxtaposed to the "anxiety" of "commerce" in Concord, Massachusetts less than three decades ago.[61]

The American South was similarly transformed. The number of southern acres given over to cotton production actually surged after the Civil War. The flood of western grains filled the gap. The "all-wheat" system fit together with the proverbial "all-cotton" system as Henry Ise's southern counterparts, black sharecroppers and white yeomen, shifted their acreage away from subsistence goods to cotton. There was it seems a national psychological dynamic at work. As a Georgia newspaper editorialized:

> We can tell a man who has corn enough a mile off. The corn man cocks his hat one side and swings along at an easy stride. The "no corn" man has his hat pulled over his eyes and shambles along with a slouching gait and a side-long look as if he expected every minute for someone to sing out, "I know what ails you, you haven't corn enough to last until May."

After the Civil War, the western mortgage market helped strip an existential sense of security and certainty from American agriculture. Here was another depiction of a loss of personal autonomy and control: the slouching gait of the southern farmer with all of his acres in the cultivation of cotton.[62]

"Independence," a young Henry Ise proclaimed, was as much an existential feeling as an objective economic fact. It was the feeling that one was responsible for one's own future and could control it, and that the Ise family, rather than its mortgage or anyone or anything else, was the master of its destiny. Instead, according to John Ise, western farming to his father constituted "years of anxiety." The Ises' dependence upon markets had become existential—a distinct peril of the liberal ideal of self-ownership in practice. The problem with plains farming, to repeat Rosie's mantra, was that "Nobody's responsible." The Ises felt they worked hard year after year. Regardless, the world market fluctuated, sometimes radically. In 1888, the price of corn dropped dramatically, so much so that the Ises, rather than selling it, fattened up their live-stock. In 1890 drought came, the price of corn rose 300 percent and the animals starved. Certainly the western farmer's fate had become inter-dependent with the wheat crops of Canada, Argentina, India, and Po-land. To many farmers, to pin down the mortgage as an external agent was to put a name, if not a face, on an increasingly global economic chance-world.[63]

Of course there had long been forces outside the farmer's control. But the old perils of drought, flood, and insect now took on a different mean-ing. The subsequent losses—grasshoppers assaulted western farmers in the late 1870s, followed by cinch bugs and hessian flies—were not the same on a mortgaged farm, as the world market connected the Argentine drought with the Kansas beetle. "All the uncertainties of the weather, crops and prices had been borne with heavier weight," John Ise recalled of the family mortgage. Carleton's "Tramp's Story" began: *"Worm or Beetle—drought or tempest—on a farmer's land may fall; But for first-class ruination, trust a mortgage 'gainst them all."* It was as if the risks of the economic chance-world constituted a new element in a world of un-controllable natural factors.[64]

To many, religious thinking proved incapable of making sense of the new contingencies. Rosie Ise had particular difficulty squaring her reli-gious beliefs with the western farmer's predicament. One evening a prominent evangelical minister and his wife visited the Ise household. Over supper, Rosie blurted out a question. Why would God ever bring drought? The minister stammered a nonanswer and Rosie pressed. Surely, the Ises had done their part, working hard and living right. The minister said something about minding one's responsibilities and hav-ing faith in God. Greatly embarrassing her husband, Rosie blurted out again that God was failing them. She was especially anxious for the starving farm animals and her worried children. The minister's wife re-minded Rosie that God had sent drought to smite the farmer's pride.

One must not rebel against His will. Whether or not it was the will of God at the helm, to Rosie the ruling source was no rational, let alone ethical, agent. As she looked around her the business of western farming simply made no sense. Certainly to her, confidence and faith in the ways of providence rang empty.[65]

What if the economic chance-world—with no ground for the farmer to stand upon outside of it—dispensed ill fates? George K. Holmes, the chief statistician of the 1890 census mortgage survey, queried the responsibility of the failed Kansas farmer:

> Did the mortgage cause his misfortune, or was it a miscalculation of the "bounty of Providence"? Again, by way of question, is a mortgage ever a cause of misfortune, except secondarily through the borrower's want of prescience or through his inability properly to manage the borrowed wealth?

"Providence" was now in quotation marks. In the hands of this statistician—a profession born a half century earlier—even the potential "bounty of Providence" was subject to calculation. But where was the line to be drawn between the farmer's moral responsibility and those forces outside of his control? Holmes had no answer. But in contrast to the antebellum years, there were now few celebrations of the farmer's divinely secured "independence."[66]

The farmer would have to turn elsewhere—namely to further applications of probabilistic certainty and the insurance principle. In this era, there arose a new field of scientific judgment called "forecasting": market forecasting; crop forecasting; weather forecasting. All shared a family resemblance and the model field of application for each was actuarial science. Given the new logic of American agriculture, farmers needed, in fact demanded, new forms of certainty, security, predictability, and control.[67]

For the farmer the volatility in price for a single crop now carried great consequences. Farmers could turn to the new business of market forecasting. In 1881, for instance, a self-described Ohio farmer named Samuel Benner began to yearly publish the massively popular *Benner's*

Prophecies of Future Ups and Downs in Prices. Benner proposed that prices moved according to the "ways of an inscrutable providence," newly revealed however by his "compilation of average prices" which were basically slapdash statistical inferences. Nothing in the universe happened by "chance," Benner promised, and everything by some scientific "law which will shortly be solved."[68]

New efforts at "crop forecasting" dovetailed with the new business of "crop insurance." Already in 1851, a Cincinnati merchant had proposed that it was the "uncertainty of a crop" that "compelled the farmer to pursue a multifarious system of husbandry." This had the disadvantage of preventing the commercial farmer from "reaping the full benefits of a division of labor." The merchant asked:

> Might not this be remedied in part by extending the principles of Insurance to farming operations? Why should not the farmer be protected against the destructive season, as well as the house owner against fire, or the merchant against the damages of the river? In short, why should there not be a crop insurance?

Indeed, drawing from the new field of crop forecasting, which flourished privately but also within the new U.S. Department of Agriculture (USDA), the first fleeting attempts at commercial crop insurance appeared during the 1880s.[69]

Likewise, a national system of scientific "weather forecasting" emerged after the Civil War. In 1851, the same Cincinnati merchant also spoke of the "immense losses" occasioned by the "fickle-ness of the seasons." The weather was a cause "beyond human control." But when "reasonable progress" was made in the new field of "meteorology," the "farmer will sow with a great certainty of reaping." The origins of scientific weather forecasting—a different tradition than that embodied in the long-enduring farmer's almanac—were actually on the high seas. But in 1870 Congress founded a National Weather Service, a grid of local weather observation posts relaying information by telegraph to Washington. The goal was to publish three eight-hour weather "probabilities" a day for the nation's many climate-specific regions. The benefits to the nation's "commercial interests," noted the head of the new Weather Service, were so obvious they "need not be commented upon." The Weather Service began issuing daily forecasts on February 19, 1871. Daily newspapers soon began to reprint them. The daily weather forecast was born.[70]

Many agricultural societies had been demanding a land-based system of weather forecasting ever since the 1850s. In the 1870s, the Weather Service began to publish agriculturally specific weather bulletins, predicting the likelihoods of frosts, hail storms, or tornadoes. A "flag system" relayed the weather "probabilities" from urban centers to rural locations. (A red flag with a black square in the center, for instance, indicated the "probability of stormy or dangerous weather.") In the 1880s, railroads started to display the weather flags and now farmers could simply watch them roll by. In 1890, Congress moved the National Weather Service into the USDA. In 1908, the Weather Service began to issue what farmers truly wanted, which was "long-range" weather forecasts.[71]

To many, it was another triumph for probabilistic certainty. The Weather Service published a pamphlet in 1885 on "Recent Advances in Meteorology." During the previous twenty-five years, "Many very important laws have recently been deduced theoretically and confirmed by observations and experiment." Meteorology had transformed from a descriptive to a prescriptive "science." In 1880, the Travelers Insurance Company noted that the entire nation had "come to depend upon the daily reports and prognostications with a confidence justified by their general accuracy." Now just about everyone consulted his or her morning newspaper "to see whether to take an umbrella or leave it at home." The Travelers provided its policyholders with pamphlets that decoded the national flag system. To avoid accident any prudent man should consult the weather before planning his day.[72]

No one might value the new "weather forecasting" more than the mortgaged western farmer. In 1896, the *Independent* noted that western weather made mortgaging "full of uncertainties and anxieties." "A single untimely frost may empty [a farmer's] pockets and blast his hopes." West of the 100th meridian, migrating farmers met with natural hazards that only the Old Testament might have prepared them for. Not to mention the grasshoppers, the climate alone was harsher and more volatile than in the East. If it was not draught, it was high winds and heavy rains. In 1879 the *Travelers Record* noted that the "Season of Tornadoes has come again" to the West. But of course loss of life "from a cause which can be neither foreseen nor prevented" was that "for which accident insurance provides."[73]

But now there was also weather insurance itself. During the 1880s new commercial firms developed "tornado," "wind storm," and "hail insurance." By 1889 there was $21 million of such insurance in force. Writing on the subject in 1881 the *Independent* noted that weather insurance was "one of the long-felt wants of the West." By 1890 western states accounted for over 75 percent of tornado insurance in force. In 1892, the president of the Nebraska Farmers' Alliance recommended the "Nebraska Mutual Cyclone and Tornado Insurance Company" to all Alliance members. To the farmer, commercial insurance was proving its "absolute security." Finally, in 1896 the famed actuary of New York's Metropolitan Life Insurance Company, Frederick L. Hoffman, published a small treatise called *Tornadoes and Tornado Insurance* which assembled all available Weather Service statistical records of tornado strikes as far back as 1870 in search of an elusive "law of probability." Quoting a Weather Service meteorologist, Hoffman argued tornadoes were "the result of an accidental condition of the atmosphere," which fit along a probabilistic distribution and could thus be insured for the farmer's benefit.[74]

Taking stock of all of these interconnected transformations, many American farmers declared satisfaction with their commercial lives. They described a feeling of "independence," a new sense of what it meant to be a free and secure actor, rooted in a more market-driven foundation. That foundation, the *Michigan Farmer* declared, only unleashed the farmer's "enterprise," compelling him to "develop his abilities as a business man" and to become more "industrious" and "economical." He would grow more cash crops and become far more rich. Forget the "certainty of a competence." What about striking it rich? This was the audience B. C. Keeler had in mind in 1880 when he published *Where to Go to Become Rich*. "Men are becoming rich there in all branches of farming," Keeler boasted of Kansas. Even Henry Ise once speculated in western town lots although he later regretted doing so. In addition to riches there was an existential thrill—not angst—to be found on the western prairies and plains.[75]

Further, with more cash in hand, there were new financial innovations and modes of prediction for the farmer to take advantage of. All hung together with new techniques of control in the West including novel forms of irrigation, dry farming, and drought-resistant grains. For some, there was a new sense that many of the forces once thought seemingly "beyond human control" could be mastered. Yet, for others none of this was a proper substitute and could never capture the old sense of independence once rooted in land ownership. With money lining his pockets, Henry Ise sat worriedly and anxiously in his chair wondering if he would have enough money on hand when the next note came due.

Whether farming had become better, worse, or simply just different in the decades after the Civil War was a question that finally came into sharp focus in 1890 at the height of the "western farm mortgage" craze, when the Census Bureau sought to quantify the outstanding mortgage debt of American farmers. The effort at quantification itself was emblematic of the rising epistemological authority of statistics. But the terms of the debate alone revealed the loss of *landed* independence. That is, if the farmer was to be called "independent" it now meant something completely different from before.

The 1890 census project was initiated by Keeler, author of *Where to Go to Become Rich*. By 1890 he saw things differently. Now president of the Western Economic Association of St. Louis, he wrote a circular entitled "Farm Mortgages" and subsequently distributed 2,000 copies. Because of mortgage debt, he argued, "farmers and other producers of the country do not obtain an equitable share of the wealth which they create." Keeler called upon his readers to demand a census count of what percentage of citizens actually owned their farms and how much of them they owned. The Census Bureau later reported a flood of petitions from "Single Tax Clubs, Knights of Labor assemblies, and farmer's and workingmen's associations" having adopted Keeler's language word for word. Senator Eugene Hale of Maine, chairman of the Committee on the Census, commissioned a special taskforce. Findings trickled out in late 1890, and in 1895 the Census issued a 921-page final report.[76]

The *Report of Real Estate Mortgages in the United States* counted 4.6 million farms, averaging 137 acres each, and found that 28.9 percent of all taxable farm acreage was encumbered with mortgage debt. The national percentage of mortgaged acreage was 16.67 percent. Mortgage debt had increased by 41.54 percent since 1880, mostly due to an increase in the numbers west of the Mississippi. Kansas and Nebraska were the most heavily mortgaged states and the only ones to surpass the 50 percent mark of mortgaged acreage. The average interest rate on mortgages was 7.36 percent, ranging from 10.9 percent in Arizona to 5.44 percent in Massachusetts. The average life of a mortgage was 4.54 years and the average loan $1,032. It was found that 89.82 percent of all debt was for land purchases or farm improvements.[77]

Such was the quantitative picture of American farm mortgage debt but the interpretation of its significance was another matter. The statistician George K. Holmes, charged with managing the census count, read a paper before the American Statistical Association in early 1890 setting out the task before him. He was already skeptical whether numbers alone could address the real question at hand: "What if the county containing the most prosperous people in a state has also the largest per capita mortgage debt, or the largest ration of debt valuation?" The more exact the collection of numbers the better but the figures alone could not get to the root of the issue. Indeed, the Census Bureau's findings were cited as compelling evidence on all sides of the debate over what conclusions to draw from the census count.[78]

This debate revealed two things. First, "independence" and "dependence"—along with a series of other cognates evoking a sharp binary—were still the standards for evaluating the western farmer's commercial life. The spectrum of possibilities to be found between these two poles, the subtle network of abstract financial interdependence that underlay the system, was missing. Furthermore, the farmer's purported independence, if it did indeed exist, was no different in kind than the independence of any other successful proprietary capitalist. That is, the farmer's independence was now based on his successful pursuit of a money income.

The debate was in fact carried on by two ships passing in the night. The Kansas Republican paper *The Atchison Daily Champion,* for instance, examined Holmes's preliminary numbers and concluded that the mortgage debt was neither "burdensome" nor "oppressive." Chicago's *Daily Inter Ocean* likewise concluded that western farmers were "comparatively free from debt." The *Milwaukee Journal* headlined its story on the subject as "Farmers are prosperous. More than half their lands without encumbrance of any kind." Meanwhile, the *St. Louis Republic* claimed that the Census found that eastern money-lenders had "a force of nearly two and a half million men" in the west working under a system worse than African slavery.[79]

And so the census count resolved nothing. There was no more clarity than during the 1870s and 1880s when disgruntled mortgaged farmers called themselves slaves, serfs, tenants, and hirelings—anything but "mortgaged farmers"—while champions of the western mortgage market referred to farmers as wonderfully "independent." In addressing farmers' descriptions of their dependent status, W. F. Mappin responded in the 1889 *Political Science Quarterly* by disputing claims that "the independent small farmer in the United States is in danger of extinction" because of mortgage debt. Look only at "how much of the capital invested in manufacturing was borrowed." The sum was even greater than in agriculture. Debt, in other words, was a necessary reality of any successful proprietary capitalist enterprise. Yes, western farming required an "energetic" people willing to take on "risk." But in the end western farmers were "their own employers." To compare them to "factory wage-workers" was a categorical mistake. There was difficulty reaching any common conclusions regarding western mortgages precisely because of the overriding desire to determine if farmers were either "independent" or "dependent," once stable concepts which now only generated confusion and obfuscation.[80]

Tellingly, the most widely circulated analysis of the census figures was a piece that appeared in the 1894 *Forum* written by Edward Atkinson and entitled "The True Meaning of Farm Mortgage Statistics." This was the same, now aged, Edward Atkinson who had been a Free Soil abolitionist, a funder of John Brown, a Boston textile industrialist, and an original trustee of the Freedman's Bank. During the Civil War Atkinson had found himself in the Union-occupied Sea Islands of South Carolina. Thwarting the freedpeople's desire for land and abhorring their preference for raising subsistence crops, Atkinson had insisted that they work for wages, grow cotton exclusively (for export to the northern mills), subsist off western grains, and save their money in the Freedman's Bank in order to manage their own futures. Tellingly, by 1894 this leading nineteenth-century liberal had also come around to the probabilistic worldview. Moving from industry to finance he became the president of the Boston Insurance Company, as well as a leading member of the American Statistical Association. Finally, Atkinson was a Republican gold bug and an influential amateur economist and public intellectual. In 1894 he looked west and, in spite of the agrarian protest, saw the fulfillment of freedom's promise.[81]

Atkinson concluded that "the burden of farm mortgages is a very light one." He first noted, correctly, that the surge in mortgage debt in the 1880s mirrored the diminishment of the national debt incurred during the Civil War. That war debt was first recycled into western railroad bonds but after the panic of 1873 it had fled into the new western mortgage market. The war for the "principle of personal liberty" produced much "useful capital," creating so many new western homesteads. The postbellum decades, Atkinson happily noted, had featured "a more rapid accumulation of capital than had ever before occurred in this country."[82]

But when Atkinson looked at the farm mortgage statistics he judged that there was no "class in this country" that was "so free of debt" and "so absolutely independent as the Western farmers of the grain-growing states." Despite the recent bust of eastern mortgage companies, American homesteads were actually underutilized as collateral. Atkinson was evaluating western farming as if it were a business like his own. He knew what it was like to be in debt. Never mind the "few shallow and discontented persons who prate about cheap money."[83]

Atkinson's essay was actually written as a rejoinder to another geriatric abolitionist, Daniel Goodloe. Goodloe was a native of North Carolina but also a Republican and a prolific journalist and writer as well. Writing in the *Forum,* Goodloe had previously invoked emancipation by calling mortgaged farming a new form of slavery. To Atkinson, the land was just another capital asset. To Goodloe, Free Soil was an ideology in which land had not only economic and existential significance but also profound social and political importance: the old Jeffersonian dream of a

landed, commercial republic. "The tiller of the soil," Goodloe had reminded, "has been the ideal American citizen." But that world no longer
existed and the mortgaged farmer was essentially forced to engage in
"speculation." With the new basis of American farming, Goodloe explained, "If the crop fails, or if the price of the product, or of the articles
in which he deals or speculates, falls suddenly, he is ruined, and the
mortgage must be foreclosed." Farming had become a "risky business."
Atkinson's response was, in effect, what business was not?[84]

The polemic between Goodloe and Atkinson guaranteed that such
heated binaries as freedom and slavery obscured any adequate view of
the complex, abstract nature of new financial forms of social interdependence. Corporate risk management generated a whole new material and
psychological reality that many observers at the time could not quite
find the right conceptual vocabulary to account for.

Of course, this was not only a conceptual problem. It was also a momentous political conflict that culminated in the failure of the Populist Revolt
in the presidential election of 1896. Mortgage debt was at the center of that
revolt, warranting the abolition of the deflationary gold standard and the
subsequent expansion of the money supply, which was supposed to reduce the farmer's debt burden. Many agrarians were more than capable of
blaming human agents for their plight—bankers, middlemen, railroad
executives, corrupt politicians. Agrarian populism also drew from late
nineteenth-century agrarian attempts at cooperative and fraternal, noncommercial mutual insurance and storage schemes. But many agrarians,
for their countermovement, began to look to the federal government.[85]

And so, on the one hand Populism looked back to the ideal of landed
independence while on the other it anticipated the federal government's
twentieth-century role as a guarantor of the citizenry's economic security. It was not a coincidence that farmers, many of whom had enjoyed a
nonmarket hedge against their commercial lives longer than other groups
within the American population, were the first to turn to the federal government once that hedge was lost. Regardless, landed independence had
given way to the world market. A successful Populism might have changed
the terms of that engagement but it did not have the tools to end it, assuming that it would have wanted to. After 1870 a bridge in American
agriculture had been burned.[86]

What that meant was that in the aftermath of the panic of 1893 and the collapse of the western mortgage market there was no possibility of a flight to safety outside the financial system—the way that farmers, even slave holders, had once recoiled after the panic of 1837. After 1896, however, with the agrarian revolt going up in smoke, the world market turned. The prices offered for American farm staples soared. By 1908, as the USDA noted, "the farmers of the mortgage-ridden state of Kansas of former days have stuffed the banks of that state full of money." The irony was that in Atkinson's industrial East, the depression of the 1890s pulled the rug out from under individual proprietorship, clearing the way for the corporate dominance of the industrial sector. Meanwhile, in the second decade of the twentieth century western farm proprietors entered the so-called Golden Age of American agriculture. Soon the wheel of the world market would turn yet again and the Golden Age begat the Dust Bowl.[87]

CHAPTER 6

Fraternity in the Age of Capital

A human being has a life to live, a career to run. . . . what his
chances may be . . . what his fortune may be, whether to suffer
major or little—are questions of his personal destiny which he must
work out and ensure as he can. . . . The great stream of time and
earthly things will sweep on just the same in spite of us.
—William Graham Sumner, *What Social Classes*
Owe to Each Other (1883)

IN 1865, JOHN UPCHURCH—in search of something like a "personal
destiny" to quote William Graham Sumner—quit his job as a master
mechanic on the Erie Railroad and set out for the oil regions of western
Pennsylvania. From there Upchurch was ideally placed to take into view
the enormously speculative economy of the postbellum United States.
Ida Tarbell, who spent her childhood in the oil regions, would later
write in *The History of Standard Oil Company* of the presence of so
many gamblers and speculators there at the time, all hoping to land a big
strike—men whose ears were "attuned to Fortune's call, and who had
the daring and the energy to risk everything." Upchurch himself had
caught the "oil excitement." He hoped to "soon make a fortune."[1]

It was not Upchurch's personal destiny to strike black gold. He did
however strike up a conversation with an old army captain concerning
the "relations in the country between capital and labor." He claimed it
was then that he hatched a new idea. Done with oil, he departed for the
nearby railroad hub of Meadville and proceeded to found the Ancient
Order of United Workmen (AOUW).[2]

The AOUW was not a labor union but rather a new kind of legally chartered nonprofit corporation—a "fraternal society." Mutual aid, in some organized form or another, was of course not new. But the three decades after the Civil War were a great era of fraternal organization, the so-called "Golden Age of Fraternity." Masonic and Odd Fellow lodges abounded, singing the praises of fraternity. The Noble and Holy Order of the Knights of Labor, a labor union founded in 1869, was a self-declared fraternal organization, as was the agrarian National Grange of the Order of Patrons of Husbandry, founded in 1867. Unlike them, the chief function of the AOUW (chartered in 1868) and the many fraternal societies created in its image was to remove economic security from the evolving American corporate financial system and to secure it instead through the active solidarity of the fraternal social bond. The AOUW offered its members benefits in the downside events of death, sickness, disability, or even sometimes unemployment—anything that prevented a man from being able to use his productive labor to support himself and his familial dependents. The bonds of "fraternity," like the bonds of family affection, were said to be noncommercial in kind—a new fraternal, rather than paternal, instantiation of the benevolent (rather than insurance) principle.[3]

In the wake of the financial panic of 1873, a nationwide fraternal movement arose with the specific aim of challenging corporate risk management. The new fraternalism was as novel as the financial practice of self-insurance. Departing from more local traditions of mutual aid, the AOUW for instance was a highly organized national institution. Yet, drawing from putatively timeworn communal longings, fraternal societies like the AOUW sought to decommodify risk. Fraternalism was a new collective strategy to cope with the insecurities of industrial capitalism. As the corporate financial system reeled from the panic of 1873, fraternal brothers launched yet another countermovement.

The new fraternalism was a rearguard action against the high tide of nineteenth-century liberalism, enunciated in pristine form by the Yale professor Sumner's 1883 *What Social Classes Owe to Each Other.* Sumner marshaled the rising probabilistic worldview into a pitiless gospel of personal risk—compatible with dependence upon corporate risk management, as it sanctified the emergent, class-stratified, urban industrial order. It was in this context that millions of Americans raised the benevolent banner of fraternalism.

A man's "personal destiny," Sumner wrote, was something "he must work out and ensure as he can." The only function for the State was to ensure "the conditions or chances under which the pursuit of happiness is carried on." Men "must make themselves happy in their own way, and at their own risk."[4] Life, as it were, at your own risk—and if there was any doubt as to the virtues of this ethos, Sumner wrote in 1883 "an instance right at hand of:"

> The negroes, once slaves in the United States, used to be assured care, medicine, and support; but they spent their efforts, and other men took the products. They have been set free. That means only just this; they now work and hold their own products, and are assured of nothing but what they earn. In escaping from subjection they have lost claims. Care, medicine, and support they get, if they can earn it. Will any one say that the black men have not gained? Will any one deny that individual black men may seem worse off? Will any one allow such observations to blind him to the true significance of the change?[5]

Pointing to slave emancipation, Sumner celebrated the brave new world of capitalism and risk. He declared that what "social classes owe to each other" was essentially nothing. If as old social hierarchies perished, individual pursuits of personal destinies led to the future evolution of distinct new "social classes," then so be it.

As for the moral texture of the future, in the wake of the Civil War the aftershock of Charles Darwin's 1859 *On the Origin of Species* continued to transform providentialist beliefs. To some intellectuals the cosmos came out of the evolutionary wash looking not only more chancy, but also rudderless, bereft of any external, transcendent authority. But one strain of evolutionary-influenced thought, reflected the philosopher John Dewey, "inherited all the goods of Divine Providence." To many thinkers Darwin had posited "chance" or "accident" in the "struggle for existence" as the new transcendent, first cause in the universe. In the "old problem" between "design *versus* chance" design still lurked. Sumner, who never claimed the mantle of Darwin himself, reassured that "God and Nature have ordained the chances and conditions of life on earth once for all." Sumner's "chances and conditions" just turned out to be the evolutionary tendencies of an industrializing capitalist economy.[6]

But Summer also meant "chances" as in the law of large numbers. Man was learning the "laws of Nature," he wrote, reducing the sphere of "accident" and "chance" to "computations." Statistical induction was of course the basis of an expanding actuarial science. As Frederick Hoffman, the most prominent actuary of the generation to follow Elizur Wright explained, the "struggle for existence" was the stuff from which the "law of average" was made—a law that "governs the life of men, and things, and events, and all that there is in the world, and all that there ever will be." The epistemological authority of probabilistic certainty would provide all the stability, certainty, and security that a liberal social order would ever need.[7]

Upchurch was not an intellectual. It is doubtful whether he had ever heard of Darwin when he departed from Oil City, although perhaps he too pondered the metaphysical dilemma of design versus chance. Nonetheless, fraternalism, whose fertile soil was small urban centers like Meadville, Pennsylvania, and Poughkeepsie, New York—not ivory towers like New Haven or sprawling metropolises like New York City—rejected Sumner's moral vision. Fraternal members did not want to leave economic security to the putatively evolutionary financial logic of capitalism. And at first fraternal brothers did not trust the new standard of probabilistic certainty. According to another founding father of the AOUW, M. W. Sackett, the early members "believed actuaries to be false scientists." "Scientific deductions" were then associated with the "cunning subterfuge of the Life Insurance Companies by which to enhance the profits of their business." A member of another fraternal doubted that "morality experience" could ever be reduced to "law."[8]

To the fraternals, Sackett recalled, "Life Insurance" was "looked upon as speculation." The panic of 1873 leveled not only working-class savings banks but also a bevy of commercial life insurance corporations.

Upchurch had no problem with speculation. He would have agreed with many at the time, including Sumner, that individual commercial risk-taking was much of what it meant to be free. Never was that ideal more in vogue than in the boom-and-bust economy of Gilded Age America. A man had a right to risk his own capital—if he did not have any then his own productive labor—and state and society must give him a wide berth to do so. What Upchurch and millions of other Americans did not want was the economic security of their households subject to the economic chance-world. More specifically than that, they did not trust financiers to take speculative risks with wealth they had devoted to their own economic security.[9]

The fraternal social bond would replace the insurance principle. Fraternal societies relied upon the "assessment system." When a member died, fell ill, was injured, or was unemployed members were charged an equal, *ex post facto* assessment to fund an individual benefit. Fraternity in this era was not exactly warm and fuzzy, and had ample room for racism, sexism, xenophobia, and outright fraud. But it was still a complete rejection of the abstract social logic of the insurance principle. "A society based on contract," Sumner generalized in *What Social Classes Owe to Each Other,* "gives the utmost room and chance for individual development, and for all the self-reliance and dignity of a free man." In a fraternal society there was no financial "risk" for sale. There was no double commodification. "We make no contract," declared a leading fraternal, the Royal Arcanum, in 1886. The fraternal society was a decommodified risk community.[10]

The twin rejection of actuarial science and contract actually went hand in hand. Actuarial premiums and the legal obligations of contract meant that commercial corporations had to accumulate large reserves of finance capital. It was those reserves that many firms speculated away while busting during the 1870s, clearing the ground for the rise of fraternalism. To Sumner, if not a providential design, there was a progressive *telos* to human evolution. "How has change been brought about?" he asked. "The answer is, by capital." "The reason why man is not altogether a brute is because he has learned to accumulate capital." The fraternals, by definition, accumulated no capital whatsoever. Ultimately, a new regime of financial capital accumulation was what was at stake in the Golden Age of Fraternity.[11]

In the final two decades of the nineteenth century, the insurance principle and the spirit of fraternalism engaged in what looked a lot like a Darwinian struggle for existence. The fraternals accumulated a staggering number of new members. Emerging almost out of whole cloth in the 1870s, by 1890 the fraternals had an estimated $58.10 of "insurance in force per capita" (they would have rejected the description "insurance") compared to $54.09 by the commercial firms. In 1890, the National Fraternal Congress estimated that 1.25 million fraternal "certificates" (not contracts) were in existence and that in 1889 fraternals had distributed over $20 million in benefits. A later scholarly estimate hazards that in 1890, 36 percent of the adult white male population held at least one fraternal certificate. Given that the fraternals had little reach in the countryside, the urban percentage must have been much higher.[12]

Meanwhile, insurance corporations—who did, recall, reach farmers—began to recover from the panic of 1873. Reaching more and more Americans through new-fangled policy schemes, during the 1880s the corporate risk management complex began to accumulate a staggering amount of finance capital. From $284 million of assets in 1870, the industry held $1.2 billion by 1895 (which more than doubled over the next ten years). The Gilded Age financial sector accordingly swelled. The financial interrelations ratio, or the percentage of financial assets to tangible assets, climbed from 0.47 in 1850, to 0.64 in 1875, to 0.71 in 1895. Further, a considerable percentage of this growth came from the expanding reserves of financial intermediaries, most prominently commercial life insurance corporations. The ratio of assets of financial intermediaries to all financial assets climbed from 12.5 in 1850, to 13.6 in 1875, to 20.0 in 1895.[13] Finance capital not only accumulated but also concentrated on Wall Street. Slowly firms began to move funds from the western farm mortgage market to the market in railroad bonds and industrial securities, fueling the modern American capital market in the process and capitalizing industrialization—which was why so many men were newly turning to either the insurance principle or the fraternal bond to begin with.

For the security of their families, would these men turn to the insurance principle or the spirit of fraternalism? Fraternal societies and insurance corporations engaged in a rhetorical struggle over the very meaning and adequate economic basis of security/certainty. But ultimately the question became a subject for the courts, which were forced to decide whether a fraternal pledge constituted a legally binding contract. The answer determined the fate of the fraternal countermovement.

At first the corporate life insurance industry had weathered the panic of 1873. In October 1873, a month after Jay Cooke & Co. imploded, the pro-industry *Insurance Times* declared "Secure Amidst Panic." For "when stocks of various descriptions tumble in price daily; when bank after bank closes. . . . Well, my life policies are still left, they are secure." Security existed because of probabilistic certainty. The "foundations are unchangeable." "Science has done her perfect work." The March 1874 *Christian Union*—edited by Henry Ward Beecher, a self-professed convert to Darwin's ideas—noted that the commercial world was engulfed in a "stormy sea," and that some "men are not as lucky as ships." But the "very uncertainty of business affairs" makes "life insurance valuable to everybody." Only the certitudes of science could face down the economic chance-world.[14]

But it turned out actuarial life insurance had become not only a victim, but also an agent of financial volatility. Between 1868 and 1877 ninety-eight commercial life companies closed for business and thirty-two failed outright, creating $35 million in losses. Between 1872 and 1880 the amount of commercial life insurance in the United States diminished by half. By 1877 the same *Insurance Times* bemoaned "the storm" now passing over the entire industry. "Public confidence" was "alarmed and shaken" because of the "too speculative investments" of assets.[15]

The shore was littered with wrecked insurance corporations. The *New York Times* looked to its city's firms and declared "the speculative element" to be "much too apparent," with capital reserves subject to "the risks incident" to "all the speculative contingencies of Wall Street and the stock exchange." The failure of Hartford's Charter Oak was the largest of the era. The firm had a cash deposit with a New York commercial bank, a conduit for purchasing financial assets disallowed by its charter. The bank failed in 1875 and the Charter Oak lost $1 million, only for it its president to abscond to Canada with another $2 million. A graying Elizar Wright—whose 1850s actuarial calculations after all were responsible for companies' large capital reserves—bemoaned in the press that speculation was ruining self-insurance.[16]

In truth, the large majority of life insurance policyholders had survived unscathed. In 1878, an industry advocate estimated that firms had only defaulted on 1 percent of their policies. Not a bad estimate— granted that life companies defaulted on $35 million from 1868 to 1877, it was still not quite 2 percent of the $2 billion of insurance in force in 1871. And not all companies failed because of speculative investment strategies.[17]

But public perception told its own story. There was a life insurance "panic" in 1876. In light of all the failures, a New York pamphlet entitled "Life Insurance Robbery" proposed that the government take over for the "greedy speculators." Later, the president of the Prudential Insurance Company would look back upon the late 1870s as a time when there was "very little faith in insurance principles." Many looked upon actuarial insurance as a "form of speculation or even as a game of chance." In 1877, noted actuary Sheppard Homans lamented in the pages of the *North American Review* that there was even distrust of the law of large numbers. All this when life insurance "more than any other business, depends upon confidence, both present and future."[18]

Distrust was so rampant that the larger firms demanded state examinations to restore public confidence in their solvency. New York conducted an investigation into the entire industry in 1877. But when the president of the Equitable of New York, Henry Hyde, was asked to defend the company's valuations of their policies he responded that, "There are certain fundamental rule[s] . . . which can only be understood by actuaries, and it is impossible for me to go into that here." Ultimately the certainty was in the science. In 1877, the *Insurance Times* summed up what would remain the linchpin of commercial life insurance's self-presentation:

> The science of the Actuary is just as important and indispensible to a life company as that of navigation to the safety of a ship at sea. Not a few of our life companies which have been wrecked would have been saved if the warning decision of the Actuary had been heeded and obeyed.

The actuary was the "navigator" who foresaw movement, not over the high seas but over homogenous, abstract units of time. Within the moral landscape of the future, the economic chance-world was uncertain, but the law of large numbers was not. Like the eye of God before, science clearly foresaw, in the contingent link between present and future, movements that were necessary, unconditioned, and perfect. All that was necessary was for the mass of Americans to buy into this vision.[19]

In the late 1870s and early 1880s they did not. Only in the late 1880s did the amount of commercial life insurance in force return to its pre–1873 level. Meanwhile fraternalism exploded. Upchurch founded the AOUW in 1868. But of the twenty-five largest fraternals in 1890, twenty-two were either founded or inaugurated their benefit schemes in the seven years after the life insurance "panic" of 1876 (see Table 3 in Appendix).[20]

The timing alone speaks for itself. Many commentators on nineteenth-century American fraternalism see in it the unique impulse towards voluntary association in American civil society.[21] Yet the Golden Age of Fraternity had a very specific trigger. In the wake of the panic of 1873, it was a countermovement against corporate risk management. That at least was how the fraternals made sense of themselves. An early founder of the AOUW believed the order took off when commercial insurance corporations lost "millions and millions of the people's money." The American Legion of Honor condemned the "bad investment and speculation" of the commercial firms—"they take risks wantonly, and many of them have been ruined in consequence." Whereas in a fraternal society assessments were paid only as needed, "under a system where there are no accumulations to be squandered" and in which there was "no temptation to speculation." An 1885 pamphlet of the AOUW bragged over its lack of a "Reserve Fund." Voicing a common fraternal argument, the *ex post facto* assessment system meant that fraternal funds were "safe in the pockets of our membership" and "out of the reach of speculative fingers." In 1888 the Royal Arcanum summed it all up. It characterized the man who purchased a commercial policy: "He has entered into a *speculation,* and has taken his chances." The fraternal order asked, "Is it not folly to speculate for an uncertainty when greater results can positively be obtained, without risk?"[22]

In 1890, N. S. Boynton of the Knights of the Maccabees explained that fraternalism shunned everything that "smacks a little of the speculative—just a little of the speculative." This at first included actuarial science. But it also included the issues most dear to Wright's heart: policy lapses; secondary market "assignments"; and "surrender values" (or lack thereof). The American Legion of Honor noted that "Mr. Wright holds out his hope" for industry reform. Still, hundreds of millions of dollars of life insurance accumulations were the forfeited premiums of lapsed policies. Meanwhile, front-loaded level premiums were not a factor in the assessment system, and fraternals explicitly disallowed members from "assigning" certificates. Indeed, Boynton further explained that "insurance" was a "commodity." Insurance corporations "come into the market and make all they can from it." Not so with fraternal societies, for they lacked the "profit motive." Fraternalism was an antifinancial innovation, a decommodifying enterprise.[23]

All together it meant no accumulation of finance capital. Take the American Legion of Honor. In 1883 it counted 51,906 members. According to its own statement, from 1878 through 1883 the benefit fund received and distributed $2,256,740 of assessments. But the net balance of the *entire* fraternal society, the cash on hand, was a mere $563.76. The Mutual Life of New York City, then the largest American insurance corporation, entered that same year with 110,990 policies in force. It reported over $100 million in assets. These figures tell what the Golden Age of Fraternalism was all about.[24]

The trailblazing fraternal order was the AOUW. Founded by Upchurch in 1868 for Erie Railroad workers and chartered as a nonprofit corporation in the state of Pennsylvania, it languished until the panic of 1873. By 1880 it was a truly national organization, with "lodges" in New York, Texas, Oregon, Alabama, and Nebraska, with a total membership of 79,248. The order was open to all white men ages twenty-one to fifty. A member had to be "capable of earning a livelihood" and had to have potential beneficiaries dependent upon his productive labor—"a wife, children, mother, sister, or other relatives or friends." The order was also open to "every man whose homestead or business is . . . encumbered in any way"—even the homesteader whose farm was heavily mortgaged.[25]

A "certificate" in the AOUW was worth $2,000, which became the typical fraternal benefit. The order invented the "assessment system," which was originally Upchurch's idea. When a man joined the AOUW he paid $1 into a "beneficiary fund." Upon a death, each member was "assessed" another $1. The assessment was *equal* irrespective of age. A few other fraternals might charge a member who surpassed age fifty an extra assessment or make some attempt to very roughly grade assessments to age. But there was often outright hostility to the actuarial pricing of "risks" in fraternal ranks during the 1870s and 1880s. In the AOUW the feeling was so intense that at the 1874 meeting of the "Grand Lodge" (the central executive authority of the fraternal), when one member proposed that the order keep statistics of benefits *already* distributed the measure was voted down because it smacked "too much of insurance methods."[26]

The AOUW's 1884 circular bragged that it provided insurance at "actual net cost." There were no "agents, boards of directors, presidents, vice-presidents, or attorneys" to pay. There were no "actuaries" on retainer. It estimated that carrying a $2,000 policy would likely cost around $20 a year, whereas a policy of that value in one of the "old-line" firms would cost $32.68. The perceived affordability in the lean 1870s was not insignificant. With only $1 paid in a man's dependents were suddenly entitled to a $2,000 benefit.[27]

The AOUW had a well-defined, corporate organizational structure. When a state reached 2,000 members it was established as its own separate "beneficiary jurisdiction" and collected its own assessments. Beneficiary jurisdictions still operated under the authority of the Grand Lodge. Beneath them were individual lodges. With some variation, this was the basic operating structure of the fraternal societies: the state-level incorporation; the national or at least translocal character; the federal structure; the assessment system; the openness to white men between ages twenty-one and fifty of all occupations, so long as they earned income on their productive labor from which their dependents subsisted.[28]

But what was the spirit of fraternalism at its core? What was the social logic of this new, decommodified risk community? The "fraternal bond" did share much in common with the insurance principle, including its bedrock premise of self-ownership. Life insurance enlisted a double commodification of the underlying asset of contingent male human capital. If a man possessed no human capital, if he was not able-bodied, he could neither buy a personal insurance policy nor join a fraternal society. After deliberation, in 1877 the Knights of Honor decided that a "man with one arm off" could be admitted to membership, so long as he could find gainful employment. But under the same standard a "blind man" could not. Like the life insurance corporations the fraternal societies demanded medical examinations for what they termed their "risks." Fraternalism did not violate the principle of self-ownership.[29]

The fraternals also embraced the masculinization of productive labor and the family wage. Gender and sex difference were long implicit in the ethos of fraternalism, and the local lodge continued to be a site of male fraternization. Only a few of the leading fraternals offered membership to women or created parallel female orders. In 1893, with far over 1.5 million members, the National Fraternal Congress counted 5,894 female certificates. The fraternal certificate replaced the life insurance policy but it was still premised upon the exclusion of women's work from the category of productive labor.[30]

Following the corporate life insurance industry, fraternals also practiced racial exclusion. In 1880, Dr. Thomas Skinner, a light-skinned African Methodist Episcopal minister and one-time state senator, along with a few other African-Americans successfully passed in a Mississippi lodge of the Knights of Pythias. Once discovered they were kicked out. Racial exclusion in fraternal societies hardly waned with the arrival of Jim Crow. In 1890 the Supreme Lodge of the Knights of Pythias, referring to its previous pronouncements on the subject in 1869, 1871, 1878, 1878, and 1888, reminded its members that it "has never recognized any body of colored persons as . . . members of the Order." A member "*must be a white* person." And, in response to a request for clarification from a western lodge, a "Chinaman" was in fact *not* a "Caucasian."[31]

There did emerge separate black fraternal societies. In 1880, the same Thomas Skinner founded the Colored Knights of Pythias with the same assessment system and the same ritual as the white Pythians. Skinner and others declared that, "since the exclusion of colored men violated the purpose of the order, which was to extend friendship, charity, and benevolence among men, Divine Providence had made it possible for Negroes to acquire the ritual." The black fraternal spread throughout the United States and even into Canada and the Caribbean. There were other prominent translocal black fraternals, and local black mutual-aid societies, often allied with churches and neighborhood organizations, were already common before the fraternal surge. The inclusion and often leadership of women distinguished black fraternals, as they had the black mutual-aid societies of the past. The 1880s and 1890s witnessed significant translocal fraternal activity among African-Americans although a fuller development waited for the turn of the twentieth century.[32]

Not everyone therefore was welcomed within the fraternal circle. But those within it commonly cited personal sentiments of "fraternity," "trust," "friendship," "humanity," "benevolence," and "charity." In its countermovement against risk, the fraternal bond too mobilized communal longings. But the thrust of the fraternal spirit was actually quite modern.

The German sociologist Max Weber was in fact first among the observers of American fraternalism. In the "Protestant Sects and the Spirit of Capitalism," an address delivered to the St. Louis Exposition of 1904, Weber placed the rise of fraternalism in the historical context of the "radical break away from patriarchal and authoritarian bondage." To him, American fraternalism evoked "equality," the "voluntarist principle," and the triumph of "modern individualism." To his mind the fraternals, while a phenomenon of secularization, shared a lineage with the early Protestant sect, the "prototype" fraternal association. For "Sect membership" had once involved "a certificate of moral qualification"— unlike with "membership in a 'church' into which one is 'born' and which lets grace shine over the righteous and the unrighteous alike." In a sect, instead of "proving" himself before God, one proved himself instead "before men." The original religious impulse was fast "decaying" but the sociological form remained. To join an American fraternal society, Weber correctly noted, required that existing members approve of the prospective member's moral worth. In the new fraternalism not the "ethical doctrine" of the "predestinarian Puritans" but the "ethical con-duct" of the Protestant sect persisted.[33]

The upshot was that in a secular, capitalist era men self-consciously looked directly to one another for interpersonal trust and security—not to God. The security of the social order did not filter through a religious conception of the world. Fraternal literature did make vague references to "Divine creators" and "Supreme Beings." But with the exception of the Catholic and Jewish fraternals, most were a-religious. Instead of God's will, they argued that only the fraternal social bond could stand outside the contingent sweep of time. Once again the metaphor of voyage ap-peared: "Republics, empires, and men," the Knights of Pythias explained in 1878, "sink into the dark sea of oblivion." But "the principles of our Ritual are eternal. We treat men as a social being." The Knights of Pythias did not bother with a man's "religious faith." Rather, binding the "har-monious brotherhood of men of all classes and all opinions" was "Friend-ship" and "Benevolence." Their name even derived from the "ancient friendship" between the Romans Damian and Pythias. Tapping com-munal longings, the names of most fraternals likewise connoted a vener-able, timeless, and ancient basis.[34]

It is important to consider more closely the social rituals of fraternal orders because many had existed before they began to issue certificates in the aftermath of 1873. In many instances the fraternal bond pre-dated the fraternal certificate. True, it turned out that in the large ma-jority of fraternals—the AOUW included—the ritual was copped from the Masons and Odd Fellows (organizations who then returned the favor and copped the AOUW's assessment system). But secretive handshakes, regalia, ceremonies, and passwords served a purpose. They were pal-pable, constituted at the face-to-face level of male fraternization. Often the local basis was an ethnocultural identity—the Knights of Honor, for instance, included German lodges. The social logic of the insurance principle was abstract, impersonal, and implicated in the complex and interdependent nature of the evolving financial system. It had a social basis for the law of averages required large numbers to work, and finan-cial intermediation, no matter how complex and abstract, was a form of social life. But the insurance principle operated naturally, passively—

whether the policyholders in a life insurance company liked it or not, they died according to the law of mortality.[35]

As a collective strategy for coping with the perils of industrial capitalism, fraternalism demanded a more active bond, if only due to the nature of the assessment system. In an actuarial life company, a policyholder paid a premium calculated solely to his own age or other personal characteristics. He bargained over the contractual sale of a commodity, his own personal "risk." In a fraternal, assessments were paid only when another member was afflicted. The members had to trust that their brothers would pay up. As Sackett of the AOUW put it, "confidence" in the fraternal bond derived not from "mortality tables"—let alone religious belief—but rather from the spirit of "fraternity."[36]

Nevertheless, in many fraternals the ritual soon gave way to the certificate as the main preoccupation. Take the Knights of Pythias. Initially men gathered to dress, drink, socialize, and engage in all manner of bizarre ritual. At the 1876 national meeting the Minnesota section proposed a "Widows and Orphans Relief Fund" which would adopt the AOUW's assessment system. The proposal was voted down because it smacked of an "insurance scheme." Brother F. P. Dann was so offended at the idea of mixing "pecuniary" motives with fraternalism that he literally tore the proposal to shreds. At the 1877 national meeting the supreme chancellor informed the delegates that if the assessment system was not soon adopted the Knights of Pythias would "cease to exist." Every other fraternal had one. That year the "Endowment Rank" of the Knights of Pythias was born. Brothers in that rank carried certificates and were assessed fees. Brother Dann was right, for by 1880 the Knights had abolished "ritualistic work" as a condition of holding a certificate.[37]

Rooted in local lodges, nevertheless the new fraternal societies were highly organized national institutions. To the most articulate fraternal members, this was what distinguished fraternalism from the long history of more localized forms of friendship, benevolence, and mutual aid. For this reason, Boynton of the Knights of the Maccabees claimed in 1890 that the "grand protective system founded upon fraternity" had only "sprung up within the last quarter of a century." Likewise, A. R. Savage's 1891 presidential address to the National Fraternal Congress explained how fraternalism united men "unknown to each other" across the country. It was simply a product of the times—"before the railroad, the telegraph and the telephone had annihilated space, as well as time, men failed to look beyond the narrow surroundings of their own life, either to seek or offer help." It was only when the "Atlantic was joined to the Pacific by bands of iron and steel" that there sprung forth "from the earth, full armed, this giant of beneficence." Savage did not say that those great bands of iron and steel were increasingly capitalized with funds from the archenemies of the fraternal societies, the commercial life insurance corporations—who in 1890 had $187 million invested in railroad securities.[38]

Finally, for all of its reliance upon interpersonal trust, a fraternal society carried a nonprofit corporate charter. Fraternalism too depended upon the corporate legal form. A friendship between two individuals who might aid each other when in need or a community or neighborhood that took especially good care of its own had no such institutional basis. Not surprisingly the fraternals filed their charters in the friendliest state legal environments. Massachusetts and Pennsylvania in particular were sympathetic to nonprofit corporations, affording them wide latitude. A pamphlet of the American Legion of Honor trumpeted its "legal status" as a nonprofit corporation in Massachusetts. All state insurance commissioners eventually acknowledged the distinct legal status of the fraternals. The AOUW, though first chartered in Pennsylvania, eventually acquired a charter in Kentucky, which had a special filing status for corporations not "pecuniary" in kind and devoted to "mechanical pursuits." Outside Kentucky it acted as an out-of-state corporation.[39]

Section 5 of the AOUW Kentucky charter is revealing. It reads:

> [T]he collecting, management and disbursement of the [beneficiary fund] . . . shall be controlled and regulated by the rules and by-laws of the corporation; and any such fund so provided and set apart shall be exempt from execution, and shall under no circumstances be liable to be seized, taken or appropriated by any legal or equitable process. . . .

The reason to legally incorporate was thus to establish the fraternal certificate as immune from any "legal" process, whether regulatory or judicial. This, in addition to the decommodification impulse, was why the fraternals were originally so careful to assert that a "certificate" was not a "contract," not a "policy of insurance." In some states, without a lodge and ritual fraternals could not file their nonprofit charters. No doubt over time the function of the lodge meeting was less so fraternization and more so to maintain a particular legal status. For an insurance contract meant that disputes over benefits or membership could end up in the courthouses. The 1884 *Digest of the Constitution, Laws, and Decisions of the Ancient Order of United Workmen,* published for distribution to AOUW lodges, clearly informed members that "the word insurance should not be printed in official returns or papers" and that the "Certificate" should never be referred to as a "Contract of Insurance." At first both state legislatures and courthouses granted the fraternal societies their prized self-rule, holding that the fraternal certificate was not a contract. The fraternal bond was therefore not subject to legal enforcement. What this meant, in the end, was that members' beneficiaries received their $2,000 benefit if and when enough assessments rolled in. But whether they did or did not the fraternal society was not legally liable.[40]

Truly, the 1884 *Digest of the Constitution, Laws, and Decisions of the Ancient Order of United Workmen* was a remarkable document. The genre itself was modeled after the digests of state and federal court reports. To handle an astounding variety of disputes the order had quasi-legal tribunals, from the local lodge leading up an appellate process to the Grand Lodge. Precedents were recorded in the next yearly *Digest,* creating the AOUW's own body of law. In one instance a Missouri court held that citizens could not "maintain any action at law" against a fraternal certificate so long as the society had a "tribunal to decide questions arising between the society and its members." In this way the Grand Lodge wielded its authority over the local lodges.[41]

All the leading fraternal corporations followed suit. The Knights of Pythias even claimed to have its own system of common law. In 1885, it published the 800-page *Knights of Pythias Common Law and Legal Text Book of the Order.* In 1880 the Ancient Order of Foresters published a nearly 1,000-page *Digest* with the hope that it would "secure harmony, dissolve doubt, and promote unity," along with "feelings of confidence." In the end it turned out that much of the glue of the fraternal bond was a quasi-legal internal structure, replete with a shadow appellate court system. Ultimately fraternalism depended upon the willingness of legal authorities to grant fraternal corporations self-rule.[42]

It remains to assess where the "fraternal bond" took hold in the context of postbellum American industrialization. Fraternalism emerged after the panic of 1873 among the middling commercial classes but ultimately by the late 1880s and early 1890s it began to catch in its net the burgeoning American industrial working class.

Most American fraternals began as self-consciously middle-class, if not cross-class, in their orientation. The AOUW boasted openness to "*men* of all professions and occupations . . . and every grade of wealth— from the millionaire to the day laborer." On principle, at lodge meetings "the differences between capital and labor" were "never discussed." Most early fraternal members identified themselves in the declining strata—given industrialization—of men engaged broadly in "mercantile pursuits," rather than salaried or waged occupations.[43]

Weber it turns out also correctly noted the original geographical location of most fraternal members. It was not the "modern metropolitan areas." During his travels across the United States in 1904, Weber questioned the Harvard philosopher William James about the nature of fraternalism, but apparently James "did not know anything about them." The growth of metropolises like New York City and Chicago aside, the era featured a great wave of small-scale urbanization. By 1890, 35 percent of the American population was urban, but that population was dispersed among 1,300 cities and towns. Tellingly, the hometowns of the 1890 representatives of the AOUW to the National Fraternal Congress included Meadville, Pennsylvania; Ypsilanti, Michigan; Cedar Falls, Iowa; Donnelly, Minnesota; and Hannibal, Missouri. These were urban commercial nodes where rail depots, shipping agencies, retail outlets, community banks, and crop-moving facilities flourished. They were fertile soil for fraternalism.[44]

Weber teased out one final consequence of American fraternalism. A fraternal certificate in his judgment did not restrain the drive towards "capitalist success." By contrast, in Europe another kind of voluntary association, the industrial trade union—whose roots were in medieval occupational guilds, not the Protestant sects—was newly providing economic security. But the ethos of these institutions was hostile to "the economic 'individualist' impulses of the modern capitalist ethos." In Weber's Germany, Bismarck's reforms were beginning to incorporate worker mutual-aid societies into the State.[45]

True, American labor unions lagged behind their European counterparts when it came to offering their members economic security. But the lag exhibited the strength rather than weakness of American class-consciousness in the 1870s and 1880s.[46]

In the 1880s American working-class radicalism gathered around the Knights of Labor, whose membership of 700,000 in 1885 peaked at 20 percent of the wage-earning workforce. That year witnessed the Great Upheaval, a violent wave of strikes and labor unrest. Certainly, labor radicals questioned what Weber called the ethos of "capitalist success." One Connecticut radical deplored "factoryism, bankism, collegism, capitalism, insuranceism and the presence of such lump-headed malignants as Professor William Graham Sumner." The Knights of Labor declared the "wage system of labor" and the "republican system of government" incompatible.[47]

Labor unrest was in fact the larger context to Sumner's 1883 *What Social Classes Owe to Each Other*. Sumner articulated the dominant Gilded Age gospel concerning the workingman's risk. In the wage bargain between capital and labor, it was capital, Sumner argued, that "takes all the risk." True, the worker must obey "orders"—relent control at the point of production, a flashpoint for so much of the labor unrest of the day. But in the bargain the laborer was "free from all responsibility, risk, and speculation." It was the "most advantageous arrangement" for him possible. The wage laborer in other words was averse to commercial risk-taking. Given the moral logic of risk and reward, it was only fair that labor sacrificed an upside. More profit rightfully accrued to the capitalist who shouldered more risk.[48]

Yet another German theorist of capitalism, Karl Marx, had already lampooned this moral argument. Marx detected the tendency of liberal thinkers to always stress the proletarian's "certain fixity of income more or less independent of the great adventures of capital." Marx quipped that, "Human bondage has been defended in the same way, perhaps on better grounds," and he was right. This kind of moral reasoning was, "Just as Don Quixote consoles Sancho Panza with the thought that, although of course he takes all the beatings, at least he is not required to be brave." By the 1880s, American liberals echoed the Sancho Panza defense of the new industrial wage-labor system.[49]

In this context, fraternalism influenced the trajectory of American class-consciousness. For one, the Knights of Labor was in fact organized as a fraternal society, replete with the "Knights" moniker, the "lodges," the ritual, and the rhetoric of fraternal cooperation and brotherhood. Many Knights of Labor leaders were enthusiastic members of fraternal societies like the AOUW. Which is not surprising, given that the Knights of Labor had no assessment system and offered no benefits to its members. It seems in the late 1880s many disaffected Knights flocked to the fraternal societies for economic security and to the upstart American Federation of Labor, founded in 1886, for a "pure and simple" brand of trade unionism.[50]

Furthermore, ever so slightly, after the violent 1870s and 1880s a few important American labor unions began to employ the fraternal assessment system. American workers (including ex-slaves) had once turned to savings banks in hopes of one day acquiring their own productive property. Now, for the permanent male wage laborer the assessment system provided necessary long-term supports. For perhaps industrial wage workers, relative to capitalists, were shielded from market risk. But there were the distinct risks of industrial wage work, ideologically screened out by the Sancho Panza defense. Following the legal precedent of *Farwell*, the worker still often "assumed the risk" of workplace accident all by himself. To carry it, and others associated with a hireling status, many workers turned to the assessment system of fraternalism.[51]

Notably, one fraternal society in particular that focused on the plight of the workingman was the Ancient Order of Foresters—founded in Brooklyn in 1864. Sometime in the late 1870s it adopted the assessment system but with a twist. Aside from a $100 death benefit to cover funeral expenses, its chief benefit was a "weekly allowance in case of sickness"—from $2 to $7 a week for up to fifty-two weeks. Bragging of its strong footing with the "working man," by 1893 the order counted a remarkable 110,000 members in lodges stretching from Brooklyn to California. In that year it had more members than the fleeting Knights of Labor (the American Federation of Labor now counted about 275,000). By the 1890s, with more and more of their members dependent upon the wage, most of the leading fraternal societies had begun to offer sickness and disability benefits.[52]

One of the first members of the Ancient Order of Foresters was a young immigrant cigar maker named Samuel Gompers, the future leader of the American Federation of Labor. Gompers later reflected, "In those early years the fraternal or lodge movement absorbed practically all my leisure." Soon his attention turned to his local Cigar Makers International Union. At Gompers' direction it became the first national American trade union of its era to offer benefits in the event of death ($25) but also sickness, disability, and even unemployment. The Cigar Makers International Union adopted the assessment system of the Ancient Order of Foresters. A few other national craft unions followed in the 1870s and 1880s: the Iron Molders' Union, the Granite Cutters, the Brotherhood of Carpenters and Joiners. Many railroad brotherhoods had already adopted the assessment system: the Brotherhood of Locomotive Engineers, the Order of Railway Conductors, the Switchmen's Union, and a few others. In a working-class key, all sung the praises of "fraternity."[53]

Thus, when in 1883 Congress held hearings on "Relations Between Labor and Capital" the thirty-two-year-old Gompers argued that an ideal labor union was really a "life and health assurance company," with a "strike benefit added." A union had these "beneficiary" features and also its "protective" functions, relating to working conditions. Working conditions were by far the most prominent theme of the hearings but the issue of "Insurance for Workingmen" was also discussed. Senator Henry W. Blair, Republican of New Hampshire, interrogated the notorious railroad financier Jay Gould on the topic. Violent strikes on Gould's Missouri and Texas-Pacific railroad lines had sparked the Great Upheaval. Blair asked Gould the following question:

> Do you think that the large employers of labor . . . might profitably
> ingraft upon their business some system of assurance, or some
> method by which a portion of the earnings of the laborers should be
> contributed to a fund, and perhaps a proportion of the profit of capi-
> tal also, to secure working people against want in seasons of non-
> employment, and against the disabilities resulting from accident,
> sickness, or old age?

Four years later the Interstate Commerce Commission would discover
that of the eighty-five largest railroad corporations in the country, twelve
had instituted employee insurance schemes (lagging far behind Europe).
But in 1885 the infamous financial speculator Gould—"the spider"—
answered that whoever controlled the reserve fund "would get control of
the money and spend it, in nine cases out of ten." It was a good idea in
"theory" but not in "practice." Meanwhile, in the next breath Blair explained that Gould had rightfully earned his fortune. Gould was a Don
Quixote. He earned "greater profit" because his business entailed "greater
risk" than either "ordinary farming or common labor work."[54]

That was the dominant approach of nineteenth-century American
liberals to the workingman's risk. A blinkered appeal to wage earners'
risk aversion combined with great expectations for the future of corporate risk management, which would somehow mop up the problem. At
any rate, at the close of the nineteenth century only a very small percentage of American workers received economic security from their unions,
a distinguishing characteristic of the American labor movement.

And so just when the liberal, as in financial, response to the generative
insecurities and radical uncertainties of capitalism had seemingly triumphed, the implosion of the corporate financial system after 1873 sent
Americans scurrying to a new sheet anchor outside that system. If there
was any doubt that fraternalism posed a fundamental threat to the interests of American financial corporations, the rabid hostility of the commercial life insurance industry stands as proof.

Rhetorically, insurance corporations sought to turn the tables on the
fraternals and to say that the fraternal bond, not the financial system and
certainly not actuarial science, was the true source of insecurity. In an

1878 pamphlet the president of the Connecticut Mutual, Jacob Greene, described fraternalism thus: "There can be no certainty in a contribution from an uncertain number of uncertain means, and of uncertain dispositions to pay that which there is no possible way of compelling them to pay." Because it lacked both the legal coercion of contract and the metaphysical coercion of the law of mortality a fraternal certificate was the true speculation.[55]

Unlike the fraternal certificate, life insurance policies were legally enforceable contracts. To Frederick Hoffman, actuary of the Metropolitan Insurance Company, the triumph of the insurance principle was part of the broader historical movement from "status" to "contract." Status had once been the bulwark of trust and confidence, of both social and economic security. But that world had "passed away." Status was hierarchical, contract was egalitarian; but social life without either was anarchical. Insurance contracts thus provided "certain sums" while fraternalism offered "indefinite promises." When a man "becomes a life insurance policyholder," Hoffman wrote, "a certain degree of compulsion forces him to make premium payments." The "permanence" of fraternal societies rested solely, according to the actuary Sheppard Homans in 1885, on "hope." The fraternals associated contracts with financial uncertainty. Insurance corporations drew from a strain of postbellum social thought in which contract was the only proper reconciler of individual volition and social obligation.[56]

Finally, fraternalism lacked a scientific basis, the epistemological foundation of a liberal yet predictable and certain enough social order. The fundamental basis of commercial life insurance, Homans explained, was the law of mortality, a "uniform, unvarying, certain law." From "this law there is no escape." "We must accept the inevitable." The fraternal societies were thus "doomed to disaster and wreck." The Travelers Insurance Company went so far as to call fraternalism a "revolt against the multiplication tables." Adequate social order was simply impossible without statistical induction. "True co-operation," the Travelers added, only existed when "members co-operative scientifically." The fraternals, by contrast, were "cooperative uncertainty."[57]

It was true that the fraternal societies were not immune to insecurity and even failure. During the 1880s a number of new societies explicitly rejected the lodge system. The Independent Order of United Workingmen closed its operations in 1885, leaving behind frustrated certificate holders in Ohio, Illinois, Missouri, Pennsylvania, and Michigan. And then there were fraternal societies—how many, who knows—that were outright frauds to begin with. An Illinois man named Andy Young, for instance, traveled with his brother from state to state setting up assessment societies, announcing failures, and pocketing assessments. Finally, there were assessment societies that were explicit gambling schemes. They often involved marriage—certificates promised benefits in the event of one's marriage or even the marriage of another. In 1883, the *Chicago Herald* reported a marriage in Galveston, Texas, noting that the "announcement created a stir among the marriage insurance companies throughout the country. More than 200 policies were reportedly taken out upon this marriage, representing an aggregate benefit to the amount of $800,000." Even the assessment system could succumb to speculation.[58]

Nevertheless, the assessment system of the AOUW and many similar fraternal orders was a success. All disavowed any connection with either the speculative or fraudulent assessment system. Fair-minded corporate actuaries began to admit that so long as the fraternals continued to replenish paying members the assessment system worked. The commercial firms still did their best to lump together the fraternals and the fraudulent and speculative "pure" assessment societies. But for all of that effort, and for all their sanctimonious appeals to the certitudes of contract and science, in the end the commercial life insurance corporations themselves emerged from the panic of 1873 only by appealing to the speculative allure of the upside.

A new policy known as "tontine insurance" pulled the personal insurance industry out of its late 1870s doldrums. It also positioned the leading American life insurance corporations at the very heart of the evolving national capital market, increasingly centered on Wall Street. From almost nothing in 1870, the value of tontine insurance in force by 1905 was $6 billion. The leading "Big Three" Wall Street insurance corporations— the Mutual Life, the New York Life, and the Equitable—had sold $5 billion of it. Together these three firms counted $1.2 billion in capital assets. The logic of tontine insurance was capital accumulation.[59]

Tontine insurance simply attached a speculative annuity to a standard commercial life insurance policy. The idea was that the policyholder, for the defined term—five, but usually ten or as much as twenty years—forfeited his right to either a surrender value or a yearly dividend. Those proceeds rolled together into the "tontine fund." If the policyholder died before the end of the term, his beneficiary received the life policy benefit. But they received nothing from the tontine fund. If the policyholder missed a premium payment during the term, he lapsed on both the policy and forfeited any right to the tontine fund. But if he survived the term he and his fellow cohort members split the proceeds of the tontine fund—which in the meantime the firm had invested in the capital market. Basically, the tontine policyholder hoped that his cohort members would either die or lapse on their policies. Tontine insurance promised speculation and insurance all bundled together into one financial asset.

In 1905, the $6 billion of tontine life insurance in force represented over 7.5 percent of total national wealth. That year there were 9 million tontine policies existent—for a total of 18 million American households. The growth of tontine insurance was as sudden and prodigious as that of fraternalism. No matter if they chose the insurance policy or the fraternal certificate—or both, there was no reason not to hedge one against the other—clearly millions of late nineteenth-century Americans were newly in search of economic security for themselves and their families.[60]

If the AOUW was the trailblazer for fraternalism, the Equitable Life Insurance Society was for tontine insurance. Its founder, Henry B. Hyde, was the son of a leading antebellum life insurance man. In 1859 he left the Mutual Life, then New York's largest life insurance corporation, to found his own firm. In 1867 Hyde's Equitable introduced tontine insurance. The tontine itself was not new and had been around for centuries, named after its seventeenth-century Italian inventor, the Neapolitan banker Lorenzo Tonti. Tontine was at first a tool of public finance. Hyde's genius was to combine it with a standard life insurance policy. By the panic of 1873, the Equitable wrote more new life insurance than any firm in the world. In 1880, tontine insurance accounted for half the company's new business, and by 1885 that number was five-sixths. Other corporations slowly followed suit. By 1885, the other members of the Big Three, the Mutual Life and New York Life, offered tontine insurance.[61]

The Equitable's tontine advertising campaign marketed both speculation and insurance. It was sold first to "business men" as a naked form of financial speculation, which also came with the benefit of insurance. One circular advertised "Life Insurance as an Investment." The Equitable projected a very high 10 percent return on the tontine, depending of course on the "fluctuations" of the market. Still, the tontine policy offered certain family protection. Too many men invested all of their savings in "speculation." But, the Equitable reminded, you "better not risk your *all* in such an uncertain manner." Better to "put at least some in 'insurance' as a refuge." All together, you could "hedge yourself in this way."[62]

Tontine insurance had one further advantage. Now the policyholder himself received a pecuniary benefit. And the tontine came to term when men entered old age. Tontine insurance, the Equitable reminded, offered provisions not only for "your wife and children" but also "yourself." In an era that predated both the public and private provision of old-age pensions, tontine insurance responded to a new demand: old-age security. Slowly, in the new industrial setting, the notion of a "retirement" was taking hold. In 1868, Henry Ward Beecher told his *Christian Union* readership to rely on their own devices for old age and not to "depend on Providence." And would not a continuing life policy provide the aging policyholder the leverage he needed over his children to secure their care in old age? Firms peddling tontine insurance played upon these growing sentiments and concerns.[63]

Tontine insurance was not uncontroversial. After all, the tontine holder was basically speculating on whether his fellow policyholders would die or lapse on their policies. However indirectly, lapsed policies took money intended for widows and orphans and rolled them into the tontine fund. Once again, corporate risk management created new forms of speculative risk-taking. Tontine insurance thus only threw the competing social logic of the fraternal bond in sharper relief.

Tontine insurance became a matter of public debate in the 1880s, when the president of a commercial firm that refused to sell such policies attacked the Equitable. Jacob L. Greene's firm, the Connecticut Mutual Life, was once the largest American insurance corporation. By the 1880s it was gasping for air, writing very little new business on its "ordinary" policies. And it was losing heavily on its investments in the western farm mortgage market. In 1884, Greene declared that "speculative insurance" had come to dominate the field in two guises—the one being the "assessment system" of fraternalism, the other the "Tontine scheme." Tontine insurance was "pure gambling" and "the thing gambled for is the loss of families." It was immoral risk-taking. Other voices echoed. One New York pamphlet concluded: "To call this *life insurance* is simply ridiculous." Yet another called tontine insurance "a risk too great to be run by any one."[64]

In 1885 the New York legislature appointed a five-man committee to investigate tontine insurance. One member was a New York agent of Greene's Connecticut Mutual Life, and another was his distant cousin. Yet even then Greene was far outmatched. Under pressure from Hyde's Equitable the investigation was halted after taking testimony from only two witnesses. A week later Ohio launched its own investigation, which did run its full course.

The two Gilded Age investigations focused on the morality of speculative risk-taking. The tontine corporations presented a unified moral defense of their trade. Hyde offered that Greene's criticism was a false appeal to "emotion." The only moral/legal obligations that existed were those between the two contracting parties—the firm and the policyholder. The *Independent* chirped "what business is it to anybody except the two parties to the contract?" "Who has a right to interfere?" As for the policy lapses that fattened the tontine funds, why should a man not suffer from breaking the terms of his contract? In the Ohio hearings the actuary Homans chimed in with more pop social theory: "Penalties for non-performance of contracts are essential to the well-being and security of society itself." In this vein, Hyde put forward that the Equitable had a 41.3 percent lapse rate on ordinary policies but only 23.5 percent for tontine policies.[65]

The upshot was that only by appealing to what one New York legislator approvingly referred to as "the tontine tendencies of men" could insurance corporations sell actuarial life insurance policies. The contradiction, given that commercial insurance fell on hard times in the 1870s precisely because of its association with speculation, is striking. The Equitable admitted that it sold so many policies because a man "thinks he sees a chance of making a little speculation." And the actuary David

Fackler explained to the Ohio commission that only the speculative inducement would "tend to cause a man of unsteady will to keep his policy in force, and in that way protect his family." This was a new argument. Speculative risk-taking would lead to risk management—to more insurance, and accordingly the accumulation of more financial capital.[66]

Here, consider Weber one final time. In a more celebrated essay, the 1904 "Protestant Ethic and the Spirit of Capitalism," Weber traced from early modern religious asceticism an ethos—"now cut off from its religious roots"—of instrumental rationality, the cradle of a certain kind of "economic man," but also of the "formation of capital." Tontine insurance, however convoluted, was a form of savings and in the work of the corporate insurance actuary there was an icy instrumental rationality. The cut-off root of probabilistic certainty—with its appeals to necessity, perfection, and a certain, transcendent power guiding the world's contingent workings—was providentialism. In the environment of "competitive accumulation" between the Big Three, there was a tinge of the instrumentally rational yet circularly irrational drive for the accumulation of capital for its own sake. And were those accumulations not the lifeblood of a new economic system, capitalism? Weber referred to that "mighty cosmos of the modern economic order" which "determines, with overwhelming coercion, the style of life *not only* of those directly involved in business but of every individual who is born into this mechanism."[67] In 1904, Weber visited the United States, walked across the Brooklyn Bridge, and gazed upwards in awe at the Manhattan skyscrapers, those great "fortresses of capital." No doubt he was looking at the midtown skyscrapers of the great New York life insurance corporations.

And yet, the insurance principle—its rationalization of contingency through statistical law, its heaping contributions to American capital formation—triumphed by appealing to a speculative rather than instrumentally rational impulse. It appealed to what Weber's Germany contemporary Werner Sombart called "the younger and more sanguine brother of the capitalist spirit—speculation."[68]

In this era, morally, the liberal axiom of self-ownership defended commercial speculation. To be sure, different lines in the sand were drawn distinguishing moral, productive speculation from immoral gambling. But the dominant ideology was that commercial risk-taking was a productive expression of self-ownership—the bigger the risk taken, the greater the upside, and the bigger the rightful moral/pecuniary reward. Thus, in the Ohio investigation a New York Life representative defended the tontine: "There is an element of uncertainty in Tontine precisely as there is in any business enterprise." In life there was always an "element of risk." "That is the law of every business enterprise," another testified. "Free choice at the outset; risk in any course and the greater prospective gain attended by the greater risk." Both the New York and Ohio investigations arrived at this final conclusion. Their findings stamped tontine insurance with the seal of state legitimacy. Ohio's final report offered that it could not condemn tontine insurance without "condemning all speculation" and it was "not prepared to take that advanced opinion." All market activity was a question of "risk and expectancy." "All business is more or less speculative." The future had moral texture. But it was for individuals—"rather than the public"—to determine when risk-taking became imprudent, let alone immoral.[69]

Throughout the hearings the tontine firms also brandished the fact that in the end their policies were secured by the certitudes of actuarial science. The actuarial calculations determining policyholders' individual property rights within the tontine fund however were a closed book. "To whom," a New York examiner had asked the vice president of the Equitable in 1885, does "the reserve of your tontine polices" belong? No straight answer was provided. Ohio called it a "bit of a mystery." Hyde told his examiners that such matters fell to corporate actuaries who dealt in mathematical complexities that legislators could not possibly comprehend. But in 1876 a company actuary wrote an internal memo to Hyde, asking him for "some rule of action" in determining the divisions of the retiring tontine funds. In 1888 he was still at it, pleading with Hyde for "instructions in regard to the course to be pursued," if only to avoid "possible litigation." A few disgruntled tontine holders did take their grievances to court although in almost all instances judges ruled in favor of the insurance corporations.[70]

This meant corporations paid out on tontine policies however much they wanted. The goal more or less was to keep their customers satisfied while accumulating as much capital as possible—if only to plow it back into business operations to acquire more customers or pass it along for investment to their Wall Street cronies. Since New York state laws kept its firms from investing too heavily in the western farm mortgage market, during the 1870s the Equitable acquired a majority stake in another outfit—the Mercantile Trust Company—that *did* invest in that market, although it failed to survive the post-1893 collapse of the western farm mortgage market. Regardless, through such ploys the Equitable promised returns on tontines in excess of 10 percent. A recent scholarly estimate of a twenty-year Equitable tontine policy purchased by a thirty-five-year-old man in 1871 calculated a real return of 7.8 percent, surpassing the 6.1 percent on offer at a typical New York savings bank. Indeed with the rise of tontine insurance savings banks suffered (see Table 4 in the Appendix). What the return should have been, based upon the advertised tontine scheme—how much the Equitable lopped off into its own reserves—nobody knew or knows.[71]

To run this operation the Equitable and its competitors needed a free hand from state regulators who were all too happy to oblige. After the small Greene-induced scare of 1885, the capture of the New York state legislature by the Big Three took on ridiculous proportions. That august body passed a law in 1890 prohibiting policyholders from demanding an accounting of their respective tontine fund without prior approval from the attorney general, which never happened. The measure further blocked policyholders' judicial recourses while the rolling accumulations meant that firms had more cash on hand to bribe lawmakers. Between 1895 and 1905 the New York Life dispensed over $1.3 million to their chief lobbyist in Albany.[72]

In short, more policies were sold and more capital was accumulated. By 1905, the Equitable had capital reserves of $412 million. $80 million of it was a "surplus," a figure over and above any potential legal liabilities owed to policyholders. The surpluses made Big Three executives popular figures on Wall Street.[73]

Fraternalism was a middle-class phenomenon that worked its way to the working class. Tontine insurance was first marketed to the wealthy. With 9 million policies in force by 1905 it had moved down market, reaching more ordinary Americans. But the tontine was not the only frontier for commercial, actuarial insurance in this era, as the industry regrouped after the calamitous 1870s. With the fraternal challenge still firing, Americans nonetheless funneled billions of dollars of their savings into new financial institutions.[74]

In 1885, the Travelers Insurance Company claimed to have sold its one-millionth "accident insurance" policy, reporting $232 million of insurance in force. That corporation had already begun to market policies not only to farmers but also to the industrial working class. Its big push in the 1880s was to steal business from the many "fraternal" railroad brotherhoods. By 1879, the Travelers already had 10,000 railroad men on its books. With permission from the bosses it sent out agents to canvass the railroads. The *Travelers Record* published letters supposedly from satisfied railroad laborers. In 1879, David McConoughe, a railroad worker in Huron, Ohio, explained how his fellow workers were generally distrustful of commercial insurance companies. When he was injured his fellow workers told him that "it was uncertain whether I would get it or not." But the Travelers had paid. Likewise, there was J. Furney Patterson, brakeman on the Portland and Ogdensburg Railroad, the longtime holder of policy number 273,944. In a year and a half he filed the following successful claims:

Arm broken against a freight shed: $75.00
Back bruised by timber: $6.42
Leg jammed between cars: $23.57
Collar-bone broken in railroad accident: $112.50
Finger-split pulling a coupling-pin: $15.00

The Travelers especially implored every railroad worker to be mindful of "injury from the carelessness of others," exactly the scenario at stake in *Farwell*. By 1885, the Travelers had broken down "Railroad Employees" into 130 occupational categories, each with their own specific rates.[75]

In 1884, the Travelers announced a campaign to insure American workers against the new class of "Industrial Risks." There was, the firm explained, "hardly a kind of manufacture of any sort which is not risky to the lives and limbs of the operatives engaged in it." The *Travelers Record* editorialized on the explosion of a flourmill in Minnesota.

How typical that the "new process" by which Americans received their daily bread had developed such "destructive capabilities." With the "march of improvement," as it were, "immunity from . . . risk was out of the question." Industrial life had become "environed with risks." Indeed, by 1885—the year of the Great Upheaval—the Travelers had established rate classifications not only for miners, but also for iron and steel workers. Open-hearth steelworkers for instance had different rates than those who labored in Bessemer Steel Works—the latter had fifty distinct occupational rate classes. Accident insurance was corporate risk management's financial response—and only a financial response—to the physical and psychic perils of industrialization. More than that, late nineteenth-century insurance corporations taught Americans to think about life itself in terms of risk.[76]

What finally cracked the American working class open to the insurance principle was something called "industrial insurance," specifically targeted to industrial wage earners. Here two companies took the lead: the Prudential Insurance Company of New Jersey, and the Metropolitan Insurance Company of New York. The Prudential opened for business in 1875. That year the Massachusetts Bureau of Labor Statistics, sampling 397 workingmen's families, found that only one carried any personal insurance (for a paltry value of $18). By 1885, the Prudential had sold 422,671 policies concentrated in the urban centers of the industrial Northeast. The Metropolitan counted 675,447 in 1884 and then an astounding 1.6 million in 1888. In 1891, the thirty-four companies that sold industrial policies totaled 5.6 million policyholders. From 1876 to 1905 industrial insurance in force climbed from $443,000 to $2.3 billion.[77]

The Prudential of Newark was the trailblazing corporation. John F. Dryden, a future New Jersey senator, was the founder. After attending Yale, Dryden traveled to England in 1877 and discovered the British Prudential (1854), the model for his American company. A number of features distinguished industrial insurance. It was for sale for sums as small as $10 although the average policy was $100. Second, agents traveled to the homes of the insured and collected premiums on a weekly basis. Finally and most importantly, the insurance was often not intended to replace contingent male productive labor but rather the cost of a proper funeral—for a man or woman. An industrial insurance policy prevented a pauper's burial. Accordingly, industrial insurance could be taken out on any life whatsoever. Firms in particular marketed policies to wives and children. With some controversy, the Prudential sold what they called "infantile policies." Wright's son, the actuary Walter Wright, called it analogous to "slave life insurance," as it was the commodification of death and not the double commodification of self-ownership.[78]

To Dryden industrial insurance did more than bury deceased children. It spread the gospel of the insurance principle—and thus also the gospel of personal responsibility. Dryden's pronouncements eerily echo those of John W. Alvord a decade before on the educational influences of the Freedman's Bank. Except, industrial firms resisted selling policies to African-Americans on equal terms (sometimes on any terms). When Dryden turned to the white industrial working class, which included so many fresh European immigrants, he saw that "the necessary habit of periodical savings had not been formed." The "virtues of prudent forethought" were absent. The panic of 1873 had stunted working-class education. Dryden blamed the aftermath of the panic of 1873 for the popular distrust of financial corporations. Now, through the weekly visits of his sales force, "boys and girls grow up in an atmosphere of insurance."[79]

The lapse rate of industrial policies was outrageous. Lapsed premiums lined industrial corporations' pockets. The leading corporations became financial behemoths, engaged in the competitive struggle for capital accumulation. A 1905 New York investigation discovered that in 1904, 51.46 percent of Metropolitan Life policyholders lapsed within a year and 63.74 percent lapsed within five years. Surrender values were basically nonexistent. In 1904 lapses were the firm's greatest source of income. Over two-thirds of all premiums paid to the Prudential lined its own pockets. (Lapse rates were also an increasingly large percentage of the Big Three's earnings, by 1891 exceeding their investment returns.) By the turn of the twentieth century, the Prudential and the Metropolitan Life became so large as to rival the Big Three.[80]

The cumulative effect is on display in Tables 2, 4 and 5 (see Appendix). In the latter decades of the nineteenth century, relative to other financial institutions the wealth accumulated by life insurance corporations soared. Those corporations divested themselves of federal debt and real estate, and increasingly invested in industrial securities. Richard McCurdy, the president of the New York Life, summed it all up: "We had a lot of money coming in that we did not know what to do with."

The problem of the 1870s—so many small firms speculating and then going belly-up during a bust—had been solved. Giant concentrations of capital meant that only the financial apocalypse could have brought the Big Three to their knees. Now, in fact, they held together the entire system. When the panic of 1893 struck it was the cash deposits of the great New York life insurance corporations that helped the New York banking houses hold the line. The concentration of finance capital itself, that is, was beginning to socialize risk.[81]

Meanwhile, the dominant insurance corporations reached for yields in their investments—in an era of declining nominal and real interest rates. After the 1870s debacle insurance corporations had considered industrial and financial bonds, let alone stocks, beyond their pale. Firms flocked to the western farm mortgage market, and to public debt. That changed during the 1880s and 1890s, as they moved into industrial securities, especially railroad bonds. These numbers do not tell the entire story, because Wall Street commercial and investment banks often circuitously directed the cash deposits and financial securities of life insurance corporations into industrial development. Tellingly, the rate of return in the industrial sector was less than what was available in other asset classes. New York insurance corporations desired institutional power on Wall Street as much as profits.[82]

In this way yet another financial systemization occurred, comparable to the western farm mortgage-insurance complex. This time instead of capital flooding the westward prairies and plains, Wall Street insurance corporations drew savings from the far geographical reaches of the American economy, oxygenated it into capital, and circulated it back increasingly in the form of fixed industrial investment. Life insurance companies provided finance capital for industrialization, a process which drew in more wage laborers who increasingly bought more insurance and whose premiums found their way through the corporate risk management complex back to Wall Street, becoming capital. The cycle repeated.[83]

Thus, by the turn of the twentieth century corporate risk management had not only survived the fraternal challenge but was thriving, forging new frontiers for the insurance principle and circulating billions of dollars of capital through the Wall Street financial system. In 1900, numerically the fraternal wave had not quite yet crested. Yet by then it had already fundamentally changed in character, succumbing to the twin liberal logics of science and contract, and, ever so slightly, beginning to contribute to the financial accumulation of capital. The spirit of fraternity was actuarialized and set on a contractual basis.[84]

Fraternalism transformed for reasons both internal and external. Once again the AOUW led the way. In 1885 it sent out a call to its brethren to meet in a "National Fraternal Congress" to discuss the possibility of setting fraternal corporations on an actuarial basis.[85]

The precedent was the AOUW's experience dealing with the aftermath of the yellow fever epidemic that had decimated its southern lodges in 1878. Death rates dipped lodge memberships below 2,000, meaning $1 assessments would not create $2,000 benefits. National official Sackett issued a "general appeal" to the entire order but with the "absence of law or authority to levy a general assessment" it was to no avail. At the 1879 annual meeting of the AOUW the Massachusetts delegation proposed that "The members of this Order throughout all jurisdictions are legally and morally bound for all claims for death benefits wherever they may occur." Kansas proposed the creation of a "Reserve Fund" equal to "five per centum of the gross receipts of the Order" to be held in U.S. treasury bonds, putatively the safest of investments. Both proposals failed, smacking too much of the insurance principle.[86]

A faction within the AOUW pushed again at the 1880 national gathering. With the yellow fever claims still outstanding, the order was $84,932.50 in the red. Yet, Michigan, Illinois, Iowa, and a few other states held that the Grand Lodge had no "legal right" to demand further assessments. Brother John Frizell warned that a "suit could be maintained against the Supreme Lodge, being incorporated, and judgment recovered." This was a good thing, for if the "whole Order" would be newly bound by "law," a brother would "feel that security and confidence so essential to the success of the institution." Frizell and his allies next proposed a "Relief Law." It would set "a maximum rate of mortality for each particular jurisdiction" based upon "tables of mortality." Corporate actuaries had been at work scaling rates to the perils of yellow fever. Once the maximum level was reached in a given state the new general fund could be drawn from. The Relief Law went to a vote and passed but Iowa remained "indignant" that out-of-state assessments could only be leveled as purely voluntary contributions. It was kicked out of the AOUW and a new Iowa lodge was founded. By 1882 the order had been essentially reconstituted.[87]

In 1885 the AOUW announced the creation of a "National Fraternal Congress." Through it, the AOUW would attempt to persuade all fraternal societies to adopt its new methods. Already, however, the courts were pushing the fraternal societies in this direction. This happened at a state-by-state level. There was no larger doctrinal discussion inside and outside the courts. Nevertheless, the trend was clear and the larger fraternal societies—who set aside money for litigation—were aware of the drift. A fraternal certificate was becoming a legal contract which meant that a fraternal member had an individual property right to a benefit.

Not coincidentally 1885 was the same year that the Iowa Supreme Court issued a crucial decision against the AOUW. The case was *State v. Miller* and involved a dispute between the order and a fraternal member over a benefit claim, emanating from the 1882 dismissal of the Iowa lodge. For the court it raised the important general question of whether the "Ancient Order of United Workmen is or should be classed as a fraternal organization . . . or whether it is a mutual life insurance company." Like many states Iowa had different laws governing "pecuniary" versus "non-pecuniary" corporations. The AOUW had filed its charter in Iowa in the latter classification, as a "fraternal organization." Its lawyer told the court that its certificate was not a legal contract. The court rehearsed the 1882 reconstitution and then declared that the establishment of a "benefit fund" to pay death benefits was the primary purpose of the order—exactly the same as a life insurance corporation. The fraternal elements—the ritual ceremony, the social fraternizing—were secondary. The AOUW was an insurance corporation, its certificates were legally binding contracts, and its members had a property right to a $2,000 benefit. Further, the AOUW would have to refile its corporate charter. In order to do business in the state of Iowa it would have to raise the capital reserve required by state law.[88]

Such was the background for the AOUW's 1885 call for a National Fraternal Congress, which went out to the fifty national fraternal societies with memberships over 40,000. All "speculative" concerns were not invited. The first meeting was lightly attended but the first resolution defined a "fraternal society" as an organization whose primary purpose was to work "under ritual, holding regular lodge or similar meetings." Yet another resolution called for the "careful examinations and compilation of vital statistics." For if a certificate was a contractual bargain and if societies were to be legally liable for their certificates, then actuarialized premiums became necessary. To not have enough cash on hand to pay benefits at a moment's notice could be the end of a fraternal society.[89]

By 1890 the National Fraternal Congress had acquired momentum. A "Bureau of Statistics and Information" now existed. The congress began to keep a register of legal cases determining the status of fraternal certificates in the various states; it had cobbled together a "Uniform Law" regulating fraternal societies to propose to every state legislature. In 1894 brother F. W. Sears gave a paper on the topic of a "Reserve Fund." Twenty-seven years ago, he explained, Father Upchurch had founded the AOUW without actuarial principles, "looking to and believing that an all-kind Providence would care for the future." It was nice that the original members of the order did not look upon things like the "death-rate" of members but only to the "spirit of hope and charity." But it was now also "an indisputable fact that the cost of insurance advances with increasing age"—a matter of statistical law, not providence. By now fraternal orders had come to embrace the very term "insurance." Would it not be unjust, Sears continued, to charge "the man at 21 the same as you do the one at the age of 50?" The only answer was a level premium which—as Wright had explained now five decades before—necessitated a "reserve fund." Certainly, "safeguards" could prevent the fund from being squandered in the financial system. By 1894 the National Fraternal Congress had begun to recommend a table of age-based rates for all fraternal members and the necessary attendant "Reserve Fund." The pillars of the fraternal bond were crumbling.[90]

Meanwhile, aided by hundreds of disgruntled and litigious members the courts continued to harass and push the fraternal societies in this direction. Insurance corporations paid off legislatures to have tontine lawsuits thrown out of court, but fraternal societies benefited from no such quarter. Most states had tried to pass laws so that the fraternal societies would not be legally classed as insurance corporations. In some states, especially Pennsylvania, the courts confirmed that classification.[91] A few courts continued to grant fraternal societies immunity because they lacked a "pecuniary motive" or had a "lodge system" or lacked a "legal reserve" fund.[92] But most state courts simply ignored the laws and declared that the fraternal societies were insurance companies and that fraternal certificates were binding contracts.[93] The legal metric "What is the real purpose and nature of the society?" emerged. Courts quashed a great many arguments by fraternal lawyers. No, the opinion of the state insurance commissioner did not matter.[94] No, the absence of the word "insurance" in the fraternal society's constitution and bylaws (or on the certificate itself) was immaterial.[95] No, the mere presence of "benevolent" features did not matter if the primary purpose of the order was still insurance.[96] And no, the assessment system alone did not mean the societies were benevolent, charitable institutions, rather than insurance companies.[97] The rulings only forced the fraternals into a greater embrace of the insurance principle. Once competing collective strategies for coping with the perils and insecurities of industrial capitalism now converged.

The result was that by 1900 even the commercial insurance actuaries had begun to praise the new spirit of fraternalism. In 1905 the actuary Miles Dawson commented that the fraternals "changed from incorrect and unsafe plans to more scientific methods" and had moved to "the adoption . . . of level rates correctly computed on a scientific basis." The fraternals had even begun to employ actuaries. Likewise, the social scientist B. F. Meyer added that the fraternals now "bind themselves by contract." In 1901 the Grand Lodge of the Knights of Pythias passed a resolution affirming the legal obligation of the order to pay out on certificates, on a vote of 103 to 19. And a 1900 speech of the vice president of the National Fraternal Congress declared that "mortality tables can be elaborated with mathematical precision, and that fraternal as well as 'commercial' insurance ultimately rest upon the same insurance principles."[98] The spirit of fraternalism was no longer distinct.

These men were not wrong, for something fundamental had indeed changed. The AOUW's Sackett wrote a history of fraternalism in 1914. He himself, on behalf of the AOUW, had done much of the "pioneer work" to bring to the other fraternal societies the power of "statistics." This had put fraternalism "on a scientific basis." But even Sackett wondered "if in the evolution to more practicable and scientific methods" fraternalism had "not lost some of that commendable co-operative and helpful spirit so pronounced and characteristic" of its early days. Regardless, by then corporate risk management had co-opted the fraternal countermovement.[99]

Thus in 1899 the Grand Lodge of the Knights of Honor issued a series of circulars to its lodges, informing them of changes in the order's constitution. There would be a new "table of assessment rates" scaled to age to place the society on a "probable stable basis." The Knights would embrace the moral and legal obligation of all members to pay their assessments. And, accordingly, there would be a reserve fund held on cash deposit in New York City in the Farmer's Loan and Security Trust Company.[100]

The financial trust company, which had been around for almost a century, was then a reinvigorated form of financial institution. Exploiting a loophole in the state banking regulatory framework, trusts took deposits and engaged in speculative investments restrained by no legal reserve requirements. Trust company deposits exploded after 1890 (see Table 4 in the Appendix). The largest New York trust companies became crucial cogs within the Wall Street capital market. The Farmer's Loan and Security Trust Company, a "formidable factor" in the money market according to one Wall Street observer, was the largest trust company in the United States with $41.5 million on deposit in 1900.

That year a director of the Farmers was Charles A. Peabody. Peabody also sat on the board of the Big Three firm, the Mutual Life Insurance Company of New York, as well as the boards of the Illinois Central Railroad and the Union Pacific Railroad. In 1906 he would become the Mutual's president. In 1905 the Mutual had invested $118 million of its some $500 million in assets in railroad securities while holding a large cash deposit in the Farmers through which to covertly sponsor more industrial securities underwritings. The Farmers was an ally in this business of the largest New York commercial bank, the First National Bank of New York. The head of that bank was George F. Baker, the uncle of Peabody's law partner in the firm Peabody, Baker, and Peabody. Baker was also the chum and associate of the great New York investment banker J. P. Morgan—who had the heaviest of all hands pulling on all of these strings. What Jay Cooke & Co. had once been to the American investment banking world, J.P. Morgan & Co. now was.[101]

The Farmers—which promised returns unmatched by the commercial banks, let alone the more conservative savings banks—was where the Knights of Honor decided to keep its new reserve fund. The 1900 circular sent out to the individual lodges from the Grand Lodge took a serious tone, acknowledging the fundamental ongoing transformation of the order. But the move was necessary to secure the order's future, and to ensure the security of its certificates. "Do this, my Brothers," the circular concluded, looking into the fraternal future, "and our good ship will ride safely over the billows."[102]

CHAPTER 7

Trading the Future

I stood in the center of the wheat fields of North Dakota where the wheat could be seen as far as the eye could reach, and these wheat fields as they were turning yellow in the summer were like the waves of the ocean, and I thought that the man who managed or sold or owned those immense wheat fields has not as much to say with regard to the price of wheat . . . [as] some young fellow who stands howling around the Chicago wheat pit.

— Charles Pillsbury, "Hearings Before the House Committee on Agriculture Upon the Subject of Fictitious Dealings in Agricultural Products" (1892)

S O BEGAN THE TESTIMONY of Charles Pillsbury, the largest commercial flour miller in the United States, before the United States House Committee on Agriculture's 1892 hearings *Fictitious Dealings in Agricultural Products*. According to him, the financial abstractions of the Chicago wheat pit had lost touch with the reality of the waving fields of wheat.

Pillsbury indicted commodities futures trading. Futures contracts, or derivatives contracts, arose in the decades after the Civil War, quickly becoming the cutting edge of the American corporate financial system. Marking a new chapter in risk's history, a futures contract was yet another complex financial instrument that promised to manage the uncertainties and instabilities of capitalism within the financial system itself.

Futures trading was a new form of financial exchange on future, physical commodities such as "September wheat," which had not yet been grown when first sold. For centuries, merchants had made contracts to deliver goods at some future date. But only in the final three decades of the nineteenth century did there emerge a professional class of merchants who exclusively traded "futures" (also known then as "derivatives" "options," "straddles," "scalps," "puts," and "calls"), which meant that no physical goods were ever delivered. Futures traders speculated in conceptual entities as if they were corporeal goods—future bales of cotton, future vats of lard. Notably, in the trading "pits"—circumscribed spaces where buyers and sellers traded futures—commodities were exchanged without material things ever changing hands between buyer and seller. A quick snap of the fingers might consummate a trade, and traders neither physically possessed nor even held legal title to the goods in which they trafficked. By 1890, futures trading had become by sheer volume the dominant mode of commodity exchange in the United States.

After 1870 more than twenty organized trading pits emerged across the United States, the home ground of the new financial practice.[1] Termed "organized commodities exchanges" or "futures markets," the leading pits quickly became chartered corporations, like the Chicago Board of Trade incorporated by the state of Illinois in 1875, or the New York Cotton Exchange incorporated by the state of New York in 1871. The trading pits of these financial corporations soon set the prices for most of the primary agricultural products of the world.

Futures trading thus further abstracted financial exchange from the space-time of the physical economy—from the temporal rhythms and geographical settings of production, distribution, and consumption. Transactions at the New York Produce Exchange, for instance, often involved commodities putatively to be harvested in North Dakota, bound for Minneapolis or Paris but never New York—or perhaps never harvested at all. Between 1885 and 1889 there were 8.5 billion bushels of wheat futures contracts sold at the New York exchange, but only 162 million bushels ever entered the city.[2] The American, indeed the global, economy took on a spatial and temporal configuration unimaginable decades before.

Further complicating the matter was the separate presence of "bucket shops"—unincorporated outfits where anyone could wager on the rise and fall of prices at an incorporated organized exchange. Bucket shops flourished in the 1880s and 1890s, grafting themselves onto the network of organized futures markets. There were hundreds, if not thousands, of bucket shops in the United States, present in even the smallest of American rural communities.

To many who testified before the House Committee on Agriculture, organized futures trading, let alone bucket shop trading, was illegitimate. Did the pits, not to mention the bucket shops, bear any relation to the wheat fields of North Dakota—to the movement of real things through the economy? According to the chairman of the House Committee on Agriculture, the intent of the 1892 hearings on "fictitious dealings" was "to get the difference . . . between an illegitimate and a legitimate sale."[3] The legal and political fate of futures hinged on this difference, as the moral problem resonated both inside and outside the halls of Congress, commanding the attention of judges, farmers, lawyers, merchants, novelists, social scientists, and journalists.[4] At stake in the public debate was the very reality of the economy itself. For in the words of critics the pits were a metaphysical economy, possessing "neither form, nor substance, nor reality."[5] Futures trading was "unnatural," "deranged," and "evil" because it was detached from the "selling of wheat actually in sight."[6] What was a legitimate financial abstraction? When did financial speculation, the rightful risk-taking of a free economic agent, pass an elusive threshold and become immoral, unproductive gambling?[7] Ultimately, these became political questions.

In the end, the incorporated futures exchanges survived and the bucket shops perished. The compromise rested upon a new legal doctrine: "contemplating delivery." According to the courts, futures traders could deal in conceptual entities so long as they "contemplated" corporeal goods in their minds while doing so. As it abolished the bucket shops, the law stamped incorporeal exchange with legitimacy, blurring the line between thoughts and things.

Yet the tortured legal doctrine of contemplating delivery still recognized the great break in risk's history ushered in by American futures trading. With the insurance principle, the rule of double commodification had long struggled to keep financial "risks"—not matter how circuitously—tied down to primary, underlying commodities. With this new tool of corporate risk management, the futures dealer had no "interest" in the underlying commodity, even if he "contemplated" its delivery. In the pits, the financial abstractions took on lives of their own. Relationships between abstractions began to power the American financial system—increasingly just as much as relationships between abstractions and their original underlying physical assets. Risk now took full flight from its corporeal foundations. Trading the future created its own present reality.

Nevertheless, futures traders and their public advocates argued that futures speculation was a form of productive labor and risk-taking. But their moral argument was as novel as the practice itself. The futures trader, according to his defenders, assumed what the American economist Henry Crosby Emery in 1896 called "conjuncture risk"—the risk of sudden and violent future price swings in a capitalist economy. The pits signaled and leveled-out future price fluctuations.[8] Therefore, in the act of speculation the futures trader actually assumed conjuncture risk for the benefit of the entire American economy. This instrumental *social* function—not the futures trader's self-ownership, his rightful commercial risk-taking— justified his moral/pecuniary reward. Frenzied and unabashed speculation in risk was now an explicit part of the financial countermovement against the perils and insecurities of capitalism. The argument was both pragmatic and social in character: futures trading might be gambling, but its result was a new kind of financial and social "insurance." The increasingly protean insurance principle was put to work.

Risk management was no longer leading to new forms of speculative risk-taking. Supposedly, new forms of speculative risk-taking were unintentionally causing risk management. Commodities derivatives trading handed down to later centuries a form of financial speculation whose only moral justification was its promise to financially stabilize an inherently unstable capitalism. Of course, to the incorporated exchanges—the Chicago Board of Trade, the New York Produce Exchange—the bucket shops did no such thing. They were the gambling dens. Risk might take full flight from the physical economy—but only in their trading pits.

In the end, it was U.S. Supreme Court Justice Oliver Wendell Holmes, Jr. who decided the legitimacy of futures trading. In 1905, Holmes delivered the majority opinion in the U.S. Supreme Court case *Board of Trade v. Christie*, elaborating his own version of contemplating delivery, which declared futures trading legal, but bucket shops illegal.[9] Understanding how Holmes grappled with the epistemological issues at stake entails addressing his intellectual milieu, one in which the relationship between thoughts and things—in the context of capitalist transformation—was especially pressing.[10] That leads to the chance-infatuated American philosopher William James, Holmes's friend and fellow intellectual traveler, whose thought further clarifies the pragmatic epistemological logic of futures trading. But in the middle—between the farmer and the philosopher—was Justice Holmes.

In the 1870s American futures traders developed a form of commodity exchange that eliminated the need for a physical object of sale—the method of "setting off." In the pits of organized futures exchanges a buyer and seller would enter a contract on a given day, say August 1, for the delivery of a specified quantity of a physical good, say 50,000 bushels of wheat, at a specified price (the subsequent "contract price"), and at a specified future date, say September 1. But they would not consummate the transaction with physical delivery on September 1; there would neither be a distribution of physical goods nor a transfer of title. Instead, traders in futures contracts would execute contracts by setting off the price differential between the original "contract price" and that day's "market price" in the pit. And traders could set off at any time before the putative date of physical delivery—one week later, one day later, one minute later. To "sell short" was to bargain that the market would fall; to "go long" was to predict a rise.

The "short sell" was (and is) the most perplexing transaction. Suppose, for example, that on August 1 trader A sold to trader B 50,000 bushels of "September wheat" "short" at $1 per bushel. Then suppose come September 1 the price of "September wheat" had fallen to $.90 per bushel. If need be trader A could go into the pit and purchase 50,000 bushels of real "September wheat" from a third party, trader C, at $.90 per bushel, to deliver to trader B who had agreed to buy it at $1. Trader A, by this practice of selling short, profited $.10 by a factor of 50,000 bushels, or $5,000. But if the price had instead risen to $1.10, trader B would have stood to profit the same amount on his "long" position. Eventually, traders A and B dispensed with trader C altogether and simply set off the difference between "contract price" and "market price," with no physical commodities ever trading hands.

Accordingly, contemporaries often referred to futures contracts as "time contracts."[11] In other words, this was not trade across space but rather trade in increments of abstract, homogenous time. Futures trading was a concrete labor of continual abstraction.

The enterprise of one prominent dealer in futures, Andrew J. Sawyer, reveals the inner workings and transformative economic implications of commodities futures trading. Sawyer testified before the House Committee on Agriculture in February 1892.[12] Called to explain how futures worked and well qualified to do so, Sawyer resided in Minneapolis and was a member of the two Minnesota exchanges—the Duluth Board of Trade and the Minneapolis Chamber of Commerce—as well as the Chicago Board of Trade. In 1881, he had been the Duluth exchange's first president. He was also the proprietor of a 5,000-acre wheat farm in Minnesota and ran one of the largest grain elevator operations in the Northwest. He had commission houses in Minneapolis, Duluth, and Buffalo, and a broker who bought and sold for him on the New York Produce Exchange. He conducted his banking in Boston. Sawyer's business ventures encompassed all of the disparate aspects of commodity exchange—both the incorporeal exchange of futures trading and the physical arena of production and distribution—at a time of intensifying animosity between producers, merchants, and financiers.

Sawyer was a large capitalist farmer and dealt exclusively in wheat.[13] Harvest season began in July and, when the crop was ready to move, Sawyer's 175 country elevators began to take in wheat from his farm and other northwestern farmers. Once Sawyer had gathered all of this wheat, it was destined for either Duluth or Minneapolis. From Minneapolis, he sold to local millers like Pillsbury or to commission merchants at the Chamber of Commerce. Duluth, however, was situated on Lake Superior and was an export market. Sawyer telegraphed his agents in Chicago, New York, and Europe to determine the going prices in a truly global market: Montreal, Liverpool, Paris, Antwerp, Berlin, St. Petersburg, Calcutta, Winnipeg, and Buenos Aires, among others, were all possible destinations for, or competitors in, his product.[14]

Sawyer was both a producer of wheat and a futures trader. He explained the crucial function that futures trading could provide for his physical business. Futures markets entered his business only when none of the "markets of the world" could take his wheat. "Suppose we are handling 100,000 bushels a day and we can sell in Minneapolis, Buffalo, Montreal, or New York only 75,000 bushels a day. . . . We have then 25,000 bushels left on our hands which we can not sell, there being no market for it." Sawyer wanted to hold the 25,000 bushels back until the market became liquid. But that came, he explained to Congress, with a "risk." What if in the meantime the market plummeted? "We are taking this risk of carrying this wheat in our elevators from the time we receive it," he explained. To hedge that risk Sawyer's solution was to sell wheat "short" for future delivery to buyers in the pit of the Chicago Board of Trade. But Sawyer never delivered wheat to Chicago. Instead, these sales were financially set off on or before the putative date of delivery. If the market had fallen, Sawyer had profited on his futures transaction. He thus had working capital to continue to store his physical wheat—to "pay interest and insurance"—while holding it back from a tepid market. If the market had risen, Sawyer had lost on his futures transaction— "that is a risk we take," he testified. But in that event his losses would be offset by the actual sale of his 25,000 bushels of physical wheat stored in Minnesota. Futures trading provided him a "hedge" against market price volatility.[15]

For sake of simplicity, Sawyer told Congress that he used the board to "insure" his physical wheat in storage against price fluctuations. One congressman asked him: "In other words, you use this absolutely as insurance?" "Certainly, it is protecting me against advance or decline in the markets of the world." "That is all I want of it; it insures me against loss." In February of 1892, Sawyer had 4 million bushels of physical wheat stored in Minneapolis with 15 million bushels of wheat futures contracts outstanding at the Chicago Board of Trade. And yet, as a member of the Chicago Board, if Sawyer thought wheat futures were undervalued there was no reason why he could not go "long." Rather than hedging his physical wheat, he could become an outright speculator on futures contracts. Or, once he sold his physical wheat, Sawyer could choose to maintain his futures position. Futures could hedge his physical product. But the line between hedging and naked speculation could be something hard to see.[16]

Regardless, Sawyer never delivered a speck of wheat to Chicago. In Chicago there was a class of traders who only speculated on price swings—the "scalpers" or "locals" as they were sometimes called—who unlike Sawyer had no feet in the physical economy. Their function, putatively, was to provide sufficient market liquidity—ever present willing buyers and sellers—so that men like Sawyer had counterparties to transact with. Sawyer explained that he needed the "gambler" in the Chicago wheat pit to "sell these contracts back again." Scalpers traded not only with producers like Sawyer but also with each other. In 1888, American farmers harvested 415 million bushels of wheat. That year, one contemporary estimated, there were some 25,000 trillion bushels of wheat sold in futures contracts in the United States that were set off, never delivered.[17]

Sawyer's business grew out of a series of changes first combined in Chicago after the Civil War. The railroads integrated city and hinterland as the steam-power grading system of elevator storage replaced selling by physical sample. The telegraph provided near-instantaneous communication for men like Sawyer to wire their trades. By 1868, traders in the Chicago pits had already ceased to exchange physical commodities and had begun to exchange "elevator receipts," which denoted title to a quantity and "grade" of a physical commodity stored in the city's sprawling network of elevators. Technically, each receipt could be taken out from the pit and redeemed at an elevator. But this system still had a lingering physical foundation: the actual presence of the commodities transacted upon in Chicago.[18] At some point in the 1870s Chicago traders stopped transferring not only physical commodities but also elevator receipts as well. Other incorporated futures exchanges followed a similar trajectory. The April 5, 1877, minutes of the Board of Managers at the New York Produce Exchange report a revision in a "Supplementary Rule" whereby "on sales of graded grain, the tender of elevator receipts of the grade sold, having a free delivery afloat, shall constitute a delivery of the grain as between sellers and buyers." Six weeks later the New York Produce Exchange dispensed with the transfer of elevator receipts. Futures trading came to Sawyer's Minnesota exchanges sometime in the 1880s.[19] Everywhere the speed and volume of transactions exploded as futures contracts were now repeatedly bought, sold, and then set off in a dizzying cycle. The Chicago wheat pit, which opened at 9:15 a.m., began to close at 1:15 p.m. and until 4:00 p.m. a group of "settlement clerks" gathered to account for that day's increasingly complex web of transactions. Provided with sufficient liquidity and volatility in price, two members of the board could now trade 1 million bushels of wheat back and forth to each other a hundred times an hour, "setting off" each individual transaction. Written contracts in turn became too cumbersome. Traders (by 1900 in Chicago, upward of 1,800 individuals) stalked the pits, instantly consummating transactions with a knuckle tap or a single chalk mark.[20]

Notably, the futures market in wheat remained rooted in Chicago even after the physical market's geography shifted. In 1880, Chicago received more than 23 million bushels of physical wheat. Duluth and Minneapolis together took in over 13 million. By 1890, as the wheat belt spread west, over 60 million bushels of wheat moved through Minneapolis and Duluth next to 14 million in Chicago.[21] Futures trading had transformed the space-time of the American, indeed global, economy. Physical wheat moved through one geographical circuitry, that is, while wheat futures moved through another. Referring to his futures contracts, Sawyer explained, "I have got to sell them in Chicago" but "I can not deliver in Chicago."[22] The telegraph was the crucial innovation. Wiring his trades from his offices in Minneapolis, Sawyer never set foot in Chicago.

The new system spread from Chicago to the other new U.S. exchanges—from New York to New Orleans, from Duluth to San Francisco. And futures encompassed more than wheat, corn, and cotton. A profusion of goods—horses, mules, cows, oxen, sheep, swine, pork, lard, beef, dairy, tallow, greases, barley, hops, corn, oats, rye, flax seed, clover seed, hay, cotton, coffee, straw, vegetable oils, butter, cheese, oil, gas, petroleum—entered the new system of financial exchange.[23] By 1890 anyone with access to a broker on an organized, incorporated commodities exchange could sell or buy a product for future delivery, only to set off the transaction at a profit or loss. An "interest" in—even plausible access to—the physical commodities themselves was no longer a prerequisite for transacting upon them.

Financial abstraction, of course, was not born in the pits of the post-bellum United States. The transactional innovation of setting off had episodic precedents in the early modern world and even other regions of the nineteenth-century American financial system.[24] But futures traders themselves were fully aware of the rupture in the history of commerce ushered in by their trade.

In 1892, for instance, William Matthews, a St. Louis futures trader, reflected on the novelty of derivatives. Matthews explained that he had been "educated and actively engaged under the old routine at a time when option trading was unknown." Then the "merchant princes" of Boston, Norfolk, Baltimore, and New York "filled their ships with miscellaneous cargoes," sending them to all "parts of the globe." "It was a blind venture . . . between distant parts of the world, entailing great risk and requiring many months before the result could be known." Back then it was "the forecast of the merchant as between places that made or lost him a fortune." Matthews was referring to the world of long-distance trade in the age of sail. But the introduction of the "telegraph" ended the "old methods" and "destroyed all opportunities for gain between places." Within the span of one lifetime the telegraph had made it so that merchants knew prices in markets at the port of destination before they shipped their goods. The only "blind venture" now left was a futures transaction across time.[25]

Of course, the old "merchant prince" had insured his "risks" against the "perils of the seas." Yet, with the rule of double commodification, he could only sell the "risk" on his own "interest" in an underlying material commodity to which he held legal title. Futures traders however conjured their "risks" seemingly out of thin air. The pits appeared to sever the world of finance from its moorings in the real world.

The "scalper" was the truly revolutionary figure. Unlike Sawyer (the farmer/merchant/futures trader), he practiced nothing but trading future commodities extant only in his mind, trafficking in the very guts of the American economy. As risk took full flight, agricultural products, the food on supper tables, the seemingly most solid, melted into thin air.

In the pits, speculative trade in incorporeal things stood newly naked before the wider public. But the wider public in fact consisted of active participants. The proliferation of bucket shops in the 1890s brought futures to the masses.[26] Bucket shops were separate places of business from incorporated futures exchanges. Anyone could buy and sell futures at a bucket shop. One did not have to pay for a membership or act through a broker who was a member, as in the pits. Transactions were between the proprietor of the shop and his or her customer, and one could deal in far less volume. Prices—mostly from commodity futures markets but also from stock markets—were continually wired to the shops over the telegraph and marked on a giant blackboard. At a typical bucket shop, customers placed a margin with the proprietor of the shop to secure the transaction. If the market price moved in the shop's favor, the transaction was closed out as soon as the fluctuation equaled the margin. If the market price went in the customer's favor, he or she could close the transaction at will and collect the difference.[27]

Bucket-shop trading was a national phenomenon at the close of the nineteenth century, existing in at least thirty-three states and in all regions.[28] Some shops were in large cities, perhaps appearing no different from organized exchanges, and even had national clienteles. Others were secretive, dimly lit, and seedy. Bucket shops were always closing their doors under a cloud of suspicion regarding their financial solvency, and the presence of women in the shops was a common scandal.[29]

Bucket-shop trading however was a mostly rural phenomenon, centered in the West and South. Shops were located, for example, in Grand Forks, North Dakota; Elkhart, Indiana; Cumberland, Pennsylvania; and Winnsboro, South Carolina. Many big-city firms specialized in "bucket orders" from "country" customers. In 1895, the *New York Times* reported that one Chicago bucket-shop firm had twenty-seven "country" branch offices in cities as far-flung as Colfax, Iowa, and Boone, Nevada. Were customers gambling on the market's rise and fall? Or were homesteaders, given the fate of landed independence—and with, say, 120 acres at their disposal, not the 5,000 acres of Sawyer—hedging their physical products against market price volatility like Sawyer claimed before Congress? Only they knew.[30]

Bucket-shop trading was easy according to one customer of the Christie Grain & Stock Company of Kansas City:

I went to the office of the Christie Company on the morning of the 25th. I made two trades, one in May corn and one in July oats. I stepped up to the counter to a man whom I since know was Mason, and told him I wanted to buy a thousand bushels of corn at 39 1/8 and a thousand July oats at 23 5/8. Mason glanced up at the board and made out a ticket . . . there was nothing else said at the time these trades were opened.[31]

That was how a great many ordinary Americans came in contact with the novel and complex world of incorporeal commodity exchange—whose legitimacy hardly went uncontested.

Public scrutiny of futures trading began in courthouses. Organized exchanges were private institutions incorporated under state charters, each with rules governing members' transactions. Any trade required a formal contract sanctioned by the corporation wherein the language explicitly called for physical delivery. Nowhere in the contract was the informal practice of financial setting off acknowledged.[32]

The Illinois State Supreme Court invented the aforementioned doctrine of contemplating delivery to adjudicate the legality of setting off in a series of cases decided in September of 1875. Each case was a principal-agent dispute between members of the Chicago Board of Trade who were trading futures as brokers on behalf of nonmember principals. In *Pickering v. Cease* (1875), for instance, Pickering was a member of the board who sold corn short for Cease in the corn pit of the Chicago Board. Pickering and Cease had a mutual understanding with their buyer that no transfer of a physical commodity was ever to take place. On the putative date of delivery Pickering did set off the contract in the pit, at a loss. Cease refused to compensate his broker. Pickering sued Cease for recovery.

Cease argued that because no transfer of a physical commodity ever occurred, no exchange ever really took place—the trade was "fictitious," and Pickering could not expect recovery.[33] Like so many defendants in this first round of cases, Cease was simply avoiding payment. Litigants were a diverse group—farmers, merchants, but also those with no prior experience in the grain business, much less in futures trading. Each cast their lot in the new financial marketplace, lost, and then refused to pay the broker who had granted them access. To mount a legal defense each invoked the long-standing principle—rooted in Anglo-American common law—alluded to by Cease: the legitimate exchange of a commodity required a foundation in the transfer of a corporeal good across space, not an imaginary one through time.[34] Outside insurance markets there was no such thing as a purely conceptual commodity, and even there, given the doctrine of "insurable interest," the "risk" was rooted in an underlying corporeal asset. The legal probity of futures trading thus confronted the court with questions unmistakably epistemological in character.

The Illinois court in *Pickering* did not deny the legality of an "executory contract" which required some future action, such as the delivery of a commodity, for its consummation. The problem occurred when traders in the pits intended all along to set off contracts, knowingly circumventing physical delivery. Because no corporeal object of sale existed to provide an objective foundation for the exchange, the court held that "the alleged purchases are purely fictitious," and thus that "such contracts are void at common law, as being inhibited by a sound public morality." Rather than legitimate speculation, it was immoral/illegal "wagering." The Illinois court, however, did not simply abolish futures trading altogether. Rather, in a group of cases decided along with *Pickering* it formulated a judicial doctrine intended to balance "public morality" with the "legitimate purpose of commerce."[35]

This was the doctrine of contemplating delivery. First, the language of the contract had to call for physical delivery. Furthermore, at least one party had to cognitively contemplate delivery when *entering* the contract. If both parties foresaw executing the contract only by setting off, the transaction was a "wagering contract," unenforceable by law. Thus, so long as one trader contemplated the transfer of a corporeal object, the contract could be legally set off instead. It was a peculiar compromise to say the least and crucial questions remained about its application. Where should the court look to establish the original intent to contemplate delivery? Some courts said that contract language calling for delivery alone was adequate. Shortly after *Pickering,* the Illinois court moved in this direction. Other state and federal courts invoked the same doctrine but enforced stricter standards. Such courts struck down agreements between brokers and their principals if the broker set off the contract in the pits and if it was evident that no one could have reasonably contemplated the transfer of a physical commodity—that is, if traders never possessed the physical commodity, never intended to, and had no means to do so.[36]

After 1875 the doctrine of contemplating delivery swiftly appeared in courthouses throughout the country, as judges focused literally on the mind-set of traders. The tide moved against those brokers who had no resources, other than in their imaginations, to contemplate physical delivery. The most powerful statement came from the Supreme Court of Wisconsin in *Barnard v. Backhaus* (1881), a case involving the Milwaukee Chamber of Commerce. The court announced its "manifest duty" to "scrutinize closely these time contracts" to "determine whether they were really intended by the parties to be what their language imports— real contracts for the future sale and delivery of grain." Furthermore, the court had to "go behind or outside the words of the contract; to look into the facts and circumstances which attended the making of it, in order to ascertain whether it was intended as a bona fide purchase and sale of property." By this standard the court refused to acknowledge the existence, let alone legality, of the disputed transaction.[37]

The judiciary's regulatory reach had clear limits. Courts heard only principal-agent disputes between members of incorporated futures markets and nonmember principals. While the practice of setting off in the pits was at issue insofar as it affected brokers' contractual relations with their clients, controversies did not arise among members of exchanges themselves. The U.S. Supreme Court case *Irwin v. Williar* (1884) was emblematic. In a dispute between a resident of Brazil, Indiana, and a member of the Baltimore Corn and Flour Exchange, Justice Stanley Matthews affirmed the strict standard of *Barnard,* but his ruling did not extend to transactions between pit traders themselves. After *Irwin,* the limits to the courts' reach became increasingly evident, as incorporated futures markets flourished and expanded. What made the courts' tepid intervention noteworthy was that, as it grappled with the elusive difference between speculation and gambling, it distilled the fundamental conceptual problem of futures trading: were objects existing only in the minds of pit traders "fictitious" or as real as the bushels of grain moving through the physical economy?[38]

The above question—whether traders' thoughts were tantamount to things—evoked rising political controversy outside the courts in the 1880s and 1890s. The litigation that generated the doctrine of contemplating delivery involved no organized, collective effort to contest futures. However, farmers' organizations mounted just such a campaign, questioning the legitimate scope of speculative financial risk-taking, as they scrutinized the very nature of economic reality. Agrarian vanguards of the Populist Revolt had already assaulted the constituent elements of the new system of commodity exchange—the railroad corporations, the grading system, and the grain elevators—by the time they turned a critical eye to incorporated commodities futures exchanges in the late 1880s.[39] The 1891 meeting of the National Farmers' Alliance, which launched the Populist Party, proposed banning futures trading.[40] In response to farmers' agitation a few state legislatures passed laws banning futures during the 1880s. Much like jurists ignored legislative bills to protect fraternal societies, they also simply interpreted anti-futures legislation according to their own, more lenient standard of contemplating delivery, effectively nullifying the laws.[41]

Futures critics thus took the fight to Congress. In 1892, Congressman William Hatch of Missouri and Senator William Washburn of Minnesota introduced bills that would tax futures trading out of existence. The congressional hearings *Fictitious Dealings in Agricultural Products* came in response to the Hatch Bill.[42] Witnesses included representatives of the leading organized futures markets, farmers' organizations, and the "handler" class—millers, wholesalers, retailers, and commission merchants who, unlike pure financial speculators, actually "handled" physical commodities and often sided with the farmers.

The very title *Fictitious Dealings in Agricultural Products* suggested the contested legitimacy of a seemingly metaphysical financial marketplace. Preeminent during the hearings were two interrelated questions: Was futures trading "fictitious" dealing or "real" commerce? Was the practice of setting off a form of productive financial speculation with real benefits for society or were dealers playing with "imagined differences" in their own minds—engaging in an unproductive form of gambling?

No doubt many agrarians simply did not understand how futures worked. "The settlement of differences" was simply "not legitimate trading," protested critics such as Wilbur F. Boyle of St. Louis, a former judge employed by the National Alliance of Farmers and Industrial Laborers. Because, "certainly no one can claim a right to sell that which he not only does not own, but never intends to acquire, and consequently never intends to deliver." For "in that case he is selling that which nobody owns, and which, in the nature of things, has no real existence." Producers claimed that farm prices had plummeted—the final decades of the nineteenth century had witnessed a brutal long-term secular decline— because futures dealers loaded the market with products that were "fictitious," "unnatural," "fiat," "phantom," "air," and "wind." As one handler complained, "Mr. Sawyer loads the market with double quantities of wheat, one being the real grain shipped to and sold in New York and other Eastern markets, and an equal quantity of phantom wheat sold in Chicago." The only remedy was that traders must buy and sell corporeal commodities that they physically possessed and meant to distribute. To simply "contemplate delivery" was not enough.[43]

Yet, more than falling prices and an inadequate understanding of arcane financial practices were at issue. The pits, where future agricultural products were marketed without the farmer's consent, had seemingly abrogated the farmer's dominion over the fruit of his productive labor, his right to negotiate the sale of his own property. As C. Wood Davis, a Wichita grain merchant, put it, Sawyer's sales "were sales of Minnesota wind instead of Minnesota wheat, and yet help determine the price the Ohio farmer shall receive for his wheat." A principle as "old as civilization" was that the "the owner of property is the one who shall determine its prices." The farmer, complained one agrarian, was "not admitted to the board." Farmers critical of futures wanted access to the forum where commodity prices were determined.[44]

In this sense, the agrarian critique was not hostile to speculation per se. Commercial risk-taking could exist comfortably within the category of productive labor. American farmers had long chased upside commercial risks. Some came before Congress and celebrated the virtues of manual labor, hyperbolically denigrating parasitic financial speculation.[45] Yet, "We want all the legitimate speculation that we can get," said one advocate of antifutures legislation. The producer "desires speculation," said one agrarian—"that laudable form of speculation which buys real products, not contracts." Another argued that Congress should remove the "gamblers" but "permit those who only sought legitimate speculation to continue to speculate." The scalper stole the farmer's upside risk, his profit. The farmer, according to one testifier, "instead of . . . getting the benefits of his labor . . . is robbed by a system of trade over which he has no control." Speculation with "evidence of ownership" was as "old as commerce itself." It was because scalpers did not ever own physical commodities that futures markets were immoral "gambling dens."[46]

Representatives of the incorporated commodities exchanges too responded that risk-taking was of the essence of commerce itself. But futures trading remained adequately rooted in the physical economy. Rather than gambling, it was a morally legitimate form of productive risk-taking. In fact, it was speculation that acted as "insurance," performing a social function for all interested parties in American agriculture—the producer, the distributor, and the consumer. The futures "speculator" was in fact the "farmer's best friend."[47]

Indeed, the pits defended futures trading with a by now longstanding moral argument. "Speculation is as old as the world," one futures trader reminded, "and while it may be immodest in a layman in the law to suggest it, has the question of a man's right to speculate with his own money ever been fully adjudicated?" Another futures trader spoke of man's inherent desire:

> . . . to take chances, to speculate; he is a gambler. The Indian will bet his blanket and his squaw on a pony race, the "negro" will risk his last dime and his chances of getting into prison on a game of "craps," and the prince of one of the most powerful nations of enlightened Europe will risk his reputation and perhaps his crown to play baccarat.

"We are preeminently a bright speculative nation," another proclaimed before Congress. "And are we not all free and equal? Can not we all deal in grain when any of us may choose?" Prevent a man from "speculating

in railroad stocks" and "railroads could not be built." Financial speculation was the rightful activity of a free, self-owning individual. The risk
taken was an element of that self-ownership, and warranted a moral/
pecuniary reward.[48]

The legal doctrine of contemplating delivery informed yet another
line of argument. A member of the Chicago Board of Trade, admitting
that the volume of futures commodities dwarfed the actual grain received in Chicago in 1891, nonetheless insisted that there was a "legitimate basis all the time for our business." The acting president of the
board declared that "a sacred and exact observance of contracts is insisted upon" where "actual delivery was contemplated." "Setting off"
constituted a form of delivery as "real" and "legitimate" as the physical
distribution of a corporeal commodity. When a Michigan congressman
described setting off as evidence that "there is never any grain delivered" in the majority of commodity exchanges, a New York futures
dealer retorted, "I beg your pardon sir, it is delivered." Two very different notions of what constituted actual delivery, a "real" economy, were
on the table before Congress.[49]

Incorporated commodities exchanges further argued that only real
events—the condition of the French crop, the curtailing of Russian
exports, or the weather in California—determined futures prices, not
whatever whims were in traders' minds. Futures traders argued their
business was a science requiring intelligence and great skill. The incorporated exchanges were great consumers of public and private
weather and crop forecasting reports, and the big exchanges in Chicago
and New York published reams upon reams of their own statistical
studies for their members' benefit. "This short selling has in recent years
been reduced to a science," explained one trader. If not yet a probabilistic science, futures speculation was becoming more scientific and therefore more professional and respectable.[50]

Yet, futures traders knew well that their transactions were detached
from the space-time of the physical economy. They warned that if Congress eradicated futures in the United States, the business would simply
move to the other futures markets of the world: Liverpool, Le Havre,
Bremen, or perhaps elsewhere. Sawyer's capital was mobile, and unlike
his wheat through the telegraph in an instant it could reach any market-

place in the world. A New Orleans trader of cotton futures was blunt: "The world is not going to cease trading and speculating in the great staples in deference to any sentimental idea, and if it can not be done in New York, New Orleans, Chicago, Milwaukee, St. Louis, and San Francisco, it will be done where no such absurd notions exist." Legislators could tax futures dealing out of existence in the United States but not the world over.[51]

Regardless, whether futures trading took place in Chicago, San Francisco, or Buenos Aires, the organized exchanges maintained that it was of a piece with and subservient to physical production, distribution, and consumption. In this context, above all, the pits argued that futures speculation amounted to "insurance."

Sawyer's testimony was part of this rhetorical effort. Another trader sounded the same theme, comparing the antifutures bill before Congress that would prohibit "insuring against loss . . . in the market" with a law that would prohibit "insuring against loss from fire." But futures provided more than personal insurance for men like Sawyer. The collective result of all futures transactions—engaged in for whatever reason—provided "insurance," as it were, for all members of American society with an interest in the production of agricultural commodities. Futures trading signaled forward prices and eliminated their future ups and downs. "Active and continuous buying and selling for future delivery holds prices in conformity with the inexorable law of supply and demand, and prevents . . . wide fluctuations," explained one Chicago dealer. "Intelligent speculation" and "prices based upon the average opinion of the board" were in fact the best indicators of the market's future. Furthermore, in the process the men of the pits assumed the risks inherent in capitalist agricultural, removing risk from the backs of other participants in the physical market structure—both handlers, and whether they realized it or not, farmers. Corporations like the Chicago Board of Trade thus centralized, systematized, and socialized risk. This was a new argument. Organized commodities futures exchanges first mounted an explicit social defense of financial speculation. Speculation was risk management.[52]

For their part, agrarian critics of futures were not deaf to the argument that capitalist agriculture required some form of risk management.

They knew that farm products had to be raised, harvested, graded, stored, and then transported over long distances of space—during which time markets fluctuated. The futures traders were right: given the fate of landed independence and high levels of mortgage indebtedness many farmers desperately wanted to hedge against market volatility. But the Populists looked not to Chicago but to Washington, not to the pits but to the federal government.

Before Congress, agrarians made the obvious point that a corporation like the Chicago Board of Trade was fit for big capitalist farmers like Sawyer, not small western homesteaders, much less southern sharecroppers. A leader of the National Grange explained: "I do not pretend . . . to represent our farmer friend who farms on the board of trade in Chicago, who can lose $15,000" on a futures trade. The man who he represented: "if he should lose $15,000 on a deal, would be wiped out and have nothing left in the world." Without access to a telegraph or a broker, enough cash or credit for the margin requirement, the ability to financially withstand the recurrent bouts of speculative mania in the pits, or the ability to buy the smallest "wheat futures" contract, the small farmer had to sell his crop to men like Sawyer during harvest season, no matter what the price. Meanwhile, Sawyer could afford to hedge his physical wheat in Chicago with short sales. "We are told that this system of trading," offered the master of the National Grange, "affords perfect insurance to [Sawyer], and enables him to do business without risk." But "insurance" always meant that a "premium had to be paid." The farmer paid that premium, having "his products cheapened by" Sawyer's short sells. Therefore, it was not Sawyer's counterparty in the pit—the scalper—but rather the farmer who assumed his risk. Meanwhile, the southern sharecropper, black or white, whose crop was probably already mortgaged to a factor to begin with, was even less able to make use of the New Orleans or New York Cotton Exchange.[53]

In this era, many farmers experimented with their own storage, marketing, and distribution cooperatives—often invoking the spirit of fraternity.[54] Yet, before Congress in 1892 the agrarian leader Charles Macune testified on the Populists' infamous "subtreasury plan." With it the federal government would provide warehouses for farmers to store their crops. It would then issue them paper money against their crops as collateral. For one, this would increase the money supply and, in the context of the deflationary gold standard, help farmers pay back their debts, including their mortgages. But subtreasuries would also allow farmers to hold back their products from a depressed world market on their own terms. Farmers would not be forced to sell to men like Sawyer. Populists would have Congress—in effect—centralize and assume risk. In response to the generative insecurities and radical uncertainties of capitalism, the federal government would enter the business of risk management.[55]

The subtreasury plan would have two upshots. It would provide small agricultural producers with a new, noncommercial form of economic security premised upon citizenship. It would also allow small farmers to chase upside commercial risks on the backs of their own products. A sympathetic congressman asked Sawyer that "if a method could be devised by which these farmers could hold the wheat and sell it as the world needs it," would not that eliminate the need for "these gamblers" in Chicago? Sawyer responded that in that case the farmers would become the "gamblers themselves." A man would be "taking his own chances instead of putting it on the market and letting the gambler take the chance." In other words, "The farmer becomes the gambler instead of the producer." But this was exactly what many agrarians wanted. They were not hostile to markets and speculation, only to the workings of one specific kind of financial market they did not control. Futures traders, although they claimed to be assuming risk for the farmer's benefit, were accused of stealing the farmer's proprietary risks, elements of his rightful self-ownership and freedom. The scalper did so by trading things that were not real.[56]

Agrarians thus sought to abolish futures trading. They very nearly succeeded. In 1892 the Hatch Bill passed the House by a vote of 167 to 46 and the Senate by a vote of 40 to 29. The opposition came from southern senators who claimed to support the bill's purpose but viewed its tax-to-destroy method as an unconstitutional affront to states' rights. When senators from the South successfully passed amendments to the bill, the House had to vote again. But only a few days remained in the 52nd Congress. The speaker had placed the bill far down in the voting schedule and a second House vote required a first vote to suspend an obscure parliamentary rule. The vote was 172 to 124, just short of the two-thirds requirement. Southern senators convinced enough members of the House to sway the vote. The Hatch Bill died. It was brought to the floor and debated again in 1893 and 1894 but failed to pass by even wider margins.[57]

By this time the presidential election of 1896 loomed. The Democratic National Convention was held in Chicago and the great Nebraska orator William Jennings Bryan emerged at the top of the ticket, fusing Democrats and Populists. Just down the street from the pits of the Chicago Board of Trade, Bryan gave his famous "Cross of Gold" address. He declared:

> the farmer who goes forth in the morning and toils all day . . . and who by the application of brain and muscle to the natural resources of the country creates wealth, is as much a business man as the man who goes upon the board of trade and bets upon the prices of grain.[58]

The Populist commercial critique was that new, big centralizing institutions—in this case the Chicago Board of Trade—were gobbling up small, individual proprietary risks. Bryan lost the election to the Republican candidate William McKinley and the Populist Revolt subsequently collapsed. For now the pits were saved. Yet the underlying moral and conceptual problems remained unresolved and returned to the courts.

Now the bucket shops took center stage. As farmers' protests against the incorporated exchanges intensified in the late 1880s, the practice of bucket-shop trading exploded.[59] The incorporated exchanges thus confronted a new adversary. Unlike their agrarian critics the bucket-shop traders advocated a form of commodity exchange not more but rather even less rooted in the physical economy of goods. What degree of abstraction from the physical economy was legitimate? In 1905 that question came before the U.S. Supreme Court, the forum where what the organized exchanges termed the "bucket shop war" finally ended.

During the 1892 hearings members of incorporated exchanges had argued for a distinction between futures and bucket-shop trading, predicated upon the contemplation of delivery in the language of organized exchanges' contracts. Bucket-shop trades lacked that formal provision. That distinction was the basis for the war between the pits and the bucket shops. Organized exchanges attacked the shops as "gambling dens" while proprietors of bucket shops responded that transactions in the shops were no different from those in the pits. If bucket-shop trading was "gambling" then so was all futures trading, no matter where it occurred. Corporations were simply trying to monopolize the trade—to create, according to one bucket-shop proprietor, a nefarious "trust." The incorporated exchanges had successfully warded off efforts to eradicate futures trading. Now they fought efforts to democratize it.[60]

Notably, agrarian radicals largely desisted from criticizing bucket shops. Perhaps it was because they too considered them no different from the incorporated exchanges. Or perhaps it was because the shops had smaller customers, who were allowed to purchase futures in smaller increments. And one did not have to buy a membership in a corporation or pay a broker who had. The shops were open to all. For small farmers, bucket-shop trading may well have performed a hedging function much the same way the Chicago Board of Trade did for Sawyer. One Cincinnati man wrote to the House Committee on Agriculture, "It is singular that the bucket shop, which is pointed out as the nearest approach to gambling of all speculative operations should be by all odds the safest from danger to the citizen."[61] The worst of all worlds for the small farmer—especially a mortgaged farmer with every acre in one crop— would be incorporated futures markets without bucket shops.

As bucket shops competed with incorporated exchanges, members of the latter campaigned to suppress them. According to a New York futures trader who testified before Congress in 1892, "Formerly, the farmers and small dealers throughout the country used to execute their orders on the exchanges of the country." But "owing to the development of telegraphic facilities they began trading through bucket shops, where no grain is received or delivered, or can be." He insisted that, "If you crush out the bucket shops, the legitimate business of the country would be greatly benefited." Conversely, bucket-shop proprietors maintained that their shops *did* handle physical commodities.[62] Regardless, in a world where commodity transactions had been liberated from space the incorporated exchanges claimed that futures trading should be tightly restricted to specific places—the trading floors of their pits.

Complicating the conflict between the pits and the bucket shops, states began passing "anti-bucket shop" laws. Sometimes this came at the request of agrarian organizations. In the late 1890s, precocious progressive reformers began to attack the "vice" of gambling in the bucket shops.[63] But truly muddying the waters were "anti-option" bills. "Options" contracts simply gave one party the option to execute, or not execute, a futures transaction at some future date.[64] Members of organized exchanges publicly decried options as a form of gambling, no different from bucket-shop trading, as the language of options contracts did not require physical delivery. Options were formally banned in the pits, although options trading was common nonetheless—in the pits, on the street curbs, and after the market closed in the exchange hall itself.[65] But it fell to the courts to interpret vague "anti-option" legislation. The 1887 Illinois "anti-option" bill loosely condemned "pretended buying and selling," defined as a trade with no "intention" of "delivering the property so sold."[66] For the courts, there were several alternatives: Abolish the bucket shops? Abolish options trading? Abolish the pits? Abolish them all?

The Chicago Board of Trade led the fight against bucket shops. For access to the board's prices (and thus their existence) bucket shops were wholly dependent on telegraph corporations. The board's legal strategy was to block companies from distributing prices to shops by claiming, as a corporate legal actor, an individual property right in its prices. In 1889, the Illinois Supreme Court ruled against the board's claim, furthering the spread of bucket shops. Finally, in 1899, the board and the Western Union telegraph company entered into a contract prohibiting price distribution to institutions identified by the board as bucket shops. C. C. Christie of the Christie Grain & Stock Company of Kansas City filed suit against the Chicago Board of Trade in February of 1900 citing the 1890 Sherman Antitrust Act. The board sued Christie for employing spies in the pits to steal quotations, a charge Christie denied. At one point the state and federal litigation descending from Christie's 1900 lawsuit encompassed forty-six cases. Consolidated as *Board of Trade v. Christie,* the conflict reached the U.S. Supreme Court in April 1905.[67]

Christie's legal strategy highlighted the abstractions of the pits and challenged all American futures trading. Citing the 1887 Illinois legislation, Christie argued that it was in fact the Chicago Board of Trade that "kept the greatest of bucket shops . . . wherein is permitted the pretended buying and selling of grain, etc., without any intention of receiving and paying for the property so bought, or of delivering the property so sold."[68] If the court accepted Christie's argument that traders in the pits never intended to perform physical delivery, it would seemingly have to either abolish or uphold both the shops and the pits. Christie, of course, wagered on the latter.

At first Christie's plan worked. In the federal trial court even the president of the board admitted under oath that "98 per cent. [of futures trades], according to the weight of the testimony, are settled before the day of delivery by the parties paying and receiving the difference between the contract prices and the market prices." The court found that "the greater part of the dealings in futures . . . are bucket-shop transactions, and that they are permitted . . . in violation of the laws of Illinois"—a finding upheld by the appellate court. The incorporated exchanges' lawyers had argued fruitlessly that their clients contemplated delivery, whereas bucket-shop traders did not. But as Christie had countered in public, "it is difficult for the average man to understand how the dealer who sells [futures contracts] can make deliveries of, or how the dealer who buys can receive, what does not exist." Of course, the lower court decisions were equally damning of bucket shops. For his part, Christie hoped the Supreme Court would acknowledge that bucket-shop trades were also conducted for hedging purposes, validating both the pits and the shops, annulling the Illinois legislation. Meanwhile, a day before the court was to announce its decision, the Chicago Board's lobbyists tried to rush a new anti-bucket shop/pro-futures bill through the Illinois Assembly. Farmers' advocates killed it. "Exciting scenes," reported the *New York Times*, "marked the defeat of the bill." As the assembly speaker "rapped for order," Chicago Board of Trade lobbyists "who had crowded in the Chamber, were ejected from the floor by the Sergeant at Arms."[69]

It thus finally fell to the Supreme Court and to Justice Holmes to determine the fundamental legality of futures trading. Holmes appeared to brusquely resolve the question, upholding the legitimacy of trading in things with no corporeal existence: "A set-off is, in legal effect, a delivery." Holmes acknowledged that at least three-quarters of all futures trades involved "no physical handing over of any grain" but merely the practice of setting off. Nevertheless, he ruled that setting off and physical delivery were one and the same: "Set-off has all the effects of delivery." Thereafter, dealers in the pits of incorporated exchanges called *Christie* the "Magna Carta" of their trade.[70]

But Holmes did not condone all fictitious dealings. He distinguished between the pits and the bucket shops. Bucket-shop trading was merely "speculation entered into for its own sake." Legally, Holmes held that incorporated exchanges had a property right in their prices. Excluding bucket shops from access to the pits' prices effectively put them out of existence. Armed with *Christie,* between May and December of 1905 the Chicago Board of Trade would successfully seek injunctions against 197 different bucket shops.[71] As opposed to bucket-shop trading, Holmes wrote of the futures traders of organized commodities exchanges, "Speculation of this kind by competent men is the self-adjustment of society to the probable."[72]

That terse statement drew the ire of the bucket-shop king. Christie himself issued a missive immediately after Holmes's ruling came down: "I know now that this band of hypocrites are busy 'adjusting society to the probable.'"[73] Christie pointed to a seeming double standard: pit trading was competent social self-adjustment, but bucket-shop trading was immoral gambling. The phrase that Christie fastened onto was indeed the pivot of Holmes's decision. It was one that, with respect to risk's history, spoke to the epistemological transformation achieved by the triumph of futures trading. But it also reflected Holmes's personal preoccupation with the contingent link between present and future.

Years after *Christie,* Holmes wrote a letter revealing the Harvard schoolboy origins of his philosophical understanding of uncertainty. "Chauncey Wright[,] a nearly forgotten philosopher of real merit, taught me when young that I must not say *necessary* about the universe, that we don't know whether anything is necessary or not," he recalled. "So that I describe myself as a *bet*tabilitarian. I believe that we can *bet* on the behavior of the universe in its contract with us." Holmes was not the only youthful thinker transfixed by the Bostonian Chauncey Wright.[74]

It was scarcely pure coincidence that Wright's other Harvard students developed similar views on the primacy of indeterminacy and chance. There was Holmes the jurist, but also the logician Charles Sanders Peirce. In 1843, Peirce's father Benjamin, a Harvard mathematician, had produced the table of mortality for the recently chartered New England Mutual Life Insurance Company. For that matter, Oliver Wendell Holmes, Sr., a medical doctor, was in that decade a founder of the American Statistical Association. One son, Charles Peirce, led a philosophical revolt against formalism in logic. Another son, Holmes, Jr., did the same in the field of jurisprudence.[75] To Peirce, indeterminateness was at the core of the universe. As he put it in 1877 in the *Popular Science Monthly,* the search for certainty was always in some sense like being on "a ship in the open sea, with no one on board who understands the rules of navigation."[76] Certainty was a human convention, not an independent reality—whether it was the certainty of God's providential order or of statistical law, there was no transcendent, fixed point that could provide an objective foundation. The universe was shot through with chance. *Christie* had strong roots in a philosophical outlook where the only certainty was a radical uncertainty.[77]

In 1875, another of Holmes's Harvard classmates, the future philosopher William James, wrote in a letter "that of late years there has been no intellect in Cambridge of such powers and originality as [Peirce], unless one should except the late Chauncey Wright." Later, as philosopher and jurist, James and Holmes would not agree on everything. Holmes, for one, believed that over the course of time James had softened from a "bettabilitarian" like himself to a wishful thinker. In 1917, Holmes wrote a letter to the British political theorist Harold Laski that wryly rendered James's view on free will: "by yearning we can modify the multiplication table, which I doubt." Holmes would later recall to Laski in 1927, "I once told Bill James that his discourse on free will would please the ladies and unitarian parsons." Holmes thought himself far more tough-minded than James. But even the nub of their philosophical differences spoke to common concerns. As a bettabilitarian, to Holmes a bet against the multiplication tables was foolhardy, yet he had only a better bet to place in its stead. 'Two times two equals four' was still bet nonetheless. Each in their own way, James philosophically and Holmes jurisprudentially, dwelled upon uncertainty and doubt. That meant, in Holmes's words "the self-adjustment of society to the probable," and in James's words "our relations with the possible." James's philosophy of chance thus helps to clarify the path Holmes followed in *Christie*.[78]

In *Christie*, for instance, Holmes adjudicated on the epistemological relationship between financial traders' thoughts and physical things. The relationship between thoughts and things was an abiding preoccupation of James. His 1904 essay "Does Consciousness Exist?" inquired, "To begin with, *are* thoughts and things as heterogeneous as is commonly said?" James answered no. The trick was not to get thoughts and things to correspond to each other but rather to do away with that hard metaphysical dualism altogether. Instead, James argued that both could be part of the same capacious, open-ended and future-oriented reality. As James argued of thoughts, "non-perceptual experiences have objectivity as well as subjectivity."[79] In a world of chance there was no use inquiring about the supposed fixed realities (things) that corresponded to one's thoughts. The only possible authority for determining a thought's truth was to look to its human consequences in the future.[80]

That, in essence, was the distinctively American philosophy of pragmatism. James arrived to it after rejecting deterministic ways of thinking. First he had come to terms with Darwin, ridiculing the pop-Darwinist notion that "there are no accidents," that all changes in the world are "independent of individual control." In an 1880 essay, a youthful James created his own Darwinism, a mixture of evolutionary randomness and free will. His 1884 essay the "Dilemma of Determinism" went further. In it, James posited two forms of determinism: "hard" and "soft." "Hard" determinism was a ruined doctrine—a determinism that spoke of "fatality, bondage of the will, necessitation, and the like" or "even predetermination." What James felt up against was the "soft" determinism of his day. "It professes that those parts of the universe already laid down absolutely appoint and decree what the other parts shall be. The future has no ambiguous possibilities hidden in its womb." Soft determinism thus included objective probability theory—which demanded that all possible outcomes be accounted for so that they could be mathematically measured. But objective probability theory could not account for all possibilities in a radically uncertain reality. To grasp those possibilities, James pictured a world of "chance"—one that "says that the parts have a certain amount of loose play on one another," a future with "possibilities . . . in excess of actualities." A universe of "chance" meant that individuals, necessarily, were metaphysical risk-takers. By 1898, when James presented his entire philosophy in the popular lectures that became *Pragmatism,* he wrote: "the world stands really malleable, waiting to receive its final touches at our hands. Like the kingdom of heaven, it suffers human violence willingly."[81]

James's sympathies and inclinations were individualist to the core. He might have trained a generation of twentieth-century social scientists, but he had also sat at the feet of Ralph Waldo Emerson. James's famous 1897 essay on religious belief, entitled the "The Will to Believe," thus argued that we have "the right to believe at our own risk any hypothesis that is live enough to tempt our will." Belief in chance, rather than providence or any other "doctrine of objective certitude," could warrant a pragmatic belief in both free will and God. In a chance-ridden universe, to bear and cope with risk was both the price and payoff of individual freedom— what James's student W. E. B Du Bois would call the "tingling challenge of risk."[82] "The Will to Believe" no doubt contributed to Holmes's sense that James had gone soft. But the moral ethos of individual risk-taking did inform one line of argument in *Christie.* "People will endeavor to forecast the future," Holmes offered, "and to make agreements according to their prophecy."[83]

James was interested in making a new argument in defense of free will; in *Christie* pragmatism showed its more social face. How should American society adjust itself to the radical uncertainties of capitalism? The economic chance-world, as much as the aftershock of the Civil War, and as much as the aftermath of Darwin, was the context in which American philosophical pragmatism arose and flourished.[84] Holmes ruled that futures speculation by "competent men" at the Chicago Board of Trade was the "self-adjustment" not of the individual but rather of "society" to "the probable."

Critics of futures trading had argued that futures prices were, put simply, false. Trading in the pits violated the physical reality of bales of wheat. But what if the only authorities in the world were future consequences and there was no standard of evaluation outside human purposes and needs? What were the consequences of futures trading in thoughts? In a narrow sense, on the transactional score of setting off, Holmes remarked that monetarily, "the result of actual delivery would be to leave the parties just where they were before." For futures dealers, it did not matter that no physical commodities provided immediate objective foundations, which was why "set-off has all the effects of delivery."[85] In *Pragmatism,* tellingly, James presented the following financial metaphor for truth:

> Truth lives, in fact, for the most part on a credit system. Our thoughts and beliefs 'pass', so long as nothing challenges them, just as bank-notes pass so long as nobody refuses them. But this all points to direct face-to-face verifications somewhere, without which the fabric of truth collapses like a *financial system* with no cash-basis whatever. You accept my verification of one thing, I yours of another. *We trade on each other's truth.* But beliefs verified concretely by somebody are the posts of the whole superstructure.[86]

James might have had a futures trader in mind. The objective foundation of each futures transaction was purely intersubjective. Futures trades themselves did not actually require the transfer of physical commodities. But each alternative had the same consequence—dealers "trade on each other's truth." James was not making a crass commercial comparison between money and truth. Rather, the uncertainty of a particular financial transaction modeled the fundamental metaphysical uncertainty of the universe.

In *Christie,* the same philosophical outlook defended a new tool of corporate risk management. James's metaphor of traders trading truths also speaks to Holmes's understanding of incorporeal exchange as a method of financial hedging. "Hedging," Holmes explained in *Christie:*

> . . . is a means by which collectors and exporters of grain or other products . . . secure themselves against the fluctuations of the market by counter contracts for the purchase or sale, as the case may be, of an equal quantity of the product, or of the material of manufacture. It is none the less a serious business contract for a legitimate and useful purpose that it may be offset before the time of delivery in case delivery should not be needed or desired.

Thoughts and things interacted—a futures trade had a relationship with a real commodity somewhere out there—in order to hedge the future fluctuations of the capitalist price system. Of course Holmes's explanation echoed Sawyer's 1892 description of his business during the hearing on *Fictitious Dealings In Agricultural Products* to the letter.[87]

Furthermore, mounting this argument in 1905, Holmes had assistance. For in between the 1892 congressional hearings and *Christie* the pits had found new allies. Leading thinkers, including prominent journalists and academics, picked up the argument that futures speculation offered society a form of social insurance. At the 1899 meeting of the American Economic Association, the economist Henry Crosby Emery gave a paper on "The Place of the Speculator in the Theory of Distribution." He called futures speculators a special "class of risk-takers" with a "distinct function." The "results" of "speculation" in their case was a "greater stability of price." It was "insurance" against the "risks of continuous price fluctuations" that plagued a market economy—namely "conjuncture risks." It was the futures trader's job—whether he knew or intended it or not—to "assume these risks" for the benefit of society. Two years later Allan H. Willett, a Columbia-trained economist, published the first economic treatise on risk, *The Economic Theory of Risk and Insurance.* In the past, Willett wrote, insurance had been "confined to the assumption of risks in which the existence of the possession of property was involved." Now, futures speculation, which involved no such possession, was being "utilized by society" for the purpose of insurance against "fluctuations in value." Paradoxically, "it is in reducing the cost of this special kind of risk that speculators serve society as insurers." In short, futures trading was social insurance.[88]

Therefore, by 1904, the Yale economist Arthur T. Hadley could summarize the prevailing view in his economics textbook. When done by "competent" men futures trading insured against "fluctuations" in future prices. A year later Holmes called futures speculation by "competent" men the "self-adjustment of society to the probable." By then farm prices had recovered from the late nineteenth-century secular decline, removing one common late-nineteenth-century agrarian critique. Looking at it pragmatically, in a chance-ridden economic universe futures speculation accomplished the self-adjustment of society. In good Jamesian fashion, Holmes came to terms with a new level of financial abstraction by extending in time and space the possible relations between thoughts and things. Even if the scalper did not own the underlying commodity, the consequence of his futures speculation achieved a pragmatic relationship with the broader American economy. It achieved risk management.[89]

But of course not all futures trades were performed with the intent to hedge. And one man's hedge might be another man's naked wager. The scalper—the always willing speculator—was necessary for the pits to flourish. But in *Christie* Holmes dismissed not scalping but rather bucket-shop trading as "purchases made with the understanding that the contract will be settled by paying the difference between the contract and the market price at a certain time"—in other words, "merely a speculation entered into for its own sake." Conversely, trades at incorporated exchanges "with the expectation that they will be satisfied by set-off" fell into the category of hedging, in which "the object was self-protection in business." Hedging supposedly kept the world of immaterial trade in line with the physical economy. Bucket-shop trading, Holmes ruled, did not. Likewise, for his part James held that the truth process "points to direct face-to-face verifications somewhere, without which the fabric of truth collapses like a financial system with no cash-basis whatever," and that "beliefs verified concretely by somebody are the posts of the whole superstructure." In *Christie,* hedging had provided such verification in incorporated exchanges but not in bucket shops.[90]

With respect to the bucket shops, Holmes's decision was on remarkably weak footing. If scalpers could speculate with no regard for corporeal goods, why could bucket-shop traders not do the same thing? Furthermore, as Christie repeatedly insisted, small farmers might use bucket shops to financially hedge their physical products. And there was plenty of "speculation" for its own sake in the pits with little social utility to show for it.

Willett underscored the fact that insurance was only "something of a by-product" of futures speculation. He wrote in *The Economic Theory of Risk and Insurance* that some of the "operations of speculators" were of "doubtful service to society." That could not be "denied." The pits always threatened to lose touch with the physical economy. They could signal and smoothen forward prices but the degree of abstraction and the intent of the traders meant that socially unproductive, if not potentially destructive, financial speculation was necessarily built into the system. Willett concluded: "It may well be hoped that in the course of time a different method of reducing . . . risk may be evolved, which shall be as efficient as speculation and free from many of its attendant evils."[91] That has not happened. In the course of time financial derivatives have only proliferated. Indeed, Willet wrote in 1901 only at the dawn of derivatives. Whether or not they have indirectly led to greater risk management or directly led to greater market volatility remains an open question.

Nevertheless, after 1905, with the closing of many a bucket shop pit traders at incorporated exchanges began to engage in even more extensive labors of abstraction. The pits newly condoned options trading, which they had equated with bucket-shop trading prior to *Christie*. Christie was right—ultimately Holmes granted financial corporations like the Chicago Board of Trade a monopoly on all kinds of derivatives trading, a monopoly which lasted late into the twentieth century.[92]

No doubt the triumph of the pits in 1905 was a political one for those whom Holmes deemed the "competent men," the men in the pits who were capable of trading thoughts as things, capable of contemplating delivery. Holmes expressed the emergence of a new way of thinking about the contingent link between present and future, but the problem of commodity exchange lay originally in the simple fact that Sawyer had to get his wheat from the fields of North Dakota, which were like the "waves of the ocean," to the mills on the other side of the Atlantic Ocean—hopefully at a nice profit.

CHAPTER 8

The Trust Question

As a matter of fact, we were all in a sinking ship, if existing cut-throat competition continued, and we were trying to build a life-boat to carry us all to the shore. You don't have to threaten men to get them to leave a sinking ship in a lifeboat. . . . The Standard [Oil Company] was an angel of mercy, reaching down from the sky, and saying 'Get into the ark. Put in your old junk. We'll take all the risks!

—John D. Rockefeller, Sr. (1917)

"[I]N THE VERY BEGINNING," explained George Walbridge Perkins, Sr., "the universe was organized." Perkins was lecturing an assembled group of academic economists at Columbia University in 1907 on the topic of the "Modern Corporation." Perkins however was no academic. A partner in J.P. Morgan & Co., normally he was downtown at 23 Wall Street organizing modern, industrial corporations—including the biggest so-called "trust" of them all, the United States Steel Corporation.[1]

Nothing that man "has done in society," Perkins continued, would ever bring "to pass so complete a form or organization," so "vast a trust," as the "all-including system of organization called the universe." From "chaos" and "competition" the universe's original design wrought "organization," "control," and "co-operation." It was "perfect." But trust lords like Perkins were giving the universe a run for its money, hoping to consign the economic chance-world to the past. By organizing industrial trusts they were attempting to build a new, corporate form of economic life. When Perkins finished his address the president of Columbia quickly ran him off the stage, realizing that he had unwittingly invited to Morningside Heights a "dangerous radical."[2]

Part of what made a leading partner in the House of Morgan appear to the president of Columbia a "dangerous radical"—hardly trustworthy—was his avowed hostility to an atomized commercial individualism. Not too many financiers have felt the need to announce a grand conceptualization of the universe to justify their daily work to the world, but Perkins was one of them. Neither the universe nor Perkins liked uncertainty which meant that both disliked the individualist ethos of market-based competition. "How should we get on," he pushed the metaphor, "if there were incessant competition between day and night, or a constant struggle for supremacy between the seasons?" Perkins wanted more chance squeezed out of the existing social universe and believed that a new, industrial form of organizational life, the "Modern Corporation," was up to the task. Before the business-minded Progressive reform group he called home, the National Civic Federation (NCF), Perkins concluded in another 1907 address that corporatization would lead to "a form of socialism of the highest" which still "preserves the right of private property." Indeed corporatization would preserve the right of private property. In 1910 Perkins, one of America's leading finance capitalists, would cash out $5.5 million from his J.P. Morgan & Co. partnership.[3]

Perkins's reference to "socialism" in his NCF address was a rhetorical flourish; there were actual socialists around at the time and he was not one of them. Rather, his 1907 addresses were early expressions of a twentieth-century corporate welfare capitalism, which was distinct in some ways from the capitalism that came before. Nineteenth-century liberal capitalism celebrated, in fact demanded, a link among freedom, self-ownership, and the personal assumption of risk. But life at your own risk, Perkins decided, had become too risky. Offloading personal risks onto a corporate financial system was not enough to adequately stabilize capitalism's radically uncertain future. Risk would have to be incorporated by society, rather than enclosed and borne by individuals. The American economy now demanded outright corporatization. Working from within the very citadel of American finance capital, Perkins sought allies to mount a wholesale corporate countermovement against the instabilities and insecurities of industrial capitalism. He placed his hopes with the new industrial corporations—known then as "trusts."

What Perkins wanted mattered because of his position of power within a financial system that had accumulated vast stores of financial capital. Perkins first reached the pinnacle of the American business community via a financial rather than industrial corporation—as the vice president and chairman of the Finance Committee of the New York Life Insurance Company. In 1905, the New York Life held $391 million in assets, representing 4.7 per cent of total private American savings.[4] Perkins all but single-handedly invested the New York Life's reserves in the Wall Street capital market, which was why, in 1901, J.P. Morgan offered him a partnership in the House of Morgan. His investments on behalf of the New York Life contributed to his wished-for corporate consolidation of American manufacturing. In this way, Perkins's "corporation idea" was the fruit of nineteenth-century financial risk management.

Financial risk management had also bequeathed to Perkins's generation a protean approach to both thinking about and institutionally managing uncertainty: the insurance principle. Perkins—who had cut his teeth at the New York Life, one of the great financial corporations of the nineteenth century—sought to newly apply a financial concept to the instabilities of industry. From men like Perkins industrial corporations began to learn to think and act in terms of risk.[5]

The new industrial trusts would insure industrial *society* as a whole. Corporate ownership, not self-ownership, would be the new premise of economic security. But to do so corporations would need to exist prior to, over, and above flesh-and-blood individuals who found a new functional place within a new institutional matrix. Financiers like Perkins organized corporations; the visible hand of corporate managers eliminated markets and vertically and horizontally organized production and distribution; wage workers kept the machines running "full," benefitting from steady employment and profit-sharing schemes along with company-sponsored insurance and pension benefits. Giant industrial corporations would employ new collective strategies to become freestanding risk communities.

The result would be less insecurity for society—corporatization, Perkins heralded, would minimize "to almost nothing the chance of financial collapse and failure." The old regime of "competition" meant "uncertainty always." But trust lords, "substantially public servants," would end that. It was reducing social risk, not taking personal risk, that justified Perkins's immense pecuniary reward.[6]

In this way Perkins, along with many in his generation, sought to write a new chapter in risk's history. Risk would no longer belong only to individuals but also to society. Perkins's idealized "universe" harbored obvious traces of providentialism mixed with pop-Darwinian ideas about evolution—which to him made the industrial trust's rise natural and inevitable. But his preoccupation with "the social" was in step with broader intellectual trends. The man who invited Perkins to Columbia in 1907, for instance, was the German-trained economist E. R. A. Seligman. In the 1914 edition of his *Principles of Economics,* Seligman announced there was now "room" for a "conception of social risks." To say "social risks" was to "emphasize the social causes" of "hazards." It was to "accentuate the responsibility of society as a whole" for the creation and amelioration of those hazards, rather than the "individual." Indeed early twentieth-century American intellectuals and reformers invoked the "social" with increasing fervor, granting it a power and responsibility of its own, recasting the relationship between individual and society. Perkins, no great thinker, was nonetheless one of these people. He spoke of a new era of social interdependence where "What affects one, affects all." He championed the coming "co-operative society" to be brought about by a corporatized social order where "the individual" became the master not of his own, but rather "his social fate."[7]

A corporate, truly "social fate" required that a new institution—the industrial trust—thoroughly dominate American capitalism. But these institutions would still require individuals—"public servants," as Perkins put it—to run them. The lifework of one man thus becomes a window onto the many different dimensions of what was known at the time as the "trust question." One dimension was this: Did the American public trust Perkins? That was not a mere hypothetical question. For Perkins not only reached the pinnacle of American corporate power. After his 1907 Columbia address, he would leave the world of finance and join the world of politics and social reform, even becoming the campaign manager of Theodore Roosevelt's 1912 bid for the presidency under the banner of the Progressive Party.

Like some subatomic particle, the one-man interlocking directorate could suddenly appear anywhere in the new corporate universe: lecturing academic economists at Columbia University; investing the New York Life's capital on Wall Street; running the House of Morgan; mastering the boardrooms of U.S. Steel and International Harvester; operating on the inside of a major Progressive reform clearing house; placating striking unions on the shop-floor; hobnobbing with trusted friends in the Oval Office. Everywhere he appeared so did the inexorable trust question.

The 1907 Columbia address marked a turning point in Perkins's career, the moment when he first took his campaign for the "Modern Corporation" public. That forum, however, was convened to consider appropriate responses to the financial panic of 1907, an event in which he had been a crucial player. Perkins's solution for financial panics was to have more giant industrial corporations and the connection between corporatization and financial crisis was not tenuous. On the one hand, the panic was rooted in speculation on corporate stocks, a market created by the great wave of corporate consolidations at the turn of the twentieth century. On the other, ultimately it was Perkins and Morgan who had turned back the tide of the panic of 1907. They did so only by marshalling the resources of the largest industrial corporation in the world: U.S. Steel.

Perkins was at the center of the storm during the panic of 1907, second in importance perhaps only to Morgan himself. It was a decisive moment in his career and he was so moved by what happened that he wrote a personal recollection of the events, seemingly only for himself. It was an existential as much as an economic record of the panic. Indeed the typescript evokes both his larger mind-set concerning the "corporation idea" and his moral outlook concerning issues of risk and responsibility. The operative word in Perkins's account to himself was "anxiety." The two weeks in late October and early November of 1907 were one "anxious" moment after another—Perkins was filled with "anxiety" and Wall Street in general was "anxious." He happily fulfilled what he saw as his public duty to stave off a national "disaster." But he did not revel in the financial chaos.[8]

As for the panic itself, Perkins and many others had expected something like it. It had been a miserable year for the stock market. It was crop season and credit and currency—as it did every fall—flowed westward and southward to finance the movement of farm products. And after the lean 1890s, "Western farmers and the Southern cotton growers," according to Perkins, had become "rich and rather independent financially." Farmers and middlemen held crops off the market hoping for prices to rise, no doubt many of them hedging their bets with commodities futures contracts, enabling them to turn over their loans. This year even more money was out from New York than usual because of the rebuilding effort in San Francisco following the 1906 earthquake. All in all, money and credit was tight on Wall Street.[9]

The situation was already "acute." Triggering a panic was the failed cornering of United Copper Company shares by that corporation's founder August Heinze. Heinze was also president of New York's Mercantile National Bank and he conspired to mobilize that bank's resources to create a pool of money to corner the stock. Joining him was Charles Barney, who tapped into the funds of the Knickerbocker Trust Company. When the corner failed, Barney resigned from the Knickerbocker Trust Company. Word spread, and a bank run on the Knickerbocker ensued.

The terminology demands clarification. Corporate industrial behemoths like U.S. Steel were often called "trusts." Different from U.S. Steel, the Knickerbocker Trust Company was a specific kind of financial corporation. Trust companies like the Knickerbocker had been around for decades, operating more or less outside the ambit of state regulation. They offered astronomical interest rates to lure depositors and functioned more or less like profit-hungry commercial banks. From 1897 to 1907 New York financial trust assets grew from almost $400 million to $1.4 billion (total New York state and national bank assets were then $2.3 billion). In 1907 the Knickerbocker was the third-largest trust company with assets over $60 million. To achieve the yields necessary to meet the interest payments on their deposits the trust companies turned to stock speculation. They loaned short-term money to brokers and dealers, accepting the stocks then purchased with the loans as collateral.[10]

J.P. Morgan & Co. operated in a different world. On principle, Morgan detested stock trading as vulgar and beneath him. The more staid bond market was the House of Morgan's natural home and when his firm underwrote large corporate stock issues, like the $500 million 1901 issue creating U.S. Steel, they created syndicates so that brokerage houses and other more crass firms—often "the Jews," like the budding firm Goldman, Sachs & Co.—could do the dirty work. Morgan himself had never set foot on the New York Stock Exchange.

The Knickerbocker's failure was hardly the endgame because the Wall Street financial system was thoroughly interdependent. The stock market in particular was dependent upon the call money market which in turn depended upon the activities of the financial trust companies. Runs on the trust companies meant that to raise cash they had to call in their loans. Since stocks were collateral for many of them the stock exchange became swamped with sellers. This threatened the assets of the banks, for many of them had heavy investments in the stock market and had sought alliances with the trust companies to gain access to their capital. Morgan and Perkins implored the New York financial community to find common cause in holding the line. "When a number of men are on a sinking ship," Perkins later recalled, "whatever their relations may have been before they are pretty apt to get together and state the condition of that ship about as it is."[11]

After the Knickerbocker failed, Morgan and two of his banker chums put up $3 million to head off the run. But depositors were now lined up outside doors, winding around streets, with police handing out numbers. Meanwhile, Perkins called Washington and informed the Treasury secretary George B. Cortelyou that he had better come to New York. When he arrived, Cortelyou, in an astounding (and illegal) devolution of power, agreed to move $25 million of Treasury funds into the various New York national banks. John D. Rockefeller agreed to kick in $10 million of his own money. Perkins knocked on the Treasury secretary's door in the middle of the night and found him "deep" in "his anxiety."[12]

The next day was hardly better and Morgan had to organize a lifeline for the stock exchange. That night Morgan and Perkins called together the city's leading religious figures and instructed them to preach confidence and calm from their Sunday pulpits. On Monday, the *New York Times* announced the "financial storm" but also carried excerpts from Sunday sermons. Once again the metaphor and imagery of voyage appeared. The archbishop held a special mass for businessmen on Sunday. He sermonized:

> I hopefully expect that within a few days the whole flurry will have subsided. Our vessel is passing through a storm, but she is staunch, well able to ride the waves, and strong to stand up against the winds.

All we need is to do our share in dissuading the passengers from jumping overboard or scuttling the ship.

A Brooklyn Presbyterian pastor explained to his congregation: "The strong forces of the financial world, backed by that magnificent and praiseworthy leader, J.P. Morgan . . . have mastered the situation." The House of Morgan must be, that is, should be trusted.[13]

But the situation was not mastered yet. Morgan next bailed out the city of New York since the market for municipal bonds had seized up. Then word spread that one of the largest Wall Street stock brokerage firms, Moore & Schley, was about to fail. The firm was highly leveraged and had used for loan collateral the stock of a steel corporation, the Tennessee Coal, Iron, and Railroad Company (TC&I). Given the already depressed stock market, if banks called in their loans Moore & Schley would likely collapse, perhaps triggering another wave of panic.

At this point Perkins's narrative takes a sharp turn. For out of the blue a "meeting of the Finance Committee of the Steel Corporation was called . . . to be held at the Library at half past two in the afternoon." TC&I was U.S. Steel's largest competitor. Indeed just the previous year Perkins had written Morgan complaining that TC&I was the one company interfering with the ability of U.S. Steel to "fix" prices in the steel market. In November 1907, Perkins was chairman of the Finance Committee of U.S. Steel. The inner circle of the corporation met in Morgan's library. Morgan told them U.S. Steel would purchase TC&I.[14]

Morgan next assembled 120 bank and trust company officials in his library and informed them that he would purchase all the outstanding TC&I stock, preventing the implosion of the stock market, if they would cobble together $25 million to shore up the still tottering trusts. He raised the specter of a complete financial apocalypse, left the room, locked the door, pocketed the key, and waited for their response. At 4:45 a.m. they relented.

One problem remained. Three years earlier President Theodore Roosevelt had successfully prosecuted the breakup of Morgan's Northern Securities Company, an amalgamation of northwestern railroads (including what decades ago was Jay Cooke's Northern Pacific Railroad) under the 1890 Sherman Antitrust Act. Perkins feared the antitrust consequences of buying TC&I so he telephoned Washington. Roosevelt agreed to the merger and the next week the New York Stock Exchange opened strong and the panic was over.

Morgan bought TC&I for $45 million. Later the bond rater John Moody estimated its value closer to $1 billion and called it "the best bargain . . . [any] concern or individual ever made in the purchase of a piece of property." Perkins looked back on the events with pride, a moment when he had exercised a great public duty while the Treasury secretary had whimpered in his hotel room. "In fact," he wrote to himself, "at almost every turn grave responsibility of one kind and another stared one in the face." One outcome of the panic of 1907 was a redoubled push for monetary reform and a bill was soon hatched in Congress that eventually led to the creation of the Federal Reserve System in 1914. The role Morgan and Perkins played in 1907 would no longer be possible.[15]

Another outcome of the panic was the growth of U.S. Steel. The TC&I transaction, still fresh, was the subtext to Perkins's 1907 defense of the "Modern Corporation" at Columbia University. In it Perkins announced that "competition" was "no longer the life of trade" in the industrial sector. Instead, "the spirit of cooperation is upon us." The economist Seligman took the floor and agreed. The corporation brought a "steadying influence," a "better adaptation of the present to the future" which had the effect of "moderating crises" and "minimizing depressions." The panic of 1907 was indeed an episode of social cooperation, Perkins-style. Through a deft financial maneuver the chaos of a market meltdown was averted—to the putative benefit of the public. Further, the ability of U.S. Steel to stabilize and control the industrial marketplace was solidified. And of course, by staving off panic and uncertainty J.P. Morgan & Co. reaped a windfall. For as long as he lived, and he was called many times before Congress to recount these events, Perkins never saw in any of this a contradiction or a conflict of interest. He only saw social cooperation, his own brand of socialism—which rightfully called for the public's trust.[16]

The relative calm in the industrial sector following the panic of 1907 was a striking contrast to the years of cutthroat competition and market instability that had followed the last great financial panic of 1893. The depressed 1890s had led to the Great Merger Movement, thrusting both Perkins and the corporate business form onto center stage. Before picking up Perkins's efforts after 1907, what must first be considered is the simultaneous rise to power of two distinct personalities: Perkins himself and what he called the "Modern Corporation."

Perkins was born in Chicago in 1862, descending from a long line of New England stock. He bore his father's name—a devout Presbyterian, the superintendent of a Chicago reform school, and a man filled with frustrated evangelical zeal. Needing money, in 1870 he took a job as a salesman in Cleveland for the New York Life Insurance Company. George Perkins the elder died in 1886 and as a sentimental favor his former boss gave his twenty-four-year-old son a job as a salesman.[17]

The youthful Perkins unleashed a torrent of energy and ambition. In search of opportunity he headed west, tapping a new market for the New York Life in Denver. He accounted for $2.4 million of insurance sold in one year and by 1887 he was named the roaming "Inspector of Agencies." From 1888 to 1892 he began to reorganize the company, turning formerly independent, commission-based agents into salaried salesmen integrated within a hierarchical management structure—a premonition, in a financial setting, of later industrial developments. The system worked and in 1892 Perkins was named vice president. That year he moved his young family to New York.[18]

As terrible as the decade of the 1890s was for the American economy, for the New York Life it was flush. The panic of 1873 had busted many fledgling American life insurance corporations, clearing the field for the rise of the Big Three Wall Street firms—the Equitable, the Mutual Life, and the New York Life. Fending off the fraternal challenge, it was an era of consolidation for insurance corporations.

Under Perkins's direction the sales of the New York Life skyrocketed. In 1892 it was the smallest of the Big Three, but by 1899 it would be the largest. Once in New York, Perkins's policy was to eliminate "competition" between sales agents. He created a "branch office" system under his control, standardizing bookkeeping and accounting procedures in search of "efficiency." He created incentives for the "steady" flow of sales, and inaugurated the "Nylic Association," a company-based fraternal society granting loyal salesmen bonuses, pensions, and insurance benefits. In the late 1890s Perkins traveled to Europe to install his system there.[19]

In an era when many American intellectuals and social reformers voyaged to Europe, returning with Old World-inspired state plans to tame industrial capitalism—including state social insurance schemes— Perkins rode a different current. He went to Europe to spread the Yankee gospel of personal responsibility and corporate risk management. In Europe Perkins finally came into contact with New York Life's institutional investment practices. Germany not only had the world's first government-run social insurance programs, it also prohibited life insurance companies from investing in stocks. Other European nations had similar policies. In 1898 Perkins crisscrossed Berlin, Berne, London, Paris, Vienna, Budapest, Moscow, and St. Petersburg, imploring state officials to allow the New York Life to sell insurance in their respective countries. In 1899 Germany acquiesced and from Berlin Perkins sent a boastful letter to President William McKinley before heading off to Russia to strike a deal with the czar's finance minister. The New York Life gained entry to Russia after purchasing $10 million of Russian railroad bonds. The Russian finance minister turned to Perkins because he had failed to float the bonds through "Pierpont Morgan and some of his friends" in New York. Germany and Russia were enormous coups, and on December 21, 1899, the New York Life threw a gilded testimonial dinner honoring the triumphant return of its star vice president. Perkins was a corporate climber extraordinaire.[20]

Thus by 1899 Perkins had arrived on the scene. The same could be said for another personality, the vehicle of his ascent, the modern industrial corporation. That year witnessed the peak in the greatest wave ever of corporate mergers and acquisitions. During the Great Merger Movement of 1895 to 1904, 1,800 American industrial firms consolidated into 157 corporations—a watershed institutional transformation. In 1899 sixty-three such combinations—creating industrial "trusts" as they were known at the time—occurred. The Great Merger Movement was the defensive response in the industrial sector of expanding, capital-intensive, high-fixed-cost firms to the cutthroat market competition that followed the collapse in investment, output, and demand during the depressed 1890s. For many corporate executives, it was also a rejection of the competitive business ethos that Perkins had already junked at the New York Life in the late 1880s.[21]

If Perkins was born in 1862 then the modern business corporation grew up right along with him. Gestating in American civil society ever since the Revolution, it was the fruit of nineteenth-century liberal capitalism. Fully formed by the opening of the twentieth century the giant industrial corporation seemingly turned patricidal.

Many early Americans were uneasy with business corporations—suspicious as they were of feudal privilege, monopoly, the specter of *imperium in imperio,* and concentrated political and economic power in general. In the colonial period the Crown had forbidden colonial Americans from creating their own joint-stock business corporations. After the Revolution a flurry of state-level incorporations—mostly finance and transportation, rather than manufacturing corporations—ensued. Always a subject of debate, nineteenth-century Americans did not quite know what to do with corporations. Originally clothed with a "public" interest—defined in the very wording of corporate charters—corporations occupied a nebulous intermediate space in civil society between political authority and private economic initiative.[22]

Ultimately, after the Civil War corporations transformed their long-standing immortal "legal personality." They became fully private individual economic actors. States passed general incorporation laws. The Supreme Court granted corporations the same rights under the postemancipation Fourteenth Amendment as any flesh-and-blood citizen. Corporate lawyers developed the "natural-entity" theory of corporate legal personhood. The corporation became a legitimate instrument of private economic initiative. Corporations now had private lives to lead.[23]

From its European origins the joint-stock business corporation was a collective strategy to cope with the perils of capitalist development. Some of the first American corporations were marine insurance companies. Perkins's New York Life Insurance Company, for that matter, was one of the great nineteenth-century American corporations. Furthermore, through the corporate form insurance, bank, canal, and later railroad and manufacturing corporations pooled capital, dispersing exposure to the perils of investment. In the mid-nineteenth century the principle of limited liability triumphed—limiting investor's exposure to the amount of their individual investments. The corporate legal form further reduced the hazards of investment.[24]

After the Civil War the greatest corporations were railroads. To coordinate their far-flung activities there arose within them a new class of salaried managers. But the directors of these corporations were often financial speculators who skimmed from the top while tapping government largesse. Much of the railroad grid—especially moving west—was a chaotic mess, with overextended parallel tracks produced by a speculative investment cycle that begat the great financial panics of 1873 and 1893. Morgan entered the mix, claiming he could end ruinous competition and bring stability and order. Representing European creditors he invited railroad presidents for dinners onboard his yacht, imploring them to gentlemanly coordinate prices. When that failed, "Morganization" combined railroads together into ever-larger combinations.[25]

Elsewhere, especially in the Northeast–Midwestern industrial corridor, postbellum manufacturing corporations grew. Still, in 1878 Carroll D. Wright, chief of the Massachusetts Bureau of Statistics for Labor, counted 10,395 private manufacturing firms in the state, employing 166,588 workers and producing $351 million of goods per year, whereas there were 520 corporations, employing 101,337 persons and producing $180 million of goods. Meanwhile, in the nascent oil industry Rockefeller exploited the railroads' desires for consistent flows to build a personal corporate empire. Buying out the competition he created the specific legal device of the "trust" in 1882—the Standard Oil Company. In the steel industry, producing the capital goods necessary for the railroad infrastructure, Andrew Carnegie followed suit, incorporating the Carnegie Steel Company in 1892.[26]

The subsequent triumph of the industrial corporation required another legal twist. Previously firms had joined forces through informal or even contractual "pools" that predetermined their price, output, and profit schedules. But they were "ropes of sand," as Rockefeller put it, difficult to enforce when times got tough and the temptation to cut prices intensified. Further, the 1890 Sherman Antitrust Act outlawed many pools and even Rockefeller's chosen legal device, the "trust." An 1889 New Jersey law allowed for the incorporation of "holding companies" that could amalgamate firms without violating the Sherman Act. New Jersey became the legal home to the Great Merger Movement.[27]

Still, in retrospect—and while the trend towards greater incorporation was always clear—nineteenth-century corporations were critical but nevertheless often ancillary economic actors. A far more dominant economic agent was the individual proprietor, often acting in partnership.[28] Such agents needed credit, insurance, and transportation services. Arguably, only corporate actors—banking corporations, insurance corporations, railroad corporations—could have provided these services to them. Insurance corporations bought millions of personal financial "risks." Banking corporations provided money and credit to move commodities over the vast American continent. Transportation was provided ultimately by railroad corporations. This explains why American attitudes towards nineteenth-century corporations—aggregations of power seemingly incompatible with a liberal, individualist social order—were so fraught. And, for that matter, why the figures of Rockefeller and Carnegie—and with them the corporations created in their images—were to many such terrifying augurs.

Much was at stake in risk's history during the Great Merger Movement, when the "trust question" moved to the center of American public debate. The corporate consolidation of industry came on the heels of the collapse of the largely agrarian Populist Revolt following the election of 1896. The specter of Bryanism at least still continued to haunt Perkins. Bizarrely, he filled two personal scrapbooks with notes and newspaper clippings following the trajectory of William Jennings Bryan's career. Writing to a friend in 1896 Perkins had called the People's Party platform "absolutely crazy and anachronistic." Nothing so "wicked" had occurred since "the firing on Sumter." The New York Life had donated $50,000 to the Republican candidate McKinley's campaign. Only after his victory secured a favorable political landscape did the Great Merger Movement take off.[29]

The infamous 1896 People's Party platform had furiously attacked concentrated economic power. The People's Party would place the

railroads—who discriminated against small businessmen in favor of titans like Rockefeller—under full federal government control, if not ownership. It assaulted J.P. Morgan & Co. and its cherished gold standard,
which Morgan had almost single-handedly saved during the panic of
1893 and which Populists wanted to undermine by inflating the money
supply—in part to assist mortgage-debt-burdened farmers.[30]

Populist voices continued to echo after 1896. In 1899, while Perkins
lobbied the czar's ministers in Russia the Chicago Civic Confederation
convened to take the measure of the ongoing Great Merger Movement.
The business-friendly but self-consciously middle-of-the-road reform
group would soon be rechristened the National Civic Federation, and
Perkins would soon call it home, becoming one of its prime movers and
benefactors. He donated $2,500 of seed money to the NCF, next to
Carnegie's $2,000.[31]

In 1899, Bryan, the famous orator, addressed the "Chicago Conference
on Trusts." But his was not the speech that brought down the house.
That honor was reserved for the Texas Democrat Dudley Wooten.
Against the corporation, Wooten championed the "sovereignty of individual manhood." He spoke nostalgically of:

> The loose and risky methods of personal enterprise, the legal limita-
> tions and vicissitudes of individual investments, and the motives of
> selfish caution and control that actions of men or firms engaged in
> business on their own responsibility.

Wooten celebrated the ethos of individual risk-taking in a competitive
free market. But recently, Wooten continued, in the process of industrialization man had raised an "artificial person"—the "corporation." The
corporation brought about "centralized control" of the market. It was
destroying "competition." It threatened to "crush out the divinity of
man." The Texan then read out loud the text of the Thirteenth Amendment abolishing slavery before declaring:

> [W]e confidently assert that the commercial and industrial bondage
> being rapidly imposed upon the toil and talents of seventy millions
> of American citizens by the syndicated wealth of a few great corpo-

rate monopolies, is more dire and dangerous than the slavery that once bowed the heads and burdened the backs of four millions of Southern black men.

When Wooten finished the gallery erupted in applause. Despite the hyperbole, the rise of the industrial corporation did raise inescapable moral dilemmas concerning freedom and unfreedom. Wooten was not an advocate of centralized control of the marketplace, whether by governments or corporations. He and many other agrarians wanted the federal government to break up the "trusts" and even take ownership stakes in certain industries if necessary, but this was only to restore and secure a mythologized commercial marketplace dominated by the "loose and risky methods" of personal enterprise. That was why Perkins thought the Populists were anachronistic and Roosevelt would call them "rural Tories." The journalist Walter Lippmann called Bryan the Don Quixote of American politics, who moved "in a world that no longer exists." Bryan's world was "doomed by the great organization that had come into the world."[32]

Pro-corporate voices at the 1899 Chicago Conference on Trusts also raised issues of freedom and unfreedom. But they did so not to celebrate the ethos of individual risk-taking but rather to indict the unfreedoms of the economic chance-world. Edward W. Bemis, an academic economist and social reformer, indicted the "waves of elation and depression, which at intervals seep across our ocean of commerce and throw frightful wreckage to the shore." What was worse, they were met with the "very same sentiment"—resignation—that had once prevailed "with regard" to "slavery." The economist John Graham Brooks of Rockefeller's University of Chicago argued that, "when competition has reached such terrible limits as it now has" it was the "climax of humor or pathos to talk too loudly" of the need for individual "economic independence." Was it not a "most haphazard and tottering independence," having led to hundreds of thousands of business failures in the industrial depression of the 1890s?[33]

Perkins too framed the Great Merger Movement in the context of slave emancipation. His own narrative of nineteenth-century American capitalism was this: after throwing "off the yoke of slavery," "great business risks were taken," and then "panics of a disastrous and far-reaching nature followed." The economic chance-world was a source of unfreedom—to personally hedge against that world was simply no longer enough. Only the "Modern Corporation" could adequately master and control capitalism. Perkins's favorite in the ranks of academic economists was Arthur Jerome Eddy. In 1912, Eddy described the capitalism of before the Great Merger Movement in this way:

> Business is a lottery; there is no game of chance with so many elements of uncertainty; in every other gamble the player may calculate to a fraction of one per cent the odds for or against him and take the risk with his eyes open; in commerce men "go it blind."

Institutionally and morally the corporate consolidation of industry was a full-frontal assault against the economic chance-world.[34]

Perhaps the loudest pro-corporate voices at the 1899 Chicago Conference on Trusts were, like Eddy, academic economists. John Bates Clark of Columbia and Jeremiah Jenks of Cornell were both in the audience when Wooten spoke nostalgically of the "loose and risky methods of personal enterprise." It is doubtful whether they applauded.

Clark had already in 1892 presciently analyzed the coming of the Great Merger Movement. In an article called "Insurance and Business Profit" published in the *Quarterly Journal of Economics,* he theorized that the corporation existed because actuarial insurance markets were inherently incomplete. He first assumed a competitive market economy of "small proprietors." These proprietors coped with numerous personal risks, whether it was "fire" or "shipwreck," by insuring them. But there was also what Clark called the "dynamic risks" of capitalism, namely the "terrors of business enterprise": market booms and busts; the volatility of the price system; technological disruptions; revolutions in consumer preference. But there were no insurance markets for dynamic risks because by nature they could not be calculated into objective probabilities. The point of the corporation then was to organizationally "insure" as best it could—without resort to actuarial knowledge—against dynamic risks. Tellingly, Clark reasoned that if "all risks could be distributed by means of insurance companies," then "the man in independent business" would continue to thrive. The flipside was that without personal insurance, the corporation would have long ago swept aside small proprietors. Capitalism had created dynamic risks that only corporatization could insure against. Clark applied a financial way of thinking about risk to ongoing organizational changes in American manufacturing. The industrial trust itself was thus a form of financial risk management.[35]

In a corporate industrial economy, Clark predicted, there would be three distinct risk-related functions for men formerly engaged in independent business to perform. There would be the "risk-maker," or entrepreneur who kick-started the industrial process. Then there would be the "risk-taker," or the financial owner of corporate stock. Third, there would be the "risk-reducer," or the salaried corporate manager that rationally administered economic production and distribution. In Clark's hands risk became a social, institutionally-mediated phenomenon. Only after such institutional mediation did risk establish a relationship with the individual.[36]

The notion that the industrial corporation was an institutional insurance mechanism against the economic chance-world soon became gospel among professional American economists. For the first time economists formalized risk as a social-scientific object of analysis. The young economist Frank Knight, in his brilliant 1921 book *Risk, Uncertainty, and Profit,* set the tone. Knight distinguished "risk" from "uncertainty." "Risk" referred to contingencies that were computable into quantifiable, mathematically measurable probabilities. "Uncertainty" referred to contingencies that were not (Clark's "dynamic risks"). Risk, Knight wrote, could never completely conquer uncertainty. Uncertainty under capitalism, in some form, was "ineradicable." (Knight's book thus belongs in the cannon of classic works in the American philosophy of pragmatism.) In an economy that conformed to perfect neoclassical assumptions Knight theorized that profit was the result of uncertainty—"pure luck." Modern insurance corporations, Knight continued, used actuarial knowledge to transform "uncertainty" into "risk." But the new industrial corporations, he reasoned, organizationally reduced uncertainty—even if uncertainty could never be fully extinguished. That meant however that only a very narrow class of economic actors in a corporatized industrial economy—the entrepreneurial class—were risk-takers ("uncertainty-takers" in Knight's terminology). Therefore the very basis of "freedom" in the American economy—Knight mused in a buried and characteristically metaphysical aside—was at stake. Populism, by then a vanquished political insurgency, had screamed this.[37]

Perkins was a financier. Nevertheless, at the dawn of the corporate economy he himself performed many of the new risk-related social functions theorized by Clark. Perkins was a risk-maker, a risk-taker, *and* a risk-reducer. He had all of these opportunities because for the last few years of the Great Merger Movement he had two jobs: vice president and chairman of the Finance Committee of the New York Life and partner in the House of Morgan.

After his triumphant 1899 return to America Perkins moved closer to the investment branch of the New York Life and the Wall Street capital market. He helped crush a bill in Albany that would limit the total insurance in force of any life insurance corporation, in part to restrict their financial power. Perkins told Ohio Senator Mark Hanna that the New York Life would not contribute to the 1900 Republican campaign if the bill went through. Hanna set up a meeting between Perkins and governor Roosevelt in March 1900. The two became fast friends.[38]

Later in the year Perkins made another good first impression, this time with Morgan. Perkins's direct purchase of the Russian railroad bonds had stirred up Wall Street, for a large institutional investor had bypassed brokerage houses and investment banks (and their fees). Now, in another seeming quid pro quo, Perkins bought $5 million of German government debt following the admission of the New York Life into the German market. Tired of being bypassed Morgan first offered Perkins a partnership in December 1900.[39]

Perkins did not accept at first, as a partnership in J.P. Morgan & Co. was a notorious death sentence. Recently an overworked Morgan partner had dropped dead at age forty-eight. "Anxiety" indeed—even before the panic of 1907 Perkins would watch another partner crack, resigning from J.P. Morgan & Co. to take the less taxing job of U.S. secretary of state. In February 1901 Morgan approached Perkins again. Now he wanted Perkins to become his point man in the corporate consolidation of U.S. Steel. Perkins accepted, although with one caveat. He would not resign his position at New York Life, working in the morning at that company's mid-town office and then spending the afternoons at 23 Wall Street.[40]

Perkins cut an odd figure at J.P. Morgan & Co. He was one of Morgan's youthful "golden boys" plucked from the Street by Morgan for their talents, not their bloodlines. Still, Morgan usually chose Ivy Leaguers, most often former athletes. Perkins had no roots within the East Coast establishment and had never graduated from high school. Now at the pinnacle of American finance he was almost *sui generis*—almost, except for the more than $400 million of finance capital under the New York Life's command and at Perkins's fingertips.

He went to work on the consolidation of U.S. Steel, implicating the New York Life. The United States Steel Corporation was chartered as a New Jersey holding company in February 1901. In 1898, Morgan had consolidated the Federal Steel Company which had become the largest competitor to Andrew Carnegie's Carnegie Steel Company. For a short time the two corporations had organized output and price schedules together. But then both had begun to organize vertically—Morgan buying up mines in Minnesota, Carnegie promising to fabricate finished-goods in Ohio. Morgan bought out Carnegie for $492 million of bonds and stocks in U.S. Steel and Carnegie retired the richest man in the world.[41]

To create U.S. Steel, the House of Morgan arranged a syndicate of numerous Wall Street firms to float a $500 million stock issue. It was a momentous, formative event in the creation of the New York Stock Exchange. Until the 1890s the bond market had dominated Wall Street finance; there was more volume in stock trading at the Boston Exchange, long the home of incorporated New England textile firms, than in New York. The industrial consolidations of the Great Merger Movement would leave in its wake the modern New York Stock Exchange.[42]

Demand for U.S. Steel stock was fiercer than expected but Morgan did not assume there were enough private individual investors through-out the country—and enough institutional circuitry to connect them to J.P. Morgan & Co.—to swallow $500 million. Perkins himself was personally allotted $3 million of stock to dispose of however he saw fit. What he wanted to do was purchase the stock from J.P. Morgan & Co. for the New York Life. The problem was that under the terms of its agreement with Germany the New York Life could not own stock. So

Perkins sold the $3 million block to the New York Security and Trust Company. Perkins was a director of this trust company, and the New York Life owned a controlling interest in it. In return for assuring his fellow directors in the New York Security and Trust that the New York Life would maintain its large cash deposits there, the trust company agreed to turn over 75 percent of the profits on $2,325,000 of the stock sales to the New York Life. Without it technically owning stock Perkins turned a profit for the New York Life of $435,207.71. It was another instance of Perkins-style social cooperation. If for academic economists the insurance principle provided the intellectual logic of corporate consolidation, then through Perkins it provided raw finance capital.[43]

Perkins was immensely proud of the U.S. Steel transaction. It had earned a hefty profit for the New York Life without, as he put it, any "risk." At the same time, acting for the New York Life, Perkins had, however indirectly, dispersed ownership of U.S. Steel into millions of hands—not a state-mediated but a corporate-mediated socialism. Perkins would soon represent the House of Morgan in the November 1901 negotiations that created the Northern Securities Company, which became the second-largest corporation in the world behind only U.S. Steel. Perkins again mobilized the funds of the New York Life. Meanwhile, the leader of the Republican Party, Senator Hanna, wrote to Perkins to see if he could get Northern Securities stock for himself. Hanna complained he was "on the outside" and did not "get a chance at such things while I am 'Serving the country.' I wish you would look 'a little out' for me." Meanwhile the New York *Journal,* blasting encroaching industrial monopoly, explained how "the best business brains in America" were midwives of socialism:

> They are smoothing out all the difficulties, consolidating staffs, creating one vast, smoothly running machine. When they have finished, all the Government will have to do will be to assume the debts of the system, exchange national bonds for stock, and give the general manager a commission from the President of the United States.

Perkins did not get the joke. He clipped the column and enthusiastically sent it to his friend President Roosevelt. "What is the essential difference," Perkins boomed in the newspapers, "between the United States

Steel Corporation, as it was organized by Mr. Morgan, and a Department of Steel as it might be organized by the government?" By now Perkins was proofreading Roosevelt's addresses and executive orders concerning corporate industrial policy.[44]

Then came the largest coup of Perkins's professional career. In 1902, at Rockefeller's request he personally negotiated the creation of the Chicago-based International Harvester Company, bringing together two family firms, the McCormick Harvesting Machine Company and the Deering Harvester Company. At its creation the International Harvester Company controlled 85 percent of the American market in farm machinery. Perkins chose the name International Harvester, and earned a $3 million fee for J.P. Morgan & Co. The McCormick family still owned a majority stake in the company while the Deerings controlled 30 percent. But part of the agreement was that Perkins would be the final arbiter of all corporate policy until 1912. Giddy, he wrote to Morgan, "The new company is to be organized by us; its name chosen by us; the state in which it shall be incorporated is left to us; the Board of Directors, the Officers, and the whole outfit left to us." Perkins concluded that "nobody has any right to question in any way any choice we make."[45]

Perkins was riding high when he and his machinations were first dragged under the public spotlight in 1905. There his vision for a finance-led, corporate socialism was left battered. The event was the state of New York's 1905 investigation into the life insurance industry, first sparked by the salacious details of an internal dispute in the Equitable Life's management. The newspapers revealed that company executives were throwing lavish dinners and balls on the policyholders' and stockholders' dime. The former Wall Street speculator Thomas Lawson published the best-selling *Frenzied Finance* which revealed hitherto hidden connections between the Big Three and Wall Street investment banking houses.[46]

It turned out that Jacob Schiff of the firm Kuhn, Loeb & Co.—Morgan's one true rival—was a director of the Equitable and tapped its funds for mergers and acquisitions as well. Morgan's friend George F. Baker of the National City Bank was a director of the Mutual Life Insurance Company and did the same. What Lawson did not know was that in 1901

Perkins had attempted to consolidate the Big Three altogether into one giant life insurance "trust," just like U.S. Steel. Perkins wrote to the president of the Equitable:

> Amalgamate. Become the arbitrator of life assurance in the world. Be so large as to be able to cope with foreign governments. Cut down expenses to the quick. Make everything purely mutual, and be the exponent of real and justifiable socialism. Buy out . . . everybody's stock for some millions. Buy out all general agents commissions . . . Form an executive control . . . have the whole under immediate management of one competent man.

Perkins dreamed of a global financial corporation large enough to face down the national governments of the world. An amalgamation of the Big Three never happened. But Perkins believed that the spectacular growth of the New York Life in the financial sector provided a model worthy of industrial emulation. Certainly if anyone cared to look there was no greater emblem of the role the Big Three had played during the Great Merger Movement's consolidation of industry than the vice president of the New York Life and partner in the House of Morgan.[47]

The state of New York created a committee to conduct extensive hearings and investigations into the Big Three—a dry run for the Pujo Committee's 1912–1913 Congressional investigation into a supposed "Money Trust." In 1905 the young attorney and future Supreme Court Justice Charles Evans Hughes was the lead investigator. He called Perkins before the committee and pummeled the conflicts of interest ridden in Perkins's brand of "cooperation." Hughes first all too easily goaded Perkins into admitting that he operated as the one-man Finance Committee of the New York Life. After Perkins took the bait, Hughes pounced. At end of year 1903 the New York Life carried $4 million of International Mercantile Marine bonds on its books which were trading below par. The New York Life had to produce a financial statement to its state regulators and Perkins evidently did not want these bonds on its public financial records. So on December 31 he sold them to J.P. Morgan & Co. and then on January 2 he bought them back. "You conducted that transaction with yourself?" Hughes asked. No, Perkins answered that he represented both the New York Life and J.P. Morgan & Co.[48]

Next, in excruciating detail Hughes exposed that Perkins had been using the New York Security and Trust Company as a cover to sponsor a series of railroad and industrial securities purchases. Further, 20 percent of all the New York Life's assets were either securities purchased directly from the House of Morgan or issued by the firm. But most controversial was the U.S. Steel syndicate, through which—via the New York Security and Trust—the New York Life had earned $2.3 million in profits from stock it was not supposed to own. Hughes called this "devious." Another examiner asked: "You knew you were taking that risk for the New York Life Insurance Company?" "No, sir," Perkins responded, "I beg your pardon." The beauty of the scheme was that there was no "risk" in it for the New York Life.[49]

The press had a field day with Perkins. Leading the public charge against him was the young Louis Brandeis, who represented a committee of disgruntled Big Three life insurance policyholders. Brandeis was a champion of small-producer "competition"—what was "cooperation" to Perkins was to Brandeis indeed a nefarious "money trust." Brandeis, to put it mildly, simply did not trust Perkins's professed public motives. In 1905, Brandeis harangued against "syndicates" formed by men like Perkins to "insure the financing of the great manufacturing and railroad combinations," which were blotting out the individual competitive marketplace. Brandeis lobbied for a law to prohibit the "use of [insurance] funds in speculative enterprises." Soon Brandeis would publish *Other People's Money*. It was a book inspired by the actions of men like Perkins.[50]

In 1905, Perkins, his world crumbling around him, was not convinced he had done anything wrong. He begged Hughes to let him read a prepared statement justifying the U.S. Steel transaction but Hughes would not cede the floor. He did Perkins a favor. For Perkins was prepared to not only defend the insider transaction but to boast of it. The New York Life earned over $435,000, he wanted to say, "without responsibility of any kind, and wholly without risk of any kind whatsoever." Ideally, all business should be conducted in this way, with no risk. The particular transaction at stake "was only possible because of the advantages of my connection with J.P. Morgan & Co." In fairness, at the time it was far from clear that the transaction violated any law. Regardless, Perkins simply did not believe in the competitive ethos of individual risk-taking. He could not understand why his inquisitors held up the transaction as evidence that the game was rigged in his own favor, rather than that he was acting in the public interest. He could not understand why seemingly nobody trusted him outside the narrow corridors of power that connected the House of Morgan, the New York Life, the NCF, and the U.S. Steel and International Harvester corporations.[51]

Only for one moment during his actual testimony was Perkins on the offensive. A state senator asked him when he was acting for the New York Life and when for J.P. Morgan & Co. "It depends on what the actual case is," was his reply. Hughes chirped, "The Senator is thinking of his Bible, where it says a man can't serve two masters." Perkins answered that his "master" was "the people's interests." In his transactions on behalf of the New York Life he was responsible for the security and welfare of "over a million of people." As chairman of the Finance Committee of U.S. Steel he represented "thousands of people." "My idea is that the business man of this country must to-day, and in the future, serve the people." Conflicts of interest were actually instances of "cooperation." "The old idea we were raised under, that competition is the life of trade, is exploded. Competition is no longer the life of trade, it is co-operation." Perkins had never acted out of selfish motives. He reminded the committee that "the Steel syndicate was absolutely in my hands to control." He could have placed the $3 million block and its "profits" anywhere, including with himself. Instead he chose to act in the interests of the stability of society as a whole.[52]

Even after his testimony—an unmitigated public disaster—Perkins remained undaunted. A writer from Albuquerque clipped Perkins's statement from a newspaper that competition was "no longer the life of trade," congratulating him for recognizing this "great economic truth." But now Perkins must devote his "great abilities" for the "benefit of ALL THE PEOPLE"—namely, become a "socialist." Perkins wrote back, differing on one point only. He already was a socialist, and was already acting "to the benefit of all the people."[53]

Nevertheless, in the aftermath of the 1905 investigations Perkins was forced to resign his position at the New York Life. The state of New York passed laws restricting life insurance companies' institutional investments. Deflated, Perkins went to Russia on J.P. Morgan & Co. business. Speaking of socialism, in St. Petersburg he witnessed in person the 1905

Russian revolution. He cabled Morgan one of his more memorable missives: "CZAR DISSOLVES DUMA . . . MARKET STRONG AND ACTIVE. ALL WELL."[54]

It was after he returned from Europe, in the wake of his 1905 public drubbing, that Perkins decided to go on the offensive and to publicize his activities at the House of Morgan. If only the public knew what he was up to they would surely approve. Perkins had indeed been up to a lot at U.S. Steel and International Harvester, laying the very foundations of twentieth-century American corporate welfare capitalism. Perkins taught U.S. Steel and International Harvester to think and act in terms of risk; at these corporations Perkins's countermovement comes into view at close range. He believed that corporate ownership would create new social hierarchies, new corporate risk communities, and a new ethos—what he called a "socialism of the highest form." There would be a new sense of what it meant to be a true and secure actor, as a new pattern of peril and possibility, danger and opportunity, took shape.[55]

The public relations campaign began with a 1907 address at the NCF on the topic of "Profit-Sharing Plan of the United States Steel Corporation," which Perkins had inaugurated in 1902. With the 1901 formation of U.S. Steel, Perkins declared, "individual ownership" in the steel industry had all but "ceased." And so:

> To men and students of affairs the real problem that faced the new corporation was this: Could men on salaries and wages successfully carry on this vast organization, directed only by other men on salaries,—with no proprietorship above them save a vast and scattered body of security holders?

Corporatization had solved certain problems in the industrial sector, namely the "chaos" inherent to the old regime of "competition." But in doing so it had created others, ranging from labor strife to the impersonal relationship between the corporation and its "security holders." Finally there was an even more abstract dilemma. What at bottom was to motivate the new class of salaried corporate managers to meld together, centralize, and systematize the hitherto disparate parts of the steel industry? How to motivate men to spend their days managing social risk, not taking personal risk?[56]

The new corporate economy, in the shift from individualist competition to cooperative risk management, demanded a revolution in business ethics. The individual proprietor pursued his own bottom line and had no particular concern for the social consequences that followed. That was why competition was called "ruthless." Perkins admitted that such ruthlessness had once injected "virility" in business, the "tingle that comes with success." Therefore perhaps "competition had to exist at one time." But the ethos of competition must now be transcended, replaced by "the principle of co-operation." Instead of competing corporations should "emulate" each other's best practices. They should cooperatively administer and manage industrial production and distribution, enlisting scientific rather than commercial values.[57] The new public spirit of business enterprise was to be "philanthropic" and "altruistic." It would shun the self-interested profit motive. Harking back to the early modern corporation clothed with a public interest, Perkins insisted that capitalism had gone wrong because corporate executives had failed to "realize that they were not in business as individuals, but were working for other people." In the twentieth century corporate leaders must once again become "semi-public servants."[58]

Perkins advocated corporate profit–sharing to inculcate the new business ethics. Proctor & Gamble had implemented a corporate profit-sharing scheme in 1886 and Perkins knew that in Europe many family firms had similar programs. Corporate titans like Carnegie and Cyrus McCormick were known to grant one-shot pecuniary dispensations to their employees. But during the 1900s U.S. Steel and International Harvester pioneered profit-sharing as a consistent corporate strategy.[59]

The effort began at U.S. Steel, which had been capitalized in 1901 at a staggering $1.4 billion. That figure included, by later estimates, about 40 percent water, or paper value above the corporation's actual assets. But Perkins was confident that future earnings would sop it up, given the added value "for the Company's vast organization of man"—the "coordinating, harmonizing, centralization, and . . . improving and extending [of] the various plants of the subsidiary companies." The task was daunting. In 1901, no less than 6.8 percent of the gross national product of the American economy was consolidated as U.S. Steel. It consisted of 213 different manufacturing plants, forty-one mines, and over 1,000 miles of railroad spread across the nation's Northeast–Midwest industrial corridor. (In 1907 with the purchase of TC&I, it reached into the South.) "The Corporation," as it became known, counted over 162,000 employees. Many were thunderstruck at its sheer size. *McClure's Magazine* marveled:

> It receives and expends more money ever year than any but the very greatest world's national governments; its debt is larger than that of many of the lesser nations of Europe. It absolutely controls the destinies of a population nearly as large as that of Maryland or Nebraska.

Perkins would have approved the image of the corporation as a new agent of fate. Meanwhile, a Michigan law professor noted that if the capital stock of U.S. steel was cashed out for silver dollars, edge to edge they would form "a silver girdle around mother earth" with room for a "double-bow knot" two thousand miles long and "streamers of over one thousand five hundred miles each." U.S. Steel was truly an industrial colossus.[60]

In 1901, harassing subsidiary companies for payroll information and personally conducting onsite visits, Perkins had subdivided the corporation's workforce into six groups, ranging from highest to lowest paid. He drafted a memo to Morgan in April of that year, outlining his vision for U.S. Steel's labor policy. Perkins argued to his fellow directors on the Finance Committee that for the 162,000 employees a "profit sharing scheme" would incite "the same interest in the business that individual ownership does." Through profit-sharing the interests of employer and employee would mesh.[61]

Perkins's scheme was unique because it included wage workers in addition to salaried managers. Before Perkins it was really only the craft-based Amalgamated Steelworkers that had sought to stabilize and steady output in the steel industry, through work slowdowns and stoppages and other union-enforced, mutualist work rules. Such tactics represented larger working-class efforts to manage risk—to slow down the machinery and reduce working hours might reduce, for instance, the downside risk of workplace accident. In that event, many worker fraternal societies and brotherhoods still competed against the corporate insurance industry. But the greatest risk industrial labor could pose to capitalists was the strike. Part of what made Carnegie a "ruthless competitor" was his "hard driving" of integrated steel plants, running them "full" while increasing and maintaining output at all costs no matter the market conditions or general economy-wide consequences. That meant the bosses had to control the point and pace of production and the Amalgamated had to be broken. Therefore, in U.S. Steel's corporate history was the bloody 1892 Homestead Strike, which ended in a pitched gun battle between workers and Pinkertons that left twelve dead. After Homestead, membership in the Amalgamated plummeted from 24,000 in 1892 to less than 8,000 in 1900.[62]

Secretly, in June 1901 the new directors of U.S. Steel decided they would oppose unionization. Recognition strikes by steelworkers were quickly broken. The United Mine Workers were able to extract some concessions in 1902, although not recognition, after President Roosevelt convened a commission to mediate their strike. Perkins sat on it, representing the Morgan interests. By then both the American Federation of Labor (AFL) president Samuel Gompers and the United Mine Workers president John Mitchell had joined Perkins on the board of the NCF. Perkins, although no one knew this at time, personally paid Mitchell a salary to do so.[63]

Writing personal checks to Mitchell was one way for Perkins to share the profits of U.S. Steel. His 1902 profit-sharing plan sought more formal means. That year he barraged the directors of the corporation with lengthy memos promising them that profit-sharing was the only salve for industrial class conflict. But the plan would have to include everyone from "the president to the man with pick and shovel." Perkins would put aside a portion of annual earnings for redistribution to all employees. Further, the corporation would buy back its own stock for resale to its employees on favorable terms through a five-year installment program. The lowest-paid workers were granted the best terms.[64]

It was almost exactly the same scheme Perkins had first designed at the New York Life in the 1880s—the Nylic Association. Perkins had even insinuated the tontine logic into Nylic, which he also carried over to U.S.

Steel. At U.S. Steel employees could yearly subscribe to stock but they had to remain in the employment of the Corporation for five years before they could actually purchase it. An old buddy from the New York Life wrote to him that "it is very interesting to see your old 'NYLIC' principles woven in so beautifully into [U.S. Steel]." Perkins asked the NCF in 1907:

> [Is this] not a form of socialism of the highest, best and most ideal sort—a socialism that makes real partners of employer and employee and yet preserves the right of private property—retaining the capitalist's incentive to enterprise while giving the worker a new inspiration for effort—humanizing a vast organization—promoting good will and industrial peace?"

By applying the tools and creed of financial risk management Perkins believed that he could both socialize and humanize industrial corporations.[65]

If this was socialism, it was a very undemocratic kind. Perkins, as chairman of the Finance Committee, held all the power. The policy announcing the profit-sharing program could not have been clearer:

> The question of what constitutes profits and all other questions shall be determined solely and finally by the Finance Committee, and as this Committee will have no interest whatsoever, directly or indirectly, in the profit-sharing plan, its rulings must be accepted by all as fair, impartial and conclusive.

It was yet another instance of cooperation Perkins-style. Rather than chance-ridden markets distributing moral/pecuniary rewards, Perkins did the job. There would be no freaks of fortune. And Perkins *was* the Finance Committee. After five years workers could collect their stock only with proof of a "certificate" from a "proper official" to the "effect that they have been continuously in the Corporation's service . . . and showed a proper interest in its welfare and progress." The standard was completely arbitrary and in the bosses' hands. Workers had no contractual rights whatsoever. Clearly union organizing would not be deemed in the "proper interest" of U.S. Steel. As the economist and president of

Yale Arthur Hadley warned Perkins in a letter, "the somewhat arbitrary power given the Finance Committee" was bound to cause "difficulty." It seemed the employees of U.S. Steel would simply have to trust Perkins. Brandeis characteristically called Perkins's profit-sharing a form of "strike insurance." The final kicker was a further extension of the tontine principle. For the men who, for whatever reason, did not continue "for five years" in the Corporation's employment their yearly installments would be "credited to a special fund" with interest paid on it by the company at 5 percent. The fund would be divided among those who "gave satisfactory service" to the corporation, which it defined—against labor protest—as an inhuman twelve-hour-a-day, seven-day workweek.[66]

Cooperation instead of competition perhaps, but Perkins was in the saddle. Before the NCF, he had also raised the problem of the abstract relationship between the corporation and its "security holders," which would now include its own workers. Soon there would circulate the notion of a "new proprietorship"—that American citizens, no longer risk-running independent proprietors, could now bear bits of corporate risk by owning corporate stock. That was not Perkins's vision. Shareholders had no power, no responsibility, and assumed no risk in Perkins's corporate universe. Or rather *he* did all of that for them. In one of his biweekly memos to Morgan on the daily operations of U.S. Steel, Perkins scribbled a lengthy justification of a pricing decision on steel bars, before reporting events at the annual meeting of U.S. Steel stockholders: "They sat around for a while and ate sandwiches." Likewise, years later, Perkins engaged in a lengthy, absurdist exchange with Samuel Untermyer, counsel to the 1913 congressional investigation into a "Money Trust." Untermyer asked Perkins if minority stockholders "ought to have the legal right to representation" on corporate boards. Perkins rejected the question because he already took it upon himself to represent the interests of all minority stockholders. Any law would be redundant. Perkins represented the "public's capital."[67]

In 1907, in preparation for his address to the NCF, Perkins had his secretary crunch the numbers on the first five-year cycle of profit-sharing at U.S. Steel. There had been 27,379 subscribers in 1903 purchasing a total of only 48,983 shares of stock. By 1907, 65 percent of them had cancelled, paying into a fund for the remaining 35 percent—the inequitable tontine principle at work. The large majority of the canceled install-ments had only subscribed for a mere 1 share of U.S. Steel stock anyway. The subscriptions for 1904–1907 were even less inspiring.

But as years passed, profit-sharing became a staple of corporate welfare capitalism, at U.S. Steel and elsewhere. Perkins inaugurated a similar profit-sharing plan at International Harvester in 1909 and almost nobody signed up—labor conditions at Harvester were then far more contentious than at U.S. Steel. Yet, by 1915, 63 percent of all International Harvester workers were in the fold. During the 1920s other American corporations followed. By 1927, 800,000 employees in 315 corporations had purchased over a $1 billion of stock through profit-sharing schemes. As much as any-body else Perkins could claim responsibility for this trend.[68]

Yet, as it spread, profit-sharing raised a vexing moral conundrum—the same question at the heart of Knight's *Risk, Uncertainty, and Profit.* Where did profit come from before men like Perkins divided it up? Did it come from assuming risk or reducing risk? Take the International Harvester Corporation. Again, when formed in 1902 it had 85 percent of the market in farm machinery. By 1907 it had virtually no competition whatsoever. In 1913, the Bureau of Corporations, an executive agency created by Roosevelt in 1903 in part at Perkins's behest, assessed the corporation's profit rate. It used the financial concept of insurance to make sense of industrial profit-making:

> In judging of the reasonableness of this rate of profit it is proper to consider the fact that the risk of the company's business is compara-tively small, owing to its world-wide character, which to a large de-gree is an insurance against the effects of local disturbances of busi-ness prosperity. It is also important to bear in mind the fact that the business rests in part on a monopolistic basis, which not only tends to reduce the element of risk, but also makes it desirable from a pub-lic standpoint that the rate of profit should not be higher than a rea-sonable return to the capital invested.

Where did the profit come from if it was not in some measure a rightful return for risk-taking? Certainly International Harvester should not ex-pect an excessive upside without assuming a corresponding downside.

Critics charged such profits were the ill-begotten fruits of monopoly. But Perkins believed it was a return for the corporation's institutional management of social risk, which in turn demanded some form of social redistribution.[69]

Social risk—that was the conceptual breakthrough necessary for a partner in the House of Morgan to argue that wage workers were entitled to a share of corporate profits above their market-priced wages. For the prevailing Gilded Age gospel of personal risk was that men became wage workers because they desired an unerring, fixed wage. The capitalist, who was guaranteed no such thing, and assumed personal risks in the commercial marketplace, was thus entitled to greater profits. But if the bosses were no longer taking personal risks, no longer assuming a potential downside to match their upside, then what? Perkins firmly believed that if labor did its part to stabilize the economy—by not going on strike and relenting control at the point of production—then labor was entitled to a larger share of corporate profits.

No matter the true source of profit—and in fact Perkins helped install a rather clumsy and inefficient corporate structure at U.S. Steel—by 1908 both U.S. Steel and International Harvester were profiting enough so that Perkins could roll out his entire corporate welfare package for wage earners. It consisted of profit-sharing, but also systematic downside protection against the wage earner's risk: "Insurance covering sickness, accident and death" and "Old Age pensions." Once again Perkins was not original. But the visibility of his actions and his role at the NCF, which created its "welfare work" department in 1904, meant his efforts were lasting. U.S. Steel began its employee benefit programs in 1906 and Perkins would boast of them before a congressional panel on industrial relations in 1915, reporting on the well-over $4 million spent by the corporation on welfare benefits—mostly pensions and workers' accident compensation—the year before. Yet if U.S. Steel brought Perkins's profit-sharing idea to the world, International Harvester truly brought the Perkins corporate benefit package.[70]

From 1902 to 1912 Perkins was the final arbiter of all International Harvester policy, after which time corporate control reverted back to Cyrus McCormick, Jr., whose family owned the bulk of the stock. McCormick, who was a member of the NCF, was notoriously antiunion and largely hostile to his ethnically diverse workforce, riddled with unrecognized craft unions powerful enough to sometimes negotiate contracts in piecemeal fashion. If the Homestead strike hovered over U.S. Steel, the 1886 Haymarket Riot, which came after McCormick's father had cracked down on workers striking for an eight-hour day, haunted International Harvester. In 1901, McCormick hired Gertrude Weeks—who would soon leave to work for the NCF in the same guise—to inaugurate a "welfare work" program at International Harvester, telling her to, "See what you can do to make the three hundred girls and five thousand men who work for us like to work for us."[71]

McCormick and Perkins butted heads early and often. McCormick believed welfare work should improve working conditions, as in provide clean lockers and after-work baseball clubs. Perkins focused on personalized financial benefits for male breadwinners. In 1908, he set in motion the creation of the International Harvester "Employee Benefit Association."

By now Perkins was also the chairman of the NCF's commission on "Wage Earner's Insurance." He had the NCF staff draft him lengthy memos on European welfare schemes. The NCF held a national conference to consider the various measures in the industrial world to manage the wage earner's risk—ranging from voluntary, private insurance, to employer-based programs, to state-provided social insurance. Indeed a gathering group of intellectual and social reformers—following the European example—advocated that the state enter the field.[72]

Perkins and McCormick went back and forth over the content of the Employee Benefit Association. Perkins had typically grandiose visions, but what was most important to him was that the corporation contributed out of its own funds for the provision of employee life, accident, sickness, and old-age insurance. These were—he agreed with social insurance advocates—social risks which the wage earner himself was not fully responsible for. Social statistics demonstrated the argument, voiding the possibility of personal moral responsibility. There was seemingly a newly discovered "law of average" for industrial accident and sickness, which meant that these risks could be insured. But it also meant that they were not "personal" risks at all. They were the fault of the industrial system—"social risks," as the economist Seligman put it. Morally, they did not reside within the sphere of self-ownership. With respect to industrial workplace accidents, moral conceptions of social risk assaulted the individualist logic of *Farwell*. To Perkins these social risks belonged not to the state but to the corporation.[73]

The International Harvester Employee Benefit Association went into effect September 1908. Every employee aged seventy or more with twenty or more years of service earned pensions, although employees had no contractual rights to them. In fact the plan read "this certificate may be revoked at any time" and "any pension may be increased or reduced by the Trustees." As for life, accident, and sickness insurance, the program was voluntary. Employees committed 2 percent of their wages or salaries in return for two years' pay in the event of death due to workplace accident; one year's pay for death due to sickness; and one year's half pay for permanent disability. Members received temporary benefits—in the events of sickness or accident—at half pay up to fifty-two weeks. The corporation contributed $50,000 a year to the program, and another $50,000 annually if 75 percent of employees signed up ($100,000 out of the $10.5 million of 1908 profits). It also agreed to make up any temporary deficit in the program's funding.[74]

As a collective strategy the Employee Benefit Association was in effect a corporate risk community. Perkins designed it to function like a mutual insurance company. Certainly it privileged the male productive body and the family wage.[75] Workers submitted to medical tests and exams, and rates were set after an extensive statistical investigation into the incident of industrial accidents and illness at International Harvester and elsewhere. Further, there was no question who would control the program's "Insurance Fund Reserves," as Perkins explained to the McCormick family, who disapproved of just about everything he was doing. That would be Perkins.[76]

The Employee Benefit Association was an enormous success. The NCF trumpeted the program in its reform agenda. Because it upheld the principle of employer contribution even social insurance advocates lauded it—especially after Perkins decided to fully fund the accident insurance provision in 1910 out of International Harvester's own pockets. Charles Richmond Henderson, the University of Chicago professor who had been consulted on the accident provision, included the plan's constitution in his watershed 1908 *Industrial Insurance in the United States.*

Not only did International Harvester continue to roll out stupendous profits but also, for a short while at least, its violent labor struggles receded.[77]

Perkins was the velvet glove on McCormick's iron fist. Appalling anti-union tactics were still a staple of International Harvester labor policy. But Perkins said in public that his corporate benefit packages would not only eliminate labor strife but also issue forth a new era of corporate "copartnership." As he told the congressional panel on industrial relations in 1913, in a monologue on corporate welfarism:

> One of the reasons why I believe in large corporations is that, the ownership being impersonal, you can have profit sharing, welfare work, pensions, accident, and benefit plans, which can not so well be had in small units of business where the ownership is personal.

Corporate profits from managing the social risks of industrial competition meant that the corporation could now afford to adequately manage the wage earner's risk. That is why Perkins told Congress that in the history of labor, after "owner and slave," after "master and man," after "employer and employee," there would now be "copartnership." With respect to risk at least, Perkins wanted to remove compensation from the wage earner's risk from his wage, the embodiment of his self-ownership. Security now flowed from many different forms of social claims—profit sharing, pensions, insurance benefits—on the corporation. To Perkins once individualized, *enclosed* personal risks had now been *incorporated* under the umbrella of the modern industrial corporation—an entity after all that in many respects enjoyed the same legal personality as flesh-and-blood individuals. Whether it was the risks run by flesh-and-blood individual proprietors in the marketplace or the risks of the wage earner, these were all social risks demanding corporate cooperation. Perkins, as always, would be the one who dictated the terms of the cooperating.[78]

Perkins did more than publicize the House of Morgan's corporate policy. He became actively interested in politics and social reform. Over time the "corporation idea" became more corporatist, as he adopted a larger role for the state in the task of risk management. And Perkins very nearly took the "corporation idea" all the way to the White House. For him, the trust question took on a more overtly political dimension.

In October 1908, Perkins sent a copy of a pamphlet announcing the International Harvester's creation of the Employee Benefit Association to his friend President Roosevelt, who responded with a "kind note" that was typical of the correspondence between the two. In 1903, Perkins had personally galvanized the business community in support of Roosevelt's creation of the Department of Commerce and Labor which included a new investigatory agency, the Bureau of Corporations. Roosevelt gave one of the pens he used to sign the legislation to Perkins.[79]

The politics of antitrust presented momentous questions for the new risk management functions of the industrial corporation. Perkins was of course unapologetically hostile to "competition." Would the Supreme Court interpret the 1890 Sherman Law's prohibition of "restraints of trade" as inimical to "cooperation" Perkins-style? Was there a threshold after which a particular corporation's share of the market became an illegal "restraint of trade?" If so, certainly by 1907 the International Harvester Corporation had passed it. The corporate risk community would be illegal. For Perkins the potential actions of the U.S. attorney general and the U.S. Supreme Court posed great peril.[80]

The Bureau of Corporations represented Perkins's best hope. It had no enforcement powers but it could investigate and publicize corporate behavior. Perkins was convinced that if "the public" could only see what he was up to they would realize that he truly was representing the "public interest." He tirelessly advocated for "publicity" and "transparency" in corporate affairs, specifically championing federal charters for corporations in return for a federal licensing and registering process that would preempt judicial review. If the executive administrative agency found any corporate policy objectionable it could alter corporate practice. That was enough for many trust lords to dismiss the bureau as an encroachment upon private property rights. But Perkins volunteered the cooperation of both U.S. Steel and International Harvester.[81]

No doubt Perkins hoped bureau approval would head off the risk of judicial prosecution under the Sherman Law. He enjoyed a direct line of communication with the president. In August 1907, he wrote to Morgan that he had visited Roosevelt in Oyster Bay and had spent "an hour and half with him, discussing the Harvester case and several other subjects." In 1908, in preparation for listing International Harvester securities on the New York Stock Exchange, he sent Roosevelt the corporation's annual report—in a strikingly new format. Until then corporate annual reports were vacuous (if not deliberatively dishonest). In the spirit of "publicity," Perkins decided to reveal the actual operations, including a detailed balance sheet, of the International Harvester Corporation. Just afterwards, upon recommendation from the Bureau of Corporations, Roosevelt instructed his attorney general not to prosecute the corporation under the Sherman Law.[82]

Meanwhile, the NCF was seeking to codify Perkins's personal negotiations with the president in new legislation. The NCF drafted the Hepburn Bill, which would allow corporations to voluntarily register with the Bureau of Corporations. If the bureau deemed their behavior constitutional, then they would be immune from judicial prosecution under the Sherman Law. Eight drafts later the Roosevelt administration had removed immunity from prosecution and the bill now granted strong regulatory power to executive agencies. The NCF abandoned the bill, but not Perkins, who watched in dismay as it floundered in committee during the final days of the Roosevelt administration.[83]

With Roosevelt out of office Perkins's political activities for a short time ebbed. He was still after all one of the nation's most powerful investment bankers. But he did raise over a million dollars for William Taft's 1908 presidential campaign, which included a personal loan to the Republican party of $15,000, never to be repaid. When Taft became president Perkins immediately bent his ear. Except now Perkins's views on the trust question were taking an increasingly radical, statist turn, separating him from even the more mainstream views of the NCF. He explicitly advocated "federal control." He wrote to Taft imploring him to send a federal incorporation bill to Congress. "Ultimately, he argued, "there can be but one solution" which was "national incorporation and regulation." Perkins had become more interested in Washington than Wall Street.[84]

Nevertheless, why Perkins then resigned from J.P. Morgan & Co. in 1910 is not clear. Long after rumors swirled that Morgan was unhappy with his work on a number of deals. But by now Perkins had drifted towards politics. He wrote to the financial editor of the *New York Times* in 1910 that nothing was more certain than that "ruthless and old fashioned competition is going and must go, and that co-operation must take its place. The political party that would see this and help bring it about would confer a great boon to the masses." Whatever the true reason, when baffled friends wrote to him Perkins consistently responded that he had made enough money and now wanted to devote his time to "the public."[85]

Perkins still sat on the boards of U.S. Steel and International Harvester but now free from Morgan commitments he went on a national speaking tour. Then there arrived two unexpected bolts from the blue. On October 26, 1911, the attorney general filed suit against U.S. Steel for violation of the Sherman antitrust law, specifically pointing to the corporation's acquisition of TC&I during the panic of 1907 as a "restraint of trade." To throw salt on the wound President Taft announced, "We must get back to competition." "If it is impossible, then let us go to socialism, for there is no way between." Taft granted Perkins a personal interview at the White House and Perkins left feeling hopeful.[86] But instead the Taft administration next sued the International Harvester Corporation for "restraint of trade." Perkins was now in the final year of his one-man rule at a corporation that had achieved a complete monopoly in its industry, had practically invented corporate welfare policy, and had opened up its entire books to the Bureau of Corporations. Worse, Taft leaked documents that exposed Perkins's personal negotiations with Roosevelt in 1907 that had led to the nonprosecution of International Harvester. The newspapers erupted with Perkins-bashing.[87]

These were the events that in fact initiated Roosevelt's 1912 bid for the Republican presidential nomination and ultimately his candidacy for the presidency under the banner of the new Progressive Party. Perkins told Roosevelt that his checkbook was open and he personally donated $123,000 to support Roosevelt's failed bid for the Republican nomination. He then bankrolled the Progressive Party candidacy as well. In 1912, Perkins, recently resigned as a partner in the House of Morgan, was Roosevelt's handpicked campaign manager.[88]

Many Progressives in 1912 simply could not believe that Perkins was running their shop. They did not trust him. "Roosevelt has the right idea," said the Wisconsin historian Frederick Jackson Turner, "but if he keeps Mr. Perkins as his chef, he is likely to have to take his omelet with

Mr. Morgan's spoon instead of the people's spoon." Left-wing Progressives never tired of attempting to remove Perkins from party leadership. But Roosevelt always came to his defense.[89]

The Progressive Party meant many things to many people but to its campaign manager it was about one thing only: the trust question. Some Progressives hoped to restore "competition." Perkins would have none of it. During the 1912 Progressive Convention he drafted the plank on trusts, conforming it precisely to his views. His enemies on the drafting committee rewrote it to their liking, and when Roosevelt read the revised plank out loud during his acceptance speech Perkins walked out of the convention. Roosevelt later reassured him that his wording would stand.[90] Perkins was by now singing the same song. "The very universe," he declared in one of his many public addresses in 1912, "teaches us regulation, supervision and control by one great central power." The Progressive Party was only "following the example of the great Creator in His organization and management of the world." Apparently God wanted more corporate risk management.[91]

During the campaign Perkins was indeed a political liability. On the campaign trail the Democratic nominee Woodrow Wilson read from one of Perkins's editorials for the *Progressive Bulletin*. "That is Socialism," Wilson declared. He further speculated that if the Bureau of Corporations was further empowered trust lords might "capture the Presidency of the United States." For if "Mr. Roosevelt is willing to have Mr. Perkins suggest how the corporations ought be regulated," Wilson asked before a Kansas audience, "why will he not be willing to take suggestions from the same quarter as to the detail of the regulation?" The public's distrust of Perkins had become campaign fodder. For his part, Wilson sounded familiar themes of self-ownership on the campaign trail. "I want the pigmy to have a chance to come out," he said. "America was created in order that every man should have the same chance as every other man to exercise mastery over his fortunes." Perkins—nefariously according to Wilson— wanted to socialize too much personal risk.[92]

Roosevelt lost the 1912 election. After that defeat the final chapter of Perkins's life was marked by drift, not mastery. As the Progressive Party melted away the new Wilson administration passed the 1914 Clayton Act, which created the Federal Trade Commission, a watered-down version of Perkins's vision for the Bureau of Corporations. Perkins called it "a poor law with a very good name." He no longer had any power at U.S. Steel or International Harvester. In 1916, with McCormick back in charge, a violent strike ripped through the corporation. Perkins wrote McCormick calling his confrontational labor policy a "very great disappointment and disturbance to me." Yet in these years Perkins's corporatist turn to the state continued. He joined the broader American counter-movement in favor of government-sponsored social insurance.[93]

The Roosevelt administration had supported workmen's compensation laws. The NCF, with Perkins's help, had drafted such a law in 1909. But how exactly workmen's compensation would work was another question. At International Harvester Perkins had funded compensation from the corporation's own pockets. The corporation was in effect self-insured. But smaller firms would not have that financial option. So would the state provide public insurance exchanges? Or would the business go to the private, for-profit accident insurance companies? What mix should there be of employer and employee contributions? The twenty-two separate state workmen's compensation laws passed between 1910 and 1913 offered different solutions. But by 1919 private insurance corporations would occupy 60 percent of the new market. Nevertheless, the era of *Farwell* was over.[94]

Having gained momentum, American social insurance reformers in the 1910s moved on to unemployment insurance—the one wage earner's risk that corporations by themselves could not cope with. In 1915, with the national debate over social insurance cresting, Perkins testified before a congressional panel, still advocating the corporation as the primary "social insurance" provider. But a congressman pushed him with respect to the risk of unemployment:

> But how, except under Government,—under a nationalized plan— could this army I refer to of men who work for a series of employers, through no fault of their own, ever receive any pensions, except under nationalization? How could it be done by the private employers?

Perkins answered, "Those cases can not," although "industry should bear those burdens as far as possible." But beyond that, Perkins admitted, "the State" must carry "the balance." The state had to take up the task of risk management. The nation would become a risk community. Economic security would be premised upon citizenship—rather than land ownership, slave ownership, self-ownership or corporate ownership.[95]

The American Association of Labor Legislation had drafted a 1914 unemployment insurance proposal that borrowed heavily from the 1911 British National Insurance Act. It advocated the full panoply of state employment exchanges, public works programs, incentives for corporations to reduce unemployment, and even state-provided unemployment insurance. In 1916, one reform group that endorsed the plan was the New York City Mayor's Committee on Unemployment. Perkins it turns out was knee deep in its day-to-day operations. Unusually for him, never once did his name appear on the Mayor's Committee letterhead or in its public pronouncements. The public's distrust of him was now taken for granted. A political pariah in social insurance circles, Perkins had nevertheless joined them.[96]

Regardless of Perkins's public profile the outcome would have been the same. American social insurance was stymied by 1917. Perkins's native ground, the private commercial insurance industry, fought hard to protect its turf. The business community, as illustrated by NCF's refusal to go beyond workmen's compensation, held the line at industrial accidents. The AFL's Gompers—vice president of the NCF until his death—argued at the NCF's annual convention in 1917 that "Compulsory Insurance" would threaten "the rights and freedom of wage-earners" while bearing within it "the germs of tyranny and autocratic power." Indeed there were plenty of powerful men running around still preaching the Gilded Age gospel of life at your own risk—forged originally in the context of nineteenth-century slave emancipation. Now, with the entry of America into World War I charges of German collectivism followed by Russian Bolshevism were leveled against social insurance.[97]

Perkins at least had finally begun to view the federal government as the fundamental institution for bringing corporations and labor unions together to manage social risk, if not to do the job itself. But nobody was listening and with Perkins lacking any real institutional seat of power what he thought no longer mattered. If he had once been the velvet glove on the iron fist, now he was a national punch line—the defanged corporate wolf in reformist sheep's clothing.

In these final years the only thing that brightened Perkins's mood was the collectivist tide that momentarily welled up during World War I before dissipating into the heady 1920s. America entered the war in the spring of 1917 and the nationalization of crucial industries followed. A new army of government managers descended on Washington, collecting statistics, coordinating output, and fixing prices. The federal government provided soldiers and sailors with social insurance.[98]

Perkins cheered. His final public address was entitled "The American of To-Morrow." He eulogized the "the individualist age," the era when "the freedom of the individual" was the dominant American ideal, a freedom that had "amounted to license to do almost anything that pleased the individual"—"every fellow for himself and the devil take the hindmost." It was a hollow freedom. "Money-making has been the one, all-absorbing occupation in this country for the last forty years." But "the great European war . . . is striking down individualism and building up collectivism," Perkins enthused. The American "of the future must live not for himself but for others." The root problem was inescapably moral. But the state now loomed much larger in Perkins's vision of "socialism of the highest form."[99]

Perkins had a personal interest in World War I. His son, George Perkins, Jr., shipped out to the Western front in 1918 leaving behind a pregnant wife at his physics professor father-in-law's home in Princeton, New Jersey. Near the end of her term she caught pneumonia and soon perished with her unborn child.[100] The private tragedy had a terrible effect on Perkins's psyche. In his more youthful days, when he was full of energy and ambition, he had spoken of a great break in the history of capitalism. Across "raging torrents" he pictured the building of a "bridge" from "old methods to new, from barbarous competition to humane co-operation." He had envisioned a fundamentally new form of corporate economic life. Now he wrote a cable to the Paris branch of the House of Morgan, hoping it could be the bridge to relay to his son, somewhere on the Western front, the news of the deaths of his wife and child. The cable concluded:

> Do you know, George, that often in recent years I have dreamed & wondered if the human race may not be on the verge of a glimpse into another world . . . It cannot be that women with Spirits like my mother and your dear wife can die . . . Each hour I say to myself more & more often, that there *must* be a plan in it all.

Perkins suffered a nervous breakdown before he died a shattered man in 1920.[101]

Decades ago, at the dawn of self-insurance not social insurance, the evangelical abolitionist turned atheist actuary Elizur Wright too had arrived at the end of life disenchanted by his efforts at reform. Wright left behind the infrastructure of corporate risk management that would make Perkins's lifework possible. The trust lord left behind a new corporate welfare capitalism—and a vision of the state as a risk manager of last resort for its citizens. Neither man however found spiritual sanctuary in the modern world he had helped to create. Wright died a fervent atheist. Perkins died wondering about the ways of providence. Neither tamed the freaks of fortune.

Epilogue

Freaks of Fortune

As *they* have chosen their own ways, and their soul hath pleasure
in their abominations, so will *I* choose freaks of fortune for them,
and their terrors will I bring unto them, because I called, and there
was none that answered, I spoke, and they did not hearken, but did
that which was evil in mine eyes, and that in which I had no pleasure they chose—

 —Isaiah 66:3–4, as translated by T. K. Cheyne

DURING THE 1970S, American capitalism entered rough and uncharted seas. At the opening of the twentieth century, George
Perkins's U.S. Steel had represented the rise of the twentieth-century
industrial corporation. Now its fate was emblematic of the coming postindustrial society.

In 1979, battered by global competition and a sagging national economy, the board of directors of U.S. Steel named David Roderick CEO.
Coming from the financial side of the corporation, Roderick had never
managed a steel mill. U.S. Steel radically changed course, quickly closing over a dozen mills. In 1901, Perkins had counted 166,588 U.S. Steel
employees. When Roderick took the helm in 1979 that figure stood virtually unchanged at 166,800. By 1984 the corporation employed just
88,753. In the meantime, Roderick secured a $4.7 billion loan to pur-
chase Marathon Oil for $6 billion. Steel production now accounted for

one-third of the corporation's revenues. Yet the corporation's stock price slid backward. Shareholders—many of them large institutional investors such as insurance corporations and employee pensions funds—grumbled. Financiers Carl Icahn and T. Boone Pickens circled, acquiring large blocks of stock and praising the new gospel of "shareholder value." Both threatened U.S. Steel with Wall Street's most newfangled transaction—the leveraged buyout.[1]

Meanwhile, in 1977 the investment bank Chase Manhattan had created a series of dummy corporations so that International Harvester—once the home of Perkins's trailblazing 1908 Employee Benefit Association—could absolve itself of $65 million in pensions obligations and an additional $20 million in promised factory shutdown benefits to its workers. Chase Manhattan's Wall Street competitors—Lehman Brothers—balked at executing the same deal on moral grounds.[2]

International Harvester renamed itself Navistar in 1987. By then Icahn and Pickens had failed to acquire U.S. Steel. But U.S. Steel—or USX as it was now known—had become a different animal. In response to Icahn's threatened buyout it had hired the investment banks First Boston and Goldman, Sachs to recommend "a wide range of restructuring alternatives to enhance shareholder value." Facing such strong financial headwinds, *The Wall Street Journal* declared, "Neither USX nor Roderick are masters of their own fates anymore."[3] U.S. Steel had stopped investing in steel production, reneging on a number of promises and obligations made to its workers concerning employment and wage increases, along with pensions and benefits. In this sense it was no longer the industrial behemoth of corporate welfare capitalism that Perkins had once helped to create. But in another sense it still was. Much like at the turn of the twentieth century, during the 1980s financiers took back control of American corporations. Perkins was after all a finance capitalist. During the intervening century finance capitalists had simply changed their minds about how they wanted capitalism to work. The durable structures of industrial corporations hollowed out. Corporations increasingly resembled sieves—porous containers of financial transactions.[4] More and more "financial services" took the form of speculative finance qua finance. Wall Street promised there would be adequate financial risk management. As those promises rang out the economic chance-world flourished once again.

To begin to grasp many of the defining characteristics of the financialization of American capitalism that began in the 1970s, only consider in more depth the nineteenth-century freaks of fortune.[5] By the end of the nineteenth century the freaks had exposed the limits of the moral idea—resurgent by the end of the twentieth—that by taking risks everyone got what they deserved in a capitalist economy. The freaks also taught another lesson. Capitalism cannot adequately stabilize itself through financial risk management. Risk management inherently breeds speculative risk-taking and manufactures new forms of insecurity and uncertainty.

Recall that freaks of fortune were sudden and utterly unforeseeable extreme turns of wealth in *either* direction. Brute luck, not divine providence, was their source. The freaks were economic events that came so fast and were so outsized that they could not be attributed to human responsibility. Writing in the wake of financial panic, an 1858 *Harper's Magazine* essay entitled "Freaks of Fortune" announced that the goddess Fortuna was acquiring a new lease on life. She "hangs up her banner in the busy streets of trade."[6]

The freaks' heyday was the Gilded Age—after slave emancipation and the golden age for landed independence. In this era, for daily newspapers to report on the visitation of yet another "freak of fortune" was not uncommon. Providence was waning. New applications of probability theory emerged. Corporate risk management proliferated, as Americans became increasingly dependent upon the activities of financial corporations for their economic security. In these contexts, Americans met the freaks with a mix of both fascination and unease.

To be sure, the new liberal ethos of economic freedom and security held great attraction. It promised outsized personal economic reward for risk-taking. An 1879 New Orleans newspaper, for instance, carried the account of the "Remarkable Career of a Man Once a Slave Who Died Worth $85,000." Through a series of freaks of fortune the former Louisiana slave found himself at the end of his life in possession of property on the Long Island Sound.[7] But not only did the new ethos invite Americans to take risks. It also promised that by offloading personal risks onto a new corporate financial system self-owning Americans could acquire economic security. The new individualism and the new corporate financial system had after all emerged in tandem. Unease therefore lingered over whether or not, given the new power of the economic chance-world, corporate risk management could deliver. The presence of the freaks gnawed away at such doubts.

The freaks defied every possible moral explanation for why an individual might become very rich or very poor. Such was the implication of an 1881 newspaper article entitled, "Freak of Fortune," an account of the life of an anonymous Chicago merchant. An entire life, the article mused, could constitute a freak of fortune, fully directed by the whims of chance. As a young man, out of work and sick and tired, this unnamed protagonist collapsed on the sidewalk. He awoke to find inside his hat a number of small coins. He kept up "this business" for six years, accumulating $20,000, and through a speculation in stocks turned that into $227,000. By 1881, his net worth was $800,000. He lived the life of a "gentleman."[8]

Freaks of fortune were often recounted in this narrative form—the anti-Horatio Alger plotline. A life was first depicted to illustrate that a freak came for no particularly just or unjust reason. A new life came into view to prove the freaks' transformative power. An inadvertent beggar now lounged in a gilded civic club.[9] As the same *Harper's* essay already declared in 1858:

> Never more than now have our people been more impressed with the power of time and chance; for no man among us began this year without decided proofs that his welfare is not wholly in his own keeping, and that changes have come upon the most sagacious from causes alike beyond their foresight and control.

A "wide margin of apparent chance" would now shape "human destiny," *Harper's* predicted. For there was in the world "another party quite as powerful as human will—a mighty and mysterious power." That power was the rising economic chance-world of capitalism.[10]

As a source of power what most distinguished the Gilded Age freaks was their amorality—their destruction of moral responsibility, even when they dispensed riches. At stake was the very possibility of independent personhood and autonomy, as in this 1886 poem with the title "A Freak of Fortune":

> A millionaire awoke one day, to find
> His millions turned to thousands over night—
> He died of grief. His heir from sheer delight
> At unexpected riches,—lost his mind!

The lesson of this double freak was clear: rather than expecting individual agency leading to economic reward, one had to adjust to the sudden, blind whims of chance or risk insanity, even death.[11]

There were jagged edges to the Gilded Age economy ruled by no ethical agent. Events occurred on those edges that were impervious to statistical prediction. An 1881 article in a Cincinnati paper labeled the life of Daniel Dale Haskel a "freak of fortune." Haskel once managed a successful banking house, earning a yearly income of $79,000. The bank failed after the panic of 1873, even after Haskel "gave all his means to endeavor to save the bank." He died in an almshouse, "a broken down vermininfested beggar." Meanwhile, an 1884 freak struck a young farmer of Mount Olivet, Kentucky. He had purchased a winning lottery ticket. "Was I embarrassed? Yes; a little." People crowded around "and closely watched me as I passed along the streets as though I was a wild animal that had escaped from some circus"—as if he was a freak himself.[12]

What to do about the freaks? Corporate risk management could do nothing about them. In the Gilded Age the suggested response was most often stoic. On the heels of the panic of 1873, an 1877 meditation raised the subject of economic volatility: "Many a one does not know how to adapt himself to this freakishness." This author decided, "When I am prosperous, I will not be elated," and "when it goes ill, I will not despair." His economic fate was subject to the freaks but his personality need not be. In 1887, a New York schoolteacher's lecture on "Commercial Business" informed students of the presence of the freaks. But he reminded that "the wealth most to be desired is the possession of one's self." The incipient economic chance-world of the antebellum period had appeared liberating to many parochial Americans—stuck in small worlds, perhaps stuck under the thumb of masters of many different stripes.

By the close of the nineteenth century one senses the emergence of stoical resignation to a new, perplexing kind of master.[13]

What happened then to the Gilded Age freaks of fortune? Certainly the ethos of risk and reward, demanding the personal assumption of risk, lived on as a powerful ideal of personal economic freedom—perhaps to become the most powerful by the opening of the twenty-first century. But Americans did for a short time wage war on the freaks, even if more so to salvage than to scrap this ideal. That war began with the rise of the industrial corporation to dominance in American life. But the New Deal state took aim at the freaks as well.

Following the greatest bust of all, the Great Depression, the New Deal state sought to devolatilize American capitalism. It stumbled towards constituting the nation as a risk community, thereby making baseline economic security a fundamental right of American citizenship. The administrations of President Franklin Delano Roosevelt launched a torrent of government programs designed to master and tame the economic chance-world, rolling back in the process the power of finance capitalists. The Glass-Steagall Act of 1932 erected a firewall between commercial and investment banking and insured ordinary citizens' savings accounts. After 1932, that is, deposits at the Freedman's Bank would have been federally insured. In 1934, the Securities and Exchange Commission was created to bar the kind of insider financial dealings practiced by Perkins. In the collapsed housing market the federal government began to provide government-sponsored mortgage insurance. New legislation granted the federal government the authority to regulate commodities futures trading. Roosevelt's rhetoric was telling when explaining the new policies. In a 1934 fireside chat, Roosevelt announced to the nation, "I am happy to report that after years of uncertainty, culminating in the collapse of the spring of 1933, we are bringing order out of the old chaos." Roosevelt promised American citizens that the federal government would become a new countermovement against the uncertainties and instabilities of capitalism.[14]

The centerpiece of Roosevelt's effort was the 1935 Social Security Act, which created government-sponsored old age, disability, and unemployment insurance. When Roosevelt signed the Act he claimed that the development of the American economy had "tended more and more to make life insecure." The American people required "security" and some "safeguard against misfortunes which cannot be wholly eliminated in this man-made world of ours." "I prefer," the president announced to the American public, "and I am sure you prefer that broader definition of Liberty under which we are moving toward to greater freedom, to greater security for the average man than he has ever known before in the history of America." Here was a new vision of what it meant to be a free and secure economic actor—premised upon the state providing baseline economic security to its citizens.[15]

Yet, in operation Social Security was dependent upon the instruments of corporate risk management. Social Security was an extension of the insurance principle. Therefore as a collective strategy it was predicated upon notions of male individual entitlement and right rather than the shared obligations of a truly national risk community, solidified by an egalitarian ethos of citizenship. Individual entitlement—long ago the thrust of Elizur Wright's reform efforts—clung to the decommodifying project of the twentieth-century American welfare state.[16] Through a special payroll tax Social Security maintained an accounting fiction of individual, personalized accounts. That aspect of the law limited the initial eligibility of large swathes of the American citizenry for Social Security, especially minorities. But more than that, Social Security, the very pillar of American social insurance, was itself emblematic of twentieth-century American risk management—originally private logics mobilized for public purposes.[17]

Nevertheless, in post-World War II America economic volatility strikingly declined. Social Security was expanded to more and more citizens as the quest for security persisted within the generation that lived through the Great Depression. Probability theory found an increasing field of social applications, seeping further into wider culture.[18] New forms of Keynesian macroeconomic steering promised to even out the most extreme peaks and troughs of capitalist business cycles.[19] So did an expanding bureaucratized industrial corporate sector. By 1963, 85 percent of the 200 largest U.S. industrial corporations were controlled by their managers, rather than their investors.[20] Many of these corporations proliferated private corporate welfare benefits.[21] In 1949, the United Steelworkers won pensions and health insurance from U.S. Steel, soon adding un-employment benefits and cost-of-living adjustments. All was not exactly calm. Strikes ripped through U.S. Steel in 1949, 1952, 1955, 1956, and 1959.[22] In 1966, in response to financial volatility, the Federal Reserve acted as lender of last resort for the first time since the 1930s.[23] Still, in this era trust and confidence crested in the collective decision-making and action of the nation's dominant political and economic institutions. Security and stability were watchwords of the era.

These transformations were momentous and in some respects have proven to be enduring. By the middle of the twentieth century something curious happened—the very expression "freaks of fortune" all but dropped from the American vernacular, a victim of the post-World War II imperative for stability and control. The freaks did not survive the ef-florescence of the New Deal order.

But as the subsequent fate of U.S. steel demonstrates that is not where the story ends. The post-World War II order, desirable or not, did not prove to be sustainable. The economic causes of its undoing in the 1970s are a subject of great debate. A shift in the dynamics of global capitalism no doubt occurred.[24] But is it too much of a stretch to suggest that in some quarters the freaks were still longed for? Certainly, in American thought and culture across the ideological spectrum there emerged a frustration with big, impersonal social forces—whether it was big busi-ness or big government—that promised stability, security, and control.[25] And so the left-wing sociologist C. Wright Mills bemoaned the equation of a "pensioned security" with "success" while the right-wing supply-sider George Gilder called for more "risks borne by individual citi-zens."[26] The New Deal social order bred for at least these men a desire for a more authentic, individual selfhood. That desire demanded a rein-vigoration of the old link among freedom, self-ownership, and the per-sonal assumption of risk.

That ethos always had a financial and probabilistic unconscious. It could not thrive without more and more corporate risk management. Indeed, the decades since the 1970s has been a new era of conquest for risk inside and outside the financial arena of capitalism.[27] Risk's nineteenth-century liberal history appears to have a neoliberal doppel-gänger.[28] In tandem with an individualist creed that celebrates risk-taking there has ensued a massive wave of financial innovation. The repressed not only returned but was in fact beckoned, as financiers prom-ised that more and more qualitative uncertainty could be transformed into quantifiable and thus manageable risk—obviating the need for state regulation. Capitalism was put back in charge of taming capitalism using financial instruments of its own design. Once again, corporate risk man-agement led to new forms of speculative risk-taking, and thus insecurity and uncertainty. Gilded Age style financial crises returned.

The era of the freaks of fortune, rather than coming to an end with the rise of the New Deal order was in fact a prologue for our own financial-ized times and risk-defined lives. Now as then the benefits and costs of uncertainty are not equally borne. But can there be any doubt that in our own day, even if they go by another name, something like the freaks of fortune roam among us once again? The vexing moral and political ques-tions at stake in the history of capitalism, risk, and freedom await satisfac-tory answers. Radical uncertainty rules. Only one prediction feels safe: Capitalism's future will be stormy.

Appendix

Notes

Acknowledgments

Index

Appendix: Tables

Table 1. Freedman's Bank Balances, 1866–1872

Year Ending March 1	Balance Due Depositors	Increase
1866	$199,283.42	
1867	$366,338.33	$167,064.91
1868	$638,299.00	$271,960.67
1869	$1,073,465.31	$435,166.31
1870	$1,657,006.75	$583,341.44
1871	$2,455,836.11	$798,829.67
1872	$3,684,739.97	$1,227,927.67

Source: Carl R. Osthaus, *Freedmen, Philanthropy, and Fraud: A History of the Freedman's Savings Bank* (Urbana: Illinois University Press, 1976), 100.

Table 2.   Assets of U.S. Life Insurance Corporations, 1865–1890 (Millions of Dollars)

Year	U.S. Gov. Bonds	U.S. Private Securities	Total Foreign Bonds	Mortgages	Real Estate	Other Assets	Total Assets
1865	27	2	0	21	2	30	82
1870	41	8	0	113	10	112	284
1875	65	15	0	234	25	96	435
1880	105	30	0	179	55	95	462
1885	60	135	1	222	66	80	564
1890	59	211	13	328	85	113	809
1895	115	374	26	417	128	162	1,222
1900	99	756	77	502	160	293	1,886
			percentages				
1865	32.6	2.7	0	25.2	2.8	36.8	100
1870	14.3	2.9	0	39.8	3.6	39.3	100
1875	14.9	3.4	0	53.9	5.8	22.0	100
1880	22.6	6.5	0	38.6	11.8	20.5	100
1885	10.6	23.9	0.2	39.4	11.6	14.2	100
1890	7.3	26.1	1.6	40.5	10.5	14.0	100
1895	9.4	30.6	2.1	34.1	10.5	13.3	100
1900	5.3	40.1	4.1	26.5	8.5	15.5	100

Sources: Bruce M. Pritchett, *A Study of Capital Mobilization: The Life Insurance Industry of the Nineteenth Century* (New York: Arno Press, 1977), 290–347, table A1; Lance Davis and Robert Gallman, *Evolving Financial Markets and International Capital Flows. Britain, the Americas, and Australia, 1865–1914* (Cambridge: Cambridge University Press, 2001), 288, table 3:5c-3.

Table 3.   Largest U.S. Fraternal Societies, 1890

Name	Date Fraternal Benefit Implemented	Membership in 1890	Benefits Paid During 1890 ($)
1. Ancient Order of United Workmen	1868	231,923	4,153,768
2. Knights of Honor	1873	131,753	3,421,033
3. Royal Arcanum	1877	97,992	2,146,526
4. American Legion of Honor	1878	62,467	2,246,936
5. Knights and Ladies of Honor	1877	61,324	735,000
6. Knights of the Golden Eagle	1879	48,553	128,132
7. Modern Woodmen of America	1883	39,457	220,000
8. Order of Chosen Friends	1879	39,492	864,000
9. Royal Templers of Temperance	1877	37,062	296,559
10. Equitable Aid Union	1879	27,072	469,025
11. Knights of the Maccabees	1881	26,977	208,900
12. Order of United Friends	1881	22,503	467,000
13. National Union	1881	20,879	339,000
14. Knights of Pythias	1877	20,505	513,00
15. Catholic Benevolent Legion	1881	19,778	369,000
16. Catholic Knights of America	1877	19,426	443,262
17. United Order of the Golden Cross	1876	15,519	219,611
18. United Order of Pilgrim Fathers	1879	15,223	143,200
19. Royal Society of Good Fellows	1882	15,223	295,400
20. New England Order of Protection	1887	8,848	56,000
21. Improved Order of Heptasophs	1878	8,000	123,000
22. Fraternal Legion	1881	7,000	42,500
23. Empire Order Mutual Aid	1879	6,986	164,001
24. Knights of the Golden Rule	1879	6,800	130,000
25. Order of the Golden Chain	1881	6,648	111,000

Source: Journal of Proceedings of the Fourth Annual Session of the National Fraternal Congress (Poughkeepsie, NY, 1891), 9–10, 45.

Table 4.   Accumulating Finance Capital by Major Type of U.S. Financial Institution
(Millions of Dollars)

Year	Deposits in Savings Banks	Time Deposits in Commercial Banks	Shares in Savings & Loan Associations	Deposits in Trust Companies	Reserves of Life Insurance Companies	Total Savings
1865	246	124	69	–	55	494
1875	924	211	264	–	361	1,760
1885	1,095	203	313	220	457	2,288
1895	1,811	491	430	398	1,032	4,162
1905	2,740	1,727	430	1,150	2,925	8,342
			Percents			
1865	49.8	25.1	14	–	11.1	100
1875	52.5	12.0	15	–	20.5	100
1885	47.9	8.9	13.7	9.6	20	100
1895	43.5	11.8	10.3	9.6	24.8	100
1905	32.8	20.7	5.2	13.8	27.5	100

Sources: Bruce M. Pritchett, *A Study of Capital Mobilization: The Life Insurance Industry of the Nineteenth Century* (New York: Arno Press, 1977), 290–347, table A1; Lance Davis and Robert Gallman, *Evolving Financial Markets and International Capital Flows. Britain, the Americas, and Australia, 1865–1914* (Cambridge: Cambridge University Press, 2001), 280-281 table 3:5c-1.

Table 5. Industrial Distribution of U.S. Life Insurance Companies' Holdings of Securities, 1870–1900 (Thousands of Dollars)

Year	U.S. Government	State & Local Governments	Railroads	Financial	Utilities	Industrials	Canal	Foreign	Other	Total Bonds	Total Stocks	Total Securities
1870	24,086	16,508	4,223	2,386	856	105	661	100	0	45,322	3,603	48,925
1880	40,025	64,493	21,582	4,982	1,779	143	1,275	87	177	127,816	6,727	134,543
1890	6,501	52,398	187,196	10,272	11,064	1,969	486	12,621	139	252,083	30,563	282,646
1900	7,460	91,850	648,475	37,228	45,492	14,163	34	76,615	10,318	830,550	101,085	931,635
						percents						
1870	49.2	33.7	8.6	4.9	1.7	0.2	1.4	0.2	0.0	92.6	7.4	100
1880	29.7	47.9	16.0	3.7	1.3	0.1	0.9	0.1	0.1	95.0	5.0	100
1890	2.3	18.5	66.2	3.6	3.9	0.7	0.2	4.5	0.0	89.2	10.8	100
1900	0.8	9.9	69.6	4.0	4.9	1.5	0.0	8.2	1.1	89.1	10.9	100

Sources: Lance Davis and Robert Gallman, *Evolving Financial Markets and International Capital Flows. Britain, the Americas, and Australia, 1865–1914* (Cambridge: Cambridge University Press, 2001), 289, table 3:5c-4.; Bruce M. Pritchett, *A Study of Capital Mobilization: The Life Insurance Industry of the Nineteenth Century* (New York: Arno Press, 1977), 290–347, table A1.

Notes

PROLOGUE

Epigraph: Francis Murphy, ed., *Walt Whitman: The Complete Poems* (New York: Penguin, 1986), 436.

1. See Michael Zakim and Gary J. Kornblith, eds., *Capitalism Takes Command: The Social Transformation of Nineteenth-Century America* (Chicago: University of Chicago Press, 2012).

2. Tom Baker and Jonathan Simon, eds., *Embracing Risk: The Changing Culture of Insurance and Responsibility* (Chicago: University of Chicago Press, 2002).

3. François Ewald, "Two Infinities of Risk," in Brian Massumi, ed., *Politics of Everyday Fear* (Minnesota: University of Minnesota Press, 1993), 226. See also Ulrich Beck, *Risk Society: Towards a New Modernity* (London: Sage Publications, 1992); Niklas Luhman, *Risk: A Sociological Theory* (New York: Aldine Transaction, 2005); Anthony Giddens, "Risk and Responsibility," *Modern Law Review* 62, no. 1 (January 1999): 1–10; Caitlin Zaloom, "The Productive Life of Risk," *Cultural Anthropology* 19, no. 3 (August 2004): 365–391; Bill Maurer, "Forget Locke?: From Proprietor to Risk-Bearer in New Logics of Finance," *Public Culture* 11, no. 2 (Spring 1999): 365–385.

4. See Mary Douglas, "Risk as a Forensic Resource," in E. J. Burger, ed., *Risk* (Ann Arbor: University of Michigan Press, 1993), 3.

5. "risk, n.," www.oed.com (accessed September 2011). See also Ian Hacking, "Risk and Dirt," in Richard V. Ericson and Aaron Doyle, eds., *Risk and Morality* (Toronto: University of Toronto Press, 2003), 24–26; Luhman, *Risk: A Sociological Theory,* 9; François Ewald, "Insurance and Risk," in Graham Burchell, Colin Gordon

and Peter Miller, eds., *The Foucault Effect: Studies in Governmentality* (Chicago: University of Chicago Press, 1991), 197–210.

6. Joseph A. Schumpeter, *Capitalism, Socialism, and Democracy* (New York: Harper, 1962/1942), 87.

7. On risk's "manufacture" of uncertainty see Anthony Giddens, *Beyond Left and Right: The Future of Radical Politics* (Palo Alto, CA: Stanford University Press, 1996), 152.

1. THE ASSUMPTION OF RISK

Epigraph: Elizur Wright, "Life Insurance for the Poor," *Journal of Social Science, Containing the Transactions of the American Association*, no. 8 (May 1876), 149.

1. *Farwell v. Boston and Worcester R.R. Corp.* 45 Mass. 49 (1842). The literature on *Farwell* is vast, but see Christopher Tomlins, *Law, Labor, and Ideology in the Early American Republic* (New York: Cambridge University Press 1993), ch. 17; John Fabian Witt, *The Accidental Republic: Crippled Workingmen, Destitute Widows, and the Remaking of American Law* (Cambridge: Harvard University Press, 2004), 13, 44–45; Morton J. Horwitz, *The Transformation of American Law, 1780–1860* (Cambridge: Harvard University Press, 1977), 209; Amy Dru Stanley, "Dominion and Dependence in the Law of Freedom and Slavery," *Law & Social Inquiry* 28, no. 4 (October 2003): 1127–1134.

2. Shaw cited a recent decision of his own: *Copeland v. New England Marine Ins. Co.* 43 Mass. 432 (1841).

3. *Farwell v. Boston and Worcester R.R.* The link between peril/risk and liberal selfhood in nineteenth-century America has been established by Barbara Young Welke, *Recasting American Liberty: Gender, Race, and the Railroad Revolution, 1865–1920* (New York: Cambridge University Press, 2001); Witt, *The Accidental Republic*; Roy Kreitner, *Calculating Promises: The Emergence of Modern American Contract Doctrine* (Palo Alto, CA: Stanford University Press, 2007); Arwen P. Mohun, "Designed for Thrills and Safety: Gender, Technology, and the Commodification of Risk in the Amusement Park Industry," *Journal of Design History* 14, no. 4 (Fall 2001): 296–306.

4. If anybody was at fault it was the employee who had mislaid the switch. But Shaw ruled that the corporation was not liable for the negligence of a "fellow servant." Thus the "fellow servant rule" was born.

5. On land enclosure from two different perspectives see E. P. Thompson, *Customs in Common: Studies in Traditional Popular Culture* (New York: New Press, 1993); Robert C. Allen, *Enclosure and the Yeoman: The Agricultural Development of the South Midlands, 1450–1850* (New York: Oxford University Press, 1992). On early modern landed property see Robert S. Gordon, "Paradoxical Property," in John Brewer and Susan Staves, eds., *Early Modern Conceptions of Property* (New York: Routledge, 1996), 95–110.

6. On colonial commons and enclosures see Allan Greer, "Commons and Enclosure in the Colonization of North America," *The American Historical Review* 117, no. 2

(April 2012): 365–386; Brian Donahue, *The Great Meadow: Farmers and the Land in Colonial Concord* (New Haven: Yale University Press, 2007); William Cronon, *Changes in the Land: Indians, Colonists, and the Ecology of New England* (New York: Hill and Wang, 1983), ch. 4. On collective use-rights and customary practices see Steven Hahn and Jonathan Prude, eds., *The Countryside in the Age of Capitalist Transformation* (Chapel Hill, NC: University of North Carolina Press, 1985).

7. Donald N. McCloskey, "The Open Fields of England: Rent, Risk, and the Rate of Interest, 1300–1815," in David W. Galenson, ed., *Markets in History: Economic Studies of the Past* (Cambridge: Cambridge University Press, 1989), 5–51; Gary Richardson, "The Prudent Village: Risk Pooling Institutions in Medieval English Agriculture," *The Journal of Economic History* 65, no. 2 (June 2005): 386–413.

8. Theophilus Parsons, *A Treatise on Maritime Law*, vol. 1 (Boston, 1859), 456.

9. See Witt, *Accidental Republic,* ch. 2 and Walter Licht, *Working for the Railroad: The Organization of Work in the Nineteenth Century* (Princeton: Princeton University Press, 1983).

10. *Copeland v. New England Marine Ins. Co.,* at 441. Emphasis in the original.

11. *Farwell v. Boston and Worcester R.R.*

12. *American Railway Times,* May 16, 1850.

13. On the critical distinction between risk and peril/hazard see Barbara Young Welke, "Spreading Risk, Owning Hazard: The Cowboy Suit Tragedy, the Search for Security, and the Modern American Consumer Marketplace" (photocopy, Department of History, University of Minnesota).

14. For a similar argument relating the individual assumption of risk with the collective, see Jason Puskar, *Accident Society: Fiction, Collectivity, and the Production of Chance* (Palo Alto, CA: Stanford University Press, 2012). See also Eric Wertheimer, *Underwriting: The Poetics of Insurance in America, 1722–1872* (Palo Alto, CA: Stanford University Press, 2006).

15. To invoke, that is, the "double freedom" of Marx's proletarian but with respect to risk. See Karl Marx, *Capital: A Critique of Political Economy,* trans. Ben Fowkes (New York: Vintage Books, 1977), 272. Yet, a younger Marx writing in 1845 once characterized America as a society in which "individuals were free to enjoy the freaks of fortune." "This right to undisturbed enjoyment of fortuity and chance has up till now been called personal freedom." Karl Marx and Friedrich Engels, *The German Ideology* (New York: International Publishers, 1970), 84, 86.

16. The classic statement here is Frank Knight, *Risk, Uncertainty and Profit* (Chicago: University of Chicago Press, 1921).

17. On commerce and uncertainty see Emma Rothschild, *Economic Sentiments: Adam Smith, Condorcet, and the Enlightenment* (Cambridge: Harvard University Press, 2002).

18. J.M. Keynes, "The General Theory of Employment," *The Quarterly Journal of Economics,* 51, no. 2 (February 1937), 214. See also John Maynard Keynes, *The General Theory of Employment, Interest, and Money* (London, 1936), esp. ch. 12. Knight, *Risk, Uncertainty, and Profit,* ch. 8, made the same distinction between risk and uncertainty. Marx and Engels, *German Ideology,* 84, 86; Karl Marx and Friedrich Engels, *The Communist Manifesto* (New York: Verso, 1998/1848); Karl Marx,

"Bastiat and Carey," Martin Nicolaus trans., *Grundrisse: Foundations of the Critique of Political Economy* (New York: Penguin, 1973/1858), 890–891. In comparison to his historical writings, Marx's *Capital,* by design, has a more necessitarian approach to the unfolding of capitalism. F. A. Hayek, *Law, Legislation, and Liberty, vol. 2: The Mirage of Social Justice* (London: Routledge, 1976), esp. chs. 9 and 10. Despite Weber's famous emphasis on instrumental rationality, see Max Weber, *Economy and Society,* eds. Guenther Roth and Claus Wittich (Berkeley: University of California Press, 1978/1922), esp. 159. Werner Sombart, *The Quintessence of Capitalism: A Study of the History and Psychology of the Modern Business Man* (New York: Taylor and Francis, 1998/1913), esp. 44. Joseph A. Schumpeter, *The Theory of Economic Development* (Cambridge: Harvard University Press, 1934/1912) and *Capitalism, Socialism, and Democracy* (New York: Harper 1962/1942), ch. 7. Fernand Braudel, *Afterthoughts on Material Civilization and Capitalism* (Baltimore: Johns Hopkins University Press, 1977), esp. 54–58. For a general history of capitalism written much from this perspective of unceasing change see Joyce Appleby, *The Relentless Revolution: A History of Capitalism* (New York: Norton, 2011).

19. On chance in antebellum American culture see Jackson Lears, *Something for Nothing: A History of Luck in America* (New York: Penguin, 2003); Maurice S. Lee, *Uncertain Chances: Science, Skepticism, and Belief in Nineteenth-Century American Literature* (New York: Oxford University Press, 2011). On capitalism, democracy, and a future-oriented vision see Joyce Appleby, *Capitalism and a New Social Order: The Republican Vision of the 1790s* (New York: Columbia University Press, 1984); Joyce Appleby, *Inheriting the Revolution: The First Generation of Americans* (Cambridge: Harvard University Press, 2001); Gordon S. Wood, "The Enemy Is Us: Democratic Capitalism in the Early Republic," *Journal of the Early Republic* 16, no. 2 (Summer 1996): 293–308. On the relationship between antebellum capitalism and democracy see Michael Zakim, *Ready-Made Democracy: A History of Men's Dress in the American Republic, 1760–1860* (Chicago: University of Chicago Press, 2003).

20. See Charles Sellers, *The Market Revolution: Jacksonian America, 1815–1846* (New York: Oxford University Press, 1994); Melvyn Stokes and Stephen Conway, eds., *The Market Revolution in America: Social, Political, and Religious Expressions, 1800–1880* (Charlottesville: University of Virginia Press, 1996); George Rogers Taylor, *The Transportation Revolution, 1815–1860* (New York: Rinehart, 1951).

21. See James L. Huston, *Securing the Fruits of Labor: The American Concept of Wealth Distribution, 1765–1900* (Baton Rouge: Louisiana State University Press, 1998); Daniel T. Rodgers, *The Work Ethic in Industrial America, 1850–1920* (Chicago: University of Chicago Press, 1974).

22. On the significance of this point more generally for the study of risk see Caitlin Zaloom, "The Productive Life of Risk," *Cultural Anthropology* 19, no. 3 (August 2004): 365–391.

23. House Committee on Agriculture, *Fictitious Dealings in Agricultural Products: Hearings on H.R. 392, 2699, and 3870,* 52nd Cong., 3rd sess., 1892, 158.

24. See Richard White, *Railroaded: The Transcontinentals and the Making of Modern America* (New York: W.W. Norton & Co., 2011).

25. Schumpeter, *Capitalism, Socialism, and Democracy,* 87. On nineteenth-century American economic growth see Robert E. Gallman, "Economic Growth and Structural Change in the Long Nineteenth Century," in Stanley L. Engerman and Gallman, eds., *The Cambridge Economic History of the United States, Volume II, the Long Nineteenth Century* (New York: Cambridge University Press, 2000), 1–56.

26. See Ann Fabian, *Card Sharps and Bucket Shops: Gambling in Nineteenth-Century America* (Ithaca: Cornell University Press, 1990); Lears, *Something for Nothing;* Stephen Mihm, *A Nation of Counterfeiters: Capitalists, Con Men, and the Making of the United States* (Cambridge: Harvard University Press, 2007).

27. Edwin T. Freedley, *A Practical Treatise on Business* (Philadelphia, 1856), 109, 171.

28. See Serena Olsaretti, *Liberty, Desert, and the Market* (New York: Cambridge University Press, 2004).

29. Ron Chernow, *Titan: The Life of John D. Rockefeller, Sr.* (New York: Random House, Inc., 2004), 54. See also Max Weber, *The Protestant Ethic and the Spirit of Capitalism and Other Writings,* ed. and trans. Peter Baehr and Gordon C. Wells (New York: Penguin Books, 2002/1904). On nineteenth-century religion and commerce see Stewart Davenport, *Friends of the Unrighteous Mammon: Northern Christians and Market Capitalism, 1815–1860* (Chicago: University of Chicago Press, 2008). On the scientific naturalization of market activity see Dorothy Ross, *The Origins of American Social Science* (New York: Cambridge University Press, 1991); Mary S. Morgan, "Competing Views of Competition in Late-Nineteenth Century American Economics," *History of Political Economy* 25, no. 4 (Winter 1993): 563–604.

30. "A Lucky Freak of Fortune," *Daily True Delta,* January 6, 1861. William Dean Howells, *A Hazard of New Fortunes* (New York, 1889), 252. On Howells see Puskar, *Accident Society,* ch. 1. In general see also Lorraine Daston, "Life, Chance and Life Chances," *Daedalus* 137, no. 1 (Winter 2008): esp. 6.

31. John Beauchamp Jones, *The Freaks of Fortune: or, The History and Adventures of Ned Lorn* (New York, 1854); Oliver Optic, *Freaks of Fortune: or, Half Round the World* (New York, 1868).

32. Alexis de Tocqueville, *Democracy in America,* ed. and trans. Philip Bradley (New York: Random House, 1945), 1:305; 2:165, 248–49.

33. "The Great Nation of Futurity," *The United States Magazine and Democratic Review* (November 1839).

34. Karl Polanyi, *The Great Transformation: The Political and Economic Origins of Our Time* (Boston: Beacon Press, 2001/1944), 80, 136.

35. See Davis A. Moss, *When All Else Fails: Government as the Ultimate Risk Manager* (Cambridge: Harvard University Press, 2004); White, *Railroaded.*

36. See Lears, *Something for Nothing;* Edward J. Balleisen, *Navigating Failure: Bankruptcy and Commercial Society in Antebellum America* (Chapel Hill: University of North Carolina Press, 2001); Scott A. Sandage, *Born Losers: A History of Failure in America* (Cambridge: Harvard University Press, 2005); Seth Rockman, *Scraping By: Wage Labor, Slavery, and Survival in Early Baltimore* (Baltimore: The Johns Hopkins University Press, 2009).

37. In general see Hyman P. Minksy, *Stabilizing an Unstable Economy* (New Haven: Yale University Press, 1986).
38. Freedley, *A Practical Treatise on Business,* 109, 171.

2. THE PERILS OF THE SEAS

Epigraph: From *American Ship-Masters Assistant* (Portland, ME, 1807), 176.
1. See Elizabeth Fox-Genovese and Eugene D. Genovese, *Fruits of Merchant Capital: Slavery and Bourgeois Property in the Rise and Expansion of Capitalism* (New York: Oxford University Press, 1993).
2. On community see Raymond Williams, *Keywords: A Vocabulary of Culture and Society* (New York: Oxford University Press, 1983), 75; Thomas Bender, *Community and Social Change in America* (New Brunswick: Rutgers University Press, 1982); Suzanne Keller, *Community: Pursuing the Dream, Living the Reality* (Princeton: Princeton University Press, 2005), 1–37.
3. On the colonial economy see Russell R. Menard, *The Economy of British America, 1607–1789* (Chapel Hill: University of North Carolina Press, 1985).
4. Merchant quoted in, T. S. (Merchant), *A Letter to a member of Parliament* [on marine insurance] *By a merchant* (London, 1720).
5. On the link between long-distance trade and moral perceptions of freedom see Thomas L. Haskell, "Persons as Uncaused Causes," in Thomas L. Haskell and Richard F. Teichgraeber III, eds., *The Culture of the Market: Historical Essays* (Cambridge: Cambridge University Press, 1993); Thomas Bender, ed., *The Antislavery Debate: Capitalism and Abolitionism as a Problem in Historical Interpretation* (Berkeley: University of California Press, 1992).
6. This is in line with the contributions of New World slavery to liberal notions of property and personhood. See James Oakes, *Slavery and Freedom: An Interpretation of the Old South* (New York: Knopf, 1990), esp. chs. 1 and 2. On the contributions of the Atlantic slave trade to the development of capitalism see Marcus Rediker, *The Slave Ship: A Human History* (New York: Viking, 2008).
7. Charles H. Wesley, "Manifests of Slave Shipments Along the Waterways, 1808–1864," *Journal of Negro History* 27 (April 1942): 172. On the U.S. domestic trade and westward expansion see Walter Johnson, *Soul by Soul: Life Inside the Antebellum Slave Market* (Cambridge: Harvard University Press, 1999); Robert H. Gudmestad, *A Troublesome Commerce: The Transformation of the Interstate Slave Trade* (Baton Rouge: Louisiana State University Press, 2003); Adam Rothman, *Slave Country: American Expansion and the Origins of the Deep South* (Cambridge: Harvard University Press, 2005).
8. "Log Book for the Creole," entries dated October 25, 1841, through November 8, 1841, General Manuscripts Collection, Louisiana State Museum. I recount the events of the revolt from multiple, often contradictory sources, with conflicting interests given the financial stakes of the insurance dispute. For an incisive reflection on this problem see Walter Johnson, "White Lies: Human Property and Domestic Slavery Aboard the Slave Ship *Creole,*" *Atlantic Studies* 5, no. 2 (August 2008): 237–263.

9. *Message from the President of the United States Communicating. . . . Mutiny on board the brig Creole. . . .* 27th Cong., 2nd sess., Sen. Doc. 51 (1842), 38.

10. *Mutiny on board the brig Creole,* Sen. Doc. 51, 40.

11. Ibid., 40, 41. On slaves' knowledge of Atlantic political geography see Phillip Troutman, "Grapevine in the Slave Market: African American Geopolitical Literacy and the 1841 *Creole* Revolt," in Walter Johnson, ed., *The Chattel Principle: Internal Slave Trades in the Americas* (New Haven: Yale University Press, 2004), 72–91, and Johnson, "White Lies."

12. The white commanding officer, Captain Fitzgerald, in fact told the nineteen they were "foolish" to not have killed all the whites onboard and to have run the brig ashore.

13. See "Circular Dispatch of 15 May 1839" and "Circular Dispatch of 14 January 1839," both in Records of the Colonial Office, CO 318/146, British National Archives. On the British context, see Thomas C. Holt, *The Problem of Freedom: Race, Labor, and Politics in Jamaica and Britain, 1832–1938* (Baltimore: The Johns Hopkins University Press, 1991).

14. *Mutiny on board the brig Creole,* Sen. Doc. 51, 14, 10. On the decision to release the nineteen see "To the Right Honorable Lord Stanley, 19 January 1842," Records of the Colonial Office, CO 318/154, British National Archives.

15. Merritt M. Robinson, *Reports of the Cases Argued and Determined in the Supreme Court of Louisiana, Volume X, from 1 March, to 20 June, 1845* (New Orleans, 1845), 216, 217. "Circular Dispatch of 14 January 1839."

16. See Howard Jones, "The Peculiar Institution and National Honor: The Case of the *Creole* Slave Revolt," *Civil War History* 21 (March 1975): 28–33; Edward D. Jervey and C. Harold Huber, "The *Creole* Affair," *Journal of Negro History* 65, no. 3 (Summer 1980): 196–211. See also the speeches before the Senate of Henry Clay and John C. Calhoun. January 11, 1842, *Congressional Globe,* 27th Cong., 2nd sess., 116 and February 3, 1842, *Congressional Globe,* 27th Cong., 2nd sess., 47, 115, 203–204.

17. On resistance see Walter Johnson, *Soul by Soul,* 72–76; Johnson, "White Lies"; and Troutman, "Grapevine."

18. The case was *Thomas McCargo v. The New Orleans Insurance Company* 10 Rob. 202 (1845).

19. Florence Edler de Roover, "Early Examples of Marine Insurance," *The Journal of Economic History* 5, no. 2 (November 1945): 172–200. Karl H. Van D'Elden, "The Development of the Insurance Concept and the Insurance Law in the Middle Ages," in Harold J. Johnson, ed., *The Medieval Tradition of Natural Law* (Kalamazoo: Medieval Institute Publications, 1987), 192–200, argues for an earlier date based upon the existence of bottomry and respondentia loans. See Robert Lopez, *The Commercial Revolution of the Middle Ages, 950–1350* (New York: Cambridge University Press, 1976).

20. Bacon quoted in 43 Elizabeth c. 12. For the second article of the Maritime Code of 1668 see Nathaniel B. Shurtleff, ed., *Records of the Governor and Company of the Massachusetts Bay in New England* (Boston: 1853–1854), 2:389. See Violet Barbour, "Marine Risks and Insurance in the Seventeenth Century," *Journal of Economic and Business History* 1, no. 1 (November 1928): 561–596; Frank Spooner, *Risks at Sea: Amsterdam Insurance and Maritime Europe, 1766–1780* (New York: Cambridge

University Press: 1983). On Lloyd's see Charles Wright and Ernest Fayle, *A History of Lloyd's, from the Founding of Lloyd's Coffee House to the Present* (London: Macmillan and Company, 1928). On colonial American underwriting see Mary Elizabeth Ruwell, *Eighteenth-Century Capitalism: The Formation of American Marine Insurance Companies* (New York: Garland, 1993).

21. The Navigation Acts passed between 1660 and 1696. See John J. McCusker, "British Mercantilist Polices and the American Colonies," in Stanley L. Engerman and Robert E. Gallman, eds., *The Cambridge Economic History of the United States, vol. 1 The Colonial Era* (New York: Cambridge University Press, 1996), 337–362. On the golden age of colonial commerce see David Hancock, *Citizens of the World: London Merchants and the Integration of the British Atlantic Community, 1735–1785* (Cambridge: Cambridge University Press, 1995); Cathy Matson, *Merchants and Empire: Trading in Colonial New York* (Baltimore: Johns Hopkins University Press, 1998). On the organization of American colonial trade and finance see R. C. Nash, "The Organization of Trade and Finance in the British Atlantic Economy, 1600–1830," in Peter A. Coclanis, *The Atlantic Economy during the Seventeenth and Eighteenth Centuries: Organization, Operation, Practice, and Personnel* (Columbia, SC: University of South Carolina Press, 2005), 95–151. On eighteenth-century American colonial underwriting see Christopher G. Kingston, "Marine Insurance in Britain and America, 1720–1844: A Comparative Institutional Analysis," *Journal of Economic History* 67, no. 2 (June 2007): 379–409; Glenn A. Crothers, "Commercial Risk and Capital Formation in Early America: Virginia Merchants and the Rise of American Marine Insurance, 1750–1815." *Business History Review* 78, no. 4 (2004): 607–634.

22. See Nash, "Organization of Trade," 73; Thomas M. Doerflinger, *A Vigorous Spirit of Enterprise: Merchants and Economic Development in Revolutionary Philadelphia* (Chapel Hill: University of North Carolina Press, 1986), 215–267; Kevin O'Rourke, "The Worldwide Economic Impact of the French Revolutionary and Napoleonic Wars, 1793–1815," *Journal of Global History* 1, no. 1 (2006): 123–149.

23. The 1720 Bubble Act had restricted incorporations. On the general post-revolutionary wave of corporations see Robert E. Wright, "Capitalism and the Rise of the Corporate Nation," in Michael Zakim and Gary J. Kornblith, eds., *Capitalism Takes Command: The Social Transformation of Nineteenth-Century America* (Chicago: University of Chicago Press, 2012), 145–168. On the Insurance Company of North America see Ruwell, *Eighteenth-Century Capitalism*. On the general shift to insurance companies see Kingston, "Marine Insurance in America," and p. 396 for 1810 London numbers; William M. Fowler, Jr., "Marine Insurance in Boston: The Early Years of the Boston Marine Insurance Company, 1799–1807," in Conrad Edick Wright and Katheryn P. Viens, eds., *Entrepreneurs: The Boston Business Community, 1700–1850* (Boston: Northeastern University Press, 1997), 151–180; Crothers, "Commercial Risk." 1837 Boston count in "Joseph May Almanacs," Box 11, Folder 2, Manuscripts, Massachusetts Historical Society.

24. John G. Clark, *New Orleans, 1718–1812: An Economic History* (Baton Rouge: Louisiana State University Press, 1980), 335. There are no settled figures for the ownership of insurance stock in the early national period. Rothenberg finds scattered evidence for a wider ownership in Boston. Winifred Barr Rothenberg, *From Market-Places to*

a Market Economy: The Transformation of Rural Massachusetts, 1750–1850 (Chicago: The University of Chicago Press, 1992), 120–122. See also Robert E. Wright, *The Wealth of Nations Rediscovered: Integration and Expansion in American Financial Markets, 1780–1850* (New York: Cambridge University Press, 2002), 119.

25. On Balch, see the biographical entry for his son in Charles Sedgwick Rackemann, "Francis Vergines Balch," in *Transactions of the Colonial Society of Massachusetts,* vol. XII (Boston, 1911), 339–340. For Balch in Boston in 1810 see "Commercial Insurance Office," *Boston Gazette,* April 19, 1820. Merchants' Insurance Company incorporation, *Laws of the Commonwealth of Massachusetts* (Boston, 1818) 7:302. For Balch's death notice see *New York Evangelist,* December 20, 1849. For Balch's journal see "Boston, 1813–1823," in Joseph Balch Papers, Baker Library Historical Collections, Harvard Business School.

26. "To Solomon Townsend, Rhode Island, December 4, 1761," in Phillip L. White, ed., *The Beekman Mercantile Papers, 1746–1799,* 3 vols. (New York, 1956), 1:395. Balch, "Boston, 1813–1823," Baker Library Historical Collections.

27. "Rights of Northern Colored Seaman," *The Liberator,* February 24, 1843; Balch, "Boston, 1813–1823," Baker Library Historical Collections. On the post-1815 fortunes of American merchants see Nash, "Organization of Trade," 120–121.

28. Francesco Rocco, *A Manual of Maritime law* (Philadelphia, 1809), 88.

29. "Robert Pringle to Andrew Pringle in London, Charles Town, 7th January 1739," in Walter B. Edgar, ed., *The Letterbook of Robert Pringle,* 2 vols. (Columbia: University of South Carolina Press, 1972), 1:202. Charleston colonial merchants were commission agents for London principals. See S. Max Edelson, *Plantation Enterprise in Colonial South Carolina* (Cambridge: Harvard University Press, 2006), ch. 3.

30. "To James Blount. Edentown, North Carolina. Charles Town, 14th January 1742," in Edgar, *Pringle Papers,* 2:483. For gaming the system see "To Archibald Cunningham, Londonberry, November 25, 1747," in White, *Beekman Papers,* 1:33.

31. William H. Ukers, *All About Coffee* (New York, 1922), 113–127. *Gibson's Guide and Directory of the State of Louisiana and the Cities of New Orleans and Lafeyette* (New Orleans, 1838), 349–353. On information see John J. McCusker, "The Demise of Distance: The Business Press and the Origins of the Information Revolution in the Early Modern Atlantic World," *American Historical Review* 110, no. 2 (April 2005), 295–321.

32. Rocco, *A Manual of Maritime law,* 135. Hugh J. Fegan, "Notes on the Development of the Doctrine of Insurable Interest," *Georgetown Law Journal* VIII, no. 1 (December 1919): 13. On the development of insurable interest in America see Willard Phillips, *A Treatise on the Law of Insurance* (Boston, 1823), ch. 3.

33. On deviation see Phillips, *A Treatise on the Law of Insurance,* 179–188.

34. On running some risk see *Admiralty Decisions in the District Court of the Untied States, for the Pennsylvania District, By the Hon. Richard Peters . . . with an Appendix containing . . . The Marine Ordinances of Louis XIV. . . .* (Philadelphia, 1807), xliii. The two cases were *Carter v. Boehm* 3 Burr 1905 (1766), which includes the quote, and *Lewis v. Rucker* (1761) 2 Burr 1167. Balthazard Marie Emerigon, *A Treatise on Insurances,* trans. Samuel Meredith (Boston, 1850), 188.

35. See Lorraine Daston, *Classical Probability in the Enlightenment* (Princeton: Princeton University Press, 1988), 116-125.

36. Joseph Balch, "Rates of premium for marine insurance," *The Merchant's Magazine and Commercial Review* 1, no. 6 (December 1839): 491.

37. Thomas Thompson to Nathaniel Phillips, July 10, 1819, Container 1, Folder 27, Records of the Warren Insurance Company, Correspondence, 1801–1841, Manuscripts Collection, Mystic Seaport Museum.

38. Ralph Davis, *The Rise of the English Shipping Industry in the Seventeenth and Eighteenth Centuries* (London: Macmillan, 1963), 82–84; Smith, *Wealth of Nations,* 121; Theophilus Parsons, *A Treatise on Maritime Law,* vol. 1 (Boston, 1859), ch. 4 for part-ownership, ch. 6 for bottomry, and ch. 9 on general average.

39. See Barbour, "Marine Risks and Insurance," 588.

40. Vernon to Thomlinson, January 20, 1758, Container 1, Folder 14, Vernon Papers, New York Historical Society. On insurance and the Atlantic slave trade see Joseph Inikori, *Africans and the Industrial Revolution in England: A Study in International Trade and Economic Development* (New York: Cambridge University Press, 2002). On colonial American involvement see Jay Alan Coughtry, *The Notorious Triangle: Rhode Island and the African Slave Trade, 1700–1807* (Madison: University of Wisconsin, 1978); Elizabeth Donnan, *Documents Illustrative of the History of the Slave Trade to America,* 4 vols. (Washington, DC: The Carnegie Institution of Washington, 1932). For Atlantic slave trade figures, see David Ellis and David Richardson, *Atlas of the Transatlantic Slave Trade* (New Haven: Yale University Press, 2010), xvii, 200.

41. Willard Phillips, Policy of Augusta Insurance and Banking Company, Folder 17, Collection of Blank Insurance Forms from American and Foreign Insurance Companies, Manuscripts, Massachusetts Historical Society. On other policies see "Suits relating to the salve mutiny aboard the brig Creole, 1841 [Docket Nos. 4408, 4409, 4410, 4411, 4413, 4414, 4419]," 1 carton, Louisiana Commercial Court, Orleans Parish, City Archives, New Orleans Public Library; Newton Boley to William Crow, December 3, 1841, Letters to William Crow, 1841–1842, Special Collections, University of Virginia Library. On Mississippi slave insurance see *Moore & Porter v. The Perpetual Insurance Company* 16 Mo. 98 (1851).

42. See, for instance, Charles F. Hoffman, "The Poetry of Trade," *Hunt's Merchant Magazine,* November 1845, 405.

43. On Fuller see Kingston, "Marine Insurance in America," 393.

44. On reinsurance see Phillips, *Treatise on Insurance,* 56; Parsons, *Treatise on Maritime Law,* 96–103.

45. On insurance corporations and reinsurance see Parsons, *Treatise on Maritime Law,* 102–103. "Marine Insurance," *DeBow's Commercial Review* (July 1846): 3. For Boston numbers see *Commercial Directory* (Philadelphia, 1823): 97; 1823; *A. E. Wrights . . . Commercial Directory* (New York, 1840): 21 (life and fire excluded).

46. "To Solomon Townsend, Rhode Island, May 1, 1762," in White, *Beekman Papers,* 1:410. The literature on "trust" in early modern merchant communities is vast. See Francesca Trivellato, *The Familiarity of Strangers: The Sephardic Diaspora, Livorno, and Cross-Cultural Trade in the Early Modern Period* (New Haven: Yale

University Press, 2009); Peter Mathias, "Risk, Credit, and Kinship in Early Modern Enterprise," in John H. McCusker and Kenneth Morgan, eds., *The Early Modern Atlantic Economy* (Cambridge: Cambridge University Press, 2001), 15–35.

47. William David Evans, *Collection of Statutes . . . vol. 2* (London, 1836), 222.

48. 43 Elizabeth c. 12; *Carter v. Boehm* 3 Burr. at 1909 (1766).

49. Emerigon, *Treatise on Insurances,* 191; Parsons, *Treatise on Maritime Law,* 89, and 90 for the legitimacy of co-adventurers insuring. Co-adventuring was known as the "portage." See Allan A. Arnold, "Merchants in the Forecastle: The Private Ventures of New England Mariners," *American Neptune,* 41 (1981), 165–187.

50. Charles Abbot, *A Treatise of the Law Relative to Merchant Ships and Seamen. . . .* (Philadelphia, 1802), 107; Parsons, *Treatise on Maritime Law,* 456. On domestic relations and the maritime law see Daniel Vickers with Vince Walsh, *Young Men and the Sea: Yankee Seafarers in the Age of Sail* (New Haven: Yale University Press, 2005), ch. 7. See also Gautham Rao, "Administering Entitlement: Governance, Public Health Care, and the Early American State," *Law and Social Inquiry* 37, no. 3 (forthcoming Summer 2012).

51. *Admiralty Decisions in the District Court of the Untied States, for the Pennsylvania District. By the Hon. Richard Peters. . . .* (Philadelphia, 1807), 143–152.

52. John Abbott, "The Perils of the Sea," *New York Evangelist* (January 16, 1845). On mercantile retreat to land see Nash, "Organization of Trade," 103; Bernard Bailyn, *New England Merchants in the Seventeenth Century* (Cambridge: Harvard University Press, 1955), 101–103; Doerflinger, *A Vigorous Spirit of Enterprise,* 41–45. On retreat to slaves see Edelson, *Plantation Enterprise in Colonial South Carolina,* 153. On the mariner's household see Lisa Norling, *Captain Ahab Had a Wife: New England Women & the Whalefishery, 1720–1870* (Chapel Hill: University of North Carolina Press, 2000), esp. 34, 197; Seth Rockman, *Scraping By: Wage Labor, Slavery and Survival in Early Baltimore* (Baltimore: Johns Hopkins University Press, 2008).

53. See Johnson, "White Lies," and Troutman, "Grapevine." On the revolutionary Atlantic see Marcus Rediker and Peter Linebaugh, *The Many-Headed Hydra: The Hidden History of the Revolutionary Atlantic* (Boston: Beacon, 2001).

54. Robinson, *Reports,* 203. For the 1779 clause see Wright and Fayle, *History of Lloyd's,* 128.

55. Emerigon, *A Treatise on Insurances,* 285.

56. *Green v. Elmslie,* Peake N. P. 278 (1792); See, for instance, *American Ship-Masters Assistant* (Portland, 1807), 176; "Marine Insurance—Perils of the Sea," *The Chronicle: A Journal Devoted to the Interests of Insurance* 2, no. 5 (November 18, 1869): 27; *Coolidge and. Oliver v. New York Fireman Ins. Co.* 14 Johns. 308 (1817).

57. See Giovanni Ceccarelli, "Risky Business: Theological and Canonical Thought on Insurance from the Thirteenth to the Seventeenth Century," *Journal of Medieval and Early Modern Studies* 31, no. 3 (Fall 2001): 621–625.

58. Urian Oakes, "The Sovereign Efficacy of Divine Providence," in Perry Miller and Thomas H. Johnson, eds., *The Puritans: A Sourcebook of Their Writings* (New York: Dover, 2001), 350; William Hubbard, "The Happiness of a People," in Miller and Johnson, eds., *The Puritans,* 248. On Protestantism and providence see

Michael P. Winship, *Seers of God: Puritan Providentialism in the Restoration and Early Enlightenment* (Baltimore: Johns Hopkins University Press, 1996); David D. Hall, *Worlds of Wonder, Days of Judgment: Popular Religious Belief in Early New England* (Cambridge: Harvard University Press, 1990).

59. Hull quoted in Phyllis Whitman Hunter, *Purchasing Identity in the Atlantic World: Massachusetts Merchants, 1670–1780* (Ithaca: Cornell University Press, 2001), 19, 20. The classic argument linking Puritan anxiety and commercial striving is of course Max Weber, *The Protestant Ethic and the Spirit of Capitalism* (New York: Penguin, 2002/1905). See also Mark A. Peterson, *The Price of Redemption: The Spiritual Economy of Puritan New England* (Palo Alto: Stanford University Press, 1997); Mark Valeri, *Heavenly Merchandize: How Religion Shaped Commerce in Puritan America* (Princeton: Princeton University 2010); Bailyn, *New England Merchants in the Seventeenth Century.*

60. Perry Miller, *The New England Mind: From Colony to Province* (Cambridge: Harvard University Press, 1953), 171; Hunter, *Purchasing Identity,* 118.

61. Benjamin Balch to Moses Hale, December 23, 1834, Container 3, Commercial Insurance Co. Collection, Baker Library Historical Collections, Harvard Business School. Daston, *Classical Probability*, 119, provides an incisive account of marine risk pricing in early modern Europe.

62. See Toby L. Ditz, "Shipwrecked; or, Masculinity Imperiled: Mercantile Representations of Failure and the Gendered Self in Eighteenth-Century Philadelphia," *The Journal of American History,* 81, no. 1 (June 1994): 51–80.

63. Balch, "Boston, 1813–1823," Baker Library Historical Collections.

64. See, for instance, a water damage claim involving Joseph Balch. *Ellery v. Merchants' Insurance Company* 20 Mass. 46 (1825).

65. On the *Zong,* see James Walvin, *The Zong: A Massacre, the Law and the End of Slavery* (New Haven: Yale University Press, 2011); Neil Jones, ed., "Symposium: The *Zong:* Legal, Social and Historical Dimensions," *The Journal of Legal History* 28, no. 3 (December 2007): 283–370; Anita Rupprecht, "Excessive Memories: Slavery, Insurance, and Resistance," *History Workshop Journal* 64, no. 1 (Spring 2007): 6–28; Ian Baucom, *Specters of the Atlantic: Finance Capital, Slavery and the Philosophy of History* (Durham: Duke University Press, 2005); Tim Armstrong, "Slavery, Insurance, and Sacrifice in the Black Atlantic," in Bernhard Klein and Gesa Mackenthum, eds., *Sea Changes: Historicizing the Ocean* (New York: Routledge, 2004). The case was *Gregson v. Gilbert* 3 Dougl. 233 (1783).

66. No other instances according to Webster, *"Zong,"* 292. The *Zong* jettison was a general average claim; see Michael Lobban, "Slavery, Insurance and the Law," *The Journal of Legal History* 28, no. 3 (December 2007): 320.

67. A point made by James Oldham, "Insurance Litigation Involving the *Zong* and Other British Slave Ships, 1780–1807," *The Journal of Legal History* 28, no. 3 (December 2007): 310.

68. On the *Zong* and British abolitionism see Anita Rupprecht, "'A Very Uncommon Cause': Representations of the *Zong* and the British Campaign to Abolish the Slave Trade," *The Journal of Legal History* 28, no. 3 (December 2007): 329–346.

69. Robert Douthat Meade, *Judah P. Benjamin: Confederate Statesman* (Baton Rouge: Louisiana State University Press, 2001/1943); Matthew Pratt Guterl, *American Mediterranean: Southern Slaveholders in the Age of Emancipation* (Cambridge: Harvard University Press, 2008), ch. 2.

70. On slaves' dual status as property and persons at the law see Thomas D. Morris, *Southern Slavery and the Law, 1619–1860* (Chapel Hill: University of North Carolina Press, 1999), and Ariela J. Gross, *Double Character: Slavery and Mastery in the Antebellum Southern Courtroom* (Athens: University of Georgia Press, 2006).

71. Robinson, *Reports,* 266; *Supreme Court: Edward Lockett vs. Merchants' Insurance Company.* Brief of Slidell, Benjamin, and Conrad for Defendants (New Orleans, 1842), 26–27. On "inherent vices," see Emerigon, *Treatise on Insurances,* 311; and Phillips, *Treatise on the Law of Insurance,* 128. *Ellery v. Merchants' Insurance Company* 20 Mass. 46 (1825).

72. Brief of Slidell, Benjamin, and Conrad, 27. Robinson, *Reports,* 260.

73. Brief of Slidell, Benjamin, and Conrad, 27. Robinson, *Reports,* 260, 266, 286.

74. Robinson, *Reports,* 286. Meade, *Judah P. Benjamin,* 62. Guterl, *American Mediterranean,* 50, 51.

75. One of the "Maxims of the Law" Francis Bacon cited in his 1597 *Elements of the Common Laws of England.* See James Spedding, ed., *The Works of Francis Bacon* (London, 1879), 7: 327. *Jones v. Schmoll* 1 TE 130 (1795).

76. *Jones v. Schmoll* 1 TE 130 (1795). Sometimes insurrections were excluded outright. See Emma Christopher, *Slave Ship Sailors and Their Captive Cargoes, 1730–1807* (New York: Cambridge University Press, 2007), 183. On Atlantic slave revolts more generally see Rediker, *The Slave Ship.*

77. *Jones v. Schmoll* 1 TE 130 (1795).

78. Robinson, *Reports,* 296, 297.

79. On the *Comte d'Estaing,* see Emerigon, *Treatise on Insurances,* 313–316.

80. Robinson, *Reports,* 292. On the last cause is the proximate cause rule see Samuel Marshall, *A Treatise on the Law of Insurance* (Boston, 1805), 617.

81. Robinson, *Reports,* 295, 293, 289, 303, 311.

82. Ibid., 303.

83. Ibid., 314. Robert Feikema Karachuk, *A Workman's Tools: The Law Library of Henry Adams Bullard* 42, no. 2 (April 1998): 160–189.

84. Robinson, *Reports,* 318. *Commonwealth v. Aves,* 35 Mass. 193 (1836).

85. Robinson, *Reports,* 325.

86. Ibid., 328.

87. "The Creole Case," *The Southern Quarterly Review* (July 1842): 58.

88. Frederick Douglass, "The Heroic Slave," in Julia Griffiths, ed., *Autographs for Freedom* (Cleveland, 1853). Douglass had first spoken of the revolt in an 1849 address criticizing the American Colonization Society's views on racial difference. "Slavery, the Slumbering Volcano: An Address Delivered in New York, New York, on 23 April 1849," in John Blassingame, ed., *The Frederick Douglass Papers, Series One: Speeches, Debates, and Interviews, vol. 2: 1847–54* (New Haven: Yale University Press, 1982), 148–158. The commentary on *The Heroic Slave* is vast. But see Melba

P Jensen, "Frederick Douglass's 'The Heroic Slave': Text, context, and interpretation," (Ph.D. diss., UMass-Amherst, 2005). For other appropriations of the *Creole* revolt see Lydia Maria Child, "Madison Washington," in Lydia Maria Child, *The Freedmen's Book* (n.p., 1865), 147–153; William Wells Brown, *The Black Man* (Boston, 1863), 75–85.

89. Douglass, "The Heroic Slave," 178. On commerce as the intellectual premise for slaves' conceptions of rebelliousness and freedom see Douglas R. Egerton, "Slaves to the Marketplace: Economic Liberty and Black Rebelliousness in the Atlantic World," *Journal of the Early Republic*, 26, no. 4 (Winter 2006): 617–639.

90. Frederick Douglass, *Narrative of the Life of Frederick Douglass, an American Slave* (New York: Penguin, 1986/1845), 135–139. Frederick Douglass, *My Bondage and My Freedom* (New York: Seven Treasuries, 2009/1855), 120.

91. Douglass, *Narrative of the Life*, 106–107. Douglass, "The Heroic Slave," 237.

92. Douglass, *My Bondage and My Freedom*, 42–159. See also Maurice S. Lee, *Uncertain Chances: Science ,Skepticism, and Belief in Nineteenth-Century American Literature* (New York: Oxford University Press, 2011), ch. 4.

3. THE ACTUARIAL SCIENCE OF FREEDOM

Epigraph: E. N. Elliot, *Cotton is King, and Pro-Slavery Arguments* (Augusta, 1860), 821.

1. I rely heavily on an excellent biography of Wright. See Lawrence B. Goodheart, *Abolitionist, Actuary, Atheist: Elizur Wright and the Reform Impulse* (Kent, OH: Kent State University Press, 1990). See also Bruce Laurie, *Beyond Garrison: Antislavery and Social Reform* (New York: Cambridge University Press, 2005).

2. Elizur Wright, "Life Insurance," *The North American Review* (August 1886): 3–5. For another reflection see *Official Report of the Proceedings of the National Insurance Convention of the United States* (New York, 1871), 57. On London life insurance auctions, see Timothy Alborn, *Regulated Lives: Life Insurance and British Society, 1800–1914* (Toronto: University of Toronto Press, 2009), 206–209.

3. Sharon Ann Murphy, *Investing in Life: Insurance in Antebellum America* (Baltimore: Johns Hopkins University Press, 2010), 5, 300. Timothy Alborn, *Regulated Lives*, 4, 52. On antebellum U.S. life insurance, in addition to Murphy's excellent study, see the classic Viviana A. Rotman Zelizer, *Morals and Markets: The Development of Life Insurance in the United States* (New York: Columbia University Press, 1979). Outside the United States, in addition to Alborn's study see Geoffrey Clark, *Betting on Lives: The Culture of Life Insurance in England, 1695–1775* (Manchester: Manchester University Press, 1999); and Geoffrey Clark, Gregory Anderson, Christian Thomann, and J.-Matthias Graf von der Schulenberg eds., *The Appeal of Insurance* (Toronto: University of Toronto Press, 2010).

4. On the panic of 1837 see Sean Patrick Adams, "How Choice Fueled Panic: Philadelphians, Consumption, and the Panic of 1837," *Enterprise & Society* 12, no. 4 (December 2011): 761–789; Jessica M. Leper, "1837: Anatomy of a Panic," (Ph.D. diss., Brandeis University, 2007); Peter Temin, *The Jacksonian Economy* (New York:

Norton, 1969), ch. 4; Ann Fabian, "Speculation on Distress: The Popular Discourse of the Panics of 1837 and 1857," *Yale Journal of Criticism* 3, no. 1 (Fall 1989): 127–142.

5. Stanley Legerbot, *Manpower in Economic Growth: The American Record Since 1800* (New York: McGraw-Hill, 1964), 510, table A-1.

6. In attempting to situate Wright's approach to risk management in the moral imagination of abolitionism, I draw from the works of David Brion Davis, *The Problem of Slavery in the Age of Revolution, 1770–1823* (New York: Oxford University Press, 1999); Davis, *Slavery and Human Progress* (New York: Oxford University Press, 1986); Thomas Bender, ed., *The Antislavery Debate: Capitalism and Abolitionism as a Problem in Historical Interpretation* (Berkeley: University of California Press, 1992); Amy Dru Stanley, *From Bondage to Contract: Wage Labor, Marriage, and the Market in the Age of Slave Emancipation* (New York: Cambridge University Press, 1998).

7. See Murphy, *Investing Life,* 161–166.

8. Elizur Wright, "Slavery, The Right of Northern Interference," *The Anti-Slavery Record* (April 1837): 1.

9. The literature on continuity and discontinuity in free American agriculture from colonial times to the Civil War is as contentious as it is vast. With respect to risk, not the only issue at stake in the debates, I am arguing for continuity over this long period. See Naomi R. Lamoreaux, "Rethinking the Transition to Capitalism in the Early Northeast," *Journal of American History* 90, no.2 (September 2003): 437–461; Allan Kulikoff, "Households and Markets: Toward a New Synthesis of American Agrarian History," *William and Mary Quarterly* 50, no.3 (April 1993): 340–355; Jeremy Atack and Fred Bateman, *To Their Own Soil: Agriculture in the Antebellum North* (Ames, IA: Iowa State University Press, 1987); Allan Kulikoff, *From British Peasants to Colonial American Farmers* (Chapel Hill: University of North Carolina Press, 2000); Richard Lyman Bushman, "Markets and Composite Farms in Early America," *William and Mary Quarterly* 55, no. 3, (July 1998): 351–374; Allan Kulikoff, *The Agrarian Origins of American Capitalism* (Charlottesville: University of Virginia Press, 1992); Christopher Clark, *The Roots of Rural Capitalism: Western Massachusetts, 1780–1860* (Ithaca: Cornell University Press, 1992); Winifred B. Rothenberg, *Farm Market-Places to a Market Economy: The Transformation of Rural Massachusetts, 1760–1850* (Chicago: University of Chicago, 1992); James A. Henretta, *The Origins of American Capitalism: Collected Essays* (Boston: Northeastern University Press, 1991); Daniel Vickers, "Competency and Competition: Economic Culture in Early America," *William and Mary Quarterly* 47, no. 1 (January 1990): 3–29; Joyce Oldham Appleby, *Capitalism and a New Social Order: The Jeffersonian Vision of the 1790s* (New York: Columbia University Press, 1984); Michael Merrill, "Cash Is Good to Eat: Self-Sufficiency and Exchange in the Rural Economy of the United States," *Radical History Review* 3 (Winter 1977): 42–71; Clarence Danhoff, *Change in Agriculture: The Northern United States, 1820–1870* (Cambridge: Harvard University Press, 1969).

10. Claire Priest, "Creating an American Property Law: Alienability and its Limits in American History," *Harvard Law Review* 120, no.2 (December 2006): 385–469.

11. "Mixed Husbandry," *The Genesee Farmer and Gardener's Journal* (January 6, 1838).

12. "W.W.B.," *The Genesee Farmer and Gardener's Journal* (January 13, 1838). "Farming," *The American Farmer*, August 5, 1840. *An Address, Delivered Before an Agricultural Meeting at Jefferson County, N.Y. on the 26th September, 1838, by Josiah T. Marshall* (Watertown, NY, 1838), 10.

13. See Dalit Baranoff, "Shaped By Risk: Fire Insurance in America, 1790–1920," (Ph.D. diss., The Johns Hopkins University, 2003). Balch led the Merchants' Insurance Company.

14. *Address Delivered Before the Agricultural Society of Westborough and Vicinity, at Westborough, October the 6th, 1841, by John Sleeper* (Boston, 1841), 37. For an estimate of land to total national wealth see James L. Huston, *Securing the Fruits of Labor: The American Concept of Wealth Distribution, 1765–1900* (Baton Rouge: Louisiana State University Press, 1998), 92, table 3. Rothenberg has found evidence of farmers in close proximity to Boston holding financial assets in the early republic. See Winifred B. Rothenberg, "The Emergence of a Capital Market in the Rural Economy of Massachusetts: Middlesex Country, 1730–1838," *Journal of Economic History* 45, no. 4 (December 1985): 781–808.

15. George S. Boutwell, *Address Before the Middlesex Society of Husbandmen and Manufacturers* (Boston, 1850), 6, 15, 17, 18. On Concord agriculture see Robert A. Gross, "Culture and Cultivation: Agriculture and Society in Thoreau's Concord," *Journal of American History* 69, no. 1 (June 1982): 42–61.

16. See Hendrik Hartog, *Someday All This Will Be Yours: A History of Inheritance and Old Age* (Cambridge: Harvard University Press, 2012); Elizabeth Blackmar, "Inheriting Property and Debt: From Family Accumulation to Corporate Accumulation," in Michael Zakim and Gary J. Kornblith, eds., *Capitalism Takes Command: The Social Transformation of Nineteenth-Century America* (Chicago: University of Chicago Press, 2012), 93–118.

17. Boutwell, *Address*, 18. On farm credit see Tamara Plakins Thornton, "'A Great Machine' or a 'Beast of Prey': A Boston Corporation and Its Rural Debtors in an Age of Capitalist Transformation," *Journal of the Early Republic*, 27, no. 4 (Winter 2007): 567–597; Allan G. Bogue, "Land Credit for Northern Farmers, 1789–1940" *Agricultural History* 50, no. 1 (January 1976): 68–100. On the coming of scientific agriculture see Alan L. Olmstead and Paul W. Rhode, *Creating Abundance: Biological Innovation and American Agricultural Development* (New York: Cambridge University Press, 2008). Danhoff first identified the 1850s as a tipping point for commercial specialization. Danhoff, *Change in Agriculture*.

18. For econometric evidence for farmer's risk-aversion see Atack and Bateman, *To Their Own Soil*, 267–273. Lee Soltow, *Men and Wealth in the United States, 1850–1870* (New Haven: Yale University Press, 1975), ch. 3, finds that farmers were wealthier than nonfarmers in 1860 by a factor of 1.58 to 1. See also Huston, *Securing the Fruits of Labor: The American Concept of Wealth Distribution, 1765–1900*.

19. On homestead laws see Paul Goodman, "The Emergence of Homestead Exemption in the United States: Accommodation and Resistance to the Market Revolution, 1840–1880," *The Journal of American History* 80, no. 2 (September 1993): 470–498.

20. Frederick Butler, *The Farmer's Manual* (Hartford, 1819), 108, 129. Boutwell, *Address*, 6. Edwin Freedley, *Practical Treatise on Business* (Philadelphia, 1853), 71, 74, 213.

21. *Hunts Merchants Magazine* 1 (1840): 11. For urbanization statistics see Stuart M. Blumin, "The Social Implications of Economic Growth," in Stanley L. Engerman and Robert E. Gallman, *The Cambridge Economic History of the United States, Volume 2: The Long Nineteenth Century* (New York: Cambridge University Press, 2008), 824, 835. On middle class formation see Stuart M. Blumin, *The Emergence of the Middle Class: Social Experience in the American City* (New York: Cambridge University Press, 1989). On antebellum commercial specialization see Thomas C. Cochran, "The Business Revolution," *American Historical Review* 79, no.4 (December 1974): 1449–1466.

22. See "Boston, 1813–1823," in Joseph Balch Papers, Baker Library Historical Collections, Harvard Business School. Balthazard Marie Emerigon, *A Treatise on Insurances,* trans. Samuel Meredith (Boston, 1850), 157. On European prohibitions see Clark, *Betting on Lives,* 13–33.

23. On eighteenth-century British life insurance see Clark, *Betting on Lives* and, with respect to probability theory, Lorraine Daston, *Classical Probability in the Enlightenment* (Princeton: Princeton University Press, 1988), ch. 3. On the nineteenth century see Alborn, *Regulated Lives.*

24. Willard Phillips, *Treatise on Insurance* (Boston, 1823).

25. For a fuller account see Murphy, *Investing in Life,* ch. 4.

26. See *Charters of American Life Insurance Companies* (New York, 1906) for the original charters of the 1840s firms, including the New England Mutual (p. 98). For the New England Mutual's early policies see Policy Applications, New England Mutual 1844 Prospectus, Volume 1, New England Mutual Life Insurance Company Collection, Baker Library Historical Collections, Harvard Business School. On the issue of suicide, see Susanna Blumenthal " 'Death by His Own Hand' ": Accounting for Suicide in Nineteenth-Century Life Insurance Litigation," in Andrew Parker, Austin Sarat, and Martha Merrill Umphrey eds., *Subjects of Responsibility: Framing Personhood in Modern Bureaucracies* (New York: Fordham University Press, 2011): 98–144.

27. See Elizur Wright, Jr., *Massachusetts Reports on Life Insurance, 1859–1865* (Boston, 1865), 289. On risk selection, which varied firm to firm, and the general trend of increased laxity see Murphy, *Investing in Life,* ch. 2. See also Daniel Bouk, "The Science of Difference: Designing Tools for Discrimination in the American Life Insurance Industry, 1830–1930," (Ph.D. diss., Princeton University, 2009). On the marketing system see J. Owen Stalson, *Marketing Life Insurance: Its History in America* (Cambridge: Harvard University Press, 1942).

28. Julius L. Mayne to Elizur Wright, Elizur Wright Papers, Correspondence, Volume 9, Library of Congress. See Zelizer, *Morals and Markets,* chs. 4 and 5, for the original argument relating life insurance to religious scruples. Murphy is skeptical of religious antipathy to life insurance. For her account see Murphy, *Investing in Life,* ch. 8.

29. Mayne to Wright; "Life Insurance," *Christian Advocate and Journal* (April 19, 1848).

30. "Mutual Life Insurance," *Merchant's Magazine and Commercial Review* (December 1849); "Life Insurance," *The Independent* (December 27, 1849); "Life Assurance," *The Columbian Lady's and Gentleman's Magazine* (January 1846).

31. See Perry Miller, *The New England Mind: The Seventeenth Century* (Cambridge: Harvard University Press, 1982/1939), 15.

32. The literature on the Second Great Awakening is vast. For a recent synthesis see Mark A. Noll, *America's God: From Jonathan Edwards to Abraham Lincoln* (New York: Oxford University Press, 2002), esp. 161–367. With respect to commerce see Mark A. Noll, *God and Mammon: Protestants, Money, and the Market, 1790–1860* (New York: Oxford University Press, 2001); Stuart Davenport, *Friends of the Unrighteous Mammon: Northern Christians and Market Capitalism* (Chicago: University of Chicago Press, 2008).

33. "The Folly of Delay," *New York Evangelist*, November 30, 1848.

34. Charles Grandison Finney, *Lectures on Revivals of Religion* (New York, 1835), 97.

35. See, for instance, George M. Marsden, *Jonathan Edwards: A Life* (New Haven: Yale University Press, 2004).

36. William Lloyd Garrison, *Thoughts on African Colonization* (Boston, 1832); Elizur Wright, *Sin of Slavery* (New York, 1833). On radical antislavery, see Richard S. Newman, *The Transformation of American Abolitionism: Fighting Slavery in the Early Republic* (Chapel Hill: University of North Carolina Press, 2002); John Stauffer, *The Black Hearts of Men: Radical Abolitionists and the Transformation of Race* (Cambridge: Harvard University Press, 2002).

37. Elizur Wright, "Slavery and its Ecclesiastical Defenders," *Quarterly Antislavery Magazine* 1, no. 4 (July 1836): 357.

38. "Life Insurance," *Christian Advocate and Journal* (April 19, 1848); "The Diadem of Life Insurance," Box 4A, Container 11, Equitable Archives, AXA Financial Corporation(hereafter cited as "EAXA").

39. Wright, *Massachusetts Reports on Life Insurance*, 303.

40. *Life Insurance: Its Principles, Operations, and Benefits, As Presented by the Connecticut Mutual Life Insurance Company of Hartford, Conn.* (Hartford, 1846), 5, 6. Emphasis in the original. Edward Jarvis, "The Production of Vital Force," *Massachusetts Medical Society Medical Communications* (January 1854), A; "Life Insurance in the United States," *Hunts Merchants Magazine and Commercial Review* (February 1843): 23.

41. Elizur Wright, "Are Slaveholders Man-Stealers?" *The Anti-Slavery Record* (September 1837): 1. "Insurance," *The Liberator* (February 8, 1850), 25; "Life Assurance," *The Columbian Lady's and Gentleman's Magazine* (January, 1846), 8.

42. Willard Philips, *Treatise on the Law of Marine Insurance* (Boston, 1840), 191–194.

43. Elizur Wright, "The Term and Amount of Insurance," *Weekly Chronotype* (February 18, 1846); Wright, "Slavery and its Ecclesiastical Defenders," 356 (emphasis in the original).

44. *Loomis v. Eagle Life and Health Insurance Company* 72 Mass. 396 (1856). On California see, for instance, "California Expeditions," *The Independent* (January 18, 1848), 26. On insurable interest see Roy Kreitner, *Calculating Promises: The Emergence of Modern American Contract Doctrine* (Palo Alto, CA: Stanford University Press, 2007), 131–146; Murphy, *Investing in Life*, 80–85.

45. *Loomis v. Eagle Life and Health Insurance Company* 72 Mass. 396 (1856). Shaw's ruling mirrored Justice Mansfield's 1760s rulings that merchants could value their

insured cargoes at the estimated price at the cargoes' port of delivery. It was also in line with the emergent at will theory of contract. See Morton J. Horwitz, *The Transformation of American Law, 1780–1860* (Cambridge: Harvard University Press, 1977), esp. 180–192; Stanley, *Bondage to Contract*.

46. The figure $2,000–$3,000 is my own impressionistic estimate. See also Murphy, *Investing Life*, 181. *Hunt's* quoted in Blumin, *Emergence of the Middle Class*, 116, 321. For $500 estimate for lower-middle class see Legerbott, *Manpower in Economic Growth*, 300. For figures on wealth-holding see Soltow, *Men and Wealth in the United States, 1850–1870*, 35, 65, 77.

47. Circular found in Policy Applications, New England Mutual 1844 Prospectus, New England Mutual Life Insurance Company Collection, Baker Library Historical Collections, Harvard Business School.

48. On early actuarial English life insurance see Daston, *Classical Probability*, ch. 3.

49. See Gerd Gigerenzer, Zeno Swijtink, Theodore Porter, Lorraine Daston, John Beatty, Lorenz Kruger, *The Empire of Chance: How Probability Changed Science and Everyday Life* (New York: Cambridge University Press, 1989); Theodore M. Porter, *The Rise of Statistical Thinking, 1820–1900* (Princeton: Princeton University Press, 1986); Ian Hacking, *The Taming of Chance* (New York: Cambridge University Press, 1990); Alain Desrosières, trans. Camille Naish, *The Politics of Large Numbers: A History of Statistical Reasoning* (Cambridge: Harvard University Press, 1998); Daston, *Classical Probability*.

50. Wright, *Massachusetts Reports on Life Insurance*, 8.

51. Wright, *Massachusetts Reports on Life Insurance*, 360. "Appendix," *Massachusetts Medical Society Medical Communications* 8 (January 1, 1854), 49.

52. Under pressure from the new American Statistical Association, Massachusetts began to collect vital statistics in 1842 and other states followed. Gerald R. Grob, *Edward Jarvis and the Medical World of Nineteenth-Century America* (Knoxville: University of Tennessee Press, 1978), 83–108. On mortatilty statistics, see James Wynne, *Report of the Vital Statistics of the United States, Made to the Mutual Life Insurance Company of New York* (New York, 1857); Murphy, *Investing in Life*, ch. 1; Bouk, "Science of Difference." On the rise of statistics in general see Patricia Cline Cohen, *A Calculating People: The Spread of Numeracy in Early America* (Chicago: University of Chicago Press, 1982); Michael Zakim, "Inventing Industrial Statistics," *Theoretical Inquiries in Law* 11, no. 1 (January 2010): 283–318.

53. Elizur Wright, *Traps Baited With Orphans* (Boston, 1877), 28.

54. On the distribution of antebellum life insurance assets and their regulation see Lester Zartman, *The Investments of Life Insurance Companies* (New York, 1906), esp. chs. 2 and 6. See also Bruce Michael Pritchett, *A Study of Capital Mobilization: The Life Insurance Industry of the Nineteenth Century* (New York: Arno Press, 1977), 93, table 7; Lance E. Davis and Robert E. Gallman, *Evolving Financial Markets and International Capital Flows: Britain, the Americas, and Australia, 1865–1914* (New York: Cambridge University Press, 2001), 285.

55. Elizur Wright, "Life Insurance," *Daily Chronotype* (March 28, 1846); Joseph Balch, "Rates of premium for marine insurance," *The Merchant's Magazine and Commercial Review* (December 1839). *Merchants Magazine and Commercial Review* (February

1847). Ralph Waldo Emerson, *The Collected Works of Ralph Waldo Emerson: The Conduct of Life,* vol. VI (Cambridge: Harvard University Press, 2003), 9. See also Eric Wertheimer, *Underwriting: The Poetics of Insruance in America, 1722–1872* (Palo Alto, CA: Stanford University Press, 2006), ch. 5.

56. Samuel Smith, "Importance of Life Assurance, Illustrative Facts and Incidents," Box 67A, Folder 6, EAXA.

57. "Life Insurance," *The Christian Register* (September 21, 1844): 151; "1857 Equitable Circular," Box 67, Folder 9, EAXA. Elizur Wright, "The United States Statistical Journal," *Chronotype* (May 20, 1847). In a sense the old Calvinist bifurcation of "ordinary" versus "special" providences gave way to statistical regularity and economic chance.

58. Henry David Thoreau, in Nancy L. Rosenblum, ed., *Thoreau: Political Writings* (New York: Cambridge University Press, 1996), 108, 7. See also Maurice S. Lee, *Uncertain Chances: Science, Skepticism, and Belief in Nineteenth-Century American Literature* (New York: Oxford University Press, 2011), ch. 5.

59. Wright, *Massachusetts Reports on Life Insurance,* 303.

60. "Society on the Basis of Mutual Insurance," *Hunt's,* 152. On mutualism see Murphy, *Investing in Life,* ch. 6.

61. On the delinking of community from place in the nineteenth century see Thomas Bender, *Community and Social Change in America* (New Brunswick, Rutgers University Press, 1982).

62. Wright, *Massachusetts Reports on Life Insurance,* 303–304. "Life-Assurance," *New England Family Magazine* (December 1, 1845). Emphasis in the original. Zelizer, *Morals and Markets,* ch. 6, and Murphy, *Investing in Life,* ch. 5, deal with these themes. On the value of women's work in this period, see Amy Dru Stanley, "Home Life and the Morality of the Marketplace," in Melvyn Stokes and Stephen Conway, eds., *The Market Revolution in America: Social, Political, and Religious Expressions, 1800–1880* (Charlottesville: University of Virginia Press, 1996), 74–96; Jeanne Boydston, *Home and Work: Housework, Wages, and the Ideology of Labor in the Early Republic* (New York: Oxford University Press, 1990). On the ideology of domesticity, see Nancy F. Cott, *The Bonds of Womanhood: "Woman's Sphere" in New England, 1780–1835* (New Haven: Yale University Press, 1997); Mary P. Ryan, *Cradle of the Middle Class: The Family in Oneida County, New York, 1790–1865* (New York: Cambridge University Press, 1983). Still, antebellum firms insured a small percentage of women. See Pritchett, *Study of Capital Mobilization,* 32–39.

63. Murphy, *Investing in Life,* 142–150. Justice Lemuel Shaw, in *Loomis v. Eagle Life and Health Insurance Company* 72 Mass. 396 (1856), had set the precedent for this interpretation of insurable interest which was upheld by the Supreme Court in *Warnock v. Davis* 104 U.S. 775 (1881).

64. *St. John v. The American Mutual Life Insurance Company* 13 NY 31 (1855). On the widespread nature of the practice see also *Valton v. National Fund Life Assurance Company* 20 NY 32 (1859); *Ruse v. Mutual Benefit Life Insurance Company* 23 NY 516 (1861). On the law of assignment see Kreitner, *Calculating Promises,* 131–146.

65. The literature on capitalism and slavery is too vast to summarize here. For a recent treatment, see Robin Blackburn, *The American Crucible: Slavery, Emancipation*

and Human Rights (New York: Verso, 2011). My own understanding, which emphasizes the dynamics of owning slaves as a particular kind of physical capital, draws heavily from Gavin Wright, *Slavery and American Economic Development* (Baton Rouge: Louisiana State University Press, 2006); Roger Ransom and Richard Sutch, "Capitalists Without Capital: The Burden of Slavery and the Impact of Emancipation," in Morton Rothstein and Daniel Field, eds., *Quantitative Studies in Agrarian History* (Ames, IA: Iowa University Press, 1993), 130–157; Elizabeth Fox-Genovese and Eugene D. Genovese, *Fruits of Merchant Capital: Slavery and Bourgeois Property in the Rise and Expansion of Capitalism* (New York: Oxford University Press, 1993).

66. "Insurance Companies," *DeBow's Review* (June 1852): 700.

67. On the southern yeoman, see Steven Hahn, *The Roots of Southern Populism: Yeoman Farmers and the Transformation of the Georgia Upcountry, 1850–1890* (New York: Oxford University Press, 1985); Lacy K. Ford Jr., *Origins of Southern Radicalism: The South Carolina Upcountry, 1800–1860* (New York: Oxford University Press, 1991).

68. On slaves as collateral for bank loans and mortgaging see Richard H. Kilbourne, Jr., *Debt, Investment, Slaves: Credit Relations in East Feliciana Parish, Louisiana, 1825–1885* (Tuscaloosa: University of Alabama Press, 1995); Bonnie Martin, "Slavery's Invisible Engine: Mortgaging Human Property," *Journal of Southern History* 76, no. 4 (November 2010): 817–866; Edward E. Baptist, "Toxic Debt, Liar Loans, Collateralized and Securitized Human Beings, and the Panic of 1837," in Zakim and Kornblith, eds., *Capitalism Takes Command*, 69–92.

69. On paternalism see Eugene D. Genovese, *Roll, Jordan, Roll: The World the Slaves Made* (New York: Vintage, 1972).

70. E. N. Elliot, *Cotton is King, and Pro-Slavery Arguments* (Augusta, 1860), 821. On late antebellum proslavery see Elizabeth Fox-Genovese and Eugene D. Genovese, *The Mind of the Master Class: History and Faith in the Southern Slaveholders' Worldview* (New York: Cambridge University Press, 2005), esp. part 4; Michael O'Brien, *Conjectures of Order: Intellectual Life and the American South, 1810–1860*, vol. 2 (Chapel Hill: University of North Carolina Press, 2005), esp. ch. 18. On Hodge and Finny, see Hodge's "Review of Finney's Lectures on Revivals of Religion and Sermons on Various Subjects," *Biblical Repertory and Theological Review* (July 1835).

71. Elliot, *Cotton is King*, 821; James Henley Thornwell, *The Rights and Duties of Masters* (Charleston, 1850), 24, 15, 12, 14. On contract, see Stanley, *From Bondage to Contract*.

72. Elliot, *Cotton is King*, vii. Thornwell, *Rights and Duties*, 5. See also Elizabeth Fox-Genovese and Eugene D. Genovese, *Slavery in White and Black: Class and Race in the Southern Slaveholders' New World Order* (New York: Cambridge University Press, 2008).

73. Fitzhugh, *Sociology for the South*, 167, 168, 27–28; Fitzhugh, *Cannibals All!*, 65, 67, 190; Geo. Fitzhugh, "Southern Thought (cont'd)," *Debow's review, Agricultural, commercial, industrial progress and resources* (November 1857), 459. See also Eugene D. Genovese, *The World the Slaveholders Made: Two Essays in Interpretation* (New York: Pantheon Books, 1969), ch. 1.

74. Henry Hughes, *Treatise on Sociology, Theoretical and Practical* (Philadelphia, 1854), vii, 170, 154, 155, 290. On the "social" in proslavery thought see Jeffrey Sklansky, *The Soul's Economy: Market Society and Selfhood in American Thought, 1820–1920* (Chapel Hill: University of North Carolina Press, 2001), Ch. 3.

75. Fitzhugh, *Sociology for the South,* ch . 16, 167; William John Grayson, *The Hireling and the Slave* (Charleston, 1855), 18, 38, 53, 52; George S. Sawyer, *Southern Institutes, or, An Inquiry into the Origins and Early Prevalence of Slavery and the Slave Trade* (Philadelphia, 1858/1859), 216, 232. See also Genovese and Fox-Genovese, *Slavery in White and Black,* esp. ch. 1.

76. On the Old South and the question of modernity see L. Diane Barnes, Brian Schoen, Frank Towers eds., *The Old South's Modern Worlds: Slavery, Region, and Nation in the Age of Progress* (New York: Oxford University Press, 2011); Anthony E. Kaye, "The Second Slavery: Modernity in the Nineteenth-Century South and the Atlantic World," *Journal of Southern History* 75, 3 (August 2009): 627–650.

77. Hughes, *Treatise on Sociology,* 155. On safety-first, see Wright, *Slavery and American Economic Development,* ch. 3; Gavin Wright, *Political Economy of the South: Households, Markets, and Wealth in the Nineteenth Century* (New York: Norton, 1978), ch. 3; Fox-Genovese and Genovese, *Fruits of Merchant Capital,* esp. chs. 1 and 2; William N. Parker, ed., *The Structure of the Cotton Economy in the Antebellum South* (Washington: Agricultural History Society, 1970). See Baptist, "Toxic Debt," on the panic of 1837 in the South.

78. Slaves entered the workforce as young as age three and on average began turning profits for their masters at age nine. They continued to do so until age seventy. See Robert William Fogel, *Without Consent or Contract: The Rise and Fall of American Slavery* (New York: Norton, 1994/1989), 52–53, figure 7. Annual net earnings are a different measure than the profitable realization of a capital investment. For the latter, the slaveholders broke even at age nineteen. See Robert William Fogel and Stanley L. Engerman, *Time on the Cross: The Economics of American Negro Slavery* (New York: Norton, 1995/1974), 154. On "Negro plots" see Ira Berlin and Phillip D. Morgan, *The Slaves' Economy: Independent Production by Slaves in the Americas* (New York: Routledge, 1995); Dylan Penningroth, *The Claims of Kinfolk: African American Property and Community in the Nineteenth-Century South* (Chapel Hill: University of North Carolina Press, 2003), esp. chs. 2 and 3.

79. Fitzhugh, "Southern Thought (cont'd)," 459.

80. For capital stock figures see James L. Huston, *Calculating the Value of the Union: Slavery, Property Rights, and the Economic Origins of the Civil War* (Chapel Hill: University of North Carolina Press, 2003), 28, table 2.3. Wright, *Slavery and American Economic Development,* 58, 61. Pritchett, *A Study of Capital Mobilization,* 93, table 7. On the concentration of southern assets in slaves and its developmental limits see Ransom and Sutch, "Capitalists Without Capital." On the westward spread of slavery see Adam Rothman, *Slave Country: American Expansion and the Origins of the Deep South* (Cambridge: Harvard University Press, 2005).

81. Murphy is much more impressed by the reach of life insurance into the South. See Murphy, *Investing in Life,* esp. ch. 7. On slavery and the fellow-servant rule and other free-labor legal doctrines see Paul Finkelman, "Slaves as Fellow Servants:

Ideology, Law, and Industrialization," *American Journal of Legal History* 31, no. 4 (October 1987): 269–305; Jenny Bourne Wahl, *The Bondsman's Burden: An Economic Analysis of the Common Law of Southern Slavery* (New York: Cambridge University Press, 1998), ch. 3; Amy Dru Stanley, "Dominion and Dependence in the Law of Freedom and Slavery," *Law & Social Inquiry* 28, no. 4 (Autumn 2003): 1127–1134.

82. On small slaveholders see Walter Johnson, *Soul by Soul: Life Inside the Antebellum Slave Market* (Cambridge: Harvard University Press, 1999).

83. Thornwell, *Rights and Duties*, 13. See also Fox-Genovese and Genovese, *Mind of the Master Class*, ch. 4.

84. On Douglass's world in Baltimore, see Seth Rockman, *Scraping By: Wage Labor, Slavery, and Survival in Early Baltimore* (Baltimore: The Johns Hopkins University Press, 2009), esp. 33, 65–66.

85. Douglass, *My Bondage and My Freedom*,(New York: Seven Treasuries, 2009/1855), 78. Herbert Gutman and Richard Sutch, "The Slave Family: Protected Agent of Capitalist Masters or Victim of the Slave Trade?" in Paul A. David, ed., *Reckoning with Slavery: A Critical Study in the Quantitative History of American Negro Slavery* (New York: Oxford University Press, 1976), 110–111. See also Johnson, *Soul by Soul.*

86. Douglass, *My Bondage and My Freedom*, 78.

87. On the extension of Wright's antislavery mindset to life insurance reform, see Goodheart, *Abolitionist, Actuary, Atheist* and Laurie, *Beyond Garrison.*

88. *Chronotype*, March 4, 1847. On Wright and free labor see Laurie, *Beyond Garrison.* On antebellum proletarianization see Sean Wilentz, *Chants Democratic: New York City and the Making of the American Working Class* (New York: Oxford University Press, 2003/1984).

89. *Chronotype*, March 4, 1847; Wright, *Massachusetts Reports on Life Insurance*, 303; Wright, "The United States Statistical Journal"; "Health Insurance," *Chronotype*, May 2, 1846.

90. On savings banks see Sheldon Garon, *Beyond Our Means: Why American Spends While the World Saves* (Princeton: Princeton University Press, 2011), esp. chs. 1 and 3; See also R. Daniel Wadhwani, "Citizen Savers: Family Economy, Financial Institutions, and Public Policy in the Nineteenth-Century Northeast," *Journal of Policy History* 18, no. 1 (January 2006): 126–145; George Alter, Claudia Goldin, and Elyce Rotella, "The Savings of Ordinary Americans: The Philadelphia Savings Fund in the Mid-Nineteenth Century," *The Journal of Economic History* 54, no. 4 (December 1994): 735–767; Nicholas Osborne, "Little Capitalists: The Social Economy of Saving in the United States, 1816–1941," (Ph.D. diss., Columbia University, forthcoming).

91. E. W., "The regulation of life insurance," *Merchants Magazine and Commercial Review* (November 1852): 541.

92. "Life Insurance," *American Railway Times* (January 16, 1858): 2. Elizur Wright, *Valuation Tables on the "Combined Experience" or "Actuaries" Rate of Mortality* (Boston, 1854). On the bill see Goodheart, *Abolitionist, Actuary, Atheist*, 148.

93. Wright, *Massachusetts Reports on Life Insurance*, 67. See also Murphy, *Investing in Life*, 255–257.

94. D. P. Fackler to Elizur Wright, 26 July 1869, Carton 1, Folder 37, Elizur Wright Business Papers, Baker Library Historical Collections, Harvard Business School. Wright, *Massachusetts Reports on Life Insurance,* 255. For arguments against see *Official Report of the Proceedings of the National Insurance Convention of the United States* (New York, 1871), esp. 57.

95. See, for instance, Elizur Wright, *The Lesson of St. Domingo* (Boston, 1861), and Elizur Wright, *The Program of Peace* (Boston, 1862).

96. Elizur Wright, *The "Bible of Life Insurance"; being a complete photographic reprint of the original studies and official reports of Elizur Wright, the "father of life insurance."* (Chicago, 1932). Murphy, *Investing in Life,* 5 and ch. 10.

97. On this episode, see Goodheart, *Abolitionist, Actuary, Atheist,* 155.

98. See Elizur Wright, "Life Insurance for the Poor," *Journal of Social Science* (May, 1876); Elizur Wright, *Life Insurance: The Way to Make it a Public Benefit with the Least Injury to Individuals* (Boston, 1871); Elizur Wright, *Savings Bank Life Insurance* (Boston, 1872).

99. *New York Life Insurance Company v. Statham* 93 U.S. 24 (1876).

100. Ibid.

101. Ibid.; Joseph Bradley to Elizur Wright, October 26, 1876, Carton 1, Folder 66, Elizur Wright Business Papers, Baker Library Historical Collections.

102. See "Life Insurance as it Should and Will Be," Container 28, Scrapbooks, Elizur Wright Papers, Library of Congress; Elizur Wright, *Insurance and self-insurance: What is meant by chapter 232 of the acts of 1880* (Boston, 1880). On the failure in New York see Goodheart, *Abolitionist, Actuary, Atheist,* 167.

103. Elizur Wright, "The Index, February 28, 1877. Read before the Second Radical club of Boston, December 31st, 1877," in Container 23, Folder 2, Elizur Wright Papers, Library of Congress; Elizur Wright, "Second Address at Third Annual Congress of the National Liberal League, Held at Cincinnati, O. 1879," in Container 23, Folder 2, Elizur Wright Papers, Library of Congress; Wright, "Life Insurance for the Poor."

4. THE FAILURE OF THE FREEDMAN'S BANK

1. See Harry S. Stout, *Upon the Altar of the Nation: A Moral History of the American Civil War* (New York: Viking, 2006); Mark Knoll, *The Civil War as a Theological Crisis* (Chapel Hill: The University of North Carolina Press, 2006).

2. Lawrence W. Levine, *Black Culture and Black Consciousness: Afro-American Folk Thought From Slavery to Freedom* (New York: Oxford University Press, 1977), 138; William B. Gravely, "James Lynch and the Black Christian Mission during Reconstruction," in David W. Wills and Richard Newman, eds., *Black Apostles at Home and Abroad* (New York: G.K Hall, 1982), 165, 170.

3. Charles Hodge, "President Lincoln," *Biblical Repertory and Princeton Review* 37 (July 1865): 435.

4. See "Meditation on Divine Will," "Second Inaugural Address," and "Gettysburg Address" in Michael P. Johnson, ed. *Abraham Lincoln, Slavery, and the Civil War:*

Selected Writings and Speeches (New York: St. Martin's Press, 2001), 168, 320, 263. See also Knoll, *Civil War as a Theological Crisis,* 94.

5. On the Civil War as a secular pivot in American history see George M. Frederickson, *The Inner Civil War: Northern Intellectuals and the Crisis of the Union* (Urbana: University of Illinois, 1993/1965). On preoccupations with chance see Louis Menand, *The Metaphysical Club* (New York: Farrar, Straus and Giroux, 2001). On religious regeneration see Jackson Lears, *The Rebirth of a Nation: The Making of Modern America, 1877–1920* (New York: Oxford University Press, 2009). See also Richard Hofstader, *Social Darwinism in American Thought* (Boston: Beacon Press, 1992/1944).

6. Steven Hahn, Steven F. Miller, Susan E. O'Donovan, John C. Rodrigue, and Leslie S. Rowland, eds., *Freedom: A Documentary History of Emancipation, 1861–1867, Series 3, Volume 1: Land and Labor, 1865* (Chapel Hill: The University of North Carolina Press, 2008), 107. *Final Report of the American Freedmen's Inquiry Commission to the Secretary of War,* 38th Cong., 1st sess., Sen. Exec. Doc. 53 (1864), 13.

7. *Orders issued by Commissioners and Assistant Commissioners of the Freedmen's Bureau,* 39th Cong., 1st sess., House Exec. Doc. 70 (1865), 92.

8. I have relied heavily in this chapter upon an outstanding account of the Freedman's Bank's history. See Carl R. Osthaus, *Freedmen, Philanthropy, and Fraud: A History of the Freedman's Savings Bank* (Urbana: Illinois University Press, 1976). See also Walter Fleming, *The Freedmen's Savings Bank* (Chapel Hill, 1927).

9. Whitelaw Reid, *After the War: A Tour of the Southern States* (New York, 1866), 59.

10. In underscoring the ambiguities of slave emancipation and the economic unfreedoms it engendered this chapter attempts to extend the analysis, among others, of Frederick Cooper, Thomas C. Holt, and Rebecca J. Scott, *Beyond Slavery: Explorations of Race, Labor, and Citizenship in Postemancipation Societies* (Chapel Hill: University of North Carolina Press, 2000); Amy Dru Stanley, *From Bondage to Contract: Wage Labor, Marriage, and the Market in the Age of Slave Emancipation* (New York: Cambridge University Press, 1998); Julie Saville, *Work of Reconstruction: From Slave to Wage Laborer in South Carolina, 1860–1870* (New York: Cambridge University Press, 1994); Thomas C. Holt, *The Problem of Freedom: Race, Labor, and Politics in Jamaica and Britain, 1832–1938* (Baltimore: The Johns Hopkins University Press, 1991); Holt, "'An Empire over the Mind': Emancipation, Race, and Ideology in the British West Indies and the American South," in J. Morgan Kousser and James M. McPherson, eds., *Region, Race, and Reconstruction: Essays in Honor of C. Vann Woodward* (New York: Oxford University Press, 1982), 283–313; Holt, *Black Over White: Negro Political Leadership in South Carolina during Reconstruction* (Urbana: University of Illinois Press, 1977); Eric Foner, *Nothing But Freedom: Emancipation and Its Legacy* (Baton Rouge: Louisiana State University Press, 2007/1983); Gerald Davis Jaynes, *Branches Without Roots: Genesis of the Black Working Class in the American South, 1862–1882* (New York: Oxford University Press, 1989).

11. Edward Atkinson, *On Cotton* (Boston, 1865), 40. The commanding account of Reconstruction is Eric Foner, *Reconstruction: America's Unfinished Revolution, 1863–1877* (New York: Harper, 2002/1988). On the triumph of industrial capital at this moment see Sven Beckert, *The Monied Metropolis: New York City and the*

Consolidation of the American Bourgeoisie, 1850–1896 (New York: Cambridge University Press, 2001), ch. 5.

12. Francis Williamson, *Edward Atkinson: The Biography of an American Liberal, 1827–1905* (New York: Ayer, 1972), 2, 3.

13. Lance Davis and Robert Gallman, *Evolving Financial Markets and International Capital Flows: Britain, the Americas, and Australia, 1865–1914* (Cambridge: Cambridge University Press, 2001), 288, table 3:5c-3. Williamson, *Edward Atkinson,* 55–56.

14. On the mind-set of Yankee emancipators at this moment, see Holt, "'An Empire over the Mind': Emancipation, Race, and Ideology in the British West Indies and the American South" and Stanley, *Bondage to Contract,* ch. 1.

15. John W. Alvord, *First Semi-Annual Report on Schools for Freedmen* (Washington, 1866), n.p.

16. George Fitzhugh, "What's to be Done with the Negroes?" (June 1866): 577–581.

17. Ira Berlin, Steven F. Miller, Joseph P. Reidy, and Leslie S. Rowland, eds., *Freedom: A Documentary History of Emancipation, 1861–1867, Series 1, Volume 2: The Wartime Genesis of Free Labor: The Upper South* (New York: Cambridge University Press, 1990), 224; *Final Report of the Secretary of War,* 8; W. C. Gannett, "The Freedmen at Port Royal," *The North American Review,* July 1865, 11. On slave time-reckoning see Mark Michael Smith, *Mastered by the Clock: Time, Slavery, and Freedom in the American South* (Chapel Hill: University of North Carolina Press, 1997), esp. 131.

18. *Orders issued by Commissioners and Assistant Commissioners of the Freedmen's Bureau,* 92.

19. *Final Report of the Secretary of War,* 34, 10; Ira Berlin, Thavolia Glymph, Steven F. Miller, Joseph P. Reidy, Leslie R. Rowland, and Julie Saville, eds., *Freedom: A Documentary History of Emancipation, 1861–1867, Series 1, Volume 3: The Wartime Genesis of Free Labor: The Lower South* (New York: Cambridge University Press, 1990), 136. See also Ira Berlin, Barbara J. Fields, Thavolia Glymph, and Joseph P. Reidy, eds., *Freedom: A Documentary History of Emancipation, 1861–67, Series 1, Volume 1: The Destruction of Slavery* (New York: Cambridge University Press, 1985), 217.

20. Berlin et al. (eds.), *Freedom, Series 1, Volume 3,* 239–240; *Final Report of the Secretary of War,* 14.

21. N. P. Banks, *Emancipated Labor in Louisiana* (Boston, 1864), n.p..

22. Ibid.; Berlin et al. (eds)., *Freedom, Series 1, Volume 3,* 408, 502. On wartime Louisiana see Lawrence N. Powell, *New Masters: Northern Planters During the Civil War and Reconstruction* (New York: Fordham University Press, 1999/1980) and John C. Rodrigue, *Reconstruction in the Cane Fields: From Slavery to Free Labor in Louisiana's Sugar Parishes, 1862–1880* (Baton Rouge: Louisiana State University Press, 2001).

23. Berlin et al. (eds.), *Freedom, Series 1, Volume 3,* 520, 462. On freedpeople's expectation of a right to subsistence see Hahn et al. (eds.), *Freedom, Series 3, Volume 1,* esp. 24. See also Susan Eva O'Donavan, *Becoming Free in the Cotton South* (Cambridge: Harvard University Press, 2007).

24. Banks, *Emancipated Labor,* n.p. On employment at will see Stanley, *Bondage to Contract* and Robert J. Steinfeld, *Coercion, Contract, and Free Labor in the Nineteenth Century* (New York, 2001).

25. Banks, *Emancipated Labor,* n.p.
26. *New York Times,* May 12, 1865.
27. See Henrietta M. Larson, *Jay Cooke: Private Banker* (Cambridge: Harvard University Press, 1936), 130, 167. *Orders issued by Commissioners and Assistant Commissioners of the Freedmen's Bureau,* 370. On Cooke's wartime efforts see Richard White, *Railroaded: The Transcontinentals and the Making of Modern America* (New York: W.W. Norton, 2011), 9–16.
28. *Final Report of the Secretary of War,* 13, 99, 109, 15.
29. Senator and congressman both quoted in Heather Cox Richardson, *The Greatest Nation of the Earth: Republican Economic Policies During the Civil War* (Cambridge: Harvard University Press, 1997), 234, 248. On the expansion of federal power during the Civil War see also Richard Franklin Bensel, *Yankee Leviathan: The Origins of Central State Authority in America, 1859–1877* (New York: Cambridge University Press, 1990).
30. Charles Sumner, *The Works of Charles Sumner,* vol. 8 (Cambridge, 1873), 476, 479. On the wartime Pacific Railroad Acts see White, *Railroaded,* 17–24.
31. Alvord, *First Semi-Annual Report,* n.p. The group was Peter Cooper, W. C. Bryant, Hiram Barney, Charles Collins, Thomas Denny, Walter S. Griffith, William Allen, Abraham Baldwin, A. S. Barnes, S. B. Caldwell, R. R. Graves, A. S. Hatch, Walter S. Hatch, E. A. Lambert, W. S. Lambert, Roe Lockwood, R. H. Manning, R. W. Ropes. H. H. Wallace, George Whipple, and Albert Woodruff. For a fuller account see Ostheus, *Freedmen, Philanthropy, and Fraud,* 1–21.
32. On antebellum banking see Howard Bodenhorn, *A History of Banking in Antebellum America: Financial Markets and Economic Development in an Era of Nation-Building* (New York: Cambridge University Press, 2000).
33. William Lawrence, *Life of Amos A. Lawrence* (Boston, 1889), 30. Emerson W. Keyes, *A History of Savings Banks in the United States,* 2 vols. (New York, 1878), 1:365. Keyes gathered that whereas by 1876 1 person in 5 was a depositor in Massachusetts and 1 in 14 in New York, it was only 1 in 20 in Great Britain. See Keyes, *Savings Banks,* 1:21, 72. On the broader transnational origins see Sheldon Garon, *Beyond Our Means: Why America Spends While the World Saves* (Princeton: Princeton University Press, 2011), ch. 1. See also R. Daniel Wadhwani, "Citizen Savers: Family Economy, Financial Institutions, and Public Policy in the Nineteenth-Century Northeast," *Journal of Policy History* 18, no. 1 (January 2006): 126–145; Nicholas Osborne, "Little Capitalists: The Social Economy of Saving in the United States, 1816–1941," (Ph.D. diss., Columbia University, forthcoming).
34. On this early ethos see Garon, *Beyond Our Means,* 86–87.
35. Bowery bank president quoted in Keyes, *Savings Banks,* 1:163. Nine out of the thirteen original trustees of the Bowery were directors of the Butcher's and Drover's. For general New York numbers and Bowery numbers see Alan L. Olmstead, *New York Mutual Savings Banks in the Antebellum Years, 1819–1861* (Madison: University of Wisconsin Press), 183, 159. In 1830, 91.5 percent of New York savings banks' $2,098,394 in assets was invested in conservative government bonds with the rest mostly on deposit in reputable commercial banks. By 1861, of the $51,333,270 in assets 54 percent was in government bonds (spiked by the new availably of Union debt), 36 percent was in

mortgage loans, 5 percent was in commercial bank deposits, and almost 2 percent was in call loans. Olmstead, *New York City Mutual Savings Banks,* 184–185. In 1856 the fifty-six commercial banks of New York counted $66.1 million in deposits. That year the sixteen New York savings banks counted $28.2 million. See Cormac Ó Gráda and Eugene N. White, "The Panics of 1854 and 1857: A View from the Emigrant Industrial Savings Bank," *Journal of Economic History* 63, no. 1 (March 2003): 216.

36. Walter T. Hatch and Alfred S. Barnes, for instance, two original Freedman's Bank trustees, were also trustees of the Dime Savings Bank of Brooklyn. In 1865 the Dime had 13,362 open accounts and $1.6 million on deposit. Emerson W. Keyes, *A History of Savings Banks in New York* (New York, 1870), 237–240.

37. The bank's founding charter: *Statutes at Large . . . of the United States of America* 13 (Boston, 1866), 510–512.

38. The Old South had a thriving banking system, but it was dominated by large planters and cotton factors and the asset basis was slaves and land. With the destruction of slavery and the subsequent decline in land values, the asset basis of the southern credit economy collapsed. See Harold D. Woodman, *King Cotton and His Retainers: Financing and Marketing the Cotton Crop of the South, 1800–1925* (Lexington: University of Kentucky Press, 1968); Roger L. Ransom and Richard Sutch, *One Kind of Freedom: The Economic Consequences of Emancipation* (New York: Cambridge University Press, 1977), esp. ch. 6; Jaynes, *Branches Without Roots.* On the lack of savings banks in the West see Keyes, *Savings Banks,* 2:sect. 17; Garon, *Beyond Our Means,* 104.

39. Ketchum quoted in Paul Cimbala, *Under the Guardianship of the Nation: The Freedmen's Bureau and the Reconstruction of Georgia, 1865–1870* (Athens, GA: University of Georgia Press, 1997), 133. On the Christmas rumor see Steven Hahn, *A Nation Under Our Feet: Black Political Struggles in the Rural South from Slavery to the Great Migration* (Cambridge, MA: Harvard University Press, 2003), ch. 3. On the land question generally see William S. McFeely, *Yankee Stepfather: General O. O. Howard and the Freedmen* (New York: Norton, 1994/1968); Claude F. Oubre, *Forty Acres and a Mule: The Freedmen's Bureau and Black Land Ownership* (Baton Rouge: Louisiana State University Press, 1978); Hahn et al. (eds.), *Freedom, Series 3, Volume 1,* ch. 4.

40. Berlin et al. (eds.), *Freedom, Series 1, Volume 3.* 334. For Special Field Order 15 see ibid., 338. Sherman also granted loans of draft animals to the freedpeople, thus the saying "40 acres and a mule."

41. "Freedmen at Port Royal: Captain Saxton's Letter," *Independent,* March 6, 1862. Berlin et al. (eds.), *Freedom, Series 1, Volume 2,* 325. The $80,000 is cited in Williamson, *Atkinson,* 11. Ketchum quoted in *The Freedmen's Advocate,* July/August 1864.

42. Edward Atkinson, *Cheap Cotton by Free Labor* (Boston, 1861). For two outstanding accounts of this moment see the classic Willie Lee Rose, *Rehearsal for Reconstruction: The Port Royal Experiment* (New York: Oxford University Press, 1976) and the more recent Saville, *Work of Reconstruction* (24, for 3.8 percent estimate). On wartime Union-controlled lands and their sale see U.S. Congress, House of Representatives, "Report of the Secretary of the Treasury on the State of the Finances for the Year 1865," *House Executive Documents,* 39th Cong., 1st sess., No. 3 (serial no.

1254), 90–92. On land restoration in the larger Yankee imagination see Eric Foner, "Thaddeus Stevens, Confiscation, and Reconstruction," in *Politics and Ideology in the Age of the Civil War* (New York: Oxford University Press, 1980), ch. 7.

43. "Freedmen's Bureau, Orders issued by Commissioners and Assistant Commissioners," *House Executive Documents,* 39th Congress, 1st sess. (serial no. 1256), 267. For Circular 13 see Hahn et al. (eds.), *Freedom, Series 3, Volume 1,* 423–425. For Georgia numbers see Cimbala, *Under the Guardianship of the Nation,* 167. On the administration of Sherman's reserve see Saville, *Work of Reconstruction,* 72–102.

44. Thus Yankee women taught perplexed freedwomen accustomed to corn to make bread from wheat grist. See Rose, *Rehearsal for Reconstruction,* 226–227. See also Atkinson's account of the goods consumed on Philbrick's plantation in *Freedmen's Record,* May 1865, 85.

45. Saville, *Work of Reconstruction,* 17, is skeptical of the continuity. On the slave's economy see Ira Berlin and Phillip D. Morgan, *The Slaves' Economy: Independent Production by Slaves in the Americas* (New York: Routledge, 1995). Dylan Penningroth, *The Claims of Kinfolk: African American Property and Community in the Nineteenth-Century South* (Chapel Hill: University of North Carolina Press, 2003), esp. chs. 2 and 3.

46. "Parker-Gallman Southern Farms Study, 1860" quoted in Gavin Wright, *Slavery and American Economic Development* (Baton Rouge: Louisiana State University Press, 2006), 100. *Census & Acres of Cotton & provision ground planted on Edisto, Jehossee, Fenwicks, Little Edisto Islands, 28 Aug. 1865,* Abandoned Land Reports, ser. 2932, SC Asst. Commr., RG 105 [A-14089]. On the southern yeoman, see Steven Hahn, *The Roots of Southern Populism: Yeoman Farmers and the Transformation of the Georgia Upcountry, 1850–1890* (New York: Oxford University Press, 1985).

47. *Census & Acres of Cotton & provision ground.* In Mississippi, where Union officials had placed 1,750 freedpeople on Jefferson Davis's former plantation and a few other surrounding ones, 181 "companies" cultivated over 5,000 acres. See Thavolia Glymph, "The Second Middle Passage: The Transition from Slavery to Freedom at Davis Bend, Mississippi" (Ph.D. diss., Purdue University, 1994), chs. 3 and 4. On land-buying groups see, for instance, Paul A. Cimbala, "A Black Colony in Dougherty County: The Freedmen's Bureau and the Failure of Reconstruction in Southwest Georgia," *Journal of Southwest Georgia History* 4 (Fall 1986): 72–89 and more generally Hahn et al. (eds.), *Freedom, Series 3, Volume 1,* ch. 7. On the communal dimensions of land ownership see Saville, *Work of Reconstruction.*

48. Elizabeth Ware Pearson, *Letters from Port Royal* (Boston, 1906), 274. Bureau agent quoted in Saville, *Work of Reconstruction,* 17. Northern freeholds were usually 60–120 acres, whereas in the Sea Islands survey there were three acres per family. On the reconstitution of cotton production at this moment see Sven Beckert, "Emancipation and Empire: Reconstructing the Worldwide Web of Cotton Production in the Age of the American Civil War," *American Historical Review* 109, no. 5 (December 2004): 1405–1438.

49. Jim Cashman quoted in Leon Litwack, *Been in the Storm So Long: The Aftermath of Slavery* (New York: Vintage, 1980), 202. See generally Hahn et al. (eds.), *Freedom, Series 3, Volume 1,* and esp. 705, 708.

50. On this episode see McFeely, *Yankee Stepfather,* 130–149. For the amnesty procla- mation see *Statutes at Large,* 758–760. For Circular 15 see Hahn et al. (eds.), *Free- dom, Series 3, Volume 1,* 431–433.

51. Mary Ames, *From a New England Woman's Diary in Dixie in 1865* (Boston, 1906), 97. Petitions in Hahn et al. (eds.), *Freedom, Series 3, Volume 1,* 440–444. *Census & Acres of Cotton & provision ground.* On Moultrie see Charles Spencer, *Edisto Is- land, 1861 to 2006: Ruin, Recovery, and Rebirth* (New York: The History Press, 2008), 112.

52. Berlin et al. (eds.), *Freedom, Series 1, Volume 3,* 527–528. See McFeeley, *Yankee Step- father,* 220–28; and Hahn et al. (eds.), *Freedom, Series 3, Volume 1,* ch. 4. On black militias see Hahn, *Nation Under Our Feet* and Saville, *Work of Reconstruction.* For Saxton's removal see his own account, U.S. Congress, *Report of the Joint Committee on Reconstruction* (Washington, 1866), 2:216–231.

53. See Samuel P. Low to John Alvord, September 14, 1865, National Archives, *Records of the Education Division of the Bureau of Refugees, Freedmen, and Abandoned Lands, 1865–1871,* RG 105, pub. No. 803, Roll 14, 102, 103. *Orders issued by Commis- sioners and Assistant Commissioners of the Freedmen's Bureau,* 352, 348. For Moult- rie's account see *Records of the Freedman's Savings and Trust Company* (hereafter *"FSTC"*), Charleston Signature Books, No. 4673, opened in 1870 which refers to an original account no. 2123. No direct record exists for no. 2123 but that account would have been opened in 1868, most likely during the summer.

54. U.S. Congress, House of Representatives, *Report of the Commissioners of the Freed- man's Savings and Trust Company,* 43rd Congress, 2nd sess., House Misc. Doc. No. 16 (1874), 91.

55. *Orders issued by Commissioners and Assistant Commissioners of the Freedmen's Bu- reau,* 4, 20.

56. Ibid., 2, 124, 125, 59.

57. Ibid., 348. On this moment see Jaynes, *Branches Without Roots,* ch. 7.

58. On the withdrawal of labor see Ransom and Sutch, *One Kind of Freedom,* 45, which estimates a decline of 28 to 37 percent. Schwalm disputes the disproportionate fe- male withdrawal. Leslie A. Schwalm, *A Hard Fight For We: Women's Transition from Slavery to Freedom in South Carolina* (Chicago: University of Illinois Press, 1997), ch. 6. On the household see also Thavolia Glymph, *Out of the Household of Bondage: The Transformation of the Plantation Household* (New York: Cambridge University Press, 1998); Nancy Bercaw, *Gendered Freedoms: Race, Rights, and the Politics of the Household in the Delta, 1861–1875* (Gainesville: University of Florida Press, 2003); O'Donovan, *Becoming Free in the Cotton South,* esp. 195–197.

59. On the decline of the plantation and the origins of sharecropping see Jaynes, *Branches Without Roots,* ch. 9; Ransom and Sutch, *One Kind of Freedom*; Barbara J. Fields, "The Nineteenth-Century American South: History and Theory," *Plan- tation Society in the Americas* 2 (April 1983): 7–27.

60. See Osthaus, *Freedmen, Philanthropy, and Fraud,* 143, 36. For the Texas agent see *Orders issued by Commissioners and Assistant Commissioners of the Freedmen's Bu- reau,* 348. *Third Semi-Annual Report on Schools for Freedmen* (Washington, 1867).

61. On this move see Osthaus, *Freedmen, Philanthropy, and Fraud*, 142.

62. Quote in ibid., 140.

63. Larson, *Jay Cooke*, 186. On the Cookes' moral universe see White, *Railroaded*, esp. 10–14.

64. On the national capital market see Davis and Gallman, *Evolving Financial Markets*, ch. 3, and Bensel, *Yankee Leviathan*, ch. 4.

65. *FSTC*, Journal of the Board of Trustees, May 9, 1867.

66. U.S. Congress, U.S. Senate, *Report of the Select Committee to Investigate Freedmen's Savings & Trust Co.*, 46th Cong., 2nd Sess., S. Rept. 440 (1880), 179.

67. Osthaus, *Freedmen, Philanthropy, and Fraud*, 100, 215; *National Savings Bank* (June 1, 1868).

68. On the savings rate see Lance E. Davis and Robert E. Gallman, "Savings, Investment, and Economic Growth: The United States in the Nineteenth Century," in John A. James and Mark Thomas, *Capitalism in Context: Essays on Economic Development and Cultural Change in Honor of R. M. Hartwell* (Chicago: University of Chicago Press, 1994), 202–229. Garon, *Beyond Our Means*, 92, cautions against reading too much into these numbers.

69. On the advertising effort see *FSTC*, Minutes of the Agency Committee, May 30, 1867; circulation estimate in *Old and New* (August 1870): 246.

70. *Freedman's Savings and Trust Company* (Washington, 1867); *National Savings Bank* (June 1, 1868).

71. *Freedman's Savings and Trust Company* (Washington, 1867). See, for instance, "Letter to Charles Howard, 3 September 1867," *Records of the Field Offices for the District of Columbia, Bureau of Refugees, Freedman, and Abandoned Lands, 1865–1870*, M1902, RG101, Roll 20, 133. On Washington, DC, see Kate Masur, *An Example for All the Land: Emancipation and the Struggle over Equality in Washington, D.C.* (Chapel Hill: University of North Carolina Press, 2010).

72. Emphasis in the original. *Freedman's Savings and Trust Company* (Washington, 1867); *The Charter and By-Laws of the Freedmen's Savings and Trust Company* (Washington, 1872); Alvord in Minutes of the Board of Trustees, February 10, 1879. See also Walter Fleming, "The Freedman's Bank," *Yale Review* (May and August 1906), 46.

73. *FSTC*, Minutes of the Finance Committee, January 23, 1868. For deposit figures see Larson, *Jay Cooke*, 225.

74. *FSTC*, Minutes of the Board of Trustees, February 13, 1868; Minutes of the Finance Committee, February 26, 1868; Minutes of the Finance Committee, June 8, 1868; Journal of the Board of Trustees, December 10, 1868.

75. Mobile cashier in *National Savings Bank* (June 1, 1868); Alvord, *Letters from the South*, letters dated "January 17, 1870" and "January 18, 1870"; Alvord, *Ninth Semi-Annual Report on Schools for Freedmen*, 68.

76. U.S. Congress, House of Representatives, *Report of the Select Committee on the Freedman's Bank*, 44th Cong., 1st sess., House Report No. 502 (1876), 37.

77. In 1866 Congress passed the Southern Homestead Act which opened up 46,000,000 acres of southern public lands. In practice, it had little effect. See Michael L. Lanza,

"One of the Most Appreciated Labors of the Bureau: The Freedmen's Bureau and the Southern Homestead Act," in Paul A. Cimbala and Randall M. Miller, *The Freedmen's Bureau and Reconstruction: Reconsiderations* (New York: Fordham University Press, 1999), 67–92. On Stevens see Foner, "Thaddeus Stevens."

78. Robert Somers, *The Southern States Since the War, 1870–1871* (New York, 1871), 54–55. For branch figures see Alvord, *Ninth Semi-Annual Report on Schools for Freedmen,* 66–67. For Green account see *FSTC,* Beaufort Signature Books, No. 3830. For black male demographic see Osthaus, *Freedmen, Philanthropy, and Fraud,* 87. For general descriptions of the sharecropping and the agricultural ladder and variations see Jaynes, *Branches Without Roots,* ch. 12; Gavin Wright, *Old South, New South: Revolutions in the Southern Economy Since the Civil War* (Baton Rouge: Louisiana State University Press, 1996); and Ransom and Sutch, *One Kind of Freedom,* chs. 7 and 8.

79. Alvord, *Ninth Semi-Annual Report on Schools for Freedmen,* 66–67. Alvord, *Letters from the South,* letter dated "January 13, 1870." Loren Schweninger, *Black Property Owners in the South, 1790–1915* (Chicago: University of Illinois Press, 1990), 146, table 9. On such political issues see Holt, *Black Over White.*

80. Theodore Rosengarten, *All God's Dangers: The Life of Nate Shaw* (Chicago: University of Chicago Press, 2000/1974), xxi, 27.

81. Schweninger, *Black Property Owners in the South,* 146, table 9; and 153, table 12. For requests for branch openings see Osthaus, *Freedmen, Philanthropy, and Fraud,* 81.

82. Keyes, *Savings Banks,* 1:237–240. *FSTC,* Beaufort Signature Books, Nos. 3765, 3766, 3831. On children at the Freedman's Bank see Osthaus, *Freedmen, Philanthropy, and Fraud,* 87, 92, 95. On the "target savings" of northern workers see George Alter, Claudia Goldin, and Elyce Rotella, "The Savings of Ordinary Americans: The Philadelphia Savings Fund in the Mid-Nineteenth Century," *The Journal of Economic History* 54, no. 2 (1994): 735–767.

83. Keyes, *Savings Banks,* 1:237–240. On women at the Freedman's Bank see Osthaus, *Freedmen, Philanthropy, and Fraud,* 87, 92, 95. On the "targeting savings" of northern workers see George Alter, Goldin, and Rotella, "The Savings of Ordinary Americans."

84. *FSTC,* Charleston Signature Books, No. 7065; Beaufort Signature Books, No. 3829; Charleston Signature Books, No. 5038; Beaufort Signature Books, No. 3764. On black mutual-aid societies, see Tera W. Hunter, *To 'Joy My Freedom: Southern Black Women's Lives and Labors After the Civil War* (Cambridge: Harvard University Press, 1997), esp. 67–73; Armstead L. Robinson, "Plans Dat Comed from God: Institution Building and the Emergence of Black Leadership in Reconstruction Memphis," in Orville Vernon Burton and Robert C. McMath, Jr., eds., *Toward a New South?: Studies in Post-Civil War Southern Communities* (Westport: Greenwood Press, 1982), 87, 88. See also Osthaus, *Freedmen, Philanthropy, and Fraud,* ch. 4. On traditions of black mutual-aid under slavery and after see W. E. B. Du Bois, *Some Efforts of Negroes for their own Social Betterment . . .* (Atlanta, 1898), 18–21. On uses of the bank in the Washington, DC, community and continuities with slave traditions see Barbara P. Josiah, "Providing for the Future: The World of the African American Depositors of Washington DC's Freedman's Savings

Bank, 1865–1874," *The Journal of African-American History* 89, no. 1 (Winter 2004): 1–16.

85. Larson, *Jay Cooke,* 211, 225.

86. Ibid., 225, 303.

87. See ibid., ch. 14, esp. 260, 277; White, *Railroaded,* 26.

88. Oliver Howard, "The Freedmen's Savings Bank," *The American Missionary* (November 1869): 45. Osthaus, *Freedmen, Philanthropy, and Fraud,* 144–147. On northern savings bank competition at this time see Keyes, *Savings Banks,* 2:546.

89. *Congressional Globe,* 41st Cong., 2nd sess., 1871, 2334.

90. On the Nichols and Seneca Stone Company loans see *Report of the Select Committee on the Freedman's Bank,* 74, 104.

91. On the transferring of liabilities from First National to Freedman's Bank see *Report of the Select Committee to Investigate Freedmen's Savings & Trust Co.,* 161; *Report of the Select Committee on the Freedman's Bank,* 77. Deposit figures are according to the recollection of black trustee Charles Purvis, *Report of the Select Committee to Investigate Freedmen's Savings & Trust Co.,* 179.

92. For Northern Pacific overdrafts see Larson, *Jay Cooke,* 383. *Christian Union,* February 15, 1871. See also White, *Railroaded,* 66–84.

93. White, *Railroaded,* 50, 68.

94. See Larson, *Jay Cooke,* 386, 389.

95. *FSTC,* Journal of the Board of Trustees, March 9 and May 11, 1871, April 11, 1872. See also the testimony of Purvis, *Report of the Select Committee to Investigate Freedmen's Savings & Trust Co.,* 74.

96. On the political and economic reverberations of the panic of 1873 see Beckert, *The Monied Metropolis,* ch. 8. On the financial causes of the panic see Charles W. Calomoris and Gary Gorton, "The Origins of Banking Panics: Models, Facts, and Bank Regulation," in R. Glenn Hubbard, ed., *Financial Markets and Financial Crises* (Chicago: University of Chicago Press, 1991), 69–108; Elmus Wicker, *Banking Panics of the Gilded Age* (New York: Cambridge University Press, 2000), 16–52.

97. On the immediate impact of the panic, depletion of funds, and the nomination of Douglass see Osthaus, *Freedmen, Philanthropy, and Fraud,* 176–180, 185. *Report of the Select Committee to Investigate Freedmen's Savings & Trust Co.,* 74.

98. Frederick Douglass, *The Life and Times of Frederick Douglass* (London, 1882), 354. Frederick Douglass to ?, March 30, 1974, FSTC Letters, Reel no. 2, Frederick Douglass Papers, Library of Congress.

99. Comptroller of the Currency, *Report,* 42nd Cong., 3rd sess., Sen. Mis. Doc. 88 (1873), 2–10. See also Abby L. Gilbert, "The Comptroller of the Currency and the Freedman's Savings Bank," *The Journal of Negro History* 57, no. 2 (April 1972): 125–143.

100. Three investigations: *Report of the Commissioners of the Freedmen's Savings & Trust Co.; Report of the Select Committee on the Freedman's Bank; Report of the Select Committee to Investigate Freedmen's Savings & Trust Co.* For southern press see *New York Times,* September 15, 1874. For final figures see Osthaus, *Freedmen, Philanthropy, and Fraud,* 215. On federal subsidization of capitalists' risks and the lack of a government safety net for working-class people in the nineteenth century, see

358 � Notes to Pages 147–151

Davis A. Moss, *When All Else Fails: Government as the Ultimate Risk Manager* (Cambridge: Harvard University Press, 2004).

101. Keyes, *Savings Banks,* 2:533, 540, 555, 557, 161. *Report . . . To Investigate the Savings Banks of the State* [of Connecticut] (Norwich, 1874), 184. *Annual Message of Governor J. F. Hartranft of Pennsylvania* (Harrisburg, 1878), 7. Samuel Rezneck, "Distress, Relief, and Discontent in the United States during the Depression of 1873–78," *The Journal of Political Economy* 58, no. 6 (December 1985): 497. Garon, *Beyond Our Means,* 104, argues that 1870s savings-bank failures had long-term, negative effects on the instituionalization of savings in the United States, especially in the South.

102. A cultural process already at work in the antebellum period, now accelerated. See Ann Fabian, "Speculation on Distress: The Popular Discourse of the Panics of 1837 and 1857," *Yale Journal of Criticism* 3 (1989): 127–142. On the religious response to the economic transformations of the postbellum decades see George M. Marsden, *Fundamentalism and American Culture: The Shaping of Twentieth Century Evangelicalism, 1870–1925* (New York: Oxford University Press, 2006).

103. "The Great Panic," *Independent,* September 25, 1873; "The Panic," *New York Evangelist,* September 25, 1873.

104. *Report of the Select Committee to Investigate Freedmen's Savings & Trust Co.,* 52. *New York Times,* October 1, 1874. On the causes of the 1873 panic, weighing fraud against sudden declines in the marketable values of securities, see Gary B. Gorton, *Slapped by the Invisible Hand: The Panic of 2007* (New York: Oxford University Press, 2010), 26, table 2.4.

105. For the 1 in 5 estimate see Schweninger, *Black Property Owners in the South,* 183.

5. BETTING THE FARM

Epigraph: *Wisconsin Farmer's Institutes, A Hand Book of Agriculture* 6 (Madison, 1892), 65.

1. John Ise, *Sod and Stubble: The Story of a Kansas Homestead* (Lawrence: University Press of Kansas, 1996/1940). Ise, an Iowa State University agricultural economist, published his narrative in dramatized form in the third person. He constructed the memoir from memory, a series of oral histories taken from his mother Rosie Ise, and research he conducted from 1924 to 1932 on Central-Western Kansas in the late nineteenth century. Ise's editor, Von Rothenberger, has researched and confirmed the factual details of the account, including such details as the Ises's 1887 mortgage. He calls it a "work of astonishing historical accuracy." See Ise, *Sod and Stubble,* xvii.

2. Ise, *Sod and Stubble,* 229.

3. *Report on Real Estate Mortgages in the United States at the Eleventh Census: 1890* (Washington, DC, 1895), 315–323, table 104. On the western farm mortgage market see Kenneth A. Snowden, "The Evolution of Interregional Mortgage Lending Channels, 1870–1940: The Life Insurance-Mortgage Company Connection," in Naomi Lamoreaux and Daniel Raff, eds., *Coordination and Information: Historical*

Perspectives on the Organization of Enterprise (Chicago: University of Chicago Press, 1996), 209–247; Kenneth A. Snowden, "Mortgage Securitization in the U.S.: 20th Century Developments in Historical Perspective," in Michael Bordo and Richard Sylla, eds., *Anglo-American Financial Systems: Institutions and Markets in the Twentieth Century* (New York: New York University Press, 1995), 261–298; Allan G. Bogue, *Money at Interest: The Farm Mortgage on the Middle Border* (Ithaca: Cornell University Press, 1955); H. Peers Brewer, "Eastern Money and Western Mortgages in the 1870s," *Business History Review* 50, no. 3 (Autumn 1976): 356–380.

4. B. C. Keeler, *Where to Go To Become Rich* (Chicago, 1880).

5. Ise, *Sod and Stubble*, 229, 268, 53.

6. Ibid., 254. *Report on Real Estate Mortgages*, 26, table 4.

7. On reduced cost of capital see Barry Eichengreen, "Interest Rates in the Populist Era," *The American Economic Review* 74, no. 5 (December 1984): 995–1015. On rising land values see Peter H. Lindert, "Long-Run Trends in American Farmland values," *Agricultural History* 62, no. 3 (Summer 1988): 45–85. For a positive account of the western farmer's market position see Douglass North, *Growth and Welfare in the American Past* (New York: Prentice-Hall, 1966), ch. 8. On Populist farmer's discomfort with market risk see Anne Mayhew, "A Reappraisal of the Causes of Farm Protest Movements in the United States, 1870–1900," *Journal of Economic History* 32, no.2 (June 1972): 464–475; James A. Stock, "Real Estate Mortgages, Foreclosures, and Midwestern Agrarian Unrest, 1865–1920," *Journal of Economic History* 44, no.1 (March 1984): 89–106.

8. According to H. W. Chaplin in 1890: "As it reads upon the records in Boston and in Portland, so it read in England in the thirteenth century." H. W. Chaplin, "The Story of Mortgage Law," *Harvard Law Review* 4, no. 1 (1890): 9. Robert C. Allen, *Enclosure and the Yeoman: The Agricultural Development of the South Midlands, 1450–1850* (Oxford: Clarendon Press, 1992); Allan Kulikoff, *From British Peasants to Colonial American Farmers* (Chapel Hill: University of North Carolina Press, 2000). On land banks see Mary M. Schweitzer, *Custom and Contract: Household, Government, and the Economy in Colonial Pennsylvania* (New York: Columbia University Press, 1987), ch. 4.

9. George S. Boutwell, *Address Before the Middlesex Society of Husbandmen and Manufacturers* (Boston, 1850), 6, 18. On the antebellum farm mortgage see Tamara Plakins Thornton, " 'A Great Machine' or a 'Beast of Prey': A Boston Corporation and Its Rural Debtors in an Age of Capitalist Transformation," *Journal of the Early Republic* 27, no. 4 (Winter 2007): 567–597. On Concord see Robert A. Gross, "Culture and Cultivation: Agriculture and Society in Thoreau's Concord," *Journal of American History* 69, no. 1 (June 1982), 42–61.

10. Henry David Thoreau, *Walden: Or, Life in the Woods* (New York: Alfred A. Knopf, 1992/1854), 7, 29, 5, 50.

11. With the Homestead Act of 1862, households, to claim a quarter, needed only to file an application, improve the land for five years, and then refile for the deed. Railroads and eastern speculators also offered land for sale. Numbers in Richard White, *"It's Your Misfortune and None of My Own": A New History of the American West* (Norman: University of Oklahoma Press, 1993), 143. See also Paul Wallace

Gates, Allan G. Bogue, and Margaret Beattie Bogue, *The Jeffersonian Dream: Studies in the History of American Land Policy and Development* (Albuquerque: University of New Mexico Press, 1996).

12. For agricultural workforce and capital numbers Stanley Legerbot, *Manpower in Economic Growth: The American Record Since 1800* (New York, 1964), 510, table A-1; and James L. Huston, *Securing the Fruits of Labor: The American Concept of Wealth Distribution, 1765–1900* (Baton Rouge: Louisiana State University Press, 1998), 91, table 2. On the broad outlines of industrialization see Walter Licht, *Industrializing America: The Nineteenth Century* (Baltimore: Johns Hopkins University Press, 1995).

13. U.S. Congress 47:2, House Miscellaneous Document, 13:3, *Report on the Production of Agriculture (10th Census), 1880*, 25; Huston, *Securing the Fruits of Labor,* 91, table 2; James L. Huston, *Calculating the Value of the Union: Slavery, Property Rights, and the Economic Origins of the Civil War* (Chapel Hill: University of North Carolina Press, 2003), 28, table 2.3.

14. W. F. Mappin, "Farm Mortgages and the Small Farmer," *Political Science Quarterly* 4, no. 3 (September 1889): 436; U.S. Congress 49:1, House Executive Document 378, *Report of the Commissioner of Agriculture,* 1886, 423; James Willis Gleed, "Western Mortgages," *Forum* (March 1890): 180.

15. On the old ecological logic see Brian Donahue, *The Great Meadow: Farmers and the Land in Colonial Concord* (New Haven: Yale University Press, 2004). On the new see William Cronon, *Nature's Metropolis: Chicago and the Great West* (New York: Norton, 1992).

16. *Where to Go to Become Rich,* 43. Most farm-making estimates are for a slightly earlier time period. See Jeremy Atack, "Farm and Farm-Making Costs Revisited," *Agricultural History* 56, no. 3 (October 1982): 663–676.

17. In a sample of 219,291 households. *Report on Real Estate Mortgages,* 278, diagram 12. In 1880, nationwide 25 percent of farmers were tenants. Gates made much of this fact, see Paul W. Gates, *Landlords and Tenants on the Prairies Frontier* (Ithaca: Cornell University Press, 1973). Recent studies have emphasized tenancy as a temporary status. See Jeremy Atack, "Tenants and Yeomen in the Nineteenth Century," *Agricultural History* 62, no. 3 (Summer 1998): 6–32. On wage labor and the agricultural ladder see Gavin Wright, "American Agriculture and the Labor Market: What Happened to Proletarianization?" *Agricultural History* 62, no. 3 (Summer 1998): 182–209.

18. On rural consumerism see David B. Danbom, *Born in the Country: A History of Rural America* (Baltimore: Johns Hopkins University Press, 2006), 131–161; David Blanke, "Consumer Choice, Agency, and New Directions in Rural History," *Agricultural History* 81, no.2 (Spring 2007): 182–203.

19. Jeremy Atack, Fred Bateman, and William N. Parker, "The Farm, the Farmer, and the Market," in Stanley L. Engerman and Robert E. Gallman, eds., *The Cambridge Economic History of the United States, volume II: The Long Nineteenth Century* (New York: Cambridge University Press, 2000), 259.

20. See Wright, "American Agriculture and the Labor Market," 194.

21. See *Willis A. Olmsted and Mary E. Olmsted v. The New England Mortgage Security Company* 11 Neb. 487 (1881).

22. Emphasis in the original. Ibid. "The Late Austin Corbin's Buffalo," *New York Times,* December 12, 1897; A. N. Harbert, "Austin Corbin," *Iowa Historical Record* 14, no. 1 (January 1898): 193–201. Sections 8 and 28 are the relevant sections of the 1864 Banking Act. The Supreme Court case *Fortier v. New Orleans National Bank* 112 U.S. 439 (1884) held that mortgage loans were not violations of the Act. But national banks still largely avoided owning mortgages. See Richard H. Keehn and Gene Smiley, "Mortgage Lending by National Banks," *Business History Review* 51, no. 4 (Winter 1977): 474–491. On European capital see Larry McFarlane, "British Investment in Midwestern Farm Mortgages and Land, 1875–1900: A Comparison of Iowa and Kansas," *Agricultural History* 48, no. 1 (January 1974): 183.

23. Ise, *Sod and Stubble,* 199; Edward Darrow, *A Treatise on Mortgage Investments* (Minneapolis, 1892), 8. See Alison D. Morantz, "There's No Place Like Home: Homestead Exemption and Judicial Constructions of Family in Nineteenth-Century America," *Law and History Review* 24, no. 2 (Summer 2006): 245–295.

24. *Ten Per Cent First Mortgages on Improved Farms in Iowa and Kansas, Negotiated by the Corbin Banking Company* (New York, 1872). "The Usury Laws of the United States," *The Bankers Magazine,* March 1861. *Report on Real Estate Mortgages,* 170, 259.

25. Richard H. Dana, Jr., *Speech . . . On the Repeal of Usury Laws* (New York, 1872), 20, 10. James Avery Webb, *A Treatise on the Law of Usury* (St. Louis, 1899), 14. Eichengreen, "Interest Rates in the Populist Era," holds that the regional variance in interest rates was a rational adjustment to the risk of repayment. Snowden is skeptical. Kenneth A. Snowden, "Mortgage Rates and American Capital Market Development in the Late Nineteenth Century," *Journal of Economic History* 47, no. 3 (September 1987): 671–691.

26. Ise, *Sod and Stubble,* 199. On the local nature of usury disputes and commissions charges see George K. Holmes, "Usury in Law, in Practice and in Psychology," *Political Science Quarterly* 7 (September 1892), 431–467. See also *Report on Real Estate Mortgages,* 168–173.

27. "Western Mortgages," *Boston Daily Advertiser,* November 13, 1877. On the 1870s capital market see Lance Davis and Robert Gallman, *Evolving Financial Markets and International Capital Flows. Britain, the Americas, and Australia, 1865–1914* (Cambridge: Cambridge University Press, 2001), esp. 20.

28. Jane Addams, "The Snare of Preparation" (1912) in Jean Bethke Elshtain, ed., *The Jane Addams Reader* (New York: Basic Books, 2002), 108.

29. Darrow, *Treatise on Mortgage Investments,* 38, 43.

30. Gleed, "Western Mortgages," 96; *Independent,* April 4, 1889; *Ten Per Cent First Mortgages; Independent,* May 31, 1889. For 1893 figure, see Snowden, "The Evolution of Interregional Mortgage Lending Channels," 227.

31. Gleed, "Western Mortgages," 102; *Congregationalist,* April 21, 1887. On spreads see Beers, "Eastern Money." On Iowa and New York regulators see D. M. Frederiksen, "Mortgage Banking in America," *The Journal of Political Economy* 2, no. 2 (March 1894): 212–213. Mappin, "Farm Mortgages and the Small Farmer," for instance, claimed Kansas and Nebraska had 134 incorporated companies with another 200 companies chartered out of those states doing business there.

32. Darrow, *Treatise on Mortgage Investments,* 25. On the originator's lack of skin in the game see Snowden, "Mortgage Securitization in the U.S." The case was *Teal v. Walker* 111 U.S. 242 (1882). After 1893 it seems farmers succeeded politically in acquiring the right to prepayment, making bonds far more difficult to price. See Samuel Armstrong Nelson, *The Bond Buyer's Dictionary* (New York, 1907), 129.

33. For figures see Snowden, "Evolution," 220. With "western" including the states of IA, MN, NB, SD, WY, and MT.

34. See Davis and Gallman, *Evolving Financial System,* 280, table 3:5c-1.

35. On life insurance investments and state laws governing them see Lester Zartman, *The Investments of Life Insurance Companies* (New York, 1906), esp. ch. 6. On savings banks see Davis and Gallman, *Evolving Financial Markets,* 279–283.

36. *Travelers Record,* June 1879, December 1881, April 1882, March 1878, August 1883; Hatch and Woodman to George E. Todd, May 31, 1879, Box 17, Collection 60, Warshaw Collection of Business Americana, Insurance Collection, Smithsonian National Museum of American History (hereafter cited as "Warshaw").

37. Travelers Insurance Companies, *Accident Department, The Travelers Insurance Company* (Hartford, 1871); *Travelers Record,* March 1887, November 1880; *Christian Union,* April 22, 187; *Seventh Biennial Report of the Bureau of Labor, Census and Industrial Statistics State of Wisconsin 1895–1896* (Madison, 1896), 110.

38. See Harold Williamson and Orange A. Smally, *Northwestern Mutual Life: A Century of Trusteeship* (Evanston, IL: Northwestern University Press, 1957).

39. *Seventeenth Annual Report of the Superintendent of Insurance of the State of Kansas, for the year ending December 31, 1886* (Topeka, 1887), 329, 330; *Twenty-Eighth Annual Report of the Superintendent of Insurance of the State of Kansas, for the year ending December 31, 1897* (Topeka, 1898), xvi–xix.

40. *Travelers Record,* August 1884; *The Advocate,* April 23, 1890 (the Topeka Kansas Farmer's Alliance newspaper).

41. On assignment see Travelers Insurance Companies, *Accident Manual* (Hartford, 1885), 12. On generational succession see Mark Friedberger, *Farm Families and Change in 20th-Century America* (Lexington: University of Kentucky Press, 1988). More traditional practices remained in ethnic enclaves. See Kathleen Neils Conzen, "Peasant Pioneers: Generational Succession among German Farmers in Frontier Minnesota," in Steven Hahn and Jonathan Prude, eds., *The Countryside in the Age of Capitalist Transformation: Essays in the Social History of Rural America* (Chapel Hill: University of North Carolina Press, 1985), 259–292.

42. *Travelers Record,* November 1880. On old age see Hendrik Hartog, *Someday All This Will Be Yours: A History of Inheritance and Old Age* (Cambridge: Harvard University Press, 2012).

43. *Travelers Record,* April 1881, November 1878.

44. Ise, *Sod and Stubble,* 53. *First Biennial Report of the Bureau of Labor and Industrial Statistics of Nebraska, 1887 and 1888* (Omaha, 1888); *Seventh Biennial Report of the Bureau of Labor, Census and Industrial Statistics State of Wisconsin 1895–1896* (Madison, 1896), 116–119.

45. Emphasis in the original. Will Carleton, *Farm Festivals* (New York, 1881), 118–121.

46. Ise, *Sod and Stubble,* 229. For comparison with industrial wage work see Herbert G. Gutman, *Work, Culture, and Society in Industrializing America: Essays in American Working-Class and Social History* (New York: Vintage, 1976), 23.

47. *Seventh Biennial Report,* 117, 114; *First Biennial Report,* 210, 218; Ise, *Sod and Stubble,* 217. On nineteenth-century farm productivity see Alan L. Olmstead and Paul W. Rhode, *Creating Abundance: Biological Innovation and American Agricultural Development* (New York: Cambridge University Press, 2008), esp. chs. 1 and 2.

48. A. H. J, "Paying the Mortgage," *Michigan Farmer,* August 22, 1882; Ise, *Sod and Stubble,* 215.

49. Ise, *Sod and Stubble,* 217, 209.

50. On early railroad-traveler accident insurance see "Accident Insurance," *The American Law Review* 7, no. 4 (July 1872): 586. For examples of early railroad accident "tickets" see Box 17, Collection 60, Warshaw.

51. *Travelers Record,* July 1885.

52. Emphasis in the original. Travelers Insurance Companies, *Accident Department;* Travelers Insurance Companies, *Accident Manual,* sects. 10, 14, 15; *Travelers Record,* November 1879. On increased attention to the sale of labor time in this period see Amy Dru Stanley, *From Bondage to Contract: Wage Labor, Marriage, and the Market in the Age of Slave Emancipation* (New York: Cambridge University Press, 1998), esp. 89.

53. Travelers Insurance Companies, *Accident Department; Travelers Record,* March 1881, February 1880.

54. *Travelers Record,* March 1879; "Examples Accident Losses Paid" and "Records of Claims Paid in Cash," both in Box 17, Collection 60, Warshaw.

55. "Accident Insurance," *American Law Review,* 586, 588; William C. Niblack, *The Law of Voluntary Societies, Mutual Benefit Insurance and Accident Insurance* (Chicago, 1894), sects. 363, 364, 365; *United States Mutual Accident Association v. Barry* 131 U.S. 100 (1889). See also *Hutchcraft's Ex'r v. Travelers' Insurance Co.* 87 Ky. 300 (1888).

56. Travelers Insurance Companies, *Accident Department,* 1871; Travelers Insurance Companies, *Accident Manual,* sect. 19. On "limitation of risk" see "Accident Insurance," 606; *Stone v. United States Casualty Company* 34 NJL 371 (1871).

57. *The Travelers Record,* January 1883, May 1880; Niblack, *Law,* section 363; Travelers Insurance Companies, *Accident Manual,* section 40. For Wright's consulting, see Rodney Dennis to Elizur Wright, 10 January 10, 1871, Carton 1, Folder 36, Elizur Wright Business Papers, Baker Library Historical Collections, Harvard Business School. See also Arwen P. Mohun, "On the Frontier of the *Empire of Chance*: Statistics, Accidents, and Risk in Industrializing America," *Science in Context* 8 (September 2005): 337–357.

58. Travelers Insurance Companies, *Accident Manual,* "Classification of Risks." *Travelers Record,* November, 1880.

59. See Edward Atkinson, "The True Meaning of Farm Mortgage Statistics," *Forum,* May 1895. On monoculture see also John Gjerde, *The Minds of the West: Ethnocultural Evolution in the Rural Middle West, 1830–1917* (Chapel Hill: University of North Carolina, 1997), 146.

60. On specialization see Allan G. Bogue, *From Prairie to Corn Belt: Farming on the Illinois and Iowa Prairies in the Nineteenth Century* (Ames: Iowa State University Press,

1994/1963); Mary Eschelbach Gregson, "Specialization in Late-Nineteenth Century Midwestern Agriculture," *Agricultural History* 67, no.1 (Winter 1993): 16–35.

61. Winifred B. Rothenberg, *From Market-Places to a Market Economy: The Transformation of Rural Massachusetts, 1760–1850* (Chicago: University of Chicago Press, 1992), 98; C. Knick Harley, "Transportation, and the World Wheat Trade, and the Kuznets Cycle," *Explorations in Economic History* 17, no.3 (July 1980): 246–247; *Fourth Annual Report of the Bureau of Labor Statistics of the State of Connecticut, for the Year Ending 1888* (Hartford, 1889), 140–144; George S. Boutwell, "Feeding Cattle," *Massachusetts Ploughman and New England Journal of Agriculture,* January 19, 1878. On changes in northeastern farming see Hal S. Barron, *Mixed Harvest: The Second Great Transformation in the Rural North, 1870–1930* (Chapel Hill: University of North Carolina Press, 1997).

62. [Hamilton, GA] *Weekly Visitor,* February 7 1873, quoted in Gavin Wright, *Old South, New South: Revolutions in the Southern Economy Since the Civil War* (New York: Basic Books, 1986), 114. On corn versus cotton see Gavin Wright and Howard Kunreuther, "Cotton, Corn, and Risk in the Nineteenth Century," *Journal of Economic History* 35, no. 3 (September 1975): 526–551. On the southern yeoman see Steven Hahn, *The Roots of Southern Populism: Yeoman Farmers and the Transformation of the Georgian Upcountry, 1850–1890* (New York: Oxford University Press, 1983).

63. Ise, *Sod and Stubble,* 276, 254. It is possible that immigrants such as the Ises were more risk averse than native Yankee farmers. See Kathleen Neils Conzen, *Making Their Own America: Assimilation Theory and the German Peasant Pioneer* (New York: Berg, 1990): esp. 20, 21; and Kathleen Neils Conzen, "Immigrants in Nineteenth-Century Agricultural History," in Lou Ferleger, ed., *Agriculture and National Development* (Ames: Iowa University Press, 1990), 303–342.

64. Ise, *Sod and Stubble,* 276, 254. *The Independent,* October 22, 1896; Carleton *Farm Festivals,* 118.

65. Ise, *Sod and Stubble,* 254.

66. George K. Holmes, "Mortgage Statistics," *Publications of the American Statistical Association* 2, no. 9 (1890): 20.

67. On forecasting see Jamie Pietruska, "Propheteering: A Cultural History of Prediction in the Gilded Age," (Ph.D. diss., Massachusetts Institute of Technology, 2009).

68. Samuel Benner, *Benner's Prophecies of Future Ups and Downs in Prices* (Cincinnati, 1884), 30, 136.

69. William D. Emerson, "On the Relations which the Agricultural, Manufacturing and Mechanical Interests, Sustain to Each Other," in *Fifth Annual Report of the Board of Agriculture of the State of Ohio* (Columbus, 1851), 536. On crop insurance see *Report on Insurance Business in the United States at the Eleventh Census: 1890,* Part I: Fire, Marine, and Inland Insurance (Washington, DC, 1894), 1108, table 7.

70. *Fifth Annual Report of the Board of Agriculture of the State of Ohio,* 535–536. See Katherine Anderson, *Predicting the Weather: Victorians and the Science of Meteorology* (Chicago: University of Chicago Press, 2005); Erik D. Craft, "Private Weather Organizations and the Founding of the United States Weather Bureau," *Journal of Economic History* 59, no. 4 (December 1999): 1063–1071.

71. *Annual Report of the Chief Signal-Officer to the Secretary of War for the year 1875* (Washington, 1875), 102; *Annual Report of the Chief Signal Officer to the Secretary of War for The Fiscal year Ended June 30, 1885* (Washington 1885), 13 and appendices 56, 58.

72. *Annual Report of the Chief Signal Officer to the Secretary of War for The Fiscal year Ended June 30, 1885* (Washington 1885), 7; *Travelers Record,* October 1880; Travelers Insurance Companies, *Weather Signals Displayed by Flags,* Box 17, Collection 60, Warshaw.

73. H. Hepworth, "Old Badger's Mortgage," *Independent,* October 22, 1896; *Travelers Record,* July 1879.

74. *Report on Insurance Business in the United States at the Eleventh Census: 1890,* 1101–1103, tables 1–3; "Tornado Insurance," *Independent,* August 4, 1881; "The Nebraska Alliance," *The American Farmer,* December 15, 1892; Frederick L. Hoffman, *Tornadoes and Tornado Insurance* (New York, 1896), 19.

75. "Some Remarks About Mortgages," *Michigan Farmer,* July 6, 1889; Keeler, *Where to Go to Become Rich,* 39. Ise, *Sod and Stubble,* 424.

76. *The Advocate,* November 9, 1889; Holmes, "Mortgage Statistics," 13.

77. *Report on Real Estate Mortgages,* 122, 121, 309, 26, 259, 312, 310.

78. Holmes, "Mortgage Statistics," 21.

79. *Atchison Daily Champion,* October 25, 1888; *Daily InterOcean,* May 5, 1893; *Milwaukee Journal,* May 8, 1893; *Daily Picayune,* August 6, 1891.

80. Mappin, "Farm Mortgages and the Small Farmer," 451.

81. See Willie Lee Rose, *Rehearsal for Reconstruction: The Port Royal Experiment* (New York: Oxford University Press, 1964), 226.

82. Atkinson, "True Meaning," 312, 313.

83. Ibid., 313. See also Edward Atkinson, "Farm Ownership and Tenancy in the United States," *Publications of the American Statistical Association* 5, no. 40 (December 1897): 329–344.

84. Daniel R. Goodloe, "Western Mortgages," *Forum* (November 1890), 346.

85. See Elizabeth Sanders, *Roots of Reform: Farmers, Workers, and the American State, 1877–1917* (Chicago: University of Chicago Press, 1999). Charles Postel, *The Populist Vision* (New York: Oxford University Press, 2007).

86. William Parker once wrote that after 1870 a "bridge was burned" in American agriculture. See William N. Parker, "The True History of the Northern Farmer," in *Europe, America and the Wider World: Essays on the History of Western Capitalism, Volume 2, America and the Wider World* (New York: Cambridge University Press, 1991), 172. See also Gavin Wright, "American Agriculture and the Labor Market," 85.

87. *Annual Report of the U.S. Department of Agriculture* (Washington, 1908), 151–152.

6. FRATERNITY IN THE AGE OF CAPITAL

Epigraph: William Graham Sumner, *What Social Classes Owe to Each Other* (New York, 1883), 34.

1. J. J. Upchurch and Sam Booth, *The Life, Labors and Travels of Father J. J. Upchurch, Founder of the Ancient Order of United Workmen, Written By Himself* (San

Francisco, 1887), 23; Ida M. Tarbell, *The History of the Standard Oil Company,* 2 vols. (New York, 1904), 1:12.

2. Upchurch, *Life, Labors,* 24.

3. On the fraternal movement see Jason Kaufman, *For the Common Good? American Civic Life and the Golden Age of Fraternity* (New York: Oxford University Press, 2002); John Fabian Witt, *The Accidental Republic: Crippled Workingmen, Destitute Widows, and the Remaking of American Law* (Cambridge: Harvard University Press, 2004), ch. 3; David T. Beito, *From Mutual Aid to the Welfare State: Fraternal Societies and Social Services, 1890–1967* (Chapel Hill: University of North Carolina Press, 2000); Mark C. Carnes, *Secret Ritual and Manhood in Victorian America* (New Haven: Yale University Press, 1991); George Emery and J. C. Herbert Emery, *A Young Man's Benefit: The Independent Order of Odd Fellows and Sickness Insurance in the United States and Canada, 1860–1929* (Montreal: McGill-Queen's University Press, 1999); Mary Ann Clawson, *Constructing Brotherhood: Class, Gender, and Fraternalism* (Princeton: Princeton University Press, 1989); David Buffum and Robert Whaples, "Fraternalism, Paternalism, the Family, and the Market: Insurance a Century Ago," *Social Science History* 15, no. 1 (Spring 1991): 97–112. Golden Age of Fraternity according to W. S. Harwood, "Secret Societies in America," *North American Review* (May 1897), 623.

4. William Graham Sumner, *What Social Classes Owe to Each Other* (New York, 1883), 36, 35.

5. Ibid., 65.

6. John Dewey, "Progress," in Jo Ann Boydston ed., *The Middle Works, 1899–1924 of John Dewey: Volume 10, 1916–1917* (Carbondale: Southern Illinois Press, 1980), 238; John Dewey, *The Influence of Darwin on Philosophy* (New York, 1910), 9; Sumner, *What Social Classes Owe to Each Other,* 14. On Social Darwinism see Richard Hofstadter, *Social Darwinism and American Thought* (Boston: Beacon Press, 1992/1944); Robert C. Bannister, *Social Darwinism: Science and Myth in Anglo-American Social Thought* (Philadelphia: Temple University Press, 1989).

7. Sumner, *What Social Classes Owe to Each Other,* 14; Frederick L. Hoffman, "The Law of Average," in *Insurance Science and Economics* (New York, 1911), 344.

8. See "Constitution of the Supreme Lodge of the A.O.U.W.," quoted in *State v. Miller* 66 Iowa 26 (1885); M. W. Sackett, *Early History of Fraternal Benefit Societies in America* (Meadville, PA: Tribune Publishing Company, 1914), 130, 42; B. H. Meyer, "Fraternal Insurance in the United States," *Annals of the American Academy of Political and Social Science* 17 (March 1901): 261.

9. Sackett, *History of Fraternal Benefit Societies,* 74; Lester W. Zartman, *The Investments of Life Insurance Companies* (New York, 1906), 131.

10. Sumner, *What Social Classes Owe to Each Other,* 26; T. H. McCann, *A Brief History of Life Insurance and the Application of its Laws to the Royal Arcanum and Kindred Fraternal Life Insurance Associations* (New Jersey, 1886), 19. On the central place of contract in postbellum social thought see Amy Dru Stanley, *From Bondage to Contract: Wage Labor, Marriage, and the Market in the Age of Slave Emancipation* (New York: Cambridge University Press, 1998).

11. Sumner, *What Social Classes Owe to Each Other*, 60, 62, 69, 61. On the age of capital in the United States see Sven Beckert, *The Monied Metropolis: New York City and the Consolidation of the American Bourgeoisie, 1850–1896* (New York: Cambridge University Press, 2001).

12. Per capita figures in Witt, *Accidental Republic*, 102, table 3.2; *Journal of Proceedings of the Fourth Annual Session of the National Fraternal Congress* (Poughkeepsie, NY, 1891), 45; Estimate of Kaufman, *For the Common Good?*, 42.

13. For life insurance companies assets see Bruce M. Pritchett, *A Study of Capital Mobilization: The Life Insurance Industry of the Nineteenth Century* (New York: Arno Press, 1977), 290–347, table A1; For financial sector numbers see Raymond W. Goldsmith, *Comparative National Balance Sheets: A Study of Twenty Countries, 1688–1978* (Chicago: University of Chicago Press, 1985), 45, table 19; and 136, table 47.

14. "Secure Amidst Panic," *The Insurance Times,* October 1873; "Weather the Cape," *Christian Union,* March 18, 1874.

15. Sharon Murphy, "Life Insurance in the United States through World War I". *EH.Net Encyclopedia,* ed. Robert Whaples, http://eh.net/encyclopedia/article /murphy.life.insurance.us (accessed August 15, 2002). Miles M. Dawson, "Assessment Life Insurance," *Annals of the American Academy of Political and Social Science* 26 (September 1905): 123; "The Prospect of Life Insurance," *The Insurance Times,* February 1877.

16. "Reform in Life Insurance," *New York Times,* May 6, 1876. On the Charter and other failures in this era see Zartman, *Life Insurance Investments,* ch. 5. Elizur Wright, *The Necessity of Reform in Life Insurance* (Boston, 1878), 1.

17. A. D. Brigham, *Is Life Insurance Management Economical, Just and Safe?* (New York, 1878), 12. See Zartman, *Life Insurance Investments,* ch. 5 for various other causes.

18. Richard Johnson, *Life Insurance Robbery,* (New York, 1878), 12; John F. Dryden, *Addresses and Papers on Life Insurance and other Subjects* (Newark, 1909), 15; Sheppard Homans, "The Insurance Crisis," *North American Review,* March/April 1877, 254.

19. *Report and testimony taken before the Committee on Insurance, relative to Life insurance companies . . .* (Albany, 1877), 382; "The Actuary," *Insurance Times,* October 1877.

20. See J. Owen Stalson, *Marketing Life Insurance: Its History in America* (Cambridge: Harvard University Press, 1942), ch. 17.

21. Kaufman, *For the Common Good?;* Gerald Gamm and Robert D. Putnam, "The Growth of Voluntary Associations in America, 1840–1890," *Journal of Interdisciplinary History* 29, no. 3 (Winter 1999): 511–557.

22. Sackett, *History of Fraternal Benefit Societies,* 74; W. E. Hallenbeck, *Facts Fraternal vs. Regular Life Insurance, or the Royal Arcanum Compared with the Leading Life Insurance Companies* (New York, 1887), 5; John Hoffman, *A Treatise on the American Legion of Honor, Its Organization, Aims and Objects* (Passaic, NJ: 1883), 29; *Object and Aims of the Ancient Order of United Workmen* (Milwaukee, WI: 1885),

11; W. E. Hallenbeck, *Words to Thinking Men Regarding the Royal Arcanum* (New York, 1888), 22. Emphasis in the original.

23. A. R. Savage, *Digest of the Official Decisions of the Knights of Honor* (Boston, 1890), 53. Section 212 declared of the certificate: "It is not a policy of insurance, and cannot be assigned as security." The American Legion of Honor stamped "Not Assignable" on its certificates.

24. Hoffman, *Treatise on the American Legion of Honor,* 20; Mutual Life's statement in *Thirteenth Annual Report of the Insurance Commissioner of the State of Minnesota* (Minneapolis, 1884), 284–286.

25. See Sackett, *History of Fraternal Benefit Societies,* 54–161; *Origin and Aims of the Ancient Order of United Workmen* (St. Louis, 1884).

26. Sackett, *History of Fraternal Benefit Societies,* 171. The figure of $2,000 was typical but there was some variation. For their $2,000 benefit, for instance, the Knights of Honor charged a $1.00 assessment from age twenty-one to forty-five which then scaled all the way up to $4.00 for those above age fifty-five. See Alfred Matthias, *Digest of the Constitution, Laws, and Decisions of the Supreme Lodge of the Knights of Honor* (Boston, 1880), 9, 30.

27. *Origin and Aims of the Ancient Order of United Workmen.*

28. Sackett, *History of Fraternal Benefit Societies,* 54–161, goes into exhaustive detail of the federal structure.

29. Matthias, *Digest of the Constitution,* 10, 35. See "Selection of Risks" in *Journal of Proceedings of the Fourth Annual Session of the National Fraternal Congress* (Poughkeepsie, NY, 1891), 17–24. Risk selection is a point emphasized by Witt, *Accidental Republic,* ch. 5. On able-bodiedness see Barbara Young Welke, *Law and the Borders of Belonging in the Long Nineteenth Century United States* (New York: Cambridge University Press, 2010).

30. *Journal of Proceedings of the Fourth Annual Session of the National Fraternal Congress,* 20. *Journal of Proceedings of the Sixth Annual Session of the National Fraternal Congress* (Poughkeepsie, NY, 1893), 74. On gender and fraternalism see Carnes, *Secret Ritual and Manhood.* More generally, see Carol Pateman, *The Sexual Contract* (Palo Alto, CA: Stanford University Press, 1988), ch. 4.

31. *Official Digest of the Supreme Lodge of the Knights of Pythias for 1890* (1891), 94. See David M. Fahey, "Colored Knights of Pythias," in Nina Mjagkij, ed., *Organizing Black America* (New York: Garland Publishing, 2001), 168. On racial exclusion and life insurance see Daniel Bouk, "The Science of Difference: Designing Tools for Discrimination in the American Life Insurance Industry, 1830–1930," (Ph.D. diss., Princeton University, 2009).

32. Quote from Theda Skocpol, Ariane Liazos, Marshal Ganz, *What a Mighty Power We Can Be: African American Fraternal Groups and the Struggle for Racial Equality* (Princeton: Princeton University Press, 2006), 37 and 24–29, table 2.1. On the role of women see Elsa Barkley Brown, "Womanist Consciousness: Maggie Walker and the Independent Order of Saint Luke," *Signs: Journal of Women in Culture and Society* 14, no. 3 (Spring 1989): 610–633; Tera Hunter, *To 'Joy My Freedom: Southern Black Women's Lives and Labors After the Civil War* (Cambridge: Harvard University Press, 1997), ch. 6.

33. Max Weber, "Protestant Sects and the Spirit of Capitalism" (1904), in H. H. Gerth and C. Wright Mills, eds. *From Max Weber: Essays in Sociology* (New York: Routledge, 1991), 321, 310, 316, 311, 305, 319, 321.

34. *The Knights of the Pythias Complete Manual and Textbook* (Philadelphia, 1878). See also McCann, *A Brief History . . . Royal Arcanum,* 19.

35. Kaufman found that the Knights of Pythias stole Masonic rituals. Kaufman, *For the Common Good?,* 109. Matthias, *Digest of the Constitution,* 18, 102.

36. Sackett, *History of Fraternal Benefit Societies,* 83.

37. William D. Kennedy, *Pythian History: Birth and Progress of the Order* (Chicago, 1904), 136, 139.

38. *Journal of Proceedings of the Third Annual Session of the National Fraternal Congress* (Poughkeepsie, NY, 1890), 46; *Journal of Proceedings of the Fourth Annual Session of the National Fraternal Congress,* 7. Pritchett, *A Study of Capital Mobilization,* 290–347, table A1.

39. Hoffman, *A Treatise on the American Legion of Honor,* 8. On the AOUW's Kentucky charter see *Digest of the Constitution, Laws, and Decisions of the Ancient Order of United Workmen* (Buffalo, 1879), 161.

40. For examples of cases see *Digest of the Constitution, Laws, and Decisions of the Ancient Order of United Workmen* (Buffalo, 1884), 245, 427.

41. *Digest of the Constitution, Laws, and Decisions of the Ancient Order of United Workmen of Michigan* (Detroit, 1891). *State vs. Citizens Benefit Association,* 6 Mo. Appeals, 163 (1883).

42. J. S. Shropshire, *Knights of Pythias Common Law and Legal Text Book . . .* (Omaha, Nebraska, 1885); M. L. Marks et. al., *Ancient Order of Forester's Manual: A Digest and Commentary on the General Laws and Customs of the A.O.F. . . .* (New York, 1880), v.

43. *Origin and Aims of the Ancient Order of United Workmen.* Emphasis in the original.

44. Weber, "Protestant Sects," 307, 308; *Journal of Proceedings of the Third Annual Session of the National Fraternal Congress,* 5. Urban figures cited in Stuart M. Blumin, "The Social Implications of Economic Growth," in Stanley L. Engerman and Robert E. Gallman, *The Cambridge Economic History of the United States, volume 2 the Long Nineteenth* (New York: Cambridge University Press, 2008), 840. On Weber in the United States see Lawrence A. Scaff, *Max Weber in America* (Princeton: Princeton University Press, 2011).

45. Weber, "Protestant Sects," 322. Kaufman, *For the Common Good?,* ch. 5, explores the relationship between fraternalism and the American labor movement. On Weber's Germany see George Steinmetz, *Regulating the Social: The Welfare State and Local Politics in Imperial Germany* (Princeton: Princeton University Press, 1993).

46. Mutual aid in various forms was not unknown to nineteenth-century American labor unions. See Bruce Laurie, *Artisans into Workers: Labor in Nineteenth-Century America* (Urbana: University of Illinois Press, 1997/1989), esp. 50 and Sean Wilentz, *Chants Democratic: New York City and the Rise of the American Working Class, 1788–1850* (New York: Oxford University Press, 2004/1984), 56, 346.

47. Quotes in Leon Fink, *In Search of the Working Class: Essays in American Labor History and Political Culture* (Urbana: University of Illinois Press, 1994), 19, 20. On the Knights of Labor and their downfall see Kim Voss, *The Making of American Exceptionalism: The Knights of Labor and Class Formation in the Nineteenth Century* (Ithaca, NY: Cornell University Press, 1993); Leon Fink, *Workingman's Democracy: The Knights of Labor and American Politics* (Urbana: University of Illinois Press, 1983).

48. Sumner, *What Social Classes Owe To Each Other*, 86.

49. Karl Marx, "Bastiat and Carey," Martin Nicolaus trans., *Grundrisse: Foundations of the Critique of Political Economy* (New York: Penguin, 1973), 890, 891.

50. *Origin and Aims of the Ancient Order of United Workmen.* Kaufman, *For the Common Good?*, ch. 5, makes the claim concerning Knights of Labor defections. See also Martin Shefter, "Trade Unions and Political Machines: The Organization and Disorganization of the American Working Class in the Late Nineteenth Century," in Ira Katznelson and Aristide R. Zoberg, eds., *Working-Class Formation: Nineteenth-Century Patterns in Western Europe and the United States* (Princeton: Princeton University Press, 1986), esp. 221–222.

51. See Witt, *Accidental Republic,* ch. 3. Witt demonstrates the ideological screening out of the wageworker's risk.

52. Mariner Kent, *Handbook and Directory of the Ancient Order of Foresters of America . . .* (New York, 1893), 18, 19, 23. On the fraternal response to illness see Whaples and Buffum, "Fraternalism, Paternalism, the Family, and the Market," table 4.

53. Samuel Gompers, *Seventy Years of Life and Labor: An Autobiography of Samuel Gompers,* Nick Salvatore, ed. (Ithaca, NY: ILR Press, 1984/1925), 16. James B. Kennedy, *Beneficiary Features of American Trade Unions* (Baltimore, 1908) 12, 43.

54. U.S. Congress, *Report of the Committee of the Senate upon the Relations between Labor and Capital, and Testimony Taken by the Committee* (4 vols., Washington, DC, 1885): 1:396, 1090, 1094. On railroad brotherhoods see Walter Licht, *Working for the Railroad: The Organization of Work in the Nineteenth Century* (Princeton: Princeton University Press, 1983), 207. On Jay Gould and risk see also Richard White, *Railroaded: The Transcontinentals and the Making of Modern America* (New York: W.W. Norton & Co., 2011), 191.

55. Jacob Greene, *Cooperative Life Insurance,* (Hartford, 1878), 5.

56. Frederick Hoffman, *History of the Prudential Insurance Company of America, 1875–1900* (Newark, 1900), 113, 316. On contract and social thought see Stanley, *From Bondage to Contract.*

57. Homans, "Assessment Life Insurance"; "The Revolt Against the Multiplication Table," *Travelers Record,* July 1881; "True Co-operation," *Travelers Record,* April 1886.

58. The "pure" assessment societies often went by the name "Cooperative Life Insurance." "Eleven Thousand Victims of Miscalculation," *Insurance Times,* December 1885; "The Marriage Insurance Game," *Travelers Record,* March 1882; *Chicago Herald* quoted in "Matrimonial Insurance in Tennessee," *Travelers Record,* August 1883.

59. *Testimony Taken before the Joint Committee of the Senate and Assembly of the State of New York to Investigate and Examine into the Business and Affairs of Life Insurance Companies* (Albany, 1905), 11–14; Roger L. Ransom and Richard Sutch, "Tontine Insurance and the Armstrong Investigation: Case of Stifled Innovation, 1868–1905," *The Journal of Economic History* 47, no. 2 (June 1987): 385. See also Douglass North, "Capital Accumulation in Life Insurance Between the Civil War and the Investigation of 1905," in William Miller, ed., *Men in Business* (Cambridge: Harvard University Press, 1952), 238–253; Morton Keller, *The Life Insurance Enterprise, 1885–1910* (Cambridge: Harvard University Press, 1963), esp. 53, table 1; and 63, table 2; Lance Davis and Robert Gallman, *Evolving Financial Markets and International Capital Flows: Britain, the Americas, and Australia, 1865–1914* (New York: Cambridge University Press, 2001), 283–291.

60. Figures cited in Ransom and Sutch, "Tontine Insurance," 385.

61. On the origins of tontine see David R. Weir, "Tontines, Public Finance, and Revolution in France and England, 1688–1789," *The Journal of Economic History* 49, no. 1 (March 1989): 95–124. For Equitable figures see *Report of Senate Committee Appointed to Investigate Tontine Insurance* (Columbus, OH, 1885), 11.

62. See "Life Insurance As an Investment," Box 4A, Folder 2, Equitable Archives, AXA Financial Corporation(hereafter cited as "EAXA"); "Popular Fallacies Regarding Life Assurance Considered and Objections Answered," Box 67A, Folder 2, EAXA; "The Following Information is of Importance to Every Business Man," Box 4A, Folder 3, EAXA; "Words to Business Men, An Endowment Policy is the Best Investment," Box 67A, Folder 2, EAXA. Emphasis in the original.

63. "Popular Fallacies Regarding Life Assurance Considered and Objections Answered." On retirement and pensions see Hendrik Hartog, *Someday All This Will Be Yours: A History of Inheritance and Old Age* (Cambridge: Harvard University Press, 2012); Roger L. Ransom, Richard Sutch, and Samuel W. Williamson, "Inventing Pensions: The Origins of the Company-Provided Pension in the United States, 1900–1940," in K. Warner Schaie and W. Andrew Achenbaum, eds., *Societal Impact on Aging: Historical Perspectives,* (New York: Springer, 1993), 45–73.

64. "Extracts from the 39th Annual Report of the Connecticut Mutual Life Insurance Company," *Christian Union,* February 26, 1885; "The Truth About Tontines," Box4A, Folder 2, EAXA; "Facts! The Tontine Saving Fund," Box 4A, Folder 2, EAXA; "Tontine. What it Is, How it Works," Box 4A, Folder 2, EAXA. See also Jacob L. Greene, *Papers Relating to Tontine Insurance Issued by the Connecticut Mutual Life Insurance Co., 1885–1888* (Hartford, 1888). Emphasis in the original.

65. "Tontine Insurance Again," *Milwaukee Sentinel,* May 20, 1885; *Report of Senate Committee Appointed to Investigate Tontine Insurance* (Columbus, OH, 1885), 204.

66. *Report of the Special Committee to Investigate Tontine Insurance* (Albany, 1885), 66; "Five Years' Experience of the Tontine Plan of Life Assurance," Box 4A, Folder 3, EAXA; *Report of the Special Committee to Investigate Tontine Insurance,* 66.

67. Max Weber, *The Protestant Ethic and the "Spirit" of Capitalism and Other Writings* (New York: Penguin, 2002/1904), 119, 117, 120. Emphasis in the original.

68. Werner Sombart, *Economic Life in the Modern Age,* Nico Steher & Reiner Grundmann, eds. (New Brunswick: Transaction Publishers, 2001/1902), 232.

69. *Report of Senate Committee Appointed to Investigate Tontine Insurance,* 174, 43, 202.

70. *Report of the Special Committee to Investigate Tontine Insurance,* 20; "Memo for Mr. Hyde, May 15th, 1876," Carton 12, Folder 36, Equitable Collection, Baker Library Historical Collections, Harvard Business School; "Memorandum for the President December 13th, 1888," Carton 12, Folder 21, Equitable Collection. See also "Memorandum for the Vice-President, January 7th, 1888," Carton 12, Folder 21, Equitable Collection.

71. On the Mercantile Trust see H. Peers Brewer, "Eastern Money and Western Mortgages in the 1870s," *Business History Review* 50, no. 3 (Autumn 1976): 361–371. For policy estimate see Ransom and Sutch, "Tontine Insurance," 378.

72. On the Big Three and Albany see Keller, *Life Insurance Enterprise,* pt. 5. Lobbying figure cited in *Testimony Taken before the Joint Committee,* 11–14. See also *Frances H. Simons v. New York Life Insurance Company,* 38 Hun 309 (1885) and Ellerbe W. Carter, "Suits for Accounting on Tontine Life Insurance Policies," *Virginia Law Review* 2, no.1 (October 1914): 18–32.

73. *Testimony Taken before the Joint Committee,* 11–14.

74. Whaples and Buffum, "Fraternalism, Paternalism, the Family, and the Market," emphasizes how income growth fueled demand for the rise of insurance in this period.

75. On the pure assessment system and accident certificates see *Travelers Record,* July 1885, and "Insurance Notes," *Independent,* December 20, 1877. McConoughe and Patterson letters in *Travelers Record,* February 1880; *Travelers Record,* September 1878. For railroad classifications see Travelers Insurance Companies, *Accident Manual* (Hartford, 1885), 44–48. On agents' attempts to canvas railroad workplaces see Hatch and Woodman to George E. Todd, May 31 1879, Box 17, Warshaw Collection of Business Americana, Insurance Collection, Smithsonian National Museum of American History.

76. *Travelers Record,* September 1884; *Travelers Record,* June 1878; *Travelers Record,* February 1880. For miner, iron, and steel-worker classifications see "Railroad classifications" in Travelers Insurance Companies, *Accident Manual* (Hartford, 1885), 48–56. More generally, on the physical and psychic perils of industrialization in this era see Jason Puskar, *Accident Society: Fiction, Collectivity, and the Production of Chance* (Palo Alto, CA: Stanford University Press, 2012); Arwen P. Mohun, "On the Frontier of the *Empire of Chance*: Statistics, Accidents, and Risk in Industrializing America," *Science in Context* 8, no. 3 (September 2005): 337–357; Barbara Young Welke, *Recasting American Liberty: Gender, Race, Law, and the Railroad Revolution, 1865–1920* (New York: Cambridge University Press, 2001).

77. Hoffman, *History of the Prudential,* 65, 159; *The Metropolitan* 17, no. 7 (n.d., probably July 1892); Stalson, *Marketing Life Insurance,* appendix 21.

78. Wright, "Life Insurance in the United States," 149. On children's insurance in this era see Viviana A. Rotman Zelizer, *Pricing the Priceless Child: The Changing Social Value of Children* (Princeton: Princeton University Press, 1994), ch. 4.

79. John F. Dryden, *Addresses and Papers on Life Insurance,* 37, 48; and (on the 1870s) 15, 137, 86. On Hoffman, race, and industrial insurance see Bouk, "The Science of

Difference" and Beatrix Hoffman, "Scientific Racism, Insurance, and Opposition to the Welfare State: Frederick L. Hoffman's Transatlantic Journey," *The Journal of the Gilded Age and Progressive Era* 2, no. 2 (April 2003): 150–190.

80. *Testimony Taken before the Joint Committee*, 1934, 2167, 3714; *Commercial and Financial Chronicle* LII (1891): 738–739, quoted in Keller, *Life Insurance Enterprise*, 142. Industrial policies were "non-participating," that is, they paid no dividends.

81. McCurdy quoted in Keller, *Life Insurance Enterprise*, 140.

82. See Keller, *Life Insurance Enterprise*, ch. 10, on general on investment performance dynamics. On the rates of return of various investments see Zartman, *Life Insurance Investments*, 48.

83. On the role of life insurance corporations in forging a national capital market, see Davis and Gallman, *Evolving Financial Markets and International Capital Flows*, 283-291.

84. Kaufman, *For the Common Good?*, 27, identifies 1910 as the numerical peak.

85. *Journal of Proceedings of the First Annual Session of the National Fraternal Congress* (Poughkeepsie, NY, 1886), 1–2.

86. *Proceedings of the Supreme Lodge of the Ancient Order of United Workmen* . . . (Nashville, 1879), 17, 20, 25, 67, 76, 91.

87. *Proceedings of the Supreme Lodge of the Ancient Order of United Workmen* (Boston, 1880), 175, 179, 174, 181; *Proceedings of the Supreme Lodge of the Ancient Order of United Workmen* (Detroit, 1881), 370.

88. *State v. Miller* 66 Iowa 26 (1885).

89. *Journal of Proceedings of the First Annual Session of the National Fraternal Congress* (Poughkeepsie, NY, 1886), 1–2.

90. *Journal of Proceedings of the Third Annual Session of the National Fraternal Congress*, 45, 13, 49; *Journal of Proceedings of the Fourth Annual Session of the National Fraternal Congress*, 18; *Journal of Proceedings of the Seventh Annual Session of the National Fraternal Congress* (Poughkeepsie, NY, 1894), 48.

91. See, for instance, *Com. v. National Mutual Aid Association* 94 Pa. 481 (1880); *Com. V. Equitable Benefit Association* 137 Pa. 412 (1890); *Dickinson v. Grand Lodge of the Ancient Order of United Workmen* 159 Pa. 258 (1893).

92. On lack of pecuniary motive see, for instance, *Northwestern Masonic Aid Association v. Jones* 154 Pa. 99 (1893); *International Fraternal Alliance v. State* 86 Md. 550 (1898); *Tice v. Supreme Lodge of the Knights of Pythias* 123 Mo. App. 85 (1904). On the presence of a lodge see *Grand Lodge of the Ancient Order of United Workmen v. Edwards* 27 Ky. L. Rep 469 (1905); *Supreme Lodge of the Knights of Pythias v. Vandiver* 213 Mo. 187 (1908). On lack of "legal reserve" see *State ex rel. Covenant Mutual Benefit Association v. Root* 83 Wis. 667 (1893).

93. Leading cases were *Commonwealth v. Wetherbee* 105 Mass. 160 (1870); *State v. Standard Life* 38 Ohio 281 (1882); *State v. Miller* 66 Iowa 26 (1885); *Farmer v. State* 69 Tex. 561 (1888); *Drum v. Benton* 13 App. D.C. 25 (1898). See also William C. Niblack, *The Law of Voluntary Societies and Mutual Benefit Insurance* (Chicago, 1888), sects. 162, 166, 384; Frederick Hampden Bacon, *A Treatise on the Law of Benefit Societies* . . . , vol. 1 (St. Louis, 1904), esp. sect. 78; "What Constitutes Insurance," *American Law Reports* 63, 711 (1929): 30–42.

Notes to Pages 228–233

94. See *Smoot v. Bankers Life Association* 138 Mo. App. 438 (1909).
95. See *Bolton v. Bolton* 73 Me. 299 (1882); *State ex rel. Atty. Gen. v. Merchants Exchange Mutual Benevolent Society* 72 Mo. 146 (1880); *Berry v. Knights Templars' & M. Life Indemnity Co.* 46 Fed. 439 (1891).
96. *Bolton v. Bolton* 73 Me. 299 (1882).
97. *Lehman v. Clark* 174 Ill. 279 (1898).
98. Dawson, "Fraternal Life Insurance," 131–133; Meyer, "Fraternal Insurance," 260, 277. Kennedy, *Pythian History*, 216.
99. Sackett, *History of Fraternal Benefit Societies*, 44.
100. "Official Circular No. 2. Grand Lodge, New York, November, 1899," and "Finance Report for 1890," both printed in *Reports of the Knights of Honor* (1890), bound volume in the printed materials collection of the Library of Congress.
101. On the growth of trust companies, whose numbers increased from sixty-three in 1889 to 1,079 in 1909, see Davis and Gallman, *Evolving Financial Markets*, 201. On the Farmers Loan and Security Trust Company and its growth see Clay Herrick, *Trust Companies: Their Organization, Growth, and Management* (New York, 1909), 6. On Peabody see "The New President of the Mutual Life Insurance Company," *The Weekly Underwriter*, December 23, 1905
102. "Official Circular No. 1. Grand Lodge, State of New Jersey, October 15, 1898," in *Reports of the Knights of Honor* (1900), bound volume in the printed materials collection of the Library of Congress.

7. TRADING THE FUTURE

Epigraph: House Committee on Agriculture, *Fictitious Dealings in Agricultural Products: Hearings on H.R. 392, 2699, and 3870,* 52nd Cong., 3rd sess., 1892, 186.

1. Between 1875 and 1905 organized commodities futures exchanges appeared at the Chicago Board of Trade, New York Produce Exchange, New York Cotton Exchange, St. Louis Merchant's Exchange, Kansas City Board of Trade, Baltimore Corn and Flour Exchange, Toledo Board of Trade, New Orleans Cotton Exchange, Minneapolis Chamber of Commerce, Wichita Board of Trade, San Francisco Chamber of Commerce, Galveston Cotton Exchange, Detroit Board of Trade, Philadelphia Grain Exchange, Milwaukee Chamber of Commerce, Duluth Board of Trade, Omaha Grain Exchange, Seattle Grain Exchange, Portland Grain Exchange, New York Petroleum Exchange, Bradford Petroleum Exchange, and Oil City Petroleum Exchange. See Jerry W. Markhan, *The History of Commodity Futures Trading and Its Regulation* (New York: Praeger, 1987), 7, 8; S. S. Huebner, "The Function of Produce Exchanges," in Emory R. Johnson, ed., *American Produce Exchange Markets* (Philadelphia, 1911), 2; Henry D. Lloyd, "Making Bread Dear," *North American Review,* August 1883, 118; and Merrill A. Teague, "Bucket Shop Sharks," *Everybody's Magazine,* 4 pts. (June–September 1906), pt. 1 (June), 723–725.
2. House Committee on Agriculture, *Fictitious Dealings in Agricultural Products: Hearings on H.R. 392, 2699, and 3870,* 52nd Cong., 3rd sess., 1892, 11.
3. Ibid., 169.

4. The classic novel is Frank Norris, *The Pit: A Story of Chicago* (New York, 1903). For social-scientific discussions see Albert C. Stevens, "'Futures' in the Wheat Market," *Quarterly Journal of Economics* 2, no. 1 (October 1887): 37–63; and Henry Crosby Emery, *Speculation on the Stock and Produce Exchanges of the United States* (New York, 1896). For only a few examples of print journalism see Van Buren Denslow, "Board of Trade Morality," *North American Review,* October 1883, 372–388; Richard Wheatley, "The New York Produce Exchange," *Harper's Monthly Magazine,* July 1886, 189–219; Egerton R. Williams, "Thirty Years in the Grain Trade," *North American Review,* July 1895, 24–35; and Charles Conant, "The Function of the Stock and Produce Exchanges," *Atlantic Monthly,* April 1903, 434.

5. *Fictitious Dealings,* 246.

6. For uses of these terms see, for instance, *Fictitious Dealings,* 244; *Lyon v. Culbertson,* 83 Ill. 33 (1876); *McGrew v. City Produce Exchange,* 85 Tenn. 572 (1886); and Senate Committee on Agriculture, Subcommittee on Agricultural Depression, *Agricultural Depression: Causes and Remedies,* 53rd Cong., 3rd sess., 1895, S. Rep. 787, 33.

7. The epistemological stakes of both futures and bucket shop trading has been established by Roy Kreitner, *Calculating Promises: The Emergence of Modern American Contract Doctrine* (Palo Alto, CA: Stanford University Press, 2007), esp. ch. 6; Ann Fabian, *Card Sharps and Bucket Shops: Gambling in Nineteenth-Century America* (New York: Routledge, 1999), ch. 4; William Cronon, *Nature's Metropolis: Chicago and the Great West* (New York: Norton, 1992), ch. 3.

8. Henry Crosby Emery, "The Place of the Speculator in the Theory of Distribution," *Publications of the American Economic Association* 1, no. 1 (February 1900): 105.

9. *Board of Trade v. Christie,* 198 U.S. 236 (1905). See also Kreitner, *Calculating Promises,* 122.

10. In underscoring the epistemological stakes of this era of capitalist transformation, this chapter follows James Livingston, *Pragmatism and the Political Economy of Cultural Revolution, 1850–1940* (Chapel Hill: University of North Carolina Press, 1997).

11. See *Barnard v. Backhaus,* 52 Wisc. 593 (1881), 599.

12. The description of Sawyer's business throughout this section is taken from *Fictitious Dealings,* 29–40, 64–71.

13. Approximately 70 percent of the acreage in Minnesota and the Dakotas in the early 1890s was in wheat, and 85 percent of that wheat was exported. See C. Knick Harley, "Transportation, the World Wheat Trade, and the Kuznets Cycle, 1850–1913," *Explorations in Economic History* 17, no. 3 (July 1980): 232.

14. See Lloyd, "Making Bread Dear," 121; Ronald Findlay and Kevin H. O'Rourke, "Commodity Market Integration, 1500–2000," in Michael D. Bordo, Alan M. Taylor, and Jeffrey G. Williamson, eds., *Globalization in Historical Perspective* (Chicago: University of Chicago Press, 2003), 41–43.

15. *Fictitious Dealings,* 31–32, 67.

16. Ibid., 33–34, 246.

17. Ibid., 34. Any precise number is an educated guess. See *Fictitious Dealings,* 245.

18. See Cronon, *Nature's Metropolis,* 97–148.

19. Minutes, April 5, 1877, Board of Managers, New York Produce Exchange, Archives of the New York Historical Society. See also Jeffrey C. Williams, "The Origins of Futures Markets," *Agricultural History* 56, no. 1 (January 1982): 306–316.

20. The organized exchanges were tight-lipped about trading practices in the public record but fantastical descriptions of trading can be found in legal testimony. See especially the testimony throughout in U.S. Supreme Court Briefs and Records, no. 280, *Board of Trade,* 198 U.S. 236, which totals 1,562 pages. See also *Fictitious Dealings* and Emery, *Speculation,* 32–74.

21. See Board of Trade of the City of Chicago, *Twenty-fourth Annual Report of the Trade and Commerce of Chicago for the Year Ended December 31, 1881* (Chicago, 1882), 25; Board of Trade, *The Thirty-third Annual Report of the Trade and Commerce of Chicago for the Year Ended December 31, 1890* (Chicago, 1891), 155; Board of Trade of Minneapolis, *Annual Report* (Minneapolis, 1891), 43.

22. *Fictitious Dealings,* 34.

23. For a listing of commodities traded see Board of Trade of the City of Chicago, *The Thirty-fifth Annual Report of the Trade and Commerce of Chicago for the Year Ending December 31st, 1892* (Chicago, 1893), 2–249.

24. See Stuart Banner, *Anglo-American Securities Regulation: Cultural and Political Roots, 1690–1860* (New York: Cambridge University Press, 2002); Rita Birla, *Stages of Capital: Law, Culture, and Market Governance in Late Colonial India* (Durham: Duke University Press, 2009).

25. *Fictitious Dealings,* 302.

26. See David Hochfelder, "'Where the Common People Could Speculate:' The Ticker, Bucket Shops, and the Origins of Popular Participation in Financial Markets, 1880–1920," *Journal of American History* 93, no. 2 (September 2006): 335–358.

27. For descriptions of bucket shops see *Fictitious Dealings,* 53–59, 94, 125, 152, 165, 175, 180, 187, 230, 246, 281, 305; John Hill, Jr., *Gold Bricks of Speculation* (Chicago, 1904), 19–93; Patton Thomas, "Bucket Shops in Speculation," *Munsey's Magazine,* October 1900, 68–70; "Bucket Shop Sharks," pt. 1, 723–725; pt. 2, 33–43; pt. 3, 245–254; pt. 4, 398–408; C. C. Christie, "Bucket Shop vs. the Board of Trade," *Everybody's Magazine,* November 1906, 707–713; Christie, *Shall the Chicago Board of Trade . . . Be Allowed to FORM A TRUST in the Great Agricultural Staples of the United States?* (Kansas City, 1906). See also Cedric B. Cowing, *Populists, Plungers, and Progressives: A Social History of Stock and Commodity Speculation, 1890–1936* (Princeton: Princeton University Press, 1965), 25–74, and Fabian, *Card Sharps and Bucket Shops,* ch. 4.

28. Legal cases are the most effective register of the wide presence of bucket-shop trading in commodities futures. See, in Alabama, *Queen City Stock & Grain Co. v. Cunningham,* 29 So. 583 (1900); in Arkansas, *Fortenbury v. State,* 1 S.W. 58 (1886); in Colorado, *Pendleton v. Smissaert,* 29 P. 521 (Col. Ct. App. 1892); in Connecticut, *State v. Flint,* 28 A. 28 (1893); in the District of Columbia, *Lappin v. District of Columbia,* 22 App. D.C. 68 (D.C. Cir. 1903); in Georgia, *Dancy v. Phelan,* 10 S.E. 205 (1888); in Indiana, *Fleming v. Yost,* 36 N.E. 705 (1894); in Iowa, *People's Savings Bank of Des Moines v. Gifford,* 79 N.W. 63 (1899); in Kansas, *Carey v. Myers,* 141 P. 602 (1914); in Kentucky, *Smith v. Western Union Telegraph,* 2 S.W. 483 (1887); in Louisiana, *State ex. rel. v. Shakespeare,* 6 So. 592 (1889); in Michigan, *People v.*

Hess, 48 N.W. 181 (1891); in Minnesota and North Dakota, *Merchants National Bank of Grand Forks v. Sullivan,* 65 N.W. 924 (1896); in Missouri, *State v. Crab,* 26 S.W. 548 (1894); in Nebraska, *Watte v. Wickerman,* 43 N.W. 249 (1889); in North Carolina, *State v. Clayton,* 50 S.E. 866 (1905); in Ohio, *Cone v. Bright,* 68 N.E. 3 (1903); in Oregon, *Mellott v. Downing,* 64 P. 393 (1901); in Pennsylvania and Maryland, *Baxter v. Deneen,* 57 A. 601 (Md. Ct. App. 1903); in Tennessee, *McGrew v. City Produce Exchange,* 4 S.W. 38 (1886); in Texas, *Goldstein v. the State,* 36 S.W. 278 (Tex. Ct. Crim. App. 1896); in Utah, *Overholt v. Burbridge,* 79 P. 561 (1905); and in Vermont, *State v. Corcoran,* 50 A. 1110 (1901). See also Teague, "Bucket Shop Sharks" and T. Henry Dewey, *Legislation against Speculation and Gambling in the Forms of Trade, Including "Futures," "Options," and "Short Sales"* (New York, 1905), 13–14. The predominantly rural state of West Virginia actually had legislation condoning bucket shops.

29. See for instance, Teague, "Bucket Shop Sharks," pt. 2, 41; and Sereno Pratt, *The Work of Wall Street* (New York, 1903), 381.
30. Bucket shops in the East, whose heyday appears to have been after 1900, tended to deal more in stocks while bucket shops in the West usually dealt in grain futures and those in the South in cotton futures. See Dewey, *Legislation against Speculation and Gambling,* 11, "Number of Bucket Shops Closed," *New York Times* (March 28, 1895). See also Hochfelder, "'Where the Common People Could Speculate.'"
31. Quoted in Hill, *Gold Bricks,* 54.
32. For the example of the Chicago Board of Trade's regulation of itself see Jonathan Lurie, *The Chicago Board of Trade, 1859–1905: The Dynamics of Self-Regulation* (Urbana: University of Illinois Press, 1979), 23–52. On contract language see Julius Aroni, *Futures* (New Orleans, 1882).
33. *Pickering v. Cease,* 79 Ill. 328 (1875), 329.
34. On the common law of contract and wagering, see Kreitner, *Calculating Promises.*
35. *Pickering,* 79 Ill., 329. *Pixley v. Boynton,* 79 Ill. 351, 353. On "executory contracts" see Morton J. Horwitz, *The Transformation of American Law, 1870–1960: The Crises of Legal Orthodoxy* (New York: Oxford University Press, 1994), 160–210; Kreitner, *Calculating Promises.*
36. On the problem of establishing intent see Aroni, *Futures;* T. Henry Dewey, *A Treatise on Contracts for Future Delivery and Commercial Wagers, Including "Options," "Futures," and "Short Sales"* (New York, 1886); Morton John Stevenson, "Gambling Contracts," *Michigan Law Journal* 35 (1897): 35–40; and Kreitner, *Calculating Promises.* The case in which the Illinois court developed the doctrine of contemplating delivery and moved away from *Pickering* was *Pixley v. Boynton.*
37. *Barnard,* 53 Wis., 600. See also, in Illinois, *Beveridge v. Hewitt,* 8 Ill. App. 467 (Ill. Ct. App., 1881); in Alabama, *Hawley v. Bibb,* 69 Ala. 52 (1881); in Iowa, *Melchert v. American Union Telegraph Co.,* 11 F. 193 (Cr. Ct., 1882); and in Kansas, *Cobb v. Prell,* 15 F. 774 (Cr. Ct., 1883).
38. *Irwin v. Williar,* 110 U.S. 499 (1884). Post-*Irwin* decisions unfavorable to futures trading included, in Indiana, *Whitesides v. Hunt,* 97 Ind. 191 (1884); in Illinois, *Pearce v. Foote,* 113 Ill. 228 (1885); in Missouri, *Crawford v. Spencer,* 4 S.W. 713 (1887); the Supreme Court decision *Embrey v. Jemison,* 131 U.S. 336 (1889); in

Ohio, *Lester v. Buel*, 30 N.E. 821 (1892); in Iowa, *First National Bank of Creston v. Carrole*, 45 N.W. 304 (1890); in Maryland, *Billingslea v. Smith*, 26 A. 1077 (Md. Ct. App., 1893); in Missouri, *Connor v. Black*, 24 S.W. 184 (1893). Not coincidentally, the organized exchanges found it in their own interest to keep members' disputes out of the court. For the example of the Chicago Board of Trade see Lurie, *The Chicago Board of Trade*, 23–52.

39. See, for example, *The Minnesota State Farmers' Alliance: Constitution and By-laws, Declaration of Principles, Resolutions, Officials, Etc.* (St. Paul, 1890), 15.

40. See *Proceedings of the Annual Session of the Farmers and Laborers Union of America at St. Louis, Mo., December 3 to 7, 1889* (Washington, DC, 1890), 51; *Proceedings of the Annual Session of the Farmers and Industrial Union at Ocala, Florida, December 2 to 8, 1890* (Washington, DC, 1891), 33; and *Proceedings of the National Farmers' Alliance Eleventh Annual Meeting, Omaha, Nebraska, January 27, 28, and 29, 1891* (Des Moines, IA, 1891), 5.

41. See Dewey, *Legislation against Speculation and Gambling*, 13, 14; and Carl Parker, "Governmental Regulation in Produce Markets," in Johnson, ed., *American Produce Exchange Markets*, 126–155. For an example of state courts' nullifying the intent of the law through invoking "contemplating delivery," see Dewey, *A Treatise on Contracts*, 104.

42. The Senate held hearings as well in which representatives of the incorporated exchanges reiterated the same arguments. See *Dealings in "Options" and "Futures": Protests, Memorials and Arguments against Bills Introduced in the Fifty-second Congress, Issued by the New York Cotton Exchange, New Orleans Cotton Exchange, Board of Trade of the City of Chicago, New York Produce Exchange* (New York, 1892), 1–135.

43. *Fictitious Dealings*, 237, 235, 260, 268, 190; Senate Committee on Agriculture, Subcommittee on Agricultural Depression, *Agricultural Depression*, 33.

44. *Fictitious Dealings*, 282, 297, 266.

45. *Fictitious Dealings*, 282, 266; *Proceedings of the National Farmers' Alliance Eleventh Annual Meeting*, 1.

46. *Fictitious Dealings*, 55, 284, 206, 266, 206.

47. Ibid., 176.

48. Ibid., 226, 302, 303, 305.

49. Ibid., 22, 157, 123.

50. On the professionalization of speculation in general see also Fabian, *Card Sharps*, 188, 191, 195; Cowing, *Populists, Plungers, and Progressives*, 28–30; and Steve Fraser, *Every Man a Speculator: A History of Wall Street in American Life* (New York: Harper, 2006), 251.

51. *Fictitious Dealings*, 129.

52. *Fictitious Dealings*, 43, 157, 175–176. On the insurance of "society" as a whole see *Fictitious Dealings*, 139, 215, 227.

53. Ibid., 258, 274–275, 289.

54. Farmers' marketing cooperatives struggled on account of capital deficiencies. On the cooperative movement see, for example, in Sawyer's home state of Minnesota, Steven Keillor, *Cooperative Commonwealth: Co-ops in Rural Minnesota, 1859–1939* (St. Paul: Minnesota Historical Society Press, 2003).

55. See Macune's testimony in *Fictitious Dealings*, 252–255. In the twentieth century, farmers successfully lobbied for policies that involved greater state involvement in agricultural marketing. See Charles Postel, *The Populist Vision* (New York: Oxford University Press, 2007), ch. 5; Elizabeth Sanders, *Roots of Reform: Farmers, Workers, and the American State, 1877–1917* (Chicago: University of Chicago Press, 1999, part. 2; Daniel T. Rodgers, *Atlantic Crossings: Social Politics in a Progressive Age* (Cambridge: Belknap Press of Harvard University Press, 2000), ch. 8.

56. *Fictitious Dealings*, 33.

57. On the Hatch Bill vote see Cowing, *Populists, Plungers, and Progressives*, 18–22. The last hurrah in Congress for agrarian radicals critical of futures was the report on agricultural depression issued by Populist senator William A. Peffer. See Senate Committee on Agriculture, Subcommittee on Agricultural Depression, *Agricultural Depression*, 33. But see also U.S. Industrial Commission, *Report of the Industrial Commission on the Distribution of Farm Products* (Washington, DC, 1901).

58. Michael Kazin, *A Godly Hero: The Life of William Jennings Bryan* (New York: Anchor, 2007), 60.

59. For instance, in his exposé of bucket-shop trading in *Everybody's Magazine* in 1906 Teague estimated that the number of bucket shops increased from hundreds in the 1890s to easily thousands by the turn of the century. Teague, "Bucket Shop Sharks," pt. 4, 407.

60. For examples of dealers' critiques of bucket shops see *Fictitious Dealings*, 176, 125, 180, 206. Many "handlers" characterized bucket shops and boards of trade as similarly illegitimate. According to Charles Pillsbury, "in the bucket shop perhaps 99 per cent of the trading is illegitimate" whereas in the pits, "90 per cent is illegitimate." Pillsbury, in *Fictitious Dealings*, 187. See Christie, *Shall the Chicago Board of Trade*, 14.

61. *Fictitious Dealings*, 305.

62. Ibid., 125, 175. Christie, *Shall the Chicago Board of Trade*, 38.

63. See Fabian, *Card Sharps*, 150–203. Illinois, Missouri, and Ohio were the states with laws explicitly banning "options." See Dewey, *Legislation against Speculation and Gambling*, 13–14 and also Parker, "Governmental Regulation in Produce Markets."

64. The distinctions between an option and a future were inordinately confusing to contemporaries. See *Anti-Option Legislation: Paternal Interference with Business, Speech of Hon. John De Witt Warner of New York in the House of Representatives, Monday, June 18, 1894* (Washington, D.C., 1894), 6.

65. On the presence of options trading among members of organized exchanges, acknowledged by representatives of the exchanges, see *Fictitious Dealings*, 95, 167, 175, 182, 221, 245. See also Dewey, *A Treatise on Contracts*, 89. Options trading was always pervasive at the Milwaukee exchange. See "The Exchanges of Minneapolis, Duluth, Kansas City, Mo., Omaha, Buffalo, Philadelphia, Milwaukee and Toledo," in Johnson, *American Produce Exchange Markets*, 251.

66. Quoted in Dewey, *Legislation against Speculation and Gambling*, 52.

67. *New York and Chicago Grain and Stock Exchange v. Chicago Board of Trade*, 19 N.E. 855 (1889). Christie's complaint, see *Board of Trade*, 198 U.S., 236. See also Teague, "Bucket Shop Sharks," pt. 2 (July), 40, and Christie, "Bucket Shop vs. the Board of Trade," 713. On the "bucket-shop war," see also Lurie, *The Chicago Board of Trade*,

75–105, 168–199. With respect to conflict over the telegraph and monopolistic control of information see Richard Johns, *Network Nation: Inventing American Telecommunications* (Cambridge: Belknap Press of Harvard University, 2010), ch. 3.

68. *Board of Trade,* 198 U.S., 246.

69. *Board of Trade,* 198 U.S., 246. *Board of Trade v. O'Dell Commission,* 115 F. 574 (Ct. App., 1902), 587, 588. See also *Christie v. Board of Trade* 125 F. 161 (Ct. App., 1903), and *Board of Trade v. Donovan,* 121 F. 1012 (Ct. App., 1902). Christie, "Bucket Shop vs. the Board of Trade," 710. "When this species of gambling on the commercial and stock exchanges of the country ceases," that same district court held, "the bucket shops will disappear, and not before." *Board of Trade v. O'Dell Commission,* 115 F., 588. Christie, *Shall the Chicago Board of Trade,* 22. In an all-night session, the bill lost, 73–63. "Kills Board of Trade Bill," *New York Times,* May 8, 1905.

70. On the widespread legal doctrinal influence of *Christie,* see "Nature and Validity of 'Hedging' Transactions on the Commodity Market," *American Law Reports* 20 (1920): 1422; Edwin Patterson, "Hedging and Wagering on Produce Exchanges," *Yale Law Journal* 40, no. 6 (April 1931): 843–884. At the time, see "A Judicial Vindication," *Chicago Daily Tribune,* May 10, 1905; "Speculation According to the Supreme Court," *Wall Street Journal,* May 10, 1905.

71. Board of Trade of the City of Chicago, *The Forty-eighth Annual Report of the Trade and Commerce of Chicago for the Year Ended December 31st, 1905* (Chicago, 1906), xlix–li.

72. *Board of Trade,* 198 U.S., 246–249.

73. Christie, *Shall the Chicago Board of Trade,* 24.

74. Oliver Wendell Holmes, Jr. to Frederick Pollock, August 30, 1929, in Mark DeWolfe Howe, ed., *Holmes-Pollock Letters: The Correspondence of Mr. Justice Holmes and Sir Frederick Pollock, 1874–1932* (Cambridge, MA, 1941), 2:252. See Chauncey Wright, "The Winds and the Weather," *The Nation* (March 1867). On Wright's influence see Louis Menand, *The Metaphysical Club: A Story of Ideas in America* (New York: Farrar, Straus and Giroux, 2002), esp. ch. 9.

75. Morton White, *Social Thought in America: The Revolt Against Formalism* (Boston: Beacon Press, 1957). On Peirce see also Ian Hacking, *The Taming of Chance* (New York: Cambridge University Press, 1990), ch. 23. On Holmes see also Horwitz, *The Transformation of American Law, 1870–1960,* 454–463.

76. Charles Sanders Peirce, "The Fixation of Belief," *Popular Science Monthly* 12 (November 1877): 1–15.

77. On philosophical pragmatism's emphasis on uncertainty see James T. Kloppenberg, *Uncertain Victory: Social Democracy and Progressivism in European and American Thought, 1870–1920* (New York: Oxford University Press, 1988). See also John Dewey, *The Quest for Certainty: A Study of the Relation of Knowledge and Action* (New York: Capricorn, 1981/1929).

78. Ignas K. Skrupskelis and Elizabeth M. Berkeley, eds., *The Correspondence of William James: 1856–1877* (Charlottesville: University of Virginia Press, 1995), 525. For distinctions that should be made between Holmes's and James's thought, see David A. Hollinger, "The 'Tough-Minded' Justice Holmes, Jewish Intellectuals, and the Making of an American Icon," in Hollinger, *Science, Jews, and Secular Culture:*

Studies in Mid-Twentieth-Century American Intellectual History (Princeton: Princeton University Press, 1998), 44. Oliver Wendell Holmes, Jr., to Harold Laski, March 29, 1917, in Mark DeWolfe Howe, ed., *Holmes-Laski Letters: The Correspondence of Mr. Justice Holmes and Harold J. Laski, 1916–1935* (Cambridge: Harvard University Press, 1963), 1: 70; Holmes to Laski, January 28, 1927, *ibid.*, 2: 917.

79. William James, *Essays in Radical Empiricism* (New York, 1912), 28, 16–17. First published as William James, "Does Consciousness Exist?" *Journal of Philosophy, Psychology, and Scientific Methods* 1 (1904): 477–491 (emphasis in the original).

80. On the question of truth and authority in pragmatism see John Patrick Diggins, *The Promise of Pragmatism: Modernism and the Crisis of Knowledge and Authority* (Chicago: University of Chicago, 1994).

81. William James, "Great Men, Great Thoughts, and the Environment," *The Atlantic Monthly,* October 1880, 442; William James, *The Will to Believe and Other Essays in Popular Philosophy* (New York, 1897), 149; William James, *Pragmatism: A New Name for Some Old Ways of Thinking* (Boston, 1907), 149, 150. On the "Will to Believe" and James's philosophy of chance see Jackson Lears, *Something for Nothing: A History of Luck in America* (New York: Viking, 2003), ch. 5.

82. Rayford Whittingham Logan, ed., *What the Negro Wants* (Chapel Hill: University of North Carolina Press, 1944), 58. The Jamesian influence on Du Bois is illustrated by Ross Posnock, *Color and Culture: Black Writers and the Making of the Modern Intellectual* (Cambridge: Harvard University Press, 2000).

83. *Board of Trade,* 198 U.S., 236.

84. See Livingston, *Pragmatism and the Political Economy of Cultural Revolution,* esp. ch. 8. A similar argument could be made linking the revival of pragmatism with the financialization of the American economy after the economic crisis of the 1970s. See the Epilogue.

85. *Board of Trade,* 198 U.S., 249.

86. James, *Pragmatism,* 80, emphasis added.

87. *Board of Trade,* 198 U.S., 236.

88. Emery, "The Place of the Speculator in the Theory of Distribution," 105. Allan Willett, *Economic Theory of Risk and Insurance* (New York: Columbia University Press, 1901), 135.

89. Arthur Hadley, *Economics* (New York, 1904), 112. *Board of Trade,* 198 U.S., 250.

90. James, *Pragmatism,* 80; *Board of Trade,* 198 U.S., 250.

91. Willett, *Economic Theory of Risk and Insurance,* 139.

92. See Caitlin Zaloom, *Out of the Pits: Traders and Technology from Chicago to London* (Chicago: University of Chicago Press, 2006).

8. THE TRUST QUESTION

Epigraph: Ron Chernow, *Titan: The Life of John D. Rockefeller, Sr.* (New York: Vintage, 1998), 153.

1. George W. Perkins, "The Modern Corporation," in E. R. A. Seligman, ed., *The Currency Problem and the Present Financial Situation* (New York: Columbia

University Press, 1908), 155. In this chapter I rely on an excellent biography of Perkins, John Arthur Garraty, *Right-Hand Man: The Life of George W. Perkins* (New York: Greenwood Press, 1978).

2. Perkins, "Modern Corporation," 155. Garraty, *Right-Hand Man,* 216.

3. George W. Perkins, "Profit-Sharing Plan of the United States Steel Corporation" (1907), in Box 20, George W. Perkins Papers, Columbia University Rare Book and Manuscript Library (hereafter cited as "GWPP").

4. $391 million from New York (State), *Report of the Joint Committee of the Senate and Assembly of the State of New York Appointed to Investigate the Affairs of Life Insurance Companies* (Albany, 1906), 41. 4.7 percent according to Lance Davis and Robert Gallman, *Evolving Financial Markets and International Capital Flows: Britain, the Americas, and Australia, 1865-1914* (Cambridge: Cambridge University Press, 2001), table 3:5c-1, p. 280.

5. Turn-of-the-twentieth-century corporate capitalists' preferences for organization and control is well known. See, for instance, Louis Galambos, "The Emerging Organizational Synthesis in Modern American History," *Business History Review* 44 (Autumn 1970): 270–290; Alfred D. Chandler, Jr., *The Invisible Hand: The Managerial Revolution in American Business* (Cambridge: Harvard University Press, 1993); Chandler, *Scale and Scope: The Dynamics of Industrial Capitalism* (Cambridge: Harvard University Press, 1990); JoAnne Yates, *Control Through Communications: The Rise of System in American Management* (Baltimore: The Johns Hopkins University Press, 1989). Chandler appreciates the role of financiers like Perkins, but ultimately attributes managers more power in the rise of the modern industrial corporation. Works that place greater emphasis on the role of finance capitalists like Perkins include Martin J. Sklar, *The Corporate Reconstruction of American Capitalism, 1890-1916: The Market, the Law, and Politics* (New York: Cambridge University Press, 1998); William Roy, *Socializing Capital: The Rise of the Large Industrial Corporation in America* (Princeton: Princeton University Press, 1997); Neil Fligstein, *The Transformation of Corporate Control* (Cambridge: Harvard University Press, 1993); James Livingston, *Origins of the Federal Reserve System: Money, Class, and Corporate Capitalism, 1890-1913* (Ithaca: Cornell University Press, 1990); Naomi R. Lamoreaux, *The Great Merger Movement in American Business, 1895-1904* (New York: Cambridge University Press, 1988); Gabriel Kolko, *The Triumph of Conservatism: A Re-Interpretation of American History, 1900-1916* (New York: Simon and Schuster, 1977/1963). On the role life insurance specifically as a template for industrial order see JoAnne Yates, *Structuring the Information Age: Life Insurance and Technology in the Twentieth Century* (Baltimore: Johns Hopkins University Press, 2005).

6. George W. Perkins, "Modern Industrialism: An Address before the Southern Commercial Congress . . ." (1911), Box 20, GWPP.

7. E. R. A. Seligman, *Principles of Economics* (New York, 1914), 655–656. Perkins, "Modern Industrialism." George W. Perkins, "Address Delivered by George W. Perkins. . . . Fourth Annual Convention . . . New York Life . . ." (1900), Box 20, GWPP. On a notion of social risk see Anson Rabinbach, "Social Knowledge, Social Risk, and the Politics of Industrial Accidents in Germany and France," in Dietrich

Rueschemeyer and Theda Skockpol, eds., *States, Social Knowledge, and the Origins of Modern Social Policies* (Princeton: Princeton University Press, 1995), 48–89. On the "social" see Daniel T. Rodgers, *Atlantic Crossings: Social Politics in a Progressive Age* (Cambridge: Harvard University Press, 2000); Rodgers, "In Search of Progressivism," *Reviews in American History* 10, no. 4 (December 1982): 113–132; Michael Willrich, *City of Courts: Socializing Justice in Progressive Era Chicago* (New York: Cambridge University Press, 2003); Jeffrey P. Sklansky, *The Soul's Economy: Market Society and Selfhood in American Thought, 1820–1920* (Chapel Hill: University of North Carolina Press, 2002); James Livingston, *Pragmatism and the Political Economy of Cultural Revolution, 1850–1940* (Chapel Hill: University of North Carolina Press, 1997); Dorothy Ross, *Origins of American Social Science* (New York: Cambridge University Press, 1992); Morton J. Horwitz, *The Transformation of American Law: The Crisis of Legal Orthodoxy, 1870–1960* (New York: Oxford University Press, 1992); Thomas L. Haskell, *The Emergence of Professional Social Science: The American Social Science Association and the Nineteenth-Century Crisis of Authority* (Chicago: University of Illinois Press, 1977).

8. Perkins, "The Financial Crisis of October 1907," Box 8, Folder "1907 Panic," GWPP.

9. On the economic causes of the panic of 1907 see Jon Moen and Ellis W. Tallman, "The Bank Panic of 1907: The Role of Trust Companies," *The Journal of Economic History* 52, no.3 (September 1992): 611–630; Kerry A. Odell and Marc D. Weidenmier, "Real Shock, Monetary Aftershock: The 1906 San Francisco Earthquake and the Panic of 1907," *The Journal of Economic History* 64, no. 4 (December 2004): 1002–1027. For a fuller narrative account see Ron Chernow, *The House of Morgan: An American Banking Dynasty and the Rise of Modern Finance* (New York: Grove Press, 1990), ch. 7.

10. For instance, before 1906 New York trusts were not legally required to carry any reserves whereas national banks carried a 25 percent reserve in specie or legal tender, which constrained their market operations. In 1906, New York passed a law demanding that trusts keep 5 percent of their deposits in the vault but this included specie, legal tender, and also less reliable national bank notes. Furthermore, not being part of the commercial banking system trust companies did not suffer drains on their reserves during crop season. Davis and Gallman, *Evolving Financial Markets and International Capital Flows*, 296.

11. Perkins, "The Financial Crisis of October 1907." See also U.S. House of Representatives, *Hearings before the Committee on Investigation of the United States Steel Corporation*, 8 vols., 62nd Cong., 2nd sess. (1911), 1613.

12. Perkins, "The Financial Crisis of October 1907."

13. "Preachers Exhort Depositors to Calm," *New York Times*, October 28, 1907.

14. Perkins to J.P. Morgan, April 20, 1906, Box 8, Folder "April–June 1906," GWPP. The events leading to the TC&I acquisition were the subject of numerous government investigations. See *United States v United States Steel Corporation et al.*, District Court, New Jersey, 223 Federal Reporter (1915); U.S. House of Representatives, *Hearings before the Committee;* and U.S. House of Representatives, *Report on the Investigation of the United States Steel Corporation*, 3 pts., 62nd Cong., 2nd sess. (1911).

15. *Hearings before the Committee,* 8:197. Perkins, "The Financial Crisis of October 1907." See Livingston, *Origins of the Federal Reserve System.*

16. Seligman, *Crisis of 1907,* 167, xxv. See, for instance, *Hearings before the Committee,* 3:1613.

17. See Garraty, *Right-Hand Man,* ch. 1.

18. See Garraty, *Right-Hand Man,* ch. 2. For the general context in the life insurance industry at the time, see Yates, *Structuring the Information Age,* part 1.

19. See Garraty, *Right-Hand Man,* 51, 52, 54.

20. Garraty, *Right-Hand Man,* 67. See Rodgers, *Atlantic Crossings,* on the late-nineteenth-century routes taken by American social reformers rather than insurance executives in Europe.

21. Lamoreaux, *The Great Merger Movement,* 2.

22. On colonial and early national corporations see Hendrik Hartog, *Public Property and Private Power: The Corporation of the City of New York in American Law, 1730–1870* (Ithaca: Cornell University Press, 1989); Pauline Maier, "The Revolutionary Origins of the American Corporation," *William and Mary Quarterly* 50, no.1 (January 1993): 51–84; Oscar and Mary Flug Handlin, "Origins of the American Business Corporation," *Journal of Economic History* 5, no.1 (May 1945): 8–17. On antebellum business corporations see Sean P. Adams, *Old Dominion, Industrial Commonwealth: Coal, Politics, and Economy in Antebellum America* (Baltimore: The Johns Hopkins University Press, 2004), ch. 5; Colleen A. Dunlavy, "From Citizens to Plutocrats: Nineteenth-Century Shareholder Voting Rights and Theories of the Corporation," and Naomi R. Lamoreaux, "Partnerships, Corporations, and the Limits on Contractual Freedom in U.S. History: An Essay in Economic, Law, and Culture," in Kenneth Lipartito and David B. Sicilia eds., *Constructing Corporate America: History, Politics, Culture* (New York: Oxford University Press, 2004), 29–93; Robert Wright, "Capitalism and the Rise of the Corporation Nation," in Michael Zakim and Gary J. Kornblith, eds., *Capitalism Takes Command: The Social Transformation of Nineteenth-Century America* (Chicago: University of Chicago Press, 2012), 145–168.

23. New York passed the first general incorporation law in 1846 and by 1875 they were more or less universal. On legal personality see James Willard Hurst, *The Legitimacy of the Business Corporation in the Law of the United States, 1780–1970* (Charlottesville: University of Virginia Press, 1970); Gregory Mark, "The Personification of the Business Corporation in American Law," *University of Chicago Law Review* 54, 4 (Autumn 1987): 1441–1483; Horwitz, *The Transformation of American Law, 1870–1960;* Herbert Hovenkamp, *Enterprise and American Law, 1836–1937* (Cambridge: Harvard University Press, 1991).

24. See Davis A. Moss, *When All Else Fails: Government as the Ultimate Risk Manager* (Cambridge: Harvard University Press, 2004), ch. 3.

25. On the railroad managers see Chandler, *Invisible Hand,* pt. 2; and Steven W. Usselman, *Regulating Railroad Innovation: Business, Technology, and Politics in America, 1840–1920* (New York: Cambridge University Press, 2002). On railroad finance see Richard White, *Railroaded: The Transcontinentals and the Making of Modern America* (New York: W.W. Norton & Co., 2011). On Morganization see Vincent P.

Carosso and Rose C. Carosso *The Morgans: Private International Bankers, 1854–1913* (Cambridge: Harvard University Press, 1987).

26. *Ninth Annual Report of the Massachusetts Bureau of Statistics and Labor* (Boston, 1878), 87–88. On Rockefeller see Ron Chernow, *Titan: The Life of John D. Rockefeller, Sr.* (New York: Vintage, 1998). On Carnegie see Harold C. Livesay, *Andrew Carnegie and the Rise of Big Business* (New York: Pearson Longman, 2007). David Nasaw, *Andrew Carnegie* (New York: Penguin, 2006).

27. See Sklar, *Corporate Reconstruction;* Hans B. Thorelli, *The Federal Antitrust Policy* (Baltimore: The Johns Hopkins Press, 1955); Tony Freyer, *Regulating Big Business: Antitrust in Great Britain and America, 1880–1990* (New York: Cambridge University Press, 1992); Charles W. McCurdy, "The Knight Sugar Decision of 1895 and the Modernization of American Corporation Law, 1859–1903" *Business History Review* 53, no. 3 (Autumn 1979): 304–342; McCurdy, "American Law and the Marketing Structure of the Large Corporation, 1875–1890," *Journal of Economic History* 38, no. 3 (September 1978): 631–649.

28. On partnership see Lamoreaux, "Partnerships, Corporations, and the Limits on Contractual Freedom." On the vitality of proprietary capitalism in manufactures see Phillip Scranton, *Proprietary Capitalism: The Textile Manufacture at Philadelphia, 1800–1885* (New York: Cambridge University Press, 1983); Scranton, *Endless Novelty: Specialty Production and American Industrialization, 1865–1925* (Princeton: Princeton University Press, 1997).

29. See "Personal Scrapbooks," GWPP; Perkins to Mrs. D.P. Kingsley, July 10, 1896, Letterbooks, GWPP.

30. On Populist demands see Charles Postel, *The Populist Vision* (New York: Oxford University Press, 2007); Elizabeth Sanders, *The Roots of Reform: Farmers, Workers, and the American State, 1877–1917* (Chicago: University of Chicago Press, 1999); Lawrence Goodwyn, *The Democratic Promise: The Populist Moment in America* (New York: Oxford University Press, 1976).

31. Christoper J. Cyphers, *The National Civic Federation and the Making of a New Liberalism, 1900–1915* (Westport, CT: Greenwood Publishing Group, 2002), 29.

32. *Chicago Conference on Trusts: Speeches, debates, resolutions, list of the delegates, committees, etc.* (Chicago: Civic Federation of Chicago, 1899), 43–49. Theodore Roosevelt, "The Trusts, the People, and the Square Deal," *Outlook,* November 18, 1911. Walter Lippmann, *Drift and Mastery: An Attempt to Diagnose the Current Unrest* (Madison, WI: University of Wisconsin Press, 1914), 129.

33. *Chicago Conference on Trusts,* 64. In this vein see also Herbert David Croly, *The Promise of American Life* (New York, 1911), 23, 409.

34. Perkins, "Wanted—A Constructive National Policy" (1911), Box 20, GWPP. Arthur Jerome Eddy, *The New Competition: An Examination of the Conditions Underlying the Radical Change That is Taking Place in the Commercial and Industrial World—the Change from a Competitive to a Cooperative Basis* (New York, 1912), 192. Corporate executives said the same before Congress in the midst of the Great Merger Movement. See U.S. Industrial Commission, *Preliminary Report on Trusts and Industrial Combinations,* vol. 1 (Washington, 1900), esp. 45, 1050; and Lamoreaux, *Great Merger Movement,* ch. 4. See also Charles R. Flint, "Industrial Consolida-

tions: What They Have Accomplished for Capital and Labor," *North American Review* (May 1901): 673; Henry Holt, "Competition," in *Morals in Modern Business: The Page Lecture Series* (New York, 1908): 68.

35. J. B. Clark, "Insurance and Business Profit," *The Quarterly Journal of Economics* 7, no. 1 (October 1892): 40–54.

36. Ibid. See also John Bates Clark, *The Distribution of Wealth: A Theory of Wages, Interest and Profit* (New York, 1902).

37. Frank Knight, *Risk, Uncertainty, and Profit* (New York: Cosmo, 2006/1921), 44, 337, 347–351, 359.

38. Garraty, *Right-Hand Man,* 79.

39. Ibid., 84–87.

40. Ibid.

41. See Kenneth Warren, *Big Steel: The First Century of the United States Steel Corporation, 1901–2001* (Pittsburgh: University of Pittsburgh Press, 2001); Thomas K. McCraw and Forest Reinhardt, "Losing to Win: U.S. Steel's Pricing, Investment Decisions, and Market Share, 1901–1938," *The Journal of Economic History* 49, no. 3 (September 1989): 594; Livesay, *Andrew Carnegie,* 116–117; Charles Schwab, "What May Be Expected in the Iron and Steel Industry," *North American Review,* 172 (May 1901), 655–664.

42. Vincent P. Carroso, *Investment Banking in America: A History* (Cambridge: Harvard University Press, 1970), ch. 3. Thomas R. Navin and Marian V. Sears, "The Rise of a Market for Industrial Securities, 1887–1902," *Business History Review* 29 (1955): 105–138; Davis and Gallman, *Evolving Financial Markets,* ch. 3. Julia C. Ott, *When Wall Street Met Main Street: The Quest for an Investors' Democracy* (Cambridge: Harvard University Press, 2011).

43. Perkins also secured the New York Security and Trust Company the job of "registrar" for the entire stock offering, a status that came with a cash fee, but also brought with it a lot of business. See New York (State), *Joint Committee of the Senate and Assembly of the State of New York to Investigate and Examine into the Business and Affairs of Life Insurance Companies Doing Business in the State of New York: Testimony* (10 vols., Albany, 1906),3:2879.

44. Garraty, *Right-Hand Man,* 158. Edmund Morris, *Theodore Rex* (New York: Random House, 2002), 64. "The Romance of Steel and Iron," *Munsey's Magazine* 36 (October 1906), 90.

45. Garraty, *Right-Hand Man,* 140. Fred V. Carstensen, ". . . a dishonest man is at least prudent': George W. Perkins and the International Harvester Steel Properties," *Business and Economic History,* 2nd series, 9 (1980): 87–102.

46. Thomas William Lawson, *Frenzied Finance: The Story of Amalgamated* (Boston, 1904).

47. Morton Keller, *The Life Insurance Enterprise, 1885–1910: A Study in the Limits of Corporate Power* (Cambridge: Harvard University Press, 1963), 77, and see ch. 15 on 1905 investigation. At this stage 74 percent of the assets of Perkins's New York Life, 57 percent of the Equitable's, and 54 percent of the Mutual's assets were held in negotiable securities.

48. New York (State), *Joint Committee,* 1:757.

49. Ibid., 3:2908.

50. Garraty, *Right-Hand Man,* 169. Louis Brandeis, *Life Insurance: The Abuses and the Remedies: An Address Delivered Before the Commercial Club of Boston* (Boston, 1905), 7. Brandies, *Other People's Money: And How the Bankers Use It* (Boston, 1913). On Brandeis's competitive ethos see Gerald Berk, *Louis D. Brandeis and the Making of Regulated Competition, 1900–1932* (New York: Cambridge University Press, 2009).

51. Typescript "United States Steel Syndicate Transaction Memo, Box 7, Folder "Material prepared for Armstrong Hearing," GWPP.

52. New York (State), *Joint Committee,* 1:773, 3:2933.

53. W. P. Metcalf to Perkins, September 16, 1905, GWPP, Box 7, Folder "1905."

54. Garraty, *Right-Hand Man,* 160.

55. On welfare capitalism see David Brody, *Workers in Industrial America: Essays on the Twentieth Century Struggle* (New York: Oxford University Press, 1993), ch. 2; Lizabeth Cohen, *Making a New Deal: Industrial Workers in Chicago, 1919–1939* (New York: Cambridge University Press, 2008/1990), ch. 4; Sanford M. Jacoby, *Modern Manors: Welfare Capitalism Since the New Deal* (Princeton: Princeton University Press, 1997); Andrea Tone, *The Business of Benevolence: Industrial Paternalism in the Progressive Era* (Ithaca: Cornell University Press, 1997); Howard Gitelman, "Welfare Capitalism Reconsidered," *Labor History* 33, no. 1 (Winter 1992): 5–31.

56. Perkins, "Profit-Sharing Plan of the United States Steel Corporation." On corporate middle management see Oliver Zunz, *Making America Corporate, 1870–1920* (Chicago: University of Chicago Press, 1990); Jürgen Kocka, *White Collar Workers in America, 1890–1940: A Social Political History in International Perspective,* trans. Maura Kealey (London: Sage Publications, 1980). See also "The Fate of the Salaried Man," *Independent* 60 (August 20, 1903), 2002.

57. George Perkins, "Address Quill Club," (1910), Box 20, GWPP. See also Perkins's speech on scientific management before the Harvard Business School, "Some Things to Think About" (1910) and Perkins, "Efficiency in Business" (1911), Box 20, GWPP. On scientific management thought see Daniel Nelson, *Frederick W. Taylor and the Rise of Scientific Management* (Madison, WI: University of Wisconsin, 1980); Thorstein Veblen, *The Engineers and the Price System* (New York, 1912).

58. Funk to Perkins, February 20, 1909, GWPP. Perkins, "Modern Corporation." Perkins, "Efficiency in Business." With respect to these issues at U.S. Steel see also Charles Schwab, "What May be Expected in the Iron and Steel Industry," *North American Review,* 172 (May 1901), 655–664. More generally, see Croly, *Promise of American Life,* 415, 416; Lippmann, *Drift and Mastery,* 38–49.

59. See Boris Emmet, "Profit Sharing in the United States," *Bulletin of the United States Bureau of Labor Statistics,* 208, no. 13 (December 1916); Brody, *Workers in Industrial America,* ch. 2.

60. George Perkins, "Co-Partnership," (1911), Box 20, GWPP. Ray Stannard Baker, "What the U.S. Steel Corporation Really is, and How it Works," *McClure's,* 18 (November 1901), 6. Horace L. Wilgus, *A Study of the United States Steel Corporation in its Industrial and Legal Aspects* (Chicago, 1901), 4. On U.S. Steel see also *United States v. United States Steel Corporation et al.,* District Court, New Jersey, 223 Federal Reporter (1915); U.S. Department of Commerce and Labor, *Report of the*

Commissioner of Corporations on the Steel Industry, 3 pts. (Washington, DC, 1911–1913); U.S. House of Representatives, *Hearings before the Committee on Investigation of the United States Steel Corporation*; U.S. House of Representatives, *Report on the Investigation of the United States Steel Corporation.*

61. George Perkins, "Memorandum of Proposed Profit Sharing Plan of the United States Steel Corporation," Box 27, Folder "U.S. Steel 1901–1903," GWPP.

62. See David Brody, *Steelworkers in America: The Nonunion Era* (Urbana: University of Illinois Press, 1998/1960), chs. 4, 6, 7; David Montgomery, *Workers' Control in America: Studies in the History of Work, Technology, and Labor Struggles* (New York: Cambridge University Press, 1979); James B. Kennedy, *Beneficiary Features of American Trade Unions* (Baltimore, 1908); C. D. Wright, "Amalgamated Association," *Quarterly Journal of Economics* 7 (July 1893): 400–432.

63. Garraty, *Right-Hand Man,* 114.

64. Perkins, "Memorandum of Proposed Profit Sharing Plan."

65. William Harris to Perkins, February 20, 1908, Box 22, Folder "Columbia Address on The Modern Corporation," GWPP. Perkins, "Profit-Sharing Plan of the United States Steel Corporation."

66. George Perkins, "To the Stockholders of the United States Steel Corporation . . . ," Box 27, Folder "U.S. Steel 1901–1903," GWPP. Arthur Hadley to Perkins, January 10, 1903, Box 27, Folder "U.S. Steel Profit Sharing Correspondence, 1901–1903," GWPP. Perkins, "Memorandum of Proposed Profit Sharing Plan." Louis Brandeis, "Our New Peonage," in *Business: A Profession* (Boston, 1914), 73.

67. George Perkins, "New York's Responsibility" (1911), Box 20, GWPP. Perkins to J.P. Morgan, April 20, 1906, Box 8, Folder "April–June 1906," GWPP. *Money Trust Investigation, Investigation of Financial and Monetary Conditions in the United States Under House Resolutions No. 429 and 504 Before a Subcommittee of the Committee on Banking and Currency,* pt. 22 (Washington, DC, 1913), 1632. The classic text on the separation of ownership and management under the corporate form is Adolf A. Berle and Gardiner Means, *The Modern Corporation and Private Property* (New York, 1936). On the New Proprietorship and on shareholding and risk see Ott, *When Wall Street Met Main Street,* esp. 178, 215.

68. See materials in Box 27, Folder "U.S. Steel 1907–1915" and Box 20, Folder "1909–1910 Harvester" in GWPP. Robert Ozanne, *A Century of Labor-Management Relations at McCormick and International Harvester* (Madison, WI: University of Wisconsin Press, 1967), 91. Arthur W. Burrit et al., *Profit Sharing, Its Principle and Practice* (New York, 1918). Brody, "Welfare Capitalism," 54. Jacoby, *Modern Manors,* 62.

69. Bureau of Corporations, *The International Harvester Co., vol. 3* (Washington, 1913), 239.

70. Perkins's testimony: U.S. Commission on Industrial Relations, *Final Report and Testimony Submitted to Congress on by the Commission on Industrial Relations,* Senate Document No. 415, 1st sess. (1916), 8:7598–7612. On U.S. Steel welfarism see the materials in Box 27, Folder, "U.S. Steel 1907–1905," GWPP, especially typescript "United States Steel Pension Fund." On the NCF welfare efforts see Tone, *Business of Benevolence,* ch. 2; James Weinstein, *The Corporate Ideal in the Liberal State, 1900–1918* (Boston: Beacon Press, 1968), chs. 1 and 2; Margaret Green, *The Na-*

tional Civic Federation and the American Labor Movement, 1900–1925 (Washington, DC: Catholic University Press, 1956).

71. Tone, *Business of Benevolence,* 179. Ozanne, *A Century of Labor-Management Relations.*

72. On Perkins's preparatory work for the Employee Benefit Association see typescript "Benefit or Relief (Industrial) Association or Workingmen's Insurance" prepared for Perkins by Mary Goss, which explicitly alerts Perkins to the German model, in Box 9, Folder "June–Dec 1908," GWPP, and the large number of materials in Box 20, Folder "Materials 1909–1910," GWPP. On Perkins and the NCF's study of "Wage Earner's Insurance" see Ralph Easley to Perkins, November 9, 1909, Box 10, Folder "1909 July–Dec," GWPP, and *Ninth Annual Meeting of the National Civic Federation, New York, December 14–15, 1908* (New York, 1909).

73. Seligman, *Principles of Economics,* 666. On the issues of risk and responsibility at stake in workmen's compensation laws see John Fabian Witt, *The Accidental Republic: Crippled Workingmen, Destitute Widows, and the Remaking of American Law* (Cambridge: Harvard University Press, 2004). Witt demonstrates the shift from notions of risk and responsibility forged in the era of slave emancipation to new attitudes towards 'social risk' at the turn of the twentieth century.

74. See "First Annual Report o the Employee Benefit Association of International Harvester Company, 1909" and "Industrial Accident Department of International Harvester Company of New Jersey, 1910," both in Box 20, Folder "Printed and Duplicate, 1909–1910," GWPP; and Ozanne, *A Century of Labor-Management Relations,* 80–95. See also Perkins to J.P. Morgan, June 1, 1908, Box 9, Folder "Jan–June 1908," GWPP. Perkins closely monitored the workings of the Employee Benefit Association, corresponding often with its director Frank Ranney. See, for instance, Perkins to F. Ranney, October 22, 1909, Box 54, Letterbooks, GWPP.

75. On gender and social insurance see Linda Gordon, *Pitied but Not Entitled: Single Mothers and the History of Welfare, 1890–1935* (New York: Free Press, 1994); Alice Kessler-Harris, *Women, Men, and the Quest for Economic Citizenship in 20th-Century America* (New York: Oxford University Press, 2001).

76. See Perkins to Harold McCormick, November 24, 1909, Box 54, Letterbooks, GWPP.

77. Charles Richmond Henderson, *Industrial Insurance in the United States* (Chicago, 1908), 377–404.

78. U.S. Commission on Industrial Relations, *Final Report and Testimony,* 8:7600, 7623.

79. Perkins to Theodore Roosevelt, October 7, 1908, Box 8, Folder "June–Dec 1908," GWPP. Ozanne, *A Century of Labor-Management Relations,* 81. Kolko, *Triumph of Conservatism,* esp. 66, but also throughout on Perkins's relationship with the White House. See also Robert H. Wiebe, "The House of Morgan and the Executive, 1905–1913," *The American Historical Review* 65, no. 1 (October 1959): 49–60.

80. On antitrust see Sklar, *Corporate Reconstruction,* ch. 3; Freyer, *Regulating Big Business,* ch. 1; Sanders, *Roots of Reform,* ch. 8; Hovenkamp, *Enterprise and American Law,* pt 4.

81. See, for instance, Perkins, "Wanted—A Constructive National Policy." These investigations resulted in U.S. Department of Commerce and Labor, *Report of the Commission of Corporations on the International Harvester Co.* (Washington, DC, 1913)

and U.S. Department of Commerce and Labor, *Report of the Commissioner of Corporations on the Steel Industry.*

82. Perkins to J.P. Morgan, April 30, 1907, Box 9, Folder "1907 General" and August 28, 1907, Box 11, Folder "June–July 1907," GWPP. Perkins to J.P. Morgan, June 1, 1908, and Perkins to Theodore Roosevelt, June 3, 1908, both in Box 8, Folder "Jan–June 1908," GWPP.

83. Garraty, *Right-Hand Man,* 225. Sklar, *Corporate Reconstruction,* 253–285.

84. See Perkins to J.P. Morgan, November 10, 1908, Box 8, Folder "June–Dec 1908," GWPP.

85. Perkins to E. A. Bradford, October 16, 1909, Box 54, Letterbooks, GWPP. Perkins to Judson Harmon, November 14, 1910, and Perkins to John C. Greenway, December 19, 1910, Box 21, GWPP. See also Garraty, *Right-Hand Man,* 234.

86. Garraty, *Right-Hand Man,* 252, 253. Perkins to J.P. Morgan, March 11, 1909, Box 9, Folder "Jan–June 1909," GWPP.

87. Garraty, *Right-Hand Man,* 257.

88. Ibid., 256.

89. Frederick Jackson Turner and Alice Forbes Perkins, *"Dear Lady": the Letters of Frederick Jackson Turner and Alice Forbes Perkins Hooper, 1910–1932* (Pasadena: Hunting Library, 1970), 124. See Amos Pinchot, *History of the Progressive Party, 1912–1916* (Norwalk, CT: Greenwood Press, 1978), 255–261.

90. Pinchot, *History of the Progressive Party,* 174. Theodore Roosevelt, *Address before the Convention of the National Progressive Party in Chicago, August 1912* (n.p., 1912). The final plank read: "We . . . demand a strong National regulation of inter-State corporations. The corporation is an essential part of modern business. The concentration of modern business, in some degree, is both inevitable and necessary for national and international business efficiency. . . . [W]e urge the establishment of a strong Federal administrative commission of high standing, which shall maintain permanent active supervision over industrial corporations. . . . Such a commission must enforce the complete publicity of these corporation transactions which are of public interest." Donald Bruce Johnson, *National Party Platforms: 1840–1956* (Urbana: University of Illinois Press, 1978), 177.

91. Perkins, "Wanted—A Constructive National Policy"; and Perkins, "Management of the New York Life" (1905), in Box 20, GWPP.

92. Arthur Link et al., eds., *The Papers of Woodrow Wilson,* vols. 24 and 25 (Princeton: Princeton University Press, 1977 and 1978), 24:346, 25:381–384. John Wells Davidson, *A Crossroads of Freedom: The 1912 Campaign Speeches of Woodrow Wilson* (New Haven: Yale University Press, 1956), 175–176; Woodrow Wilson, *The New Freedom: A Call for the Emancipation of the Generous Energies of a People* (New York, 1913), 207, 278.

93. George Perkins, "The Sherman Law," (1915), Box 20, GWPP. On the Federal Trade Commission see Sklar, *Corporate Reconstruction,* 324–332; Thomas K. McCraw, *Prophets of Regulation: Charles Francis Adams, Louis D. Brandeis, James M. Landis, Alfred E. Kahn* (Cambridge: Harvard University Press, 1984), chs. 3 and 4. On the International Harvester 1916 strike, see Ozanne, *A Century of Labor-Management Relations at McCormick and International Harvester,* 106–112.

94. Roy Lubove, *The Struggle for Social Security, 1900–1935* (Pittsburgh: University of Pittsburgh Press, 1986), 215.

95. U.S. Commission on Industrial Relations, *Final Report and Testimony Submitted to Congress on by the Commission on Industrial Relations,* 8:7625.

96. See materials in Box 32, Folder "Unemployment Committee," GWPP. See also Rodgers, *Atlantic Crossings,* 252; John B. Andrews, "A Practical Program for the Prevention of Unemployment in America," *American Labor Legislation Review* 5 (1914): 171–192; New York Mayor's Committee on Unemployment, *Report* (New York, 1916), which lists Perkins as a member of the Executive Committee on p. 5.

97. Samuel L. Gompers, "Not Even Compulsory Benevolence Will Do," *American Federationist* 24 (January 1917): 48.

98. See *Report of the President's Conference on Unemployment, September 26 to October 13, 1921* (Washington, D.C., 1921); William J. Breen, "Foundations, Statistics, and State-Building: Leonard P. Ayers, the Russell Sage Foundation, and U.S. Government Statistics in the First World War," *Business History Review* 69, no. 4 (1994): 451–482; Udo Sautter, "Government and Unemployment: The Use of Public Works before the New Deal," *The Journal of American History* 73, no. 1 (June 1986): 59–86; Robert D. Cuff, *The War Industries Board: Business-Government Relations During World War I* (Baltimore: The Johns Hopkins University Press, 1973).

99. Elisha M. Friedman, ed., *American Problems of Reconstruction* (New York, 1918), 47, 51, 54.

100. Garraty, *Right-Hand Man,* ch. 19.

101. George Perkins, "Some Things to Think About." Perkins to George Perkins, Jr., October 15, 1918, Letterbooks, GWPP. *New York Sun,* June 19, 1920.

EPILOGUE

Epigraph: T. K. Cheyne, *The Prophecies of Isaiah,* vol. 2 (London, 1880), 124. Emphasis in the original. The King James translation reads:

> Yea, they have chosen their own ways, and their soul delighteth in their abominations. I also will choose their delusions, and will bring their fears upon them; because when I called, none did answer; when I spake, they did not hear: but they did evil before mine eyes, and chose that in which I delighted not.

The Revised Standard Version renders the word in question as "affliction."

1. See Judith Stein, *Running Steel, Running America: Race, Economic Policy, and the Decline of Liberalism* (Chapel Hill: University of North Carolina Press, 1998), esp. ch. 10 and 11; Nitin Nohria, Davis Dyer, and Frederick Dalzell, *Changing Fortunes: Remaking the Industrial Corporation* (New York: John Wiley & Sons, 2002), 169–181. On shareholder value, see William Lazonick and Mary O'Sullivan, "Maximizing Shareholder Value: A New Ideology for Corporate Governance," *Economy and Society* 29, no. 1 (February 2000): 13–35.

2. See Stein, *Running Steel, Running America,* 249. In 1992 the federal government's Pension Benefit Guaranty Corporation reached a $65 million settlement with

International Harvester, or Navistar as it was then known. See "$65 Million Settlement with Navistar," *Chicago Tribune,* August 21, 1992.

3. Nohria et. al., *Changing Fortunes,* 174

4. See Karen Ho, *Liquidated: An Ethnography of Wall Street* (Durham: Duke University Press, 2009); Gerald F. Davis, *Managed by the Markets: How Finance Re-Shaped America* (New York: Oxford University Press, 2009).

5. On financialization see Greta R. Krippner, *Capitalizing on Crisis: The Political Origins of the Rise of Finance* (Cambridge: Harvard University Press, 2011).

6. "Freaks of Fortune," *Harper's New Monthly Magazine,* August 1858, 344.

7. "Freaks of Fortune," *New Orleans Times Picayune,* January 28, 1879.

8. "A Freak of Fortune," *New Orleans Times Picayune,* July 2, 1881. On what the freaks defied see Daniel T. Rodgers, *The Work Ethic in Industrial America, 1850–1920* (Chicago: University of Chicago Press, 1974), esp. 12; Amy Dru Stanley, *From Bondage to Contract: Wage Labor, Marriage, and the Market in the Age of Slave Emancipation* (New York: Cambridge University Press 1998), esp. ch. 3; James L. Huston, *Securing the Fruits of Labor: The American Concept of Wealth Distribution, 1765–1900* (Baton Rouge: Louisiana State University Press, 1998).

9. Alger's protagonists often benefited from lucky breaks. But the author always portrayed the break as reward for virtuous moral character and a good dose of pluck. The morality is karmic. See Horatio Alger, *Ragged Dick: Or, Street Life in New York* (New York, 1868).

10. "Freaks of Fortune," *Harper's,* 344.

11. "A Freak of Fortune," *Life,* November 11, 1886.

12. "A Freak of Fortune," *Cincinnati Commercial Tribune,* December 21, 1881. "Freaks of Fortune," *National Police Gazette,* June 21, 1884.

13. "Instability of Fortune," *Messenger,* March 21, 1877; S. S. Packard, "Commercial Business," *The Chautauquan,* February 1887, 266–268.

14. Russell D. Buhite and David W. Levy, eds., *FDR's Fireside Chats* (Norman: University of Oklahoma Press, 1992), 54. On New Deal legislation see David M. Kennedy, *Freedom From Fear: The American People in Depression and War, 1929–1945* (New York: Oxford University Press, 2005), ch. 12. On the welfare state as Polanyiesque countermovement see Mark Blyth, *Great Transformations: Economic Ideas and Institutional Change in the Twentieth Century* (New York: Cambridge University Press, 2002).

15. Franklin D. Roosevelt, "Presidential Statement upon Signing the Social Security Act, August 14, 1935," in *Papers,* vol. 4, 324; Buhite and Levy, eds., *FDR's Fireside Chats,* 62. See also Paul Douglas, "Freedom and Security," *The Social Welfare Reform* 1 (1949), esp. 150. On citizenship and economic security see Alice Kessler-Harris, *In Pursuit of Equity: Women, Men, and the Quest for Economic Citizenship in Twentieth-Century America* (New York: Oxford University Press, 2003).

16. On the actuarial dynamics of Social Security see Edward D. Berkowitz, *America's Welfare State: From Roosevelt to Reagan* (Baltimore: The Johns Hopkins University, 1991), ch. 1. On decommodification see Gosta Esping-Anderson, *The Three Worlds of Welfare Capitalism* (Princeton: Princeton University Press, 1990).

17. On the public/private character of the American welfare state see Jennifer Klein, *For All These Rights: Business, Labor, and the Shaping of America's Public-Private Welfare State* (Princeton: Princeton University Press, 2003); Jacob Hacker, *The Divided Welfare State: The Battle Over Public and Private Social Benefits in the United States* (New York: Cambridge University Press, 2002).

18. See Caley Horan, "Actuarial Age: Insurance and the Emergence of Neoliberalism in the Postwar United States," (Ph.D. diss., University of Minnesota, 2011).

19. See Stephen A. Marglia and Juliet E. Schor, eds., *The Golden Age of Capitalism: Reinterpreting the Postwar Experience* (New York: Oxford University Press, 1992).

20. Nohria et. al., *Changing Fortunes*, 168.

21. See Sanford M. Jacoby, *Modern Manors: Welfare Capitalism Since the New Deal* (Princeton: Princeton University Press, 1998).

22. Stein, *Running Steel, Running America*, 16, 61.

23. See Hyman P. Minksy, *Stabilizing an Unstable Economy* (New Haven: Yale University Press, 1986), ch. 4.

24. See Robert Brenner, *The Economics of Global Turbulence: The Advanced Capitalist Economies from Long Boom to Long Downturn, 1945–2005* (New York: Verso, 2006); Andrew Glyn, *Capitalism Unleashed: Finance, Globalization, and Welfare* (New York: Oxford University Press, 2006); David Harvey, *The Condition of Postmodernity: An Enquiry into the Origins of Cultural Change* (New York: Wiley-Blackwell, 1991).

25. On thought and culture see Daniel T. Rodgers, *Age of Fracture* (Cambridge: Harvard University Press, 2011), esp. ch. 2; James Livingston, *The World Turned Inside Out: American Thought and Culture at the End of the 20th Century* (New York: Rowman & Littlefield Publishers, 2010); Harvey, *Condition of Postmodernity*.

26. C. Wright Mills, *White Collar: The American Middle Classes* (New York: Oxford University Press, 2002/1951), 285; George F. Gilder, *Wealth and Poverty* (New York: Bantam Books, 1982), 41.

27. See Tom Baker and Jonathan Simon, eds., *Embracing Risk: The Changing Culture of Insurance and Responsibility* (Chicago: University of Chicago Press, 2002).

28. See in general Jefferson Cowie and Nick Salvatore, "The Long Exception: Rethinking the Place of the New Deal in American History," *International Labor and Working Class History* 74 (Fall 2008): 3–32. With respect to risk see Jacob S. Hacker, *The Great Risk Shift: The Assault on American Jobs, Families, and Retirement* (New York: Oxford University Press, 2006).

Acknowledgments

It is a great pleasure to acknowledge the individuals and institutions that made this book possible.

The project began at the Department of History at the University of Chicago. The debt I owe to Amy Stanley, for her steady guidance, moral compass, and razor sharp criticism, is immeasurable. I am even more grateful for her unstinting loyalty, and now friendship. Thanks are due to Craig Becker, Isaac Stanley-Becker, and Thomas Stanley-Becker, as well. Thomas Holt's mentorship was equally decisive. I thank him for his composure and equanimity, and for often salvaging and reformulating my incoherent ideas. Kathleen Conzen (whose offhand remark became Chapter 5) and William Sewell both gave far more to the project than I had any right to expect.

The individuals that made my time at the University of Chicago so intellectually rewarding, and, yes, even fun, include Thomas Adams, Anita Chari, Bernard Dubbeld, Molly Hudgens, Gwennath Ickes, Grant Madsen, Kelly King-O'Brien, Sarah Potter, David Spatz, Michael Stamm, James Sparrow, Timothy Stewart-Winter, Katherine Turk, James Vaughn, Kyle Volk, Rosa Williams, and Tara Zahra. At Chicago and after, Alison Lefkovitz and Gautham Rao in particular have provided steadfast friendship and intellectual support. I learned Peter Novick died while I was completing the manuscript, even as his taunt, "But Jon what *is* risk?" still rang in my ear.

I am fortunate that research for the project was supported financially by the Division of Social Sciences at the University of Chicago, the Council on Library and Information Resources, and the American Council of Learned Societies. For letting me sleep on their couches or in their spare bedrooms for weeks, even months, at a time when conducting research I thank Jake Fuller, Erin Killory, Michael Kahney, Dana Cicerani, Tony Coyne, Matt McCarthy, and Dan Wolman. Jeff Charbeneau, Stephan Endicott, Garrett Long, and Benson Loveless are four friends in Chicago that shaped this book and deserve thanks.

Since 2008, the Department of History at Princeton University has been my intellectual home. I thank two department chairs, Jeremy Adelman and William Jordan, for making possible the research leave that led to the book's completion. For their counsel, and for incisive readings of the entire manuscript—not once but twice—I thank Hendrik Hartog, Daniel Rodgers, and Keith Wailoo. At Princeton, the book benefited from the input of Lucia Alais, Jeremy Adelman, On Barak, Dan Bouk, Henry Cowles, Angela Creager, Sheldon Garon, Caley Horan, Jamie Kreiner, Dael Norwood, Martin Reif, Rebecca Rix, Martha Sandweiss, Alison Isenberg, Wendy Warren, Sean Wilentz, and Viviana Zelizer. Thankfully, I cannot imagine working in Princeton without the additional camaraderie of Matthew Backes, Edward Baring, Margot Canaday, Eduardo Canedo, James Dun, Katja Guenther, Joshua Guild, Robert Karl, Michael Laffan, Sarah Milov, Bradley Simpson, and Max Weiss.

The bulk of the manuscript was written during academic year 2009–2010 when I was a visiting fellow at the John Kluge Center at the Library of Congress in Washington, DC. I remain grateful to its director Carolyn Brown and its wonderful administrator Mary Lou Reker for creating such a hospitable and intellectually charmed environment. Conversations with David Christian, Chiara Cordelli, Claudia Deetjen, and Matthias Freidank helped move the project forward. I thank the American Council of Learned Societies again for another year of generous fellowship support.

The manuscript benefited from the insights and encouragement of many generous colleagues. Jean-Christophe Agnew, Elizabeth Blackmar, Stanley Engerman, Jackson Lears, Walter Licht, Barbara Welke, and Michael Zakim all graciously read and critiqued the entire manuscript at various stages, while offering sage advice. James Livingston has been willing to bat around ideas since I was a second-year graduate student. Caitlin Zaloom taught me a lot about derivatives trading. Jennifer Ratner-Rosenhangen offered encouragement during a worrisome lull.

A number of venues offered the opportunity to receive feedback on portions of the manuscript. I thank Daniel Raff and Walter Licht and the Penn Economic History Forum (including commentator Paul Rhode), Viviana Zelizer and Princeton's Economic Sociology Workshop, Allan Needell and the Smithsonian Institution Contemporary History Colloquium, Susanna Blumenthal and the University of Minnesota Law School's Legal History Workshop, Angus Burgin and Louis Galambos and Johns Hopkins Institute for Applied Economics, Global Health, and the Study of Business Enterprise Workshop, and Bruce Caldwell and the History of Political Economy Workshop in the Duke Economics Department for invitations to present sections of the book. Presentations at two national meetings of the American Council of Learned Societies—one in Pittsburgh near the beginning of the project another in Philadelphia near the end—led to bursts of energy.

At Harvard University Press, Joyce Seltzer supported this book long before she had any right to. I thank her for seeing it through to the end with such expert editorial guidance and skill. At Harvard, Brian Distelberg calmingly shepherded the book through the production process. I have a much healthier relationship with the comma after Paul Vincent copyedited the manuscript. My appreciation for the research assistance provided by Jonathan Evans—a uniquely talented Princeton (now former) undergraduate—is unbounded. Brooke Fitzgerald provided critical research assistance for Chapter 5. Sean Vanatta offered a sharp-eyed reading of the manuscript during the copyediting stage. So did Sarah Milov, whose painstaking effort to add polish and clarity up to the very final moment deserves special mention.

I thank Sarah Stein and Scott Nelson, and also Alan Lessof at the *Journal of the Gilded Age and Progressive Era*, for providing forums to develop my ideas at an early stage. Portions of Chapter 2 and Chapter 5 are reprinted with permission from " 'The Mortgage Worked the Hardest': The Fate of Landed Independence in 19th-Century America," in Michael Zakim and Gary J. Kornblith, eds., *Capitalism Takes Command: The Social Transformation of Nineteenth-Century America* (University of Chicago Press, 2012), 39–68. I thank Gary Kornblith and Michael Zakim for the opportunity to contribute to the volume, and along with them fellow contributors Sean Adams, Christopher Clark, Tamara Thornton, and Robert Wright for their comments on the chapter. Portions of Chapter 7 are reprinted with permission from " 'Contemplating Delivery': Futures Trading and the Problem of Commodity Exchange in the United States, 1875-1905," *American Historical Review* 11, no.2 (April 2006): 307–335.

Writing this book has meant pursuing a career that has taken me far away from those who I care about the most, my family. If I had known the cost of that sacrifice setting out, I am not sure I would have followed the same career path. Since I did, I hope my family knows how much I miss them on a daily basis and love them. I hope they are aware of the countless ways large and small they have mattered for this book.

Chiara Cordelli probably thinks I could have written this book without her love and support. For so many reasons she could not be more wrong.

Index

Abbott, John C., 42

abolitionists, 32, 60–65, 71–77, 90–97, 107–108, 126, 188, 339n6

accident insurance, 173–175, 177, 221, 298–299, 305. *See also* insurance; perils; providence

actuaries and actuarial knowledge: agricultural markets and, 181–182, 184, 186–187; dynamic risks and, 280–281; emergence of, 60–65; fraternal orders' relation to, 205, 212–213, 225–229; futures markets and, 248; life insurance and, 70, 89, 198–199; origins of, 35; premium-setting and, 79–86; providential worldviews and, 70, 218; risk communities and, 174–177, 181, 197; speculation and, 198–200, 205, 218–219. *See also* statistical knowledge; uncertainty

Addams, Jane, 162–163, 167

advice to insure, 33, 37

African Americans. *See* landed independence; slaves and slavery; *and specific people*

Agricultural Society of Concord, 67

agriculture: continuity and discontinuity in, 339n9, 353n45; crop diversity and, 111–112, 121–122, 177–180; crop forecasting and, 181–184; farmers' cooperatives and, 250–251, 378n49; farming practices as risk taking and, 66, 68–69, 77, 94–95, 111–112, 121, 170, 181–185, 187, 189, 346n78; landed independence and, 9, 68–69; market systems and, 69, 121, 152, 158–164, 176–181, 185, 187–188, 246–247, 250, 253, 269; offsets and, 178; safety-first strategies and, 177–178; tenant farmers and, 127–129, 134–135, 140, 153, 158, 179–180, 360n17. *See also* farmers; futures contracts; landed independence

Alger, Horatio, 311, 392n9

Alvord, John W., 109, 115, 119, 125–129, 133–136, 144, 146, 223

Amalgamated Steelworkers, 291–292

America: class consciousness in, 70–71, 88, 208–209, 211, 220; corporate cooperation and, 263–307; Darwinist impulses in, 192–194, 196–197, 258–259, 267; democracy and, 14; English legal legacies and, 10, 29–30, 39, 44, 47–49, 89, 173, 243; Federal Reserve System, 272; fraternal organizations in, 191–230; freedom's definition and, 5; government bonds and, 112–115, 117–118, 129–134, 138–148, 165; Interstate Commerce Commission and, 212; Jeffersonian republicanism and, 69, 177, 188–189; landed independence in, 65–67; legal structures of, 7–14, 20, 52, 69, 71–72, 78, 89, 101, 233–235, 242–244, 248, 255–263, 275–276, 342n45, 376n28; postindustrial society in, 308–310; Pragmatism and, 235, 256–263, 281, 381n84; providence and, 17–18, 74, 104–105, 114, 147–148, 180–182; rural nature of, 3, 66–68, 155, 339n9; social